FIFTY KEY CONTEMPORARY THINKERS

In this book, John Lechte focuses both on the development of structuralist theory and on key thinkers opposed to this tendency. For the specialist and the general reader alike, it is an indispensable reference book on this century's most important intellectual revolution. In each of the fifty entries, John Lechte skilfully illuminates complex thought with unusual clarity. He also provides comprehensive bibliographical information and suggestions for further reading.

From early structuralism, *Fifty Key Contemporary Thinkers* guides us through post-structuralism, semiotics, post-Marxism and Annales history, on to modernity and postmodernity. It includes chapters on Bakhtin, Freud, Bourdieu, Chomsky, Derrida, Lacan, Kristeva, Saussure, Irigaray and Kafka among others. Literary figures who have changed the way language is conceived are considered, together with philosophers, linguists, social theorists, feminists and historians.

Fifty Key Contemporary Thinkers shows that thought in the twentieth century emphasises the relational dimension of existence rather than an essential dimension. This kind of thought leads on to nihilism, but also to the point where nihilism might be overcome. In explaining new developments in literature, art and philosophy, John Lechte helps readers to achieve a more profound understanding of the underpinnings of post-war thought and culture.

John Lechte, a former student of Julia Kristeva, teaches social theory and the sociology of representation at Macquarie University, Australia. He has also worked in the fields of history, semiotics and politics, and has an abiding interest in psychoanalysis. He has taught and published widely on many aspects of modern thought.

FIFTY KEY CONTEMPORARY THINKERS

From structuralism to postmodernity

John Lechte

London and New York

First published 1994
by Routledge
11 New Fetter Lane, London EC4P 4EE

Simultaneously published in the USA and Canada
by Routledge
29 West 35th Street, New York, NY 10001

©1994 John Lechte

Typeset in Times by Florencetype Limited, Stoodleigh, Devon
Printed and bound in Great Britain by
T J Press Ltd, Padstow, Cornwall

British Library Cataloguing in Publication Data
A catalogue record for this book is available from the British Library

Library of Congress Cataloging in Publication Data
Lechte, John.
  Fifty key contemporary thinkers: from structuralism to
  postmodernity/John Lechte.
      p.   cm.
  Includes bibliographical references and index.
    1. Philosophy, modern – 20th century. 2. Structuralism.
  3. Semiotics. 4. Feminist theory. 5. Philosophy, Marxist.
  I. Title.
  B804.L37   1994
  190'.9'04—dc20   94-996

ISBN 0-415-05727-2 (hbk)
      0-415-07408-8 (pbk)

To the memory of my grandmothers who valued education

Carolyn Lechte (1885–1978)
Muriel Garner (1896–1979)

PREFACE

This book follows the very admirable model provided by Diané Collinson's *Fifty Major Philosophers* (1987). Thus I offer the reader both an overview of each thinker's work together with biographical information. Like Ms Collinson, I also aim to introduce, sometimes in a fairly detailed way, one or more aspects of the *oeuvre* in question, and particularly as this relates to that aspect of thought inspired by structuralism. And I often engage with that thought – differ with it, or appreciate its insights. My hope is that the reader will get a real sense of the flavour, style, and, in many cases, the truly innovative character of the thought in question.

My task, however, was both easier and more difficult than Diané Collinson's, for while I did not have to treat the entire history of the Western canon of philosophy in writing my entries, I had to choose fifty *contemporary* thinkers. And although, of course, one can debate about who should be in the philosophy canon, there is less doubt about the fact that a canon has been extraordinarily influential, even to the point where people are speaking Plato, Hobbes or Sartre without knowing it. To some extent, then, Diané Collinson's task was to make explicit forms of thought which have already formed us. My task, by contrast, has been to distil key elements in the work of thinkers who are sometimes not yet widely known, but who are becoming so. Most people will at least have heard of Plato; but will they have heard of Saussure? Most will know that idealism is located somewhere in Plato's philosophy; but do they know that 'difference' is a key notion in Saussure? Clearly, I believe that the answer is 'no' in both cases.

It is not only the general reader's knowledge that I am actually alluding to here, but also my own. For the contrast that I am trying to bring out is that between a relatively stable canon with which I am familiar, if not in detail, and a series of thinkers whose thought is often still evolving, both because many are still writing and thus have not completed their work, and because, by definition, it is not possible to have a deep familiarity with thought that is essentially contemporary and innovative. In other words, whether I have chosen the most important or illuminating angle on the thinkers in question will be, and should be, a cause for debate.

In response to this difficulty, my wager on behalf of the reader is that the light that I do shine on the thought I have explicated is an informed one, but that even if it turns out to be but one possible way of understanding the thinker in question, this is still informative and educative in the sense that I intend. And this sense is that to (be able to) disagree with me is to understand me.

What of the choice of thinkers, however? Here, the subtitle of the book should convey the orientation of the choices I have made. The thinkers chosen serve to deepen an understanding of the post Second World War structuralist orientation in thought, which arose largely, if not exclusively, in France. In my expositions, I have tried not to belabour this point; for each of the fifty thinkers treated is irreducible to a movement. Although the focus is primarily on the post-war period, it is not exclusively so: I have tried to include thinkers who, chronologically, might have been of another generation (Saussure, Freud, Nietzsche), but who have been of seminal importance, and are of great contemporaneity, intellectually speaking. 'Contemporary', therefore, means more than chronologically contemporary.

As the orientation of the book is largely towards presenting those thinkers who represent a structural–post-structural, modern–postmodern, orientation, I have also included a number of indisputably important thinkers (Adorno, Habermas) who are unsympathetic, or at least less sympathetic, to this orientation.

As to the material presentation of the book, I have grouped the thinkers in nine categories: early structuralism; structuralism; structural history; post-structuralist thought; semiotics; second generation feminism; post-Marxism; modernity; and, finally, postmodernity. A short introductory note, intended to give the reader a broad overview of the intellectual orientation concerned, precedes each group of thinkers. Some may see these groupings as too reductive. My view is that they signal an orientation only, and help the reader to appreciate the global significance of this collection, a significance which should not go unnoticed and which, used intelligently, can assist understanding at a more individual level.

For each thinker, I have aimed to provide information about recent as well as early work in the listing of major works, as I have also attempted to provide recent further readings.

Finally, I should address briefly the question as to how this book might be used. It would have been farcical, I believe, to have claimed to have presented these fifty key contemporary thinkers in a way which obviated the need for the reader to do additional reading to consolidate his or her understanding. This book offers a way in to understanding the thinkers concerned; it is not a substitute for reading them oneself. After Heidegger, I am not providing learning; I am trying to let learning take place.

John Lechte

ACKNOWLEDGEMENTS

Gill Bottomley has been inspiring in discussing the issues raised by the thinkers in this book, as she has also been untiring in her material support. My deepest thanks thus go to her. Eduardo de la Fuente is becoming a world authority on Adorno, and gave me the benefit of his advice and knowledge in this regard. He also assisted in researching key bibliographical items. Several people read, and commented upon, entries. These include Gill Bottomley, Murray Domney, Eduardo de la Fuente, Barry Hindess, Ephraim Nimni, and Paul Patton. I thank them all, but of course take full responsibility for any errors that remain in the text they so generously helped to improve.

Finally, I would, very sincerely, like to thank my publisher, Richard Stoneman, for the idea for this project, and especially for his extreme forbearance in light of a project, which, I am loath to admit, went way over a number of deadlines.

Early Structuralism

To give an insight into the factors which set in motion the structuralist movement, we can see that certain tendencies in the work of a Marcel Mauss or a Georges Canguilhem had already begun to destabilise the presuppositions of phenomenology and positivism. A focus on society as a system where certain phenomena constitute a 'total social fact', or on the epistemological basis of knowledge (Canguilhem), begins to shift the emphasis away from an essentialist explanation of society or knowledge, and towards this as being the result of the structural (that is, differential, and relational) nature of these events. The history of science is thus no longer the expression of a mind; rather, through an epistemological configuration, history constructs the intellectual framework that comprehends it. In addition, changes in the present experience of a society or an individual (cf. Freud) change the meaning of the past. The past can no longer be understood in its own terms because now the past is to be understood in terms of the concerns of the present.

GASTON BACHELARD

Gaston Bachelard – epistemologist, philosopher of science, and theorist of the imagination – influenced key figures in the structuralist and post-structuralist generation of the post-war era. Through Jean Cavaillès, and especially in light of the work and guidance of Georges Canguilhem, Michel Foucault found his particular orientation in researching the history of knowledges. Again, with Louis Althusser finding inspiration in Bachelard's concept of 'discontinuity' – which he translated into 'epistemological break' – a generation of Marxist philosophers was stimulated to rethink the notions of time, subjectivity, and science.

Gaston Bachelard was born in 1884, in rural France, at Bar-sur-Aube and died in Paris in 1962. After being employed in the postal service (1903–13), he became professor of physics at the Collège de Bar-sur-Aube from 1919 to 1930. At the age of 35, Bachelard engaged in further studies – this time in philosophy, for which he completed an *agrégation* in 1922. Still later, in 1928, he published his doctoral thesis, defended in 1927: *Essai sur la connaissance approchée* (*Essay on Approximate Knowledge*) and his complementary thesis, *Etude sur l'évolution d'un problème physique, La propagation thermique dans les solides* (*Study on the Evolution of a Problem in Physics: Thermal Propagation in Solids*). In light of this work, Bachelard, in 1940, was called upon to take up the chair of history and philosophy of science at the Sorbonne, a position he held until 1954.

Three key elements of Bachelard's thought made him both a unique philosopher and thinker and also rendered his work crucial to the post-war generation of structuralists. The first element concerns the importance placed on epistemology in science. If, in this regard, scientists were to have a defective understanding of their own practice, the application of their work would be fundamentally impeded. Epistemology is the domain where the significance of scientific endeavours is comprehended. As Bachelard wrote in *The Philosophy of No*: 'The space in which one *looks*, in which one *examines* is philosophically very different from the space in which one sees.'[1] This is because the space in which one sees is always a represented space, and not a real space. Only by recourse to philosophy can one take account of this. Indeed, Bachelard goes on to advocate 'a systematic study of *representation*, the most natural intermediary for determining the relationships of noumenon and phenomenon'.[2] Closely aligned to the interaction between reality and its representation, is Bachelard's unswerving advocacy of the dialectical relationship between rationalism and realism – or empiricism, as it could also be called. Thus in perhaps what became, for a wider public, his most influential book, *The New Scientific Spirit*, this veritable poet of epistemology argues that there are fundamentally two prevailing metaphysical bases: rationalism and realism. Rationalism – which includes philosophy and theory – is the field of interpretation and reason; realism, on the other hand, provides rationalism with the material for its interpretations. Simply to remain at a naive and intuitive level – the experimental level – in grasping new facts is to condemn scientific understanding to stagnation; for it cannot become aware of what it is doing. Similarly, if one exaggerates the importance of the rationalist aspect – perhaps even claiming that, in the end, science is nothing but the reflection of an underlying philosophical system – an equally sterile idealism can result. For Bachelard, therefore, to be scientific is to privilege neither thought nor reality, but to recognise the inextricable link between them. In the following memorable expression, Bachelard captures what is at stake: '*Experimentation must give way to argument, and argument must have recourse to experimentation.*'[3] All of Bachelard's writings on the nature of science are motivated by this principle. Trained as a scientist and as a philosopher, Bachelard exemplified the position he strove to represent in his writing. As may be expected, a book like *Le Rationalisme appliqué* (*Applied Rationalism*), is geared to demonstrate the theoretical basis of different types of experimentation. A profound rationalism is thus always an applied rationalism, one that learns from reality. This is not all, however. For Bachelard also agrees that the empiricist can learn something about reality from the theorist when it happens – as with Einstein – that a theory is developed prior to its experimental correlate. Here, theory *needs* its experimental correlate in order to be confirmed. With the emphasis he placed on epistemology, Bachelard brought science and philosophy together in a way seldom seen before. The human and natural sciences in fact find their intermediary here, in the man who, in the end, comes to write a 'poetics' of science.

The second major aspect of Bachelard's work which has been particularly influential as far as structuralism is concerned is his theorisation of the history of science. In a nutshell, Bachelard proposes a non-evolutionary explanation of the development of science, where prior developments do not necessarily explain the present state of science. For example, according to Bachelard, it is not possible to explain Einstein's theory of relativity as developing out of Newtonian physics. New doctrines did not develop out of the old, says Bachelard, 'but rather, the new *enveloped* the old'. And he continues: 'Intellectual generations are nested, one within the other. When we go from non-Newtonian physics to Newtonian physics, we do not encounter contradiction but we do experience contradiction.'[4] On this basis, the concept that links later discoveries to a prior set of discoveries is not continuity, but discontinuity. There is thus a discontinuity between Euclidean and non-Euclidean geometry, a discontinuity between Euclidean space, and the theories of location, space and time put forward by Heisenberg and Einstein. Again, Bachelard points out that in the past, mass was defined in relation to a quantity of matter. The greater the matter, therefore, the greater the force thought to be needed to oppose it: velocity was a function of mass. With Einstein, we now know that mass is a function of velocity, and not the reverse. The main point made here is not that previous theories were found to be wanting and therefore opposed, but that new theories tend entirely to transcend – or are discontinuous with – previous theories and explanations of phenomena. As Bachelard explains:

> No doubt there are some kinds of knowledge that appear to be immutable. This leads some people to think that the stability of the contents is due to stability of the container, or, in other words, that the forms of rationality are permanent and no new method of rational thought is possible. But structure does not come from accumulation alone; the mass of immutable knowledge does not have as much functional importance as is sometimes assumed.[5]

In fact, Bachelard argues, it is the – sometimes radical – changes in the meaning of a concept, or in the nature of a research field which best characterise the nature of scientific endeavour. What is new in science, therefore, is always revolutionary.

As an addendum to the Bachelardian conception of scientific development, it is important to note that all scientific thought, 'is, in its essence, process of objectification' – a sentiment with which Pierre Bourdieu (a former student of Bachelard's) would entirely agree. Moreover, in speaking about the scientific thought of the modern era, Bachelard notes that it is fundamentally oriented to seeing phenomena relationally, and not substantively, or as having essential qualities in themselves. This observation clearly signals a feature present in contemporary structuralist thought. Thus, Bachelard confirms, 'the properties of the objects in

Hilbert's system are purely relational and in no way substantial'.[6]

When he argues that 'the assimilation of the irrational by reason never fails to bring about a reciprocal reorganization of the domain of rationality',[7] Bachelard confirms the dialectical nature of his approach – one that is recalled, albeit in a different context and with different aims, by Julia Kristeva and her concepts of the 'semiotic' and the 'symbolic'. Thought is always 'in the *process* of objectification';[8] it is never given and complete – never closed in upon itself and static, as some scientists used to assume.

Connected to this view of thought is Bachelard's anti-Cartesian stance. Whereas Descartes had argued that to progress, thought had to start from the point of clear and simple ideas, Bachelard charges that there are no simple ideas, only complexities, this being particularly in evidence when ideas are applied. 'Application is complication', Bachelard claims. Moreover, while the best theory seems to be the one that explains reality in the simplest way, our author retorts that reality is never simple, and that in the history of science attempts to achieve simplicity (e.g., the structure of the hydrogen spectrum) have invariably turned out to be over-simplifications when the complexity of reality is at last acknowledged. As a notion derived from Descartes, simplicity does not adequately cope with the fact that every phenomenon is a fabric of relations, and not a simple substance. As such, phenomena can only be grasped through a form of synthesis that corresponds to what Bachelard, in 1936, called *surrationalisme*.[9] Surrationalism is an enrichment and revitalisation of rationalism through reference to the material world, just as, through dream, Surrealism, from another direction, aimed to revitalise realism through dream.

Another dimension of Bachelard's thought which has been influential is his work analysing forms of the imagination, particularly the images related to the themes of matter, movement, force, and dream, as well as the associated images of fire, water, air, and earth. Bachelard, in works like *La Terre et les rêveries de la volonté* (*The Earth and Reveries of Will*) includes numerous references to the poetry and literature of the Western cultural tradition, references which he uses to illustrate the *work* of the imagination. The work of the imagination is to be distinguished from the perception of the exterior world translated into images. The work of imagination, as our author says, is more fundamental than the image-perception; it is thus a question of affirming the 'psychically fundamental character of creative imagination'.[10] Imagination is not here a simple reflection of exterior images, but is rather an activity subject to the individual's will. Bachelard thus sets out to investigate the products of this creative will – products which cannot be predicted on the basis of a knowledge of reality. In a certain sense, therefore, science cannot predict the trajectory of the imagination, for the latter has a specific kind of autonomy. Being subject to will means that the imagination – as for some of the surrealists – has to do with semi-conscious day-dreaming (*rêverie*) rather than with the unconscious processes (condensation, displacement, etc.) of dream-work. Indeed, this factor, together with his interest in archetypes, places Bachelard much closer to Jung than to Freud. Also reminiscent of Jung is the emphasis Bachelard gives in his analysis of the imagination to the four 'primary' elements of fire, water, air, and earth seen to be eternally present in a poetical alchemy. A certain mystical element is thus on the horizon (cf. Jung's *Psychology and Alchemy*). Furthermore, Bachelard's insistence on the primacy of the already given subject–object relation, which he takes, although not always willingly, from phenomenology, means that while the imagination might produce images (most often sublimations of archetypes), the work of creativity is not itself seen to produce the subject–object relation. In effect, the subject here is his Majesty the ego, as Freud said; for there is an assumption of autonomy that verges on being absolute. An element of closure, apparently absent from his scientific writings thereby enters into Bachelard's writings on imagination.

The imagination, then, is the field of the image, and as such is to be distinguished from the translation of the external world into concepts. The imagination produces images and is its images, whereas thought produces concepts. Without a surrealism that emerges in order to revivify the image, the world of the image would wither and die, so much would it be closed in upon itself. Similarly, were it not for a certain surrationalism, thought and its concepts would also wither – sick from its very completeness and simplicity. Rather, 'openness' and 'complexity' sum up Bachelard's position. In his pleiade of elements – a little too Jungian – the concept falls to the masculine side of things, whereas the image tends towards the feminine. Similarly, the concept corresponds to the *image* of the day (for it is equivalent to 'seeing'), while the image corresponds to the *image* of the night. Dominique Lecourt's astute little book on Bachelard draws attention precisely to this feature of the thinker's work: 'In short, to reiterate Bachelard's terms, between his scientific books and his books about the imagination, it is as the Day is to the Night.'[11] For the most part, Bachelard himself is coy about whether the two elements in fact come together, that is, about whether the image emerges in science, and science in the realm of images. Bachelard's writing, almost despite itself, has nevertheless come to be seen as a source of inspiration for those intent on breaking down the barrier between concept and image, so that new images can become the basis of new scientific concepts, while new concepts can emerge on the basis of new images.

More specifically, Bachelard's writings point to the fact that neither a concept nor an image is transparent, and that this opacity signals that an element of subjectivity is always in play in human affairs. This means that human beings are spoken as much as they are speaking in the frameworks of science and the symbolic that constitute their lives. As Lecourt again puts it: 'no one can read these divergent texts without sensing a *unity* which is to be looked for there beneath the contradiction'.[12] 'Unity'? – or 'synthesis'? The answer is not unimportant. For whereas unity connotes homogeneity and risks becoming a simple unity, synthesis, as Bachelard said, is to do with relations. The latter can exist between *different* elements (provided the difference is not radical), and presupposes divisions of some sort. Unity, on the other hand, tends to erase relations. In the end, Bachelard's *oeuvre* tends to embody the notion of synthesis that he propounded in his early writing. Of necessity, though, this was a synthesis that he could not see, a necessary blindness constitutive of the place (existentially speaking) from which he wrote. In this sense, then, the Night might well be seen to take precedence over the Day in this exceptional *oeuvre*.

Notes

1 Gaston Bachelard, *The Philosophy of No: A Philosophy of the New Scientific Mind*, trans. G.C. Waterston, New York, Orion Press, 1968, p. 63.
2 ibid., p. 64.
3 Gaston Bachelard, *The New Scientific Spirit*, trans. Arthur Goldhammer, Boston, Beacon Press 1985, p. 4. Bachelard's emphasis.
4 ibid., p. 60.
5 ibid., p. 54.
6 ibid., pp. 30–1.
7 ibid., p. 137.
8 ibid., p. 176. Emphasis added.
9 Gaston Bachelard, 'Le Surrationalisme', *Inquisitions*, 1 (1936).
10 Gaston Bachelard, *La Terre et les rêveries de la volonté: essai sur l'imagination des forces*, Paris, Corti, 1948, p. 3.
11 Dominique Lecourt, *Bachelard ou le jour et la nuit (un essai de matérialisme dialectique)*, Paris, Maspero, 1974, p. 32.
12 ibid. Lecourt's emphasis.

See also in this book

Althusser, Bourdieu, Canguilhem, Cavaillès, Foucault, Kristeva

Bachelard's major writings

Essai sur la connaissance approchée, Paris, Vrin, 1928. Third edn, 1970 (principal thesis for the Doctorate in literature)
La Valeur inductive de la relativité, Paris, Vrin, 1929
Le Pluralisme coherent de la chimie moderne, Paris, Vrin, 1932
L'Intuition de l'instant: étude sur la 'Siloë' de Gaston Roupnel, Paris, Stock, 1932
Les Intuitions atomistiques: essai de classification, Paris, Boivin, 1933
The New Scientific Spirit (1934), trans. Arthur Goldhammer, Boston, Beacon Press, 1984
La Terre et les rêveries de la volonté: essai sur l'imagination des forces, Paris, Jose Corti, 1948
La Dialectique de la durée, Paris, Boivin, 1936. New edn, PUF, 1950
L'Expérience de l'espace dans la physique contemporaine, Paris, PUF, 1937
La Formation de l'esprit scientifique. Contribution a une psychanalyse de la connaissance objective, Paris, Vrin, 1938. Eighth edn, 1972
The Psychoanalysis of Fire (1938), trans. Alan C. M. Ross, Boston, Beacon Press, 1964; London, Routledge & Kegan Paul, 1964
Lautréamont (1940 and 1951), trans. Robert Duprée, Dallas, The Dallas Institute of Humanities and Culture Publications, 1984
The Philosophy of No. A Philosophy of the New Scientific Mind (1940), trans. G. C. Waterston, New York, The Orion Press, 1968
Water and Dreams. An Essay on the Imagination of Matter (1942), trans. Edith Farrell, Dallas, The Dallas Institute of Humanities and Culture Publications, 1983
Air and Dreams: An Essay on the Imagination of Movement (1943), trans. Edith and Frederick Farrell, Dallas, The Dallas Institute of Humanities and Culture Publications, 1988
La Terre et les rêveries du repos. Essai sur les images de l'intimité, Paris, Jose Corti, 1948. Sixth impression 1971
Rationalisme appliqué, Paris, PUF, 1949. Third edn 1966
Le Materialisme rationnel, Paris, PUF, 1953. Second edn 1963
The Poetics of Space (1957), trans. Maria Jolas, New York, Orion Press, 1964
La Poétique de la rêverie, Paris, PUF, 1960. Third edn 1965
The Flame of a Candle (1961), trans. Joni Caldwell, Dallas, The Dallas Institute of Humanities and Culture Publications, 1990
The Right to Dream (1970), trans. J. A. Underwood, Dallas, The Dallas Institute of Humanities and Culture Publications, 1988
On Poetic Imagination and Reverie: Selections from the Works of Gaston Bachelard, trans. Colette Gaudin, Indianapolis, Bobbs-Merrill, 1971

Further reading

Ginestier, Paul, *Pour connaître la pensée de Bachelard*, Paris, Bordas, 1968
Lecourt, Dominique, *Bachelard ou le jour et la nuit*, Paris, Grasset, 1974
McAllester Jones, Mary, *Gaston Bachelard: Subversive Humanist. Texts and Readings*, Madison, University of Wisconsin Press, 1991
Smith, Roch Charles, *Gaston Bachelard*, Boston, Twayne, 1982
Tiles, Mary, *Bachelard, Science and Objectivity*, Cambridge, Cambridge University Press, 1984

MIKHAIL BAKHTIN

Mikhail Bakhtin is, according to some estimations, one of the greatest theoreticians of literature of the twentieth century.[1] Both the historical range of his writing and the political conditions under which he wrote (particularly the political repression under Stalin) have made Bakhtin a social philosopher of some magnitude.

Born in November 1895, Bakhtin took a degree in classics and philology at the University of Petrograd in 1918. Largely for political reasons, he lived much of his life in self-imposed obscurity, taking up a professorship at the remote Mordovia State Teachers College in 1936, where, apart from one interruption in the 1940s due to rumours of a political purge, he taught until 1961. Despite his low political profile, Bakhtin was arrested in 1929 for alleged involvement in the underground Russian Orthodox Church and sentenced to six years' internal exile in Kazakhstan where he worked as a bookkeeper. By the 1960s, Bakhtin had become a cult figure in Russia, his 1929 work on

Dostoyevsky having been rediscovered and his best-known book on Rabelais – initially submitted as a doctoral thesis in the 1940s – being published for the first time in the Soviet Union in 1965. With the renewed interest in his work, Bakhtin began working in the early 1970s on a number of projects – such as one on the philosophical bases of the human sciences – which remained unfinished at his death in March 1975.

Bakhtin's intellectual trajectory and his practice of writing are quite exceptional. Not only did he often rework partially completed pieces and continue to elaborate already formulated concepts in a different way – so that his trajectory is less a straight line than a spiral – but, in addition, there is a controversy concerning the authorship of a number of books suspected of having been written by him, but published under the names of his friends, V.N. Voloshinov and P.N. Medvedev. The most notable of these are *Freudianism* and *Marxism and the Philosophy of Language* by Voloshinov, and *The Formal Method in Literary Studies* by Medvedev.

Questions of attribution aside, most scholars agree that Bakhtin's work can be divided into three main periods: (1) Early essays on ethics and aesthetics; (2) Books and articles on the history of the novel; (3) Posthumously published essays which again take up the themes of the second period. Despite the careful scholarship that is now being undertaken to show the depth of his thought, it remains true that, outside a circle of specialists, Bakhtin is best known in the West, first, for his notion of carnival, which comes from his study of Rabelais; second, for the concept of the dialogical, polyphonic novel that derives from Bakhtin's study of Dostoyevsky; and finally, for terms, such as 'chronotope' and 'novelistic discourse' which derive from his collected essays on the theory of the novel.[2]

In his Rabelais study, which was his first work translated into English, Bakhtin focuses on the carnival as it existed in the pre- to mid-Renaissance period (Rabelais (1494–1553) wrote his most important works in the early 1530s). Rabelais, for Bakhtin, continues the carnival tradition, while adding his own innovations. What then is carnival?

The most important aspect of carnival is laughter. However, carnival laughter cannot be equated with the specific forms it takes in modern consciousness. It is not simply parodic, ironical, or satirical. Carnival laughter has no object. It is ambivalent. Ambivalence is the key to the structure of carnival. The logic of carnival is, as Kristeva has shown, not the true or false, quantitative and causal logic of science and seriousness, but the qualitative logic of ambivalence, where the actor is also the spectator, destruction gives rise to creativity, and death is equivalent to rebirth.

Carnival, then, is neither private nor specifically oppositional, as it is in the period just prior to, and during, Romanticism. In no sense is carnival to be understood as an event that is officially sanctioned, or simply as a holiday period – a break from the normal labour of everyday life; nor is carnival a festival which reinforces the prevailing regime of everyday life, with its power hierarchy, and striking contrast between rich and poor. Carnival, in short, is not the result of officialdom (which is always serious) reinforcing its own power on the principle of 'bread and circuses'. Rather, the people are the carnival, and officialdom, like everyone else, is subject to its rituals and its laws – the Church as well as the Crown. To put it in a nutshell: carnival is not simply negative; it has no utilitarian motive. It is ambivalent.

Consequently, rather than a spectacle to be observed, carnival is the hilarity lived by everyone. And this raises the question as to whether there can be, strictly speaking, a theory of carnival. For there is no life outside the carnival. The people in it are both actors and spectators simultaneously. And as the festival laughter of carnival is also directed against those who laugh, the people in it are both subjects and objects of laughter. This laughter is general, has a philosophical basis, and embraces death (cf. the themes of macabre laughter and the grotesque) as well as life. As such, carnival laughter is one of the 'essential forms of truth concerning the world'.[3] Bakhtin remarks, however, that with the modern era, laughter has been reduced to one of the 'low genres'. Carnival itself, on the other hand, embraces lowness. Degradation, debasement, the body and all its functions – but particularly defecation, urination, and copulation – are part and parcel of the ambivalent carnival experience. The body, then, is part of this ambivalence. It is not closed in and private, but open to the world. Similarly, the proximity between the womb and the tomb is not repressed, but, like reproduction, is celebrated, as 'lowness' in general is celebrated. The body only becomes 'finished' (that is, private) according to our author, in the Renaissance.

Carnival figures, such as the clown, who exists on the border between art and life, experiences, such as madness, and the figure of the 'mask', which does not hide but reveals, all illuminate the ambivalent, all-embracing logic of carnival. Of the mask, Bakhtin writes that it is 'connected with the joy of change and reincarnation, with gay relativity and with the merry negation of uniformity and similarity'.[4] The mask in the eighteenth century of course became a symbol – especially in the work of Rousseau – of everything that was false and inauthentic. The mask, in effect, was always the mask of hypocrisy. With carnival ambivalence, the mask is always *obviously* distorting. That it is covering up and transforming its object is clearly understood. The mask undermines the notion of being as identical with itself; it both reveals and plays with contradiction, and in so doing begins to encapsulate the ambivalence of the carnival as practice. As Bakhtin says: 'The mask is related to transition, metamorphosis, the violation of natural boundaries, to mockery and familiar nicknames. It contains the playful element of life.'[5] For Kristeva, the mask signals the loss of individuality and the assumption of anonymity, and thus the assumption of a multitude of identities. Hence the mask always plays with the symbolic so as to unhinge it from its fixed and rigid forms. The mask is the incarnation of movement and change. It is never serious unless we understand that to refuse to give seriousness absolute power is a serious matter. The exhortation of the carnival is, as a result, that we should enter the game of life, masked: that is, ambivalently, irreverently, and with a spirit of laughter.

Carnival, in its ambivalence, focuses attention on the people as the arena of participation. As participation, it is the circumvention of representation. Carnival, then, makes the people the most important element in life. The people, as participants in the carnival as participation, come to embody the universal. This is why the universal is practical and tends to escape objectification. Again, while carnival laughter can find a place for seriousness (even if this be to mock it – 'not a single saying of the Old Testament was left unchallenged', says Bakhtin[6] – seriousness cannot find a place for laughter. If we equate seriousness with objectification (all seriousness is self-conscious), this would mean that laughter cannot be objectified, cannot be theorised.

Carnival logic (the logic of ambivalence) is not restricted to the limitation of binary oppositions which set limits, but is equivalent of the power of continuum (positive *and* negative). The carnival logic is revealed closer to home when we realise that any speech act is essentially bi-valent (both One and Other), so that, for instance, the seriousness of academic discourse is based on the repression of ambivalence.

In his study of Dostoyevsky, Bakhtin argues that the Russian writer's fiction has a 'polyphonic' structure in that – like carnival – it includes the other's voice within itself. For example, with a text like *The Brothers Karamazov*, 'the other's discourse gradually, stealthily penetrates the consciousness and the speech of the hero'.

For Bakhtin, novelistic discourse should not be understood as the word of communication studied by linguistics, but is rather the 'dynamic milieu' in which the exchange (dialogue) takes place. In terms of linguistics, the word for Bakhtin is translinguistic: the intersection of meanings rather than a fixed point, or a single meaning. While parody, irony, and satire are, for instance, clear examples of the word in Bakhtin's sense (we must resort to the translinguistic/semiotic dimension in order to interpret them), Dostoyevsky's work leads us to the same kind of insight by way of the dialogical word which includes the other's word within itself. This is a polyphonic word in the sense that polyphony, too, has no fixed point but is the interpenetration of sounds. Polyphony is multiple, not singular; it includes what would be excluded by a representation of it.

Bakhtin reads Dostoyevsky in the spirit of carnival with its double logic. Justice therefore cannot be done to Dostoyevsky's writing by reducing it to a story with characters, as is typical of the closed structure of the epic, and also fundamental to what Bakhtin called a 'monological' text. Most simply understood, a monological text has a single (mono-), homogeneous, and relatively uniform logic. It lends itself very easily to an ideological appropriation; for the essential aspect of ideology is the message conveyed, and not the *way* the message arises and is articulated within the milieu of the word. For Bakhtin, Tolstoy's works are most often monological in this sense. By contrast, in *The Brothers Karamazov*, not only words create meaning, but also the contextual relationship between them (e.g., Ivan's 'poem', 'The Legend of the Grand Inquisitor', and Smerdyakov's confession).

All of Bakhtin's approach directs attention to the way the novel is constructed – its *mise-en-scène* – rather than the intrigue, or story, or the particular views, ideology, or feelings of the author. Quite simply: the author becomes the site of the *mise-en-scène* of the novel. The polyphonic novel makes this more explicit than other forms, but in almost every novelistic genre, there are a number of languages in operation, each one utilised by the author. As Bakhtin explains:

> The author is not to be found in the language of the narrator, not in the normal literary language to which the story opposes itself . . . – but rather, the author utilizes now one language, now another, in order to avoid giving himself up wholly to either of them; he makes use of this verbal give-and-take, this dialogue of languages at every point in his work, in order that he himself might remain as it were neutral with regard to language, a third party in a quarrel between two people.[7]

Although Bakhtin formally distanced himself from structuralism and semiotics, his refusal to embrace the ideology of the author's intentions as a way of explaining the meaning of a work of art, places him much closer to a structural approach than might at first appear. For Bakhtin, the author is an empty space where the drama would take place – or better: the author is the dramatisation itself. In this sense, Bakhtin founded a dynamic view of structure, certainly one with more dynamism than what developed in Russia under the aegis of the Russian formalists. Indeed, Bakhtin's concern to emphasise the open-ended, unfinished quality of Dostoyevsky's novels (and even the unfinished quality of much of his own writing, both published and unpublished), together with his concern to show that (static) form was never separable from (dynamic) content, means that his is a structural approach that refuses to be limited by a privileging of the synchronic over the diachronic. Similarly, in his critique of Saussure's distinction between *langue* and *parole*, Bakhtin claims that Saussure ignores speech genres, and that this renders doubtful the usefulness of *langue* in explaining the essential working of language. Furthermore, Bakhtin rejects what he sees as the structuralist tendency to analyse texts as though they were completely self-contained units whose meaning could be established independently of context. Rather, any attempt to understand *parole* must take into account the circumstances, assumptions and the time of the enunciation of the utterance. In effect, Bakhtin urges that account must be taken of the contingency of language.

The concern for the contingency of language led Bakhtin to formulate his theory of the 'chronotope'. As the term implies, both space and time are at issue, and Bakhtin sought to reveal the way in which the history of the novel constituted different forms of the chronotope. Inspired by Einstein's theory of relativity, Bakhtin defines the chronotope as the 'intrinsic connectedness of temporal and spatial relationships in literature'. He goes on to show the variations in the chronotope in the history of the novel. The novels of Greek Romance, for example (second and sixth centuries AD), are characterised by 'adventure time' which is played out through the obstacles (storm, shipwreck, illness, etc.) preventing the union between the two lovers taking place. The plot is often played out over several geographical locations, and the manners and customs of the people within these locations are described. In the idyllic novel (e.g., Rousseau), space and time are inseparable: 'Idyllic life and its events are inseparable from this concrete, spatial corner of the world where the fathers and grandfathers lived and where one's children will live.'[8] The idyllic world is thus self-sufficient, homogeneous, identical with itself – almost outside time and change. This implies that in the polyphonic, dialogical novel, time is a heterogeneous, almost unrepresentable element. Furthermore, time will tend to render (Euclidean) space more fluid, so that the time of relativity becomes a possible analogy.

Clearly, the chronotope is a mechanism for classifying various genres of the novel as well as a means of constituting a history and theory of the novel. And it should be remembered that for all his interest in the particular details of the speech and other events of everyday life, Bakhtin was a thinker who used the broadest canvas possible to develop his theory of literary production. In fact the effect of Bakhtin's use of macro-categories like 'chronotope' and 'genre' is to render invisible the unique, the singular, the individual, and the unclassifiable. Some critics, such as Booth, have suggested that Bakhtin generalises at the expense of a detailed exegesis of the great variety of works concerned. Moreover, in his description of genres like 'Greek romance' or the 'Idyllic novel', he adopts a formal approach very like that of the early structuralists (e.g., Propp), emphasis being placed on the individuality and distinctiveness of the homogeneous structure of the genre, with the result that the individuality of the works which make it up becomes invisible. One might go further and suggest that the problem of genre is that it risks turning individual works of art into myth. For myth exhibits a homogeneous, and relatively undifferentiated structure; this allows it to be communicated to a vast audience who, it is true, may then appropriate it in their own way.

Perhaps if Bakhtin had been more structuralist in the Lévi-Straussian sense, and had seen the structure of genres as a kind of grammar which constituted the precondition of specific works done under its aegis, he would not have given the impression of the lack of rigour which comes with a procrustean attempt to place all the works of an era under the same classificatory umbrella.

Notes

1 cf. Tzvetan Todorov, *Mikhail Bakhtin: The Dialogical Principle*, trans. Wlad Godzich, Manchester, Manchester University Press, 1984, p. ix.
2 See Mikhail Bakhtin, *The Dialogic Imagination, Four Essays by M. M. Bakhtin*, trans. Caryl Emerson and Michael Holquist, Austin, University of Texas Press, 1981.
3 Mikhail Bakhtin, *Rabelais and his World*, trans. Hélène Iswolsky, Bloomington, Indiana University Press, 1984, p. 66.

4   ibid., p. 39.
5   ibid., p. 40.
6   ibid., p. 86.
7   Bakhtin, *The Dialogic Imagination*, p. 314.
8   ibid., p. 225.

See also in this book

Kristeva, Lévi-Strauss, Todorov

Bakhtin's major writings

Problems of Dostoyevsky's Poetics (1929), trans. Caryl Emerson, Manchester, Manchester University Press, 1984

Rabelais and His World (1940), trans. Hélène Iswolsky, Bloomington, Indiana University Press, 1984

The Dialogic Imagination, Four Essays by M.M. Bakhtin (1965–1975), trans. Caryl Emerson and Michael Holquist, Austin, University of Texas Press, 1981

Speech Genres and Other Late Essays, trans. Vern W. McGee, Austin, University of Texas. Second paperback printing, 1987

Freudianism: A Marxist Critique (1927) (with V.N. Volishonov), trans. I.R. Titunik, New York, Academic Press, 1976

Marxism and the Philosophy of Language (1929) (with V.N. Volishonov), trans. L. Matejka and I.R. Titunik, New York, Seminar Press, 1973

Further reading

Kristeva, Julia, 'Word, dialogue and novel' in *Desire in Language: A Semiotic Approach to Literature and Art*, trans. Thomas Gora, Alice Jardine, and Leon S. Roudiez, Oxford, Basil Blackwell, paperback, 1982 (reprinted 1984), pp. 64–91

Morson, Gary Saul, and Emerson, Caryl, *Mikhail Bakhtin: Creation of a Prosaics*, Stanford, California, Stanford University Press, 1990

Todorov, Tzvetan, *Mikhail Bakhtin: The Dialogical Principle*, trans. Wlad Godzich, Manchester, Manchester University Press, 1984

GEORGES CANGUILHEM

According to Michel Foucault,[1] philosophy in post-war France, as well as being Marxist, or non-Marxist, phenomenological or non-phenomenological, could also be divided into two strands of a different order: one, a philosophy of sense experience and the subject, the other, 'a philosophy of knowledge, rationality and of the concept' – a more epistemologically based philosophy. While Sartre was of course was the dominant figure of the first strand, Foucault argues that the supervisor of his doctoral thesis on madness, Georges Canguilhem, was the leading figure in the other. In effect, the far from flamboyant and low-key Canguilhem, had an influence on the structural approaches to history, Marxism and psychoanalysis which far outstripped the public perception of who the main players were in intellectual and academic circles. Indeed Canguilhem paved the way for Lacan in 1956 when, in a lecture at the Collège Philosophique, he criticised the doyen of clinical psychology, Daniel Lagache. This article was republished ten years later in *Les cahiers pour l'analyse*, the journal animated in the 1960s at the Ecole Normale Supérieure (rue d'Ulm) by Jacques Lacan's son-in-law, Jacques-Alain Miller. There, Canguilhem's now famous words referred to the positivist face of psychology as being equivalent to philosophy less its rigour, as ethics less its demands, as medicine without verification.[2]

Georges Canguilhem was born in 1904 at Castelnaudary in south-west France. In 1924, along with Sartre, Nizan, and Aron, Canguilhem passed his *agrégation* in philosophy at the Ecole Normale Supérieure when he was a student of Alain. After completing his studies in philosophy, Canguilhem undertook a medical degree to enable him to teach and research in the field of the history and philosophy of science. After teaching at a lycée in Toulouse, Canguilhem taught during the war at the University of Strasbourg, where his course on *Norms and the Normal* would become the basis of his thesis defended in 1943 for his doctorate in medicine. In 1955, after a period as inspector-general of national education, Canguilhem succeeded Gaston Bachelard in the chair of philosophy at the Sorbonne. In 1961, it was Canguilhem, on the jury before which Michel Foucault defended his thesis on the history of madness, who acknowledged that his protégé had the talent of a poet in speaking about madness.

A staunch defender of Foucault against the attacks of Sartre and his supporters, Canguilhem set the scene for a history of science which clearly diverged from any inevitable evolutionism, or from any cumulative notion of knowledge as progress. He acclimatised a generation of thinkers to the idea of a structural history of the sciences, one that attempts to account for discontinuities as much as for continuities in the history of the scientific enterprise. Few have as perceptively as Michel Foucault pin-pointed the general co-ordinates of Canguilhem's project from the perspective of the structuralist angle which interests us here. Briefly, some of Foucault's key points were as follows.

Prior to Canguilhem's work, the dominant approach in the history of science was to see the past as a coherent, and continuous precursor to the present. Implied in this approach is the idea that once a science and its object is established, it henceforth becomes the guarantor of truth. Thus would the scientific disciplines established in the seventeenth and eighteenth centuries serve as the basis for those sciences as they developed in the nineteenth and twentieth centuries. The problem with such an approach is that it is based on a retrospective illusion. It assumes that the past is a lead up to the present; but more than this, it assumes that the present is static and unchanging and that, therefore, a history of science as it is written today will be just as valid tomorrow. For Canguilhem, however, what characterises science is not closure and continuity, but rather openness and discontinuity. What might have appeared to be a minor, or even invisible side issue in the history of science can suddenly become central for dealing with a newly discovered problem. Thus, Foucault points out, 'the discovery of non-cellular

fermentation – a "side" phenomenon during the reign of Pasteur and his microbiology – marked an essential break only when the physiology of enzymes developed'.[3] Because science is inevitably changing – because, for Canguilhem, it is primarily an 'open system' and thus affected by its environment – it 'spontaneously makes and remakes its own history at every instant'.[4]

This sense of science remaking its history is even more acute in those disciplines which have not reached the high degree of formalisation of mathematics. Canguilhem has thus focused almost exclusively on biology and medicine in his studies: the sciences of life. He has brought the history of science 'down from the heights' and towards those 'middle regions' where knowledge is clearly dependent on the external environment.

The upshot is that truth and error, as Nietzsche argued, are truth and error as seen from a particular point of view. Thus what is important and interesting in the history of science is what appears to be so from the perspective of the present. This is clarified by Canguilhem's statement that 'It is in the present that problems provoke reflection.'[5] For this reason alone, there can be no entirely neutral history of science. It has thus to be acknowledged, first, that a particular version of truth and error could be false, and, second, that, in any case, the fact of error – or falsity – can be just as revealing of the history of science as 'truth'. Consequently, Canguilhem's aim becomes not the discovery of truth, but the search for a way to establish a knowledge of how the true and the false are constituted at a given moment in the history of science. At this level, one mode of constituting the true–false dichotomy can be, and often is, discontinuous with another. Discontinuity, in sum, entails viewing the history of science as a series of self-corrections carried out by science.

Although, in his later work, Canguilhem has written on Darwin and Darwin's relation to his predecessors and his precursors, his best-known, and most pertinent work as an illustration of his approach to the history of medicine, is *On the Normal and the Pathological*, first published in 1943, and subsequently republished with additions in 1966. The text is concerned to make a contribution to explaining the difference between the normal and the pathological by examining the way that these concepts have been developed in physiology and biology in the course of the nineteenth and twentieth centuries. The question which guides the study is: how is the normal established in biology and medicine? By normal one could mean good health, as opposed to illness, or what is deemed to be pathological. On the other hand, if one took life as a whole, illness, or the pathological, might in some sense have to be included in the concept of 'normal'.

During the nineteenth century, medicine was considered to be the science of diseases, while physiology was the science of life. A question will arise to upset this dichotomy, however – namely: is not disease also part of life? Or, to put it another way: can a fully-fledged physiology be constituted without reference to disease? Is not disease the way the body actually becomes an object of knowledge? For the Classical Greeks, the normal was equated with harmony and equilibrium, while a malady was equated with disequilibrium, 'dysharmony', or 'anormality'. The prefixes 'dys-' and 'a-' imply a discontinuity between the normal and the pathological. Largely through the work of Claude Bernard in experimental physiology, nineteenth-century medicine developed a quantitative view (largely related to levels of excitation) of the difference between the normal (health) than the pathological (disease). Disease became a *hyper-* or *hypo-*normal state. In other words, for Bernard, there was a relationship of continuity between good health and disease. To know the physiology of the normal body was thus to be put in touch with the basis of the diseased body as well. In short, through the quantitative paradigm, good health (the normal) was a way to the knowledge of the pathological.

In the twentieth century, the work of René Leriche shakes the quantitative perspective of the positivist approach. For Leriche, health is equivalent to the 'silence of the body in its organs'. Health (the normal) now becomes what is entirely taken for granted; well-being is the body not experienced as such, or knowable as such; a knowledge of the body is now seen to be possible only by starting from the perspective of the pathological – from the perspective of medicine, and not from that of physiology.

Nevertheless, the nature of the pathological still remains to be established. Clearly, this question can be approached either from the point of view of the one who feels ill, or from the point of view of medicine itself, in which case it may be possible to establish, in strictly medical terms, the existence of a pathological condition before the person concerned has a conscious knowledge of it. While the very latest technology might have the effect of taking a knowledge of illness away from the patient, Canguilhem, in concluding a reflection that runs right through his book, points out that the physician tends to forget that, in the end, 'the patient calls him'. This reminder of something obvious will allow Canguilhem to emphasise that the distinction between physiology and pathology can only have 'clinical significance'. This is a key point. As opposed to what he designates as the positivist approach to science, in which one has to know in order to act, Canguilhem argues for the importance of 'technique'. That is, only by referring to the environment, or the conditions of existence (and not by attempting to constitute the distinction theoretically and a priori) in which good health and illness exist, can the distinction between them be sustained. Reference to conditions means that the distinction between the normal and the pathological has to remain provisional and continually open to change. Instead of closing off avenues for the expansion of human agency, Canguilhem's approach here would seem to lead to a profound enhancement of them.

Another important theme running through Canguilhem's work concerns the formal definition of the normal. One way in which the normal has been defined is in terms of the statistical norm. For Canguilhem, twentieth-century research has been able to show that a living being can be perfectly normal even though it might bear little relation to a statistical average. Indeed, a monster (an anomaly) could be quite normal in the sense that it constitutes its own norm in relation to the environment in which it is located. 'Taken separately, the living being and his environment are not normal: it is their relationship that makes them such.'[6] An anomaly can be rare and still be normal in this sense.

In his detailed discussion of the difference between disease and health, Canguilhem shows that although the boundary between the normal and pathological is imprecise, this does not imply a continuity between them. Nevertheless, when life is understood as a kind of totality it must also be recognised that disease cannot be abnormal in any absolute sense. In fact, were someone to experience no ill-health, this may well lead to deleterious results, because, given that the living being is fundamentally an open system, it requires a means of initiating new conditions through the overcoming of the sort of obstacles posed by illness. Thus 'The healthy man does not flee before the problems posed by sometimes sudden disruptions of his habits, even physiologically speaking; he measures his health in terms of his capacity to overcome organic crises in order to establish a new order.'[7]

In twentieth-century medical science, we find that health is not the total absence of disease, but rather the capacity to restore a former state through an effort that can change the structural basis of the person so affected. This change in the structural base, equivalent to the interaction of the living being with its conditions of existence, results not in abnormal states, but in a continual process of norm-changing. In this sense, Canguilhem argues, human beings are 'normative' beings, not because they conform to norms, but because they are norm-creating beings, or open systems dependent on their environment. As our author confirms: 'Norms are relative to each other in a system.'[8] Disease – the obstacle – is the necessary stimulus for the norm-making necessary for health.

Given the important place Canguilhem attributes to the pathological, he is opposed to psycho-social notions of the norm. The work of Talcott Parsons would be an example. Here, the a priori norm of a well-functioning, more or less well-ordered society is assumed as given, and opposition to the norm, if it goes beyond a certain threshold, is deemed to be pathological and dangerous to the existence of society as such. Social theory of this kind sees society as a relatively closed system whereby 'health' is maintained by subscribing to the norm, rather than by creating new forms of normality.

Overall, for Canguilhem, the history of science itself tends to be an open system – as Foucault implied. Science 'makes and re-makes its history at every instant'; it finds a norm, only in order to revise and transform it. For this reason, it tends to be a process of discontinuity; for a plurality of norms, by its very nature, entails a discontinuity between norms. History, as the history of continuity, like the notion of the transcendental subject, is a closed system and fundamentally unable to change in any fundamental sense. Discontinuous history, then, is one that always asks questions of itself, as Kant did regarding the Enlightenment. This principle of questioning, perhaps more than anything else, joins Foucault to Canguilhem, as Canguilhem himself is joined to the most important developments of twentieth-century science.

Notes

1 Michel Foucault, 'Introduction' in Georges Canguilhem, *On the Normal and the Pathological*, trans. Carolyn R. Fawcett,

Dordrecht, Holland, Reidel Publishing Company, 1978, pp. ix–xx.

2 Elisabeth Roudinesco, *Jacques Lacan and Company. A History of Psychoanalysis in France, 1925–1985*, trans. Jeffrey Mehlman, Chicago, University of Chicago Press, 1990, p. 221.

3 Foucault, 'Introduction' in Canguilhem, *On the Normal and the Pathological*, p. xiv.

4 ibid.

5 Canguilhem, *On the Normal and the Pathological*, p. 27.

6 ibid., p. 78.

7 ibid., p. 117.

8 ibid., p. 153.

See also in this book

Bachelard, Cavaillès, Foucault, Lacan

Canguilhem's major writings

On the Normal and the Pathological (1943, 1966), trans. Carolyn R. Fawcett, Dordrecht, Holland, Reidel Publishing Company, 1978

Etudes d'histoire et de philosophie des sciences, Paris, Vrin, 1975

Formation du concept de réflex aux XVII et XVIII siècles, Paris, Vrin, 1977

Ideology and Rationality in the History of the Life Sciences (1977), trans. Arthur Goldhammer, Cambridge, Mass., MIT Press, 1988

La Santé: concept vulgaire et question philosophique, Pin-Balma, Sables, 1990

Further reading

Foucault, Michel, and Burchell, Graham, 'Georges Canguilhem: Philosopher of error', *Ideology and Consciousness*, 7 (Autumn 1980), pp. 51–62

Lecourt, Dominique, *Marxism and Epistemology: Bachelard, Canguilhem and Foucault*, trans. Ben Brewster, London, NLB, 1975

Spicker, Stuart, 'An introduction to the medical epistemology of Georges Canguilhem', *Journal of Medicine and Philosophy*, 12, 4 (November 1987), pp. 397–411

JEAN CAVAILLES

While Jean Cavaillès and his key work, *Sur la logique et la théorie de la science* (*On Logic and the Theory of Science* – hereafter *Sur la logique*),[1] may not in themselves have irrevocably transformed the French intellectual landscape after the Second World War, he and his work were the precondition of such a transformation. Like Georges Canguilhem – although for quite different reasons – Cavaillès is another of the invisible (to the broader public) precursors of the structuralist movement of the 1960s. What Cavaillès brought to both life and the intellectual milieu was a unique combination of enormous courage (he was posthumously decorated twice for his bravery in the Resistance), energy and poetry on the one hand, coupled with extreme rigour and philosophical brilliance on the other. The now famous words of Cavaillès at the end of *Sur la logique*[2] calling for a non-humanist philosophy of concepts to replace the philosophy of consciousness as represented by Sartre and phenomenology, must be seen in conjunction with a commitment to the Resistance during the German occupation, and subsequent death of Cavaillès by a Nazi firing squad in 1944 at the age of 41. For those like Georges Canguilhem, Cavaillès was the living proof that a man of action could be structuralist in philosophical orientation.

Jean Cavaillès was born into a Protestant family in 1903.[3] He completed his *agrégation* in philosophy in 1927, and in 1929 attended Husserl's lectures on Descartes at the Sorbonne. With assistance of a Rockefeller bursary, he studied in Germany in the early 1930s at a number of universities, including the University of Freiburg where, in 1931, he met Husserl. After teaching in a Lycée in Amiens, Cavaillès was appointed as a lecturer in logic and general philosophy in the Faculty of Letters at the University of Strasbourg. It was there, in 1938, that he completed his doctorate in mathematics on axiomatic method and formalism, with a minor thesis on set theory. In both these works, Cavaillès begins to work out an anti-intuitionist position which argues that the development of mathematics owes nothing to existence in the Existentialist sense, but is purely formal – the development of concepts.

In 1939, Cavaillès was mobilised, first of all as an officer of the *corps franc* (irregular forces), and then as a cipher officer. When taken prisoner in June 1940, he escaped in Belgium while being transported to Germany and returned to teaching at the University of Strasbourg, then relocated to Clermont-Ferrand in the so-called free zone. In 1941, he was appointed to the Sorbonne as an associate-professor of logic. As co-founder of the resistance movement, *Libération-sud*, Cavaillès was arrested in August 1942 by French police and interned in the south of France, first at Montpellier, then at Saint-Paul d'Eyjeaux. He escaped a second time in December of the same year, and later travelled to London where he met Simone Veil. After his return from London in 1943, Cavaillès was again arrested, this time by German counter-espionage. Disowned by the Vichy government, he was tortured, then executed in February 1944 after having been condemned to death by a military tribunal. He was posthumously made a Companion of the Libération and a Knight of the Legion of Honour.

During his internment in the south of France, Cavaillès proceeded to write what has become his most important philosophical work, *Sur la logique*. To call the latter work philosophical is in one sense misleading. For while Husserl and other phenomenologists accepted Kant's view that philosophy was the arbiter of the epistemological foundations of the natural and human sciences, Cavaillès took no such view. For him, the investigation of the bases of the sciences would show that science *qua* science – for which mathematics is a privileged example – is fundamentally misunderstood if it is thought to be in need of a philosophical meta-language for clarifying its formal framework. In this regard, Cavaillès thinks through the way Kant deals with the issue of grounding thought in relation to experience, the point being to know what thought and logic are *vis-à-vis* new experiences. Here, Cavaillès quickly homes in on the relation-ship between logic and singularity. Is this relationship one where logic assumes an unchanging, transcendental character, so that new experience is filtered through an eternal formal structure? Or is it, rather, that a particular experience can overturn the edifice itself, so that logic and experience would be inextricably bound to each other – a change on one side avoidably leading to profound effects on the other?

Kant, and before him, the Port-Royal grammarians, privileged a founding ego or consciousness in their explanation of the rules of logic and grammar. The uncondi-tioned, apodictic rules of logic, like reason, would belong to the faculty of consciousness. Logic, therefore, would be the organisation of consciousness itself. Logic would be intrin-sic to human psychology. On this reading, consciousness itself is organised, but its con-tents are contingent or conditioned. Thus an unchanging and ultimately formal conscious-ness encounters a heterogeneous content of experience. Of course Kant famously argues that form and content are inseparable: there can be no experience without a concept, and no thought without a content. Despite this, Kant and later Husserl, see the formal side of the equation as having to do with the rules of logic which would be transcendental and unchanging: the content may change, but the form always remains the same. In relation to this, Cavaillès argues that 'In a philosophy of consciousness logic is transcendental or it does not exist.'[4]

A similar approach has been adopted in the sciences with regard to logic and mathe-matics. On the one side is the fixed formal basis of science, and on the other, the accu-mulation of knowledge deemed to derive from the physical, external world. Within mathematics the issue has been taken further with the intuitionists arguing that the ulti-mate basis of mathematical axioms is the physical world itself. Or rather, it is a ques-tion of arguing that as human consciousness is itself a physical entity in the world, math-ematical formalisation is, for the intuitionists, ultimately tied to consciousness. On this basis, the starting point for investigation must be the material world.

When Bolzano, in 1817, showed that science need no longer be considered as the simple intermediate between the human mind and external reality, he opened up an entirely different avenue of reflection. In following this avenue of thought, Cavaillès argues that while a theory of science cannot but be a theory of unity, this unity is one of movement, and not one of stasis – not one of a science outside of time. In this regard, the 'true meaning of a theory is not in what is understood by the scientist himself as essentially provisional, but in a conceptual becoming which cannot be halted'.[5] More generally, science is not reducible to the intentions of the scientist, as the philosophies of consciousness from Descartes to Husserl have implied; rather, the basis of science is to be found in the formation of concepts and their history. That is, science *changes* at the conceptual level; it does not remain in a fast-frozen state as it does in Kant's transcendentalism.

So as to consolidate and clarify his argument, Cavaillès employs a number of key terms. The first is 'structure'. Because investigating the nature of science is itself a scientific activity, science is the 'science of science'. Its statements are not constitutive but appear immediately in the self-illumination of the scientific movement. This movement, Cavaillès says, is equivalent to structure. Structure, then, is the manifestation of science to itself.

Revelation, in keeping with the movement of structure, is equivalent to what is revealed. There is no form of revelation separate from what is revealed. Revelation opens on to a key term in the whole of Cavaillès's project, and this is 'demonstration'.

With demonstration, Cavaillès endeavours to grasp the whole of the scientific enterprise. To illustrate the point, we can focus on the relationship between mathematics and physics. In keeping with Kantian episte-mology, the relationship between mathematics and physics would be seen as the 'pure' side of science in relation to its 'applied' side. New physical phenomena would be explained and understood in terms of the a priori mathematical framework. For Cavaillès, on the other hand, true science never leaves what it demonstrates. All of science is inseparable from demonstration. In effect, there is no purely 'pure' side of science, any more than there is an essentially 'applied' side. A demonstration is true, therefore, not through some theorem being actualised, but by way of the necessary movement of logic. The logic of science, then, is *in* its demonstration, which is the structure speaking of itself.

In order that this might be grasped more fully, Cavaillès shows how the movement of science is embedded in its process of enchaining, that is, in its logic. Rather than the metaphor of empirical content being poured into a formal container (i.e. into concepts), Cavaillès sees enchaining as the key to the relationship between form and content. The enchaining of science which is made possible through logic, is science as demonstration. There is no beginning – or ending – to the movement of enchaining; such would only be possible if Kantian epistemology is used as the basis of understanding. And there is, Cavaillès acknowledges, always the temptation to insert mathematics into the imaginative constructions of experience typical of a Kantian approach.

Cavaillès concludes his presentation with a discussion of Husserl's phenomenological philosophy of science. Here, it is shown that the basic premises of phenomenology, as far as mathematics in particular is concerned, reinforce the primacy of consciousness and the transcendental ego. For even if consciousness is always the consciousness of something, and even if Husserl was bent on constructing a rigorous (read: scientific) body of concepts for analysing the content of consciousness, consciousness, at the level of its internal structure, is fundamentally a formal entity without any particular content. This is so even though Husserl distinguishes between formal logic as it is practised in particular judgements, or arguments, and the disciplines of the *mathesis universalis* (arithmetic, pure logic, etc.) which, being absolutely formal, have no empirical basis to their validity. This fundamental separation in Husserl, Cavaillès sees as another version of the separation between the formal structure of science and its concrete content.

By way of confirming the latter point, he examines Husserl's view of mathematics. He notes that the father of phenomenology divides mathematics into a formal part and an applied part. Phenomenology, says Cavaillès, thus puts forward a position similar to that of the empiricist logician who claims that mathematics does not have its own content. Here, Cavaillès focuses on Husserl's use of the term 'nomology' used to mark out axiomatic theories in mathematics. Nomology allows for a univocal definition of a system of objects; it cannot lead to contradiction and is thus in itself tautological. Mathematics as a pure form is thus found at the nomological level, while its applied side, or content, is seen in physics. For Cavaillès the mathematician, however, the theory of numbers is not nomological. Gödel's theorem that a proposition can exist which is neither the product, nor contradiction, of axioms cannot be accommodated with the formalism of nomology. Again, Cantor's notion of infinity cannot be accommodated by a purely formal mathematics. Mathematics, says Cavaillès, begins with the infinite. In the end, therefore, Husserl's philosophical project is not unique. It may reveal that there can be a consciousness of progress, but it cannot give any insight into the progress of consciousness as such; for the latter is, in the end, purely formal, that is, nomological. Scientific progress, then, is not to be understood as the history of the accumulation of knowledge, but as the 'perpetual revision of existing content through deepening and erasure'.[6]

From the analysis just outlined, Cavaillès concludes his study by saying that there is no consciousness capable of generating its own products; rather, consciousness is immediately in the idea, and not formally separated from it. Just as science is demonstration (union of pure and applied aspects), so consciousness is the inseparability of thought and its actualisation. Finally, all this is summarised by the famous remark that: 'It is not a philosophy of consciousness but a philosophy of the concept which can give a doctrine of science.'[7]

Jean Cavaillès wrote the work for which he has become best known while he was a prisoner during the Occupation in a French gaol in the south of France. He was unable to write the Introduction which he deemed necessary for making this difficult work more accessible. He participated in history while rejecting the existentialist version of it. In short, as Canguilhem has reminded us, it was Cavaillès's activity as a combatant (a role for which he saw himself destined, one derived from a certain logical rigour) which cut short his career as a philosopher and a historian of science. The philosopher for whom science is seen as demonstration, as structure, and as a history of concepts not founded on the cogito, died in action, so to speak. As such, his death has itself come to serve as a kind of demonstration – that is, as a unique synthesis of life and intellect. As Georges Canguilhem again said, the life of Cavaillès the philosopher was not a preparation for death; rather, his death was a preparation for philosophy.

Notes

1   Jean Cavaillès, *Sur la logique et la théorie de la science*, Paris, Vrin, fourth edn, 1987. The title of this work was given by the establishers of the text, Georges Canguilhem and Charles Ehresmann.
2   ibid., p. 78.
3   The following details about the life and career of Jean Cavaillès come from Georges Canguilhem, *Vie et mort de Jean Cavaillès*, Ambialet, Pierre Laleure, 'Les carnets de

Baudasser', 1984. This text consists of three commemorative lectures by Canguilhem given at the University of Strasbourg, the Sorbonne and on Radio France-culture, in 1967, 1969, and 1974, respectively.

4 Cavaillès, *Sur la logique*, p. 10.
5 ibid., p. 23.
6 ibid., p. 78.
7 ibid.

See also in this book

Bachelard, Canguilhem, Foucault

Cavaillès's major writings

Méthode axiomatique et formalisme. Essai sur le problème du fondement des mathematiques (*Axiomatic Method and Formalism. Essay on the Problem of the Foundation of Mathematics*), Paris, Hermann, 1938
Remarques sur la formation de la théorie abstraite des ensembles (*Remarks on the Abstract Theory of Sets*), Paris, Hermann, 1938
Transfini et continu (*The Transfinite and the Continuous*) (1943), Paris, Hermann, 1947
Sur la logique et la théorie de la science (1943 and 1947), Paris, Vrin, fourth edn, 1987

Further reading

Gaston Bachelard, 'L'Oeuvre de Jean Cavaillès' ('The work of Jean Cavaillès') in Gabrielle Ferrières, *Jean Cavaillès, philosophe et combatant*, Paris, Presses Universitaires de France, 1950
Georges Canguilhem, *Vie et mort de Jean Cavaillès*, Ambialet, France, Pierre Laleure, 1976

SIGMUND FREUD

It is a cliché to say that Freud was a man of his time – that he had the values of a nineteenth-century bourgeois, that he was influenced by scientific positivism and vitalism, that certain Victorian attitudes coloured his views about sexuality. From another angle, though, it is possible to see Freud as a thinker who was, and in all likelihood will remain, both controversial in what he had to say about sexuality and the psyche, and

brilliantly disturbing in the way he founded psychoanalysis through the analysis of phenomena which were hitherto thought to be unanalysable – dreams, and slips of the tongue, for example.

Freud's text is more than challenging in what it says as a (relatively) discrete entity; it is also, and even primarily, challenging as the trace of a grand intellectual odyssey in which psychoanalysis undergoes a subtle transformation within a body of texts that is always evolving. In part, this transformation results from the fact that Freud himself is not entirely in control of the concepts (e.g., life, death, pleasure, ego) he seeks to explicate, and this because these concepts are often unstable in themselves. In short, Freud, who emphasised the importance of engaging continually in interpretation – Freud, who said that, ultimately, a psychoanalysis was interminable – this Freud must himself be interpreted in light of the notion of 'unlimited interpretation' that he inaugurated.

Consequently, perhaps one of the most interesting readings of Freud has been done by the French psychoanalyst, and student of Jacques Lacan, Jean Laplanche. Very briefly, Laplanche has suggested that, as concerns the concepts of life and death in particular, almost the whole of the Freudian corpus – from the 'Project for a scientific psychology', written in 1895, passing especially by *Beyond the Pleasure Principle* of 1920, to 'The economic problem of masochism' of 1924 – can be seen in terms of a chiasmus, where what was life (homeostasis) at the beginning becomes death (Thanatos), and what was death (unbound energy) in the beginning becomes life (Eros).[1] Laplanche shows that there is indeed no substitute for actually reading Freud.

Sigmund Freud was born into a Jewish family in 1856 in Freiburg. When he was 4, his family moved to Vienna where Freud lived and worked until 1938, when he was forced to flee to England after the Anschluss. Although he always complained about the oppressiveness of Vienna, Freud not only lived there nearly all his life, but he lived with his family at the same address for nearly fifty years: the famous Berggasse 19. Freud was a brilliant student, topping every year at the Gymnasium, and graduating with distinction in 1873. In 1881, he took out his medical degree from the University of Vienna, and in 1885 won a scholarship to go to Paris to study under the great Jean Martin Charcot, at Salpetrière. To Freud, Charcot not only opened the way to taking mental illness seriously, with his diagnosis of hysteria and the use of hypnosis; he was also a charismatic yet encouraging teacher for whom Freud had a lasting admiration. Upon his return to Vienna in 1886, Freud set up practice as a physician. He later died in London in 1939.

During his university years, the future psychoanalyst worked in the laboratory of the physiologist and positivist, Ernst Brücke. Brücke's contemporary and influential colleague, Hermann Helmholtz – who, among other things, wrote on thermodynamics – was also an early influence on the young Freud, as was the physicist and philosopher, Gustav Fechner. All three were representatives of the medical positivism and vitalism which reigned in Vienna and elsewhere during the last three decades of the nineteenth century. Their influence can be seen in particular in Freud's theory of 'bound' and 'unbound' psychical energy in the posthumously published, 'Project for a scientific psychology'. In the same year, 1895, Freud and Breuer, initially basing their work on the case of Anna O, published their *Studies in Hysteria*. Freud's research into psychical activity was thus pushed in a new direction. For what seemed to bring about Anna O's recovery through catharsis (release of tension), was, as the patient put it, the 'talking cure'. In effect, the 'talking cure' is the result of proceeding according to the physicalist or vitalist model of the psyche: tension is released (homeostasis is attained) through talking and interpretation – that is, through a manipulation of meaning(s).

As Laplanche shows, the cross-over from the vitalist model of the psyche, witnessed in the analysis of hysteria, is more dramatically seen in a case study recounted in the 1895 'Project', a text which sets out most clearly the quantitative model of the psyche – the psyche as 'a kind of economics of nervous force', as Freud wrote in a letter to Fliess. The case in question concerns a young woman, Emma, who has a fear of going into shops alone. In analysis, Emma relates her symptom to the memory of going into a shop at the age of 12, seeing two shop assistants laughing together, and fleeing in fright from the shop. Analytic investigation reveals that behind this scene, there is another: at the age of 8 Emma went into a shop to buy some sweets, and the shopkeeper fondled her genitals through her clothes. At the time, however, Emma did not find the experience traumatic. What is significant about these two scenes is that the first is traumatic as a memory, but innocent as an event, whereas the second (chronologically the first) is potentially traumatic as an event but remains innocent as a memory – precisely because it was not experienced as traumatic. It was not until the intervening period of puberty had given the violation its full significance that it became traumatic in a psychical sense, but then only as a memory trace, only through displacement, we could say. The notion of displacement here is crucial, for it makes the categorical attribution of a trauma to a physical event impossible. Rather, it suggests that any notion of trauma in a human sense has to take account of its retrospective *meaning*. In other words, a physicalist or vitalist understanding of the psyche is inadequate. Such would be the way in which the very reality of displacement – which Freud outlined most fully in *The Interpretation of Dreams* – reveals itself within the structure of Freud's own text, when he is led to modify his positivistic theory of psychical life through an encounter with the facts of the psyche itself – those of his own psyche, encountered in self-analysis, as much as those of his patients.

The psyche is thus a meaning structure before it is a physical entity. It has to do with symbolic processes, and so calls for interpretation. Once the element of interpretation is seen to be crucial to psychical life, a quantitative – and more latterly, a behaviourist – model of the psyche becomes inadequate. Perhaps more than anything else, this apparent division in Freud's work between the physical-cum-biological level, and the symbolic level has been the centre of numerous debates and misunderstandings. With regard to sexuality, for example, many Anglo-American commentators have been moved to dismiss Freud's theory of sexuality because they read it in terms of biology – that is positivistically, not symbolically.

In the *Interpretation of Dreams*, Freud begins by clearly stating that in his effort to bring about a more profound understanding of dreams his method differs from earlier ones in that he will not be relying on a pre-existing dream code. He thus proposes to consider dream material on its own terms. Broadly speaking, Freud shows that dream interpretation has to be of a particular kind because a dream is the fulfilment of a wish – broadly, the wish that it not be understood at the level of its manifest content. A dream invariably contains a disguised message relating to the dreamer's sexuality. Taken literally, many people might think (many people have thought!) that this is an incredible claim. How is it possible to be sure that a dream is essentially about sexuality? The short answer is that sexuality is essentially disguised – has to be disguised, we could add. By this is meant that sexuality has to do with signs and the symbolic. It is not an animal urge (although Freud himself at times appears to be attracted to such a view), but is imbricated in all the displacements of social and cultural life. Displacement here means circuitous path. In *The Interpretation of Dreams*, Freud defines displacement as one of the ways dream-work disguises the unconscious message of the dream. Together with condensation, it forms part of the primary process. Displacement refers to the way that an element, or elements, in the manifest content of the dream may be insignificant, or even absent, in the latent content: the dream-thoughts. Condensation refers to the way the manifest content of a dream is meagre by comparison with the wealth of dream-thoughts which may be derived from it. Each dream element may give rise to multiple lines of association. This Freud called overdetermination. Displacement and condensation, therefore, entail that a dream calls for interpretation (it cannot be equated with its manifest content). These two processes are, furthermore, two aspects of the dream-work which serve to disguise the dream's true meaning (inevitably sexual), and which thereby enable the fulfilment of a wish: the masking of unconscious thoughts.

As we noted earlier, Freud's point of departure is that there is no pre-given code for interpreting a dream. Each element (usually an image) must be interpreted as though for the first time. This is because a dream is less a product of linguistic processes, and more a language in its own right: it approximates an ideolect. It is perhaps because Freud showed how a dream stretched language and interpretation to the limit that his work has become influential in fields outside psychoanalysis dealing with the interpretation of texts

To understand the significance of disguise and distortion in dreams, Freud shows that it is also necessary to understand the role of repression. Repression, of course, is very closely linked with the unconscious. And unconscious dream thoughts are what are repressed. From one point of view, the dreamer – and, subsequently, the analysand – represses painful and traumatic memories of a sexual nature; repression, on this reading, is primarily a form of defence. However, in the wake of the work of Jacques Lacan, a more structural interpretation has been given to repression. Repression here is associated with the very formation of the subject in language and the symbolic. It would be what makes possible the very distinction between subject and object. But if this is so, why is it necessary to gain access to repressed material? If repression is a structural necessity, why does it have to be 'uncovered'? The answer, in part, is, as Freud showed, that repression can break down, resulting in a symptom (which Freud calls a compromise formation) and unconscious repetition. The former appears inexplicable to the subject, and the latter often escapes consciousness altogether. In both cases the aim becomes one of interpreting the symptom and the repetition, thereby confirming, and perhaps expanding, the domain of the symbolic. The unconscious *par excellence* is the sexual trauma: namely, that which cannot be said or symbolised, and which is known only by its effects in the symbolic. On this basis, obscenity would be the cross-over point between the symbolic and the unconscious (trauma).

Freud, of course, is also known as the formulator of the concept of the Oedipus complex. Literally speaking, this is the phenomenon observed by Freud (and it figures in his own self-analysis) where the son (like Oedipus of the Greek myth) wants to have done with his father in order to sleep with his mother. A related theme emerges in *Totem and Taboo*, where Freud refers to the myth of the killing and devouring of the violent father in Darwin's primal horde. The sons, in an act of contrition and guilt, give up immediate access to the father's women, and so institute the symbolic order: the order of the law. Oedipus and the story of the primal horde both illustrate the way that the unconscious (the primary process) is always trying to avoid repression and thus by-pass the symbolic order (the secondary process). It leaves its mark in the symbolic as a symptom (such as slips of the tongue).

A strand of Freud's thought that has caused much debate is the notion of the ego. Freud defined the ego in relation to two other terms: the id – or reservoir of affective energy – and the super-ego – the ego-ideal, or the representative of external reality. A major point of contention has been over whether the ego is equal to the whole personality – in which case it would incorporate the id and the superego within itself – or whether the ego is an agency attempting to distinguish itself from the other two (id and super-ego). While the first view opens up the possibility of an ego ultimately identical with itself, the second renders problematic the very possibility of self-identity.

Another complicating factor in relation to the ego is narcissism. Here, the ego-subject makes itself an object to itself, once again bringing into question the notion of an entity identical with itself. For its part, American ego-psychology has tended to view the ego as the centre of perception and consciousness, thus opening up the possibility of an ego with a capacity for complete self-awareness. As Laplanche and Pontalis point out, whatever else one might say, Freud's text leaves no doubt as to the ambiguity which reigns throughout it in relation to the ego, and, we can add, in relation to a good many of the key concepts of psychoanalysis. And perhaps this is only to be expected from an *oeuvre* in continual evolution, one which, in the end, seeks to throw light on the very mechanisms of its own production.

Freud left a wide-ranging and heterogeneous *oeuvre*: works based on a biological model of the psyche; meta-psychological works outlining key concepts; case studies derived from clinical practice; autobiographical and historical works; works based on anthropological and historical data; studies of everyday life, and didactic works which sought to explain psychoanalysis to a wider public. Perhaps what he left overall, however, is an *oeuvre* that does not conceal the process of its own evolution: the false starts, the discoveries, the continual modification of key concepts are all there. This means that for the contemporary reader, Freud's most enduring legacy is that his text, more than ever, calls for interpretation.

Notes

1 Jean Laplanche, *Life and Death in Psychoanalysis*, trans. Jeffrey Mehlman, Baltimore, Johns Hopkins University Press, 1976.

See also in this book

Foucault, Irigaray, Kristeva, Lacan

Freud's major writings

The standard reference for all of Freud's works in English is *The Standard Edition of the Complete Psychological Works of Sigmund Freud* (hereafter, *SE*), trans. under the general editorship of James Strachey, in collaboration with Anna Freud, assisted by Alix Strachey and Alan Tyson, London, Hogarth Press, 1962–75. Works mentioned in the above article with date of first publication and *SE* volume number are:

Studies in Hysteria (1895) (with Joseph Breuer), *SE*, 2
'Project for a scientific psychology' (1950) (posthumous), *SE*, 1
Beyond the Pleasure Principle (1920), *SE*, 18
'The economic problem of masochism' (1924), *SE*, 19
The Interpretation of Dreams (1900), *SE*, 4–5
Totem and Taboo (1912–13), *SE*, 9

Further reading

Brennan, Teresa, *The Interpretation of the Flesh: Freud and Femininity*, London and New York, Routledge, 1992
Gay, Peter, *Freud. A Life for Our Time*, New York, Anchor-Doubleday, 1989
Jones, Ernest, *The Life and Work of Sigmund Freud*, 3 vols, New York, Basic Books, 1953–7
Laplanche, Jean, *Life and Death in Psychoanalysis*, trans. Jeffrey Mehlman, Baltimore, Johns Hopkins University Press, 1976
Weber, Samuel, *The Legend of Freud*, Minneapolis, University of Minnesota Press, 1982

MARCEL MAUSS

It would be hard to underestimate the intellectual significance of Marcel Mauss for at least two generations of French thinkers. Beginning with Bataille, Dumézil, and Lévi-Strauss, Mauss has also been a crucial reference point for a new generation which would include Bourdieu, Baudrillard, Derrida and Foucault. While Mauss's theory of the gift and the nature of exchange in so-called archaic societies has particularly occupied thinkers inspired by structuralism, like Lévi-Strauss, the debt of others like Bourdieu and Foucault is more related to Mauss's thinking about techniques of the body. *Habitus* is a term that Mauss remarked upon prior to its reworking by Bourdieu; and Foucault's notion of a 'technology of the body' could easily be derived from Mauss's view that bodily techniques are, effectively, a 'technique without an instrument' – the French term, *technique* connoting technology, not just the technical. A technique of the body is thus a technology to the extent that it can be transferred across areas of activity, and because, to do this, it must be at least partially objectified (i.e. formalised).

Mauss, a nephew and pupil of Emile Durkheim, was born in Epinal in 1872, and died in Paris in 1950. Like his uncle, he grew up in a Jewish orthodox atmosphere. In 1895, he came third in the *agrégation* in philosophy, after which he studied Greek, Latin, Hebrew and Ancient Iranian at the Ecole Pratique des Hautes Etudes.[1] By 1902, Mauss had become a *maître assistant* at the Ecole Pratique des Hautes Etudes, Fifth Section, where he taught in the 'history of religions of uncivilized peoples'. At the outbreak of the First World War, Mauss volunteered for service and served as an interpreter in the British army, and was decorated for bravery with two citations and two military crosses. His experience in the army gave Mauss the opportunity to study the different bodily techniques observable in British, Australian, and French troops. Later, in his writings on the techniques of the body, Mauss will remark on the capacity of Australian soldiers for sitting on their haunches during rest periods, while he, a Frenchman, had to remain upright; for he, like many Europeans, lacked this ability. Unlike his uncle, Mauss was more of a Bohemian with socialist aspirations; he collected exotica, championed the work of Debussy and Picasso and was always open to new ways of understanding social and cultural forms. In 1925, Mauss set up the Institut d'Ethnologie, and in 1930 he was elected to the Collège de France until his retirement in 1940.

In 1899, Mauss published with H. Hubert, *Sacrifice: Its Nature and Function*. Mauss's renown and influence, however, came largely through articles he published in the Durkheimian sociological journal, *L'Année sociologique*, rather than through any monograph. He was also a highly respected and engaging teacher. According to Georges Dumézil, who had very little time for Durkheim – Mauss's mentor – Mauss rarely prepared his courses, but he had a taste for the universal supported by an enormous knowledge which knew few boundaries.

Due no doubt in part to Claude Lévi-Strauss's famous *Introduction to the work of Marcel Mauss*,[2] Mauss's best-known work is his *Essai sur le don* (trans. *The Gift*) first published in the 1923–4 volume of the *Année Sociologique*. Although, ostensibly, the gift can be distinguished from a commodity (the basis of exchange in a money economy) in that it apparently does not entail reciprocity, in fact, Mauss argues, the gift implies a threefold obligation: to give, to receive, and to reciprocate. Thus, in light of ethnographies of a wide range of societies – but particularly those describing the potlatch in America, the *kula* in the Pacific and the *hau* in New Zealand – Mauss shows that the gift is the very foundation of social life – so refined and differentiated are the forms of behaviour that are carried out in its wake. The gift, then, is never a simple exchange of goods. It involves honour and a particular use of time; it is a mechanism touching upon every aspect of life ensuring the circulation of people (women) as well as goods. Thus exchange can be seen in marriage, festivals, ceremonial rites, military service, dances, feasts, fairs and the like. Even when exchange has to do exclusively with objects of some kind, it has to be recalled that objects are not simply the dead, inanimate things they are assumed to be in highly differentiated, capitalist societies. Rather, objects have a 'soul', a spirituality, so that an object is not simply an object; conversely, while human beings have a spirituality – most often called *mana* – about them, they are also objects which can therefore be part of the exchange system.

Instead of the accumulation of wealth for the purpose of accumulating more wealth that is characteristic of capitalist societies, societies of the gift are characterised by expenditure – giving – and the gaining of prestige. The essence of the North American potlatch, for example, is the obligation to give. Prestige and honour are gained and maintained by the one who can expend to the greatest possible extent, thus placing the receiver under an obligation to match the prodigality of the giver. At least this is so for as long as the potlatch does not turn into an orgy of pure destruction, that is, into a pure expenditure without return. In general, however, gifts must be reciprocated with interest, thereby raising the stakes ever higher.

As to the nature of things exchanged in the system of the gift, it would be wrong to assume that these are limited to material goods. Indeed, a key point made by Mauss is that virtually everything – services, sexual favours, festivals, dances, etc. – is drawn into the system. For an individual or group not to engage in the obligations implied by the gift system is to run the risk of war.

While a capitalist society is not structured according to the general social obligations attached to the gift, it is, says Mauss, reasonable to say, in light of historical evidence, that Western systems of law and economy originally emerged from institutions similar to those of societies dominated by the gift. In modern capitalist societies, then, an impersonal and calculating attitude developed, whereby a notion of monetary equivalence came to supplant the moral obligation and battle for prestige integral to the gift. Rather than invading the whole of life's activities, the development of law and a money economy allowed exchange to be formalised and limited to the public domain through the separation of the public from the private sphere.

Mauss concludes his study by summarising a number of key points. First of all, he notes, the gift still permeates 'our own' societies, but in a much reduced form. Special religious occasions, weddings and birthdays can still generate a substantial gift-giving and the sense that one should reciprocate with interest, that 'we must give back more than we have received'.[3] Not to be able to reciprocate can leave the receiver in a position of inferiority *vis-à-vis* the giver. Whether the meaning of charity and social welfare should perhaps be viewed in this light is an open question; for while there may be an element of reciprocity and pride at stake, charity is also backed by a utilitarian motive that is absent in gift-exchange. Those societies whose social structure is entirely based on the gift, however, have no space which is not subject to exchange. Human beings are also part of this exchange system. This is a notion of exchange that has to be clearly separated from utilitarian motives. Much more than economic exchanges in so-called highly differentiated societies with a marked distinction between public and private, the gift is an end in itself; for even though it is indeed a question of a person's *mana*, or indefinable quality of prestige which is at stake, this is inseparable from the act of giving (and receiving) itself. 'To give is to show one's superiority.'[4] Because it animates the social structure, touching every facet of life, the gift is an example of what Mauss calls a 'total social fact'. Thus while occurring at an individual, or group, level the gift exchange is, *par excellence*, a social fact. Individual and group fortunes are inextricably tied to the fortunes of the society as a whole. To understand the implications and significance of an individual act of gift-giving, it is thus necessary to understand the nature of the whole social structure. The very triangular structure of the gift, entailing giving, receiving and reciprocating, clearly evokes the idea of the total social fact.

The notion of *mana*, deemed to be linked to the indefinable quality of prestige in the system of the gift, had been discussed in Mauss's earlier essay on magic.[5] There, the author remarks that *mana* is one of the troubling concepts of which anthropology had thought it had rid itself. *Mana* is a vague term, obscure and impossible to define rigorously. There are indeed, Mauss comments, a veritable 'infinity of manas'.[6] *Mana* is not simply a force, a being, but also 'an action, a quality and a state'. The word is at one and the same time, 'a noun, an adjective, a verb'.[7] *Mana* cannot be the object of experience because it absorbs all experience. In this, it is of the same order as the sacred. For Mauss, this is to say that *mana* has a spirituality which is equivalent to collective thought, which is the equivalent of society as such.

For its part, magic is irregular and tends towards something that is prohibited by society. Magic is a private, secret, and singular act. It is isolated, mysterious, furtive, and fragmented. It encapsulates the non-social side of the social world, and is indeed at one and the same time a threat to the social and the limit which gives it meaning. Magicians can be women, children, foreigners – any 'non-professional' being.

Mana and magic thus raise the issue of the precise nature of the social bond. For Lévi-Strauss the very fact that *mana* is difficult to define suggests that it is essentially indefinable; or rather, because *mana* can take on a multiplicity of meanings, it is a 'floating signifier' – an indefinable 'x' – analogous to the 'zero' phoneme brought to light by structural linguistics. Such a phoneme has no meaning in itself, but can take on a variety of meanings, depending on the context, and its differential relationship with other terms. This implies that *mana* can only be interpreted synchronically, at a given moment, rather than in an evolutionary sense where meaning would be derived from the past – that is, diachronically. Equating *mana* with the 'floating signifier' was Lévi-Strauss's way, at the time of his famous 1950 essay on Mauss, of claiming Mauss for structuralism.

A number of additional consequences follow from a structural interpretation of *mana* and the gift. For instance, light can be thrown on the nature of the social evoked by *mana* and the gift as a 'total social fact' if the social is understood to be analogous to the structure of language. In this way, the social would not be immediately revealed by the presentation of social facts, any more than the grammar of a natural language is immediately present to the consciousness of a native speaker. Similarly, Lévi-Strauss argues, the fact of exchange is not immediately present in empirical observation, which only furnishes three obligations: give, receive, reciprocate. The notion of exchange explains the relationship between the three elements; it does not exist transparently in the facts, but must be constructed from the facts.

In another important study, Mauss's historical and contextual approach to social phenomena is perhaps even more pronounced. Thus in his discussion of the 'techniques of the body',[8] he calls on the notion of *habitus*[9] in order to throw light on the way that bodily activities are specific to a given culture and society. Two elements must be present for there to be a bodily technique: first, the technique must be efficacious and so capable of producing a desired result; and, second, it must be inscribed within a tradition which makes its transmission possible. In short, a technique is something that can be transmitted. For Mauss, bodily techniques are not spontaneous nor are they simply anatomical or physiological. To illustrate the degree to which supposedly natural acts can in fact be the result of the technique, Mauss relates how he actually taught a child who was suffering from a cold to spit.

Every bodily technique has its form. The error of the past has been, Mauss argues, to think that there is a technique only when

there is an instrument. Bodily techniques are effectively like technology without an instrument. The framework of a technique allows one to explain the significance of the multitude of small actions carried out by each individual every day of their lives. Technique brings all these taken-for-granted instances into an explanatory framework so that they cease to be arbitrary and the result of pure chance. Michel Foucault's concept of 'techniques of the self' seems to be clearly presaged in Mauss's insights in this domain. The pertinence of Mauss is particularly in evidence for the contemporary understanding of practices when we recall that he distinguishes specific categories of behaviour from techniques of the body – from so-called mechanical acts of a 'physical-chemical' type. These are also traditional and efficacious acts in the sphere of religion, symbolic acts, juridical acts – acts relating to communal life, moral acts; in other words, acts which for Mauss cannot be reduced to a purely physical event.

Modern thought, however (cf. Foucault, Bourdieu, Althusser) has questioned the opposition between a supposedly self-conscious symbolic act, and a physical technique. In fact, following Pascal's description of acquiring faith – 'Kneel down, move your lips in prayer, and you will believe'[10] – the claim is made that even the most symbolic act is inextricably bound to a physical technique – even to the extent that the technique is seen to be prior to the symbolic meaning. And as if to confirm that he himself doubted the validity of keeping the symbolic aspect separate from the physical, Mauss concludes his reflection on bodily techniques by saying that

I believe precisely that at the bottom of all our mystical states there are techniques of the body which have not been studied but which were perfectly studied in China and in India, even in very remote periods. . . . I think that there are necessarily biological means of entering into 'communication with God'.[11]

Mauss, then, let it be reiterated, is a largely unacknowledged source of this aspect of contemporary thought concerned with the body.

Finally, we should note with Lévi-Strauss that Mauss, even more than Durkheim, showed that an individuality, while not reducible to the social, always has a social expression. In short, because social facts are only manifest in individuals, society is in the individual as much as, or even more than, the individual is in society. In reality, therefore, the tedious debate about whether the individual is prior to society, or whether society is prior to the individual comes to an end with Marcel Mauss. It now remains for those who have come after him to recognise this.

Notes

1 This and the following biographical details on Mauss are derived from Anthony Richard Gringeri, Jr., 'Twilight of the Sun Kings: French anthropology from modernism to postmodernism, 1925–1950', unpublished Ph.D. thesis, University of California, Berkeley, 1990.
2 Claude Lévi-Strauss, 'Introduction à l'oeuvre de Marcel Mauss' in Marcel Mauss, *Sociologie et anthropologie*, Paris, Presses Universitaires de France, 'Quadrige', eighth edn, 1983, pp. IX–LII. In English as *Introduction to the Work of Marcel Mauss*, trans. Felicity Baker, Routledge & Kegan Paul, 1987.
3 Marcel Mauss, *The Gift: The Form and Reason for Exchange in Archaic Societies*, trans. W.D. Halls, London, Routledge, 1990, p. 65.
4 ibid., p. 74.
5 Marcel Mauss, 'Esquisse d'une théorie générale de la magie' in Marcel Mauss, *Sociologie et anthropologie*, pp. 1–141. In English as *A General Theory of Magic*, trans. Robert Brain, London and Boston, Routledge & Kegan Paul, 1972.
6 ibid., p. 104. English trans., p. 111.
7 ibid., p. 101. English trans., p. 108.
8 Marcel Mauss, 'Les Techniques du corps' in Marcel Mauss, *Sociologie et anthropologie*, pp. 362–86. In English as 'Techniques of the body', trans. Ben Brewster, *Economy and Society*, 2, 1 (1973), pp. 70–88.
9 ibid., p. 368–9. English trans. at p. 73.
10 Quoted in Louis Althusser, *Lenin and Philosophy and Other Essays*, trans. Ben Brewster, London, New Left Books, 1971, p. 158.

11 Mauss, 'Les Techniques du corps', p. 386, and 'Techniques of the body', p. 87.

See also in this book

Bataille, Bourdieu, Dumézil, Foucault, Lévi-Strauss

Mauss's major writings

Sacrifice: Its Nature and Function (1899) (with Henri Hubert), trans. W.D. Halls, Chicago, University of Chicago Press, 1981
A General Theory of Magic (1902–3), trans. Robert Brain, London, Routledge, 1972
The Gift: The Form and Reason for Exchange in Archaic Societies (1923–4), trans. W.D. Halls, London, Routledge, 1990
'Techniques of the body' (1935), trans. Ben Brewster, *Economy and Society*, 2, 1 (1973), pp. 70–88

Further reading

Bloor, David, 'Durkheim and Mauss revisited: Classification and the sociology of knowledge', *Studies in the History and Philosophy of Science*, 13, 4 (1982)
Carrier, James, 'Gifts, commodities, and social relations: A Maussian view of exchange', *Sociological Forum*, 6, 1 (March 1991), pp. 119–36
Carrithers, Michael, Collins, Steven, and Lukes, Steven (eds), *Category of the Person: Anthropology, Philosophy, History*, Cambridge, Cambridge University Press, 1985. As well as essays on Mauss, this book contains a translation of Mauss's 'A Category of the human mind'
Gane, Mike (ed.), *Radical Sociology of Durkheim and Mauss*, London, Routledge, 1992
Lévi-Strauss, Claude, *Introduction to the Work of Marcel Mauss*, trans. Felicity Baker, London, Routledge & Kegan Paul, 1987
Ritter, Henning, 'The ethnological revolution: On Marcel', trans. John Burns, *Comparative Civilizations Review*, 22 (Fall 1990), pp. 1–18

MAURICE MERLEAU-PONTY

Even though he perhaps remained a French 'philosopher of consciousness' Maurice Merleau-Ponty separated himself gradually from the phenomenology of Jean-Paul Sartre, and perhaps also from that of Husserl. Specifically, Merleau-Ponty brought Saussure into his reflections and teachings on language in the late 1940s and early 1950s. During the 1950s, he was also well aware of Saussure's influence on the work of Lévi-Strauss and formed a close alliance with the latter, who eventually became his colleague at the Collège de France.

Merleau-Ponty was born in 1908. As with Roland Barthes's father, Merleau-Ponty's father was also killed in the First World War. He attended the Lycées Janson-de-Sailly and Louis-le-Grande, and in 1930 he successfully completed his *agrégation* in philosophy at the Ecole Normale Supérieure (rue d'Ulm). Like many intellectuals of his generation, Merleau-Ponty attended Kojève's lectures on Hegel. He was also associated for a short time with the Catholic journal, *Esprit*. When the Second World War broke out, Merleau-Ponty served in the infantry and was tortured by the Germans. During the Occupation he was associated with the ill-fated, independent Resistance group, 'Socialism and Freedom', the group with which Jean-Paul Sartre was also associated. In 1945, Merleau-Ponty's major work was published: *Phenomenology of Perception*. In 1949, he was appointed to the chair of child psychology at the Sorbonne, and in 1952 he was the youngest candidate ever to be elected to the chair of philosophy at the Collège de France, a position he held until his sudden death in May 1961.

From 1945 to 1952, Merleau-Ponty was a close friend and collaborator of Jean-Paul Sartre, and one of the founding editors of *Les Temps Modernes*. The year 1952 marked Merleau-Ponty's disillusionment with the Korean War and Sartrian politics, and he thus resigned from the editorial board of what was to become Sartre's journal. The substance of his differences with Sartre is contained in Merleau-Ponty's book, *Adventures of the Dialectic*, published in 1955. Here, his former comrade-in-arms develops an exhaustive analysis of Sartre's

relationship to communism, at the same time as he questions the privileging of the subject–object relationship in Sartre's version of phenomenology. As Vincent Descombes explains, without an 'interworld', the subject–object dichotomy leads to solipsism: 'If the subject-object dichotomy were correct, then all meaning would issue from men, and all meaning *for myself* would issue from *myself*.'[1]

From 1952, Merleau-Ponty began to develop a conception of political activity which freed itself from Sartre's naive flirtation with hard-line communism. More importantly, though, Merleau-Ponty began to sketch out a philosophical trajectory which confirmed the importance of lived experience in grasping the nature of language, perception, and the body. An outline of the main aspects of the link between perception and thought opened up in the *Philosophy of Perception* will help to clarify what is at stake here.

In the Preface to the work in question, Merleau-Ponty confirms the influence of Husserl on his own philosophy. Thus like Husserl, Merleau-Ponty emphasises the importance of the phenomenological reduction, or *epoché* (abstention; also called 'bracketing' and 'disconnection') introduced in order to open access to 'essences'. The latter are to be grasped, not as the transcendental essences given in available scientific disciplines, or in the general abstract knowledge (such as that relating to space and time) an individual may have about the world. Rather, the phenomenological *epoché* gives access to the immanent essences of the consciousness of 'lived experience'. The *epoché* is a disconnection from the given natural world in all its objectivity. This disconnection, Husserl is quick to say, is not in any sense a denial of the natural world. Indeed it, and all the knowledge provided by the sciences which study its various aspects, is entirely accepted. However, the consciousness of lived experience – the consciousness which is always a consciousness *of* something

– is fundamentally different from an acceptance of the givenness of the world, or scientific knowledge. In Husserl's words:

> we fix our eyes steadily upon the sphere of Consciousness and study what it is that we find immanent in *it*. . . . *Consciousness in itself has a being of its own which in its absolute uniqueness of nature remains unaffected by the phenomenological disconnexion.*[2]

Thus the study of the essence of things in consciousness opens up the field of the 'science of Phenomenology'.[3]

Merleau-Ponty's point of departure is Husserl's *epoché*. For him, however, the aim is not to remain with the structure of Descartes's philosophy of doubt, as Husserl tends to do in providing an explanation of phenomenology, but rather to go to the heart of embodied experience, which is what perception is. Pitting himself directly against the abstractness and emptiness of the Cartesian cogito – 'I think, therefore I am' – Merleau-Ponty shows that 'to be a body is to be tied to a certain world'; and he adds: 'our body is not primarily *in* space: it is of it'.[4] In effect, our body is always already in the world; therefore, there is no body in-itself, a body which could be objectified and given universal status. Perception, then, is always an embodied perception, one that is what it is only within a specific context or situation. Perception in-itself does not exist.

In his own explanation of his philosophical trajectory,[5] Merleau-Ponty confirms the primacy of lived experience by saying that the 'perceiving mind is an incarnated mind'.[6] Furthermore, perception is not simply the result of the impact of the external world on the body; for even if the body is distinct from the world it inhabits, is is not separate from it. Indeed, the very imbrication of the perceiving organism and its surroundings is what lies at the basis of perception. This means that there is no perception in general – a notion which would turn it into an abstract universal; there is only perception as it is

lived in the world. It is precisely the 'lived' nature of perception and the body which makes phenomenological research viable and necessary. As a result of the incarnate nature of perception, the perceiving subject is always changing, always going through a process of rebirth. Consciousness, for its part, does not relate to the world in the manner of a thinker in relation to a series of objects. There is no subject in general, in effect, one entirely autonomous and separate from its objects, as Descartes argued. Rather, consciousness is perceptual; consequently, the certainty of ideas is based on the certainty of perception. This certainty always remains to be established and confirmed by phenomenological investigation; for the phenomenologist, there are no ideal, universal certainties at the level of ideas. Descartes's cogito is thus what Merleau-Ponty's phenomenology is opposing more than anything else. To sum up: 'I perceive' is not equivalent to 'I think', nor is it universalisable. The incarnate status of the perceiving subject opens the way to a phenomenological description of the Living Present. Within such a description – that is, within the phenomenological *epoché* – the perceived thing is equivalent to what is said about it. Merleau-Ponty elaborates:

> The perceived thing is not an ideal unity in the possession of the intellect, like a geometrical notion, for example; it is rather a totality open to a horizon of an indefinite number of perspectival views which blend with one another according to a given style, which defines the object in question.[7]

Given the status of perception as incarnate, what is the real *raison d'être* of phenomenological description, and, indeed, reflection? Merleau-Ponty's answer is that, if left to itself, perception 'forgets itself and is ignorant of its own accomplishments'.[8] But the issue is not, as Merleau-Ponty seems to think, that we risk going back to an unreflected moment prior to philosophy, but that a distinction has been made quite unambiguously between the perception of an incarnate perceiving subject and the philosophy of perception – as though, after all, one were forced to accept at least some version of the universal 'I think' just at the point when the primacy given to the 'I perceive' seemed to deal it a truly mortal blow. Such perhaps would be the typically insurmountable problem faced by a philosophy of consciousness which wants to maintain a sense of its own self-presence (contained in the 'I think'), while at the same time launching into a description of the heterogeneous level of the subject incarnate. Within his phenomenological framework, Merleau-Ponty has presented a fundamental rift between consciousness and 'Lived Experience', a rift which must remain repressed.

If this were the end of the story, however, there is no doubt that the philosopher of perception would have long ceased to be of interest to a post-war generation brought up on the aporias of philosophies of consciousness, just as Merleau-Ponty's teachers (such as Brunschvicg) have ceased to be of interest. Language, and Merleau-Ponty's attempt to make it central to his later philosophical concerns via the aegis of a reading of Saussure, inspired early structuralism. For instance, Algirdas-Julien Greimas was one who attended Merleau-Ponty's inaugural lecture at the Collège de France in 1952, and came away with a sense that Saussure, and not Marx, held the key to a genuine philosophy of history.[9]

Although it is often said that Merleau-Ponty took from Saussure's theory of language what he wanted in order to confirm his phenomenology, it should also be said that he highlighted two Saussurian principles which would come to be the focus of structuralist theories of language and semiotics. These are that meaning in language arises through a diacritical relationship between signs, and that a diachronical study of language cannot explain the nature of current usage. Thus in his unfinished work, *The Prose of the World*, Merleau-Ponty writes that

'Saussure shows admirably that . . . it cannot be the history of the word or language which determines its present meaning.'[10] What the phenomenologist finds in the structural linguist is a theory which seems to emphasise the subject's lived relation to the world. Again, Merleau-Ponty writes that Saussure's notion of the primacy of the synchronic dimension of language for understanding the nature of language as such, 'liberates history from historicism and makes a new conception of reason possible'.[11] To view language synchronically, Merleau-Ponty argues, is to view it as enacted, and not as an abstract, universal entity, subject to gradual evolution over time. Language here is fundamentally the 'living present' in speech. To speak, to communicate – to use language – is in part equivalent to becoming aware that there are only successive living presents. Indeed, any discourse *on* language must come to grasp itself as an enactment of language. A linguistics worthy of the name, therefore, comes to recognise that language can only be understood from the inside. In other words, language can no more be reduced to a history of linguistics than history can be reduced to historical discourse.

Nevertheless, in by-passing Saussure's theory of *langue* (language as a system) which explains *how* speech is enacted, in favour of *parole* (the enactment itself), Merleau-Ponty is unable to show that language is doubly articulated: the level of the signifier is relatively independent of the level of the signified. And while Merleau-Ponty, with his emphasis on the 'living present', had focused on the signified (the enactment of meaning), structuralist linguistics would, almost from the moment of Merleau-Ponty's death in 1961, oppose the phenomenologist's emphasis on the embodied transparence of the signified,[12] only to become dazzled by language's opacity as a system of signifiers.

Furthermore, in focusing almost exclusively on the level of *parole* as the embodiment of language, the phenomenologist is unable to explain satisfactorily how a move can be made from the individual 'I speak', to the fact that another speaks. The usual (Sartrian) claim that the 'I speak' entails a recognition that 'we speak' fails to show how, on this reading, the 'I' is not simply being raised to the power of the 'we' – a 'we' which is effectively rendered homogeneous in the process. This issue is but the tip of the iceberg. For phenomenology (Merleau-Ponty's included) has notoriously found it difficult to cope with the general problem of otherness – of which the 'I speak' issue is an instance. Having rejected any theory of the unconscious, phenomenology treats every subjective (even if embodied) instance as a unity, present to itself. Then, in the illusion of pluralising it, it raises this instance to the power of 'we'. This 'we' then becomes a unity: the unity of the collectivity. Otherness and heterogeneity are thus done away with in a veritable wave of the phenomenologist's homogenising wand. It is perhaps to Merleau-Ponty's credit, however, that through his creative audacity the limit of phenomenology becomes visible in his work.

Notes

1 Vincent Descombes, *Modern French Philosophy*, trans. L. Scott-Fox and J.M. Harding, Cambridge, Cambridge University Press, 1980, p. 72.
2 Edmund Husserl, *Ideas. A General Introduction to Pure Phenomenology*, trans. W.R. Boyce-Gibson, New York, Collier Books, 1962, p. 102. Husserl's emphasis.
3 ibid.
4 Maurice Merleau-Ponty, *Phenomenology of Perception*, trans. Colin Smith, London, Routledge, reprinted 1992, p. 148. Merleau-Ponty's emphasis.
5 Maurice Merleau-Ponty, 'An unpublished text by Maurice Merleau-Ponty: A prospectus of his work', trans. Aleen B. Dallery in James M. Edie (ed.), *The Primacy of Perception*, Evanston, Northwestern University Press, 1964. Eighth paperback printing, 1989, pp. 3–11.
6 ibid., p. 3.
7 Maurice Merleau-Ponty, 'The primacy of perception and its philosophical consequences', trans. James M. Edie in ibid., p. 16.

8 ibid., p. 19.
9 See François Dosse, *Histoire du structuralisme I. Le champ du signe, 1945–1966*, Paris, éditions la découverte, 1991, pp. 62–3.
10 Maurice Merleau-Ponty, *The Prose of the World*, trans. John O'Neill, London, Heinemann, 1974, p. 22.
11 ibid., p. 23.
12 For example, Merleau-Ponty writes: 'A friend's speech over the telephone brings us the friend himself, as if he were wholly present in that manner of calling and saying goodbye to us' ('Indirect language and the voices of silence' in *Signs*, trans. Richard C. McCleary, Evanston, Northwestern University Press, 1964; eighth printing, 1987, p. 43).

See also in this book

Lacan, Lévi-Strauss, Saussure

Merleau-Ponty's major writings

The Structure of Behaviour (1942), trans. Alden L. Fisher, Boston, Beacon Press, 1963
Phenomenology of Perception (1945), trans. Colin Smith, London, Routledge, 1962
Humanism and Terror (1947), trans. John O'Neill, Boston, Beacon Press, 1969
Sense and Non-Sense (1948), trans. Hubert L. Dreyfus and Patricia Allen Dreyfus, Evanston, Northwestern University Press, 1964
Consciousness and the Acquisition of Language (Sorbonne course for the year, 1949/50), trans. Hugh J. Silverman, Evanston, Northwestern University Press, 1973
In Praise of Philosophy (1953), trans. John Wild and James M. Edie, Evanston, Northwestern University Press, 1963
Adventures of the Dialectic (1955), trans. Joseph Bien, Evanston, Northwestern University Press, 1973
Signs (1960), trans. Richard C. McCleary, Evanston, Northwestern University Press, 1964
The Visible and the Invisible (1964), ed. Claude Lefort, trans. Alphonso Lingis, Evanston, Northwestern University Press, 1968
The Primacy of Perception, ed. James M. Edie, Evanston, Northwestern University Press, 1964
The Prose of the World (1967), ed. Claude Lefort, trans. John O'Neill, London, Heinemann, 1974

Further reading

Barral, Mary Rose, *Body in Interpersonal Relations: Merleau-Ponty*, Lanham, University Press of America, 1965. Reprinted 1984

Basch, Thomas W., and Gallagher, Sharon (eds), *Merleau-Ponty, Hermeneutics and Postmodernism*, Albany, State University of New York, 1992

Burke, Patrick, and van der Veken, Jan, *Merleau-Ponty in Contemporary Perspective*, Boston, Kluwer Academic Books, 1993. Collection of papers presented at an international symposium on Merleau-Ponty held in 1991

Decombes, Vincent, *Modern French Philosophy*, trans. L. Scott-Fox and J.M. Harding, Cambridge, Cambridge University Press, 1980

Johnson, Galen A., and Smith, Michael B. (eds), *Ontology and Alterity in Merleau-Ponty*, Evanston, Illinois, Northwestern University Press, 1990

Langer, Monika M., *Merleau-Ponty's Phenomenology of Perception: A Guide and Commentary*, Basingstoke, Macmillan, 1989

Schmidt, James, *Maurice Merleau-Ponty: Between Phenomenology and Structuralism*, Basingstoke, Macmillan, 1985

STRUCTURALISM

Two aspects of the structural approach stand out: (1) the recognition (Chomsky not withstanding) that differential relations are the key to understanding culture and society; and, (2) that, as a result, structure is not prior to the realisation of these relations. Saussure, even if he did not recognise the full implications of what he was arguing, inspired the view that to focus on material practices is the way to come to grips with the full, and most anti-essentialist, meaning of 'structure'.

LOUIS ALTHUSSER

Louis Althusser was born in Algeria in 1918 and died in Paris in 1990, after being incarcerated for strangling his wife. In 1939, he was accepted as a candidate for an *agrégation* in philosophy at the prestigious Ecole Normale Supérieure (rue d'Ulm). The Second World War intervened, however, and Althusser was taken prisoner by the Germans, with the result that he did not proceed to the *agrégation* until 1948. Thereupon, he was appointed the 'caïman' at rue d'Ulm, a position which involved preparing candidates for the *agrégation*. For nearly forty years the 'cream' of French academic and intellectual life passed through this caïman's hands. Michel Foucault, for instance, was one such candidate, Derrida another. While Althusser's influence was always considerable within the restricted circles of the Ecole, it was not until the 1960s, with the articles subsequently published in *For Marx*, that Althusser became a 'name' as a Marxist theorist with a structuralist leaning. So by 1966, along with Foucault, Althusser had become one of the most cited French philosophers in the *agrégation*.[1]

Althusser's renown – or notoriety – had its origin in his famous 'anti-humanism'. With anti-humanism, the reader of *Capital* sought to reinvigorate a Marxism Christianised under the influence of Teilhard de Chardin,[2] humanised by the Frankfurt School, and both humanised and historicised by Sartre and Gramsci.[3] By arguing against the idea that individuals were in any sense prior to social conditions, and by conceptualising society as a structured whole consisting of relatively autonomous levels (the legal, cultural, political, etc.) whose mode of articulation, or 'effectivity' is determined, 'in the last instance', by the economy, Althusser shocked many inside as well as outside Marxism. The differences between the levels, and not their expressive unity – where each part or element would mirror the identity of the whole – became important. Gone is the individual actor consciously producing the social relation implied by the structure, and instead each subject becomes an agent of the system.

In the famous *Reading Capital*, Althusser not only 'reads' Marx, but clearly explains the difference between a 'surface' reading, which simply focuses on the actual words of the text, and a '*symptomatic*' reading, which attempts to piece together the *problematic* that informs, or governs, the real meaning of the text. Attention to reading allows Althusser to shift the focus away from both an economism – which would see Marx as the inheritor of the classical framework of political economy (Smith and Ricardo) – and a humanism and historicism that had come to rely on the authority of Marx's early works: *The Economic and Philosophic Manuscripts*, and the *Theses on Feuerbach*. Simply to see Marx as the inheritor of classical political economy, Althusser claims, is to ascribe to him a narrow and commonsensical notion of economy, one that results in an economic determinism, because, as with Hegel, it assumes that society is a social totality made up of elements which directly *express* the economic relations of society.

Even if one can point to the Hegelian, or 'political economy' language in Marx's major work, *Capital*, this is not sufficient evidence to prove that Marx can be located within the same problematic as Hegel or classical political economy. Again, when commentators point to Marx's explicit claim to have reversed the Hegelian dialectic – to have 'stood it on its head' – so that the material base becomes primary rather than the Hegelian realm of the Absolute Idea, Althusser argues that such a reversal would not at all mean that a different problematic is in operation, or that one could therefore escape the influence of the Hegelian problematic. For a problematic marks out a horizon of thought: it is the 'form in which problems must be posed'; it limits the language and concepts which are available for thought at a particular historical conjuncture; finally, the problematic constitutes the 'absolute and definite condition of possibility' of a 'definite theoretical structure'. Consequently, the radically new in Marx might be unable to find expression in much of his writing because he was forced to use concepts and language derived from the problematic which preceded him. To see Marx as having taken a negative view of classical political economy, and thus as championing the workers against the political economists who would champion the capitalists, is little different from Feuerbach's approach in relation to Hegel. To counterpose Feuerbachian humanism to Hegelian idealism is to remain trapped in the same Hegelian problematic, one which *needs* – in order to remain viable – its negative aspect (what it rejects) just as much as its positive aspect.

Althusser's strategy is thus to introduce a reading practice which can discern the way that Marx inaugurates a theoretical revolution based on an entirely new object: the mode of production. In Marx this becomes the invisible structure of the articulation of the elements of the social whole; it no longer belongs to the problematic informing Hegel's philosophy and classical political economy. Integral to this strategy is an epistemology separating a Marxist theory of knowledge from all others, but particularly from all forms of empiricism. Consequently, to discover the concept of the mode of production, Marx had to break with forms of knowledge which, to be validated, relied on the 'obviousness' of immediate experience. The mode of production (the structure of society) just does not appear in immediate experience. Nor does it appear, says Althusser, in any form of knowledge claiming to be part of the real object. Any epistemology which unites knowledge and the real object will be unable to produce a concept of that object. This applies, in Althusser's view, whether we are dealing with Hegelian idealism (the real = thought), or with classical empiricism (the real as inseparable from sense experience). Because his predecessors (and many who came after him) have been unable to avoid empiricism – have been unable to break the link between knowledge and the real object – they have also been unable to 'see' (provide a knowledge of) the mode of production as Marx did, and Marx, in his turn, was unable to elaborate the concept of the mode of production because he was still reliant on the language of empiricism. Accordingly, in only a few privileged texts (in the 1857 *Introduction*, *The Critique of the Gothe Programme*, and *Marginal Notes on Wagner*) does Marx really speak in his own name. Today's reader of Marx thus has to carry out a symptomatic reading capable of making Marx's discovery visible. This means providing the concepts for the theoretical revolution that Marx inaugurated.

Once the empiricist problematic is neutralised, knowledge and the objective world become entirely separate. From this it follows that the validity of a theory is not dependent on whether or not what it says corresponds immediately with reality, but on whether its premises are internally consistent. Similarly, a scientific truth is not derived a postiori, but entirely a priori: the theory of relativity is entirely true (or false) before it is tested in reality. On this basis, Althusser is able to make Spinoza Marx's direct predecessor because Spinoza claimed that science is true because it is successful; it is not successful because it is true. Such is the fundamental characteristic of a science which, for Althusser, distinguishes it from ideology. Consequently, the distinguishing feature of ideology is that it assumes knowledge, or ideas are derived from the way things are – whether these 'things' are God's work, as in religion, or whether they are man's work, as in Enlightenment philosophy. In short, ideology accepts the (false) obviousness of things; it discourages questions, and avoids the task of constructing the object of knowledge.

Given this preparation, what is it that

Marx discovered? Two possible answers, representing two different levels of analysis, present themselves. The first is that Marx discovered the concept of the mode of production in history and, in particular, the capitalist mode of production (surplus value, exchange value, commodity); the second answer is, according to Althusser, that Marx discovered the science of history, or historical materialism, as well as dialectical materialism – the non-empiricist philosophical framework providing the concept of this discovery. Historicism, by contrast, forgets that Marxism is also a philosophy, and humanism forgets that Marx inaugurated a new science, the science of history, where history is to be understood as the history of modes of production. Althusser never tires of repeating that the mode of production is the unique object of historical materialism, an object quite different from the object of classical political economy and Enlightenment theories of history and society. Now, with Marx, there is no 'society', only modes of production which evolve in history and are always immanent in the various relatively autonomous levels of the structured social whole.

If the mode of production is also equivalent to the determination of the economy in the last instance, how is the economy supposed to manifest itself within the social formation to which it gives rise? And if changes occur in the economy, will these become evident throughout society? At least until the mid-1930s the answer to these questions was that a change in the economy (or infrastructure) would be reflected in society and culture (the superstructure). If, therefore, capitalism was equivalent to the exploitation of labour through the extraction of surplus-value, or profit, this antagonistic relationship between capitalist and worker would also find ideological expression in social life. In other words, the worker and capitalist would become *conscious* of this antagonism and fight it out. Thus the economy would directly *determine* social and cultural life.

A little reflection reveals that if this determinist explanation were valid, there would hardly be any need to turn to Marx to understand it; instead, recourse to Feuerbachian anthropology (which placed 'Man' at the centre of the universe), and also to Hegel would be more than sufficient. For Althusser, Marx's concept of the mode of production cannot be read off from the level of consciousness or ideology. On the contrary, as a structural phenomenon, it can only exist in an overdetermined way throughout the social formation in question. 'Overdetermination' is a term Althusser borrowed from Freud (who used it in *The Interpretation of Dreams* to show how dream-thoughts exist in a displaced form in the manifest content of the dream) in order to emphasise that the reality of the economic level, or the mode of production, is not directly expressed in ideology or in consciousness, but exists in a displaced form in the social formation in question. In this sense, contradictions in the system are overdetermined. They are not immediately visible, but must be analysed, that is, rendered visible, by science.

Althusser was not the first Marxist thinker to challenge the over-simplifications of the economic–determinist position. For after the discovery of Marx's *Economic and Philosophic Manuscripts* in 1932, humanist Marxism challenged not only economic determinism, but all interpretations of social life which denied man the initiative in changing social conditions. Consciousness, ideology – politics – became, in the 1960s, the catch-cries of many radical theories of society. Althusser thus contested the idea that Marxism was a humanism, just as he contested the idea that it was an economic determinism. This is why, particularly in 1965, he wrote so insistently about the 'epistemological break' between the early and the late Marx.[4] The early Marx, Althusser agrees, is decidedly humanist, decidedly Feuerbachian; however, says Althusser, he is not Marx. The true Marx, as we have seen, is the one who broke with the Hegelian–Feuerbachian

problematic governing both economic determinism and humanism. An epistemological
break separates the early, ideological Marx
from the later, scientific Marx.

If, however, Marx's science breaks with
the problematic that privileges ideology in
social explanation, does this mean that ideology is a pure illusion, or a kind of myth,
something that has no real basis in social
life? As if to answer this question in 1967, and
thereby rectify the somewhat brutal way
ideology had been deprived of any explanatory power in his version of Marxism,
Althusser wrote as follows in the English
Preface to *For Marx*: 'In no sense was I
condemning ideology as a social reality: as
Marx says, it is in ideology that men "become
conscious" of their class conflict and "fight it
out".'[5] Three years later, Althusser went
even further in analysing ideology and, in a
famous essay, 'Ideology and ideological state
apparatuses',[6] offered a Marxist theory of
ideology. The state – which, in Leninist
fashion, is seen to intervene unambiguously
in the interests of the bourgeoisie against
the proletariat – consists of ideological
apparatuses (churches, schools, legal system,
family, communications, political parties,
etc.), as well as repressive apparatuses
(police, prisons, army, etc.). Althusser tries
to use his theory of ideology to fill what has
always been a glaring gap in Marxist theory:
the explanation of how the existing relations
of production are actually reproduced.
Ideology is the mechanism through which the
bourgeoisie is able to reproduce its class
domination. Through ideology, succeeding
generations continue to adapt to the status
quo. In Althusser's words, ideology 'represents in its necessarily imaginary distortion
not the existing relations of production (and
the other relations that derive from them),
but above all the (imaginary) relationship of
individuals to the relations of production and
the relations that derive from them'.[7]

Ideology provides the framework in which
people live their relationship to the social
reality in which they are located. Ideology

forms subjects, and in forming them locates
them in the system of relationships necessary
for the maintenance of existing class relations. Ideology 'interpellates' – or 'hails' –
individuals as subjects of the system: it gives
them the identity necessary to the functioning of the existing state of affairs. This
identity is constituted materially, concretely
in various practices – ritual practices like
shaking hands or praying. 'Obviousness' –
taken-for-grantedness – is quite characteristic of ideological practices; and it is so
because these practices are inseparable from
the way that people live out the spontaneous
and immediate aspect of their 'existence'. No
one is unaffected by ideology in this sense.
No society is without this spontaneous,
practical level of existence. Everyone is in
ideology; no one escapes it. Everyone is
constituted as a subject in these material
practices.

In all probability, Althusser's popularity
as a Marxist declined because the popularity
of Marxist theory declined in the late-1970s.
Perhaps the Althusserian intervention had
never been more than a holding operation
anyway, so that even the social doctrine he
developed, in the end, found it difficult to
shake off the nineteenth-century worldview
inspired by industrialism which partly
brought it into being.

On the other hand, there is rigor to be
marvelled at in Althusser's writing, once the
tone of the Marxist pilgrim is discounted, and
the extreme discipline of the organisation
and presentation of the text is allowed to
come into view. Moreover, it cannot be
denied that Althusser's strategies for reading
take this familiar activity out of the category
of the false obviousness of immediate experience. Few theorists of note today would
go along with the naive empiricism which was
so much the norm prior to Althusser's
intervention.

To adopt once again a more critical tone,
Althusser's theorising is in fact terribly
narrow in focus, clinging as it does to the
canon of Marxist thought. Consequently,

although Althusser is directly concerned with the concept of science, and although he claims that Marx inaugurated the science of history, exactly what is meant by science is almost impossible to determine outside the rather unilluminating fact that, contrary to ideology, science does not have a subject. In addition, while aspects of Althusser's text on ideology contain some of the best things that he wrote, the actual link between ideology, reproduction and interpellation is not sufficiently spelt out. If ideology is always present (being the immediate relationship people have to the world) but is, under the capitalist mode of production, the way exploitation is maintained, what is the link between ideology in general, and the historically specific way that individuals are constituted as subjects under capitalism? Suddenly we see that with all the emphasis on Marx's scientific discovery of the mode of production – a discovery that leaves ideology behind – the very nature of ideology as the illusory immediacy of the relationship between the human being and the world is neglected. What seems to be needed is not only a science of modes of production, but also a science of the nature of ideology. And so although Althusser has something important to say about ideology in general, it conflicts with what he wants to say as a Marxist philosopher concerned with exploitation. What precisely can a Marxist theory of ideology tell us about exploitation? Almost nothing, if we were to follow Althusser on this point – even though ideology is inextricably linked to the reproduction of the system. Gradually, it begins to dawn that perhaps the best book Althusser ever wrote was his autobiography.[8]

Notes

1 Jean Lacroix, cited by Didier Eribon in his *Michel Foucault*, Paris, Flammarion, 1989, p. 183.
2 ibid., p. 189.
3 See Althusser's illustrative remark on Gramsci in *Reading Capital*, trans. Ben Brewster, London, New Left Books (reprinted in paperback 1975), p. 130: 'It is clear that Gramsci tends to make the theory of history and dialectical materialism coincide within *historical materialism alone*, although they form two distinct disciplines.'
4 Louis Althusser, *For Marx*, trans. Ben Brewster, Harmondsworth, Penguin Books, 1969, p. 33.
5 ibid., p. 11.
6 In Louis Althusser, *Lenin and Philosophy and Other Essays*, trans. Ben Brewster, London, New Left Books, 1971, pp. 121–73. (Includes the essay 'Ideology and ideological state apparatuses'.)
7 ibid., p. 155.
8 Louis Althusser, *L'Avenir due longtemps suivi de les faits*, text established by Olivier Corpet et Yann Moulier Boutang, Paris, Stock/IMEC, 1992. In English as *The Future Lasts a Long Time*, trans. Richard Veasey, London, Chatto & Windus, 1993.

See also in this book

Foucault, Kristeva, Lacan, Lévi-Strauss

Althusser's major writings

Montesquieu: Politics and History (1959), trans. Ben Brewster, London, New Left Books, 1972
For Marx (1965), trans. Ben Brewster, Harmondsworth, Penguin Books, 1969
Reading Capital (1968) (with Etienne Balibar), trans. Ben Brewster, London, New Left Books. Reprinted in paperback 1975
Lenin and Philosophy and Other Essays, trans. Ben Brewster, London, New Left Books, 1971
Essays in Self-Criticism (1973, 1974, 1975), trans. Grahame Lock, London, New Left Books, 1976. Includes 'Reply to John Lewis', 'Elements of self-criticism' and 'Is it simple to be a Marxist in Philosophy?'
Philosophie et philosophie spontanée des savants, Paris, Maspero, 1973
Positions, Paris, Editions Sociales, 1976
L'Avenir due longtemps suivi de les faits, text established by Olivier Corpet and Yann Moulier Boutang, Paris, Stock/IMEC, 1992

Further reading

Benton, Ted, *The Rise and Fall of Structural Marxism*, London, Macmillan, 1984
Callincos, Alex, *Althusser's Marxism*, London, Pluto Press, 1976

Kaplan, E. Ann, and Sprinker, Michael, *The Althusserian Legacy*, London, Verso, 1993

Smith, Steven, *Reading Althusser: An Essay on Structural Marxism*, Ithaca, Cornell University Press, 1984

EMILE BENVENISTE

Born in Cairo in 1902, Emile Benveniste was professor of linguistics at the Collège de France from 1937 to 1969, when he was forced to retire due to ill-health. He died in 1976. After being educated at the Sorbonne under Ferdinand de Saussure's former pupil, Antoine Meillet, Benveniste's early work in the 1930s continued Saussure's interest in the history of Indo-European linguistic forms, particularly the status of names. Because of the specialist, technical nature of this early work, Benveniste was little known outside a relatively narrow circle of scholars.

This situation changed with the publication of the first volume of his *Problèmes de linguistique générale* in 1966. A second volume appeared in 1974. The book brings together Benveniste's most accessible writings of a period of more than twenty-five years, and looks at language as a linguistic and semiotic object, as an instrument of communication, as a social and cultural phenomenon, and as a vehicle of subjectivity. In the wake of this work, Benveniste became an important figure in the evolution of the structuralist tendency in the social sciences and humanities. Lacan, for instance, recognises in his *Ecrits* that it is Benveniste who deals a behaviourist interpretation a mortal blow with the insight that, unlike the communication of bees, human language is not a simple stimulus-response system. And Kristeva, for her part, has seen that Benveniste's theory of pronouns – especially the relationship between 'I' and 'you' – or what is called the I–you polarity – is of fundamental importance for developing a dynamic conception of subjectivity. Roland Barthes, similarly, clearly saw Benveniste's writings on the 'middle voice' of the verb as being of seminal importance for understanding the position of the writer today – the writer who now writes intransitively (middle voice).

In his work on pronouns, Benveniste developed a theory of the difference between the *énoncé* (statement independent of context) and the *énonciation* (the act of stating tied to context). Given the phenomenon of 'shifterisation', as elaborated by Roman Jakobson, no meaning of an *énoncé* containing pronouns and other markers of the shifter (such as 'here', 'there', 'this', 'that', etc.) can be understood without reference to context, equivalent here to the act of enunciation. Granted that it is difficult to give an example of an *énonciation* because in fact an *énoncé* is always the necessary vehicle of any example (an example being an instance of a speech act taken out of its context), it is important to recognise that the subject in language is inseparable from its realisation. In other words, the subject is not equivalent to the status attributed to it in the formal, grammatical structure. In terms of the latter, the subject is always the fixed, static entity given in the *énoncé*. In sum, then, Benveniste's insight is that any linguistics which wants to do justice to the dynamics of language must see it as a 'discursive instance' – as discourse, in short. Discourse is the enactment of language.

A key element of Benveniste's theory of language as discourse is his theory of pronouns, and in particular, the theory of the I–you polarity. Grammatically, this polarity constitutes the first and second person pronouns, with he–she–it constituting the third person. Benveniste's insight is that the third person functions as the condition of possibility of the first and second person; the third person is a 'non-person', a status revealed by the neutral voice of narration, or description – the voice of denotation. Kristeva will come to see this polarity as the key to understanding the dynamics of the subject–object (I = subject, you = object) relation in language. The upshot is that, now, the I–you polarity has meaning uniquely in relation to the present instance of discourse. As our author explains when discussing the 'reality' to which *I* or *you* refers: '*I* signifies "the person who is uttering the present instance of the discourse containing *I*." This instance is unique by definition and has validity only in its uniqueness. . . . *I* can only be identified by the instance of discourse that contains it and by that alone.'[1] *You*, for its part, is defined in the following way:

> by introducing the situation of 'address', we obtain a symmetrical definition for *you* as the 'individual spoken to in the present instance of discourse containing the linguistic instance of *you*'. These definitions [Benveniste adds] refer to *I* and *you* as a category of language and are related to their position in language.[2]

More generally, Beveniste sees language as essentially a dialogue between two or more parties, unlike a signal system where there is no dialogue. Again, in language a message can be passed on to a third person, in contrast to a signal system where the 'message' goes no further than the receiver. Finally, human language is a form that makes possible an infinite variety of contents, while a simple communication system based on a signal is invariably limited to what is programmed (e.g., the signal system of bees relates exclusively to honey). An important implication deriving from these insights is that human language can be used in an ironical way, or in a way requiring the constant interpretation and reinterpretation of the potentially multiple meanings latent in the *énonciation*. This means that human language has an undeniable poetic and fictive side to it. Connected to this is the further implication that, *qua énonciation*, human language never repeats itself exactly, as is the case with a signal system.

While he did not ever claim that thought and language were identical, Benveniste would not accept either the position of Hjelmslev, for whom thought was entirely separate from language. For his part, Benveniste pointed out that in practice it is impossible to separate thought from language for, at minimum, language must be the vehicle for thought. As Benveniste says, 'whoever tries to grasp the proper framework of thought encounters only the categories of language'.[3]

Although a strong advocate of the importance of Saussure for the history of modern semiotics and linguistics, Benveniste also recognised the need to modify Saussure's theory, in particular in terms of the relationship Saussure drew between linguistics and semiotics. Linguistics, Saussure said in the *Course in General Linguistics*, would one day be subsumed by semiotics, the discipline which studies sign-systems. Such a prediction, Benveniste recognised, needs to be carefully thought through. In doing this, Benveniste notes that linguistic systems such as Morse code, braille, or sign language for the deaf and dumb can be translated between themselves, while semiotic systems are characterised by their non-redundance and therefore are not mutually translatable. As our author explains, 'there is no "synonymy" between semiotic systems; one cannot "say the same thing" through speech and through music, which are systems each having a different basis'.[4] Again, two semiotic systems may well have the same constituent base and yet still be mutually untranslatable – such as, to cite Benveniste, the red in the traffic code and the red in the French tricolore. Consequently, Benveniste concludes, there is no single system of signs which would transcend all other systems; the possibility of an all-embracing semiotics which would include linguistics is therefore greatly reduced. The reverse is perhaps much more likely, namely that the linguistic system is the basis of translation of all semiotic systems.

Further to his analysis of the difference between the semiotic and the linguistic systems is Benveniste's discussion of the difference between the semiotic and the semantic dimensions of language. The semiotic (*le sémiotique*) dimension is the mode of significance proper to the sign. Fundamentally, the semiotic exists when it is recognised. It is independent of any reference. The semantic aspect, on the other hand, is to be understood, rather than recognised. As a result, it is entirely referential and engendered by discourse.

Benveniste also became influential during the 1960s with his writings about the nature of language. Like Lévi-Strauss, he pointed out that language is constitutive of the social order, rather than the other way round. Furthermore, it was Benveniste who showed that language's unique and paradoxical aspect in its social setting is its status as a super-individual instrument which can be objectified (hence linguistics), and which, as an instance of discourse, is constitutive of individuality. Indeed, the I–you polarity implies that the individual and society are no longer contradictory terms; for there is no individuality without language and no language independently of a community of speakers. Although Benveniste recognised that it is perfectly possible to study the history of national languages – just as it is possible to study the history of societies – it is not possible to study the history of language as such, or the history of society as such, because it is only within language and society that history is possible.

> For humanity, language (*langue*) and society are unconscious realities. . . . Both are always inherited, and we cannot imagine in the exercise of language and in the practice of society that, at this fundamental level, there could ever have been a beginning to either of them. Neither can be changed by human will.[5]

Consequently, important changes certainly occur within social institutions, but the social bond itself does not change; similarly, the designations of language can change, but not the language system. This, Benveniste tried to impress upon those who, like Freud in some of his writings, would explain language and society at the level of ontogenesis. The risk is that the 'primitive' form (of society, language, culture) is made to serve as an explanation for the more advanced form. In this sense, 'primitive' societies were deemed by Rousseau, and certain anthropologists who were influenced by him, to be the 'childhood' of mankind, and so hold the key to a knowledge of the foundations of Western society. Benveniste, in 1956, to his credit, demonstrated that Freud, too, was not free of the temptation to call upon an ontogenesis in order to explain dream, primal words, and language in general. Benveniste's response is to point out that

> confusions seem to have arisen in Freud from his constant recourse to 'origins': origins of art, of religion, of society, of language. . . . He was constantly transposing what seemed to him to be 'primitive' in man into an original primitivism, for it was indeed into the history of this world that he projected what we could call a chronology of the human psyche.[6]

By drawing attention to the risks involved in allowing ontogenesis to have a strong influence in social theory, Benveniste shows himself to be one of those who opened the way towards a structuralist (and later post-structuralist) approach to the analysis and interpretation of social phenomena. He showed conclusively that language has no origin precisely because it is a system. There can, therefore, be no primitive language. Language changes, but it does not progress. Linguistically, every natural language without exception is complex and highly differentiated. With Benveniste, then, the ethnocentrism of early enthnography is dealt a mortal blow.

Notes

1 Emile Benveniste, *Problems in General Linguistics*, trans. Mary Elizabeth Meek, Coral Gables, Florida, University of Miami Press, 'Miami Linguistics Series No. 8', 1971, p. 218.
2 ibid.

3 ibid., p. 63.
4 Emile Benveniste, *Problèmes de linguistique générale*, Volume 2, Paris, Gallimard, TEL, 1974, p. 53.
5 ibid., p. 94.
6 Benveniste, *Problems in General Linguistics*, p. 72.

See also in this book

Barthes, Greimas, Kristeva, Lacan, Lévi-Strauss, Saussure

Benveniste's major writings

Problems in General Linguistics, trans. Mary Elizabeth Meek, Coral Gables, Florida, University of Miami Press, 'Miami Linguistics Series No. 8', 1971. Trans. of Vol. 1 of *Problèmes de linguistique générale*, Paris, Gallimard, 1966
Problèmes de linguistique générale, Volume 2, Paris, Gallimard, 1974
Indo-European Language and Society, trans. Elizabeth Palmer, London, Faber & Faber, 'Studies in General Linguistics Series', 1973
Origines de la formation des noms en indo-européen, Paris, A. Maisonneuve, 1935
Les Infinitifs avestiques, Paris, A. Maisonneuve, 1935
Noms d'agent et noms d'action en indo-européen, Paris, A. Maisonneuve, 1948
Titres et noms propres en iranien ancien, Paris, Klincksieck, 'Travaux de l'Institut d'Etudes Iraniennes de l'Université de Paris, I', 1966

Further reading

Lotringer, Sylvèrer, and Gora, Thomas (guest eds), 'Polyphonic linguistics: The many voices of Emile Benveniste', special supplement of *Semiotica*, The Hague, Mouton, 1981

PIERRE BOURDIEU

Given the complexity of Pierre Bourdieu's work, there is always the risk that his project will be misinterpreted. Care is needed in reading this *oeuvre* – the same care Bourdieu himself puts into his writing.

That said, certain things stand out: a concern to analyse inequality and class distinction at a structural rather than at an ideological level, but without succumbing to the (as Bourdieu puts it) 'objectivist' illusion of structuralism; a concern to enable science to go beyond its reliance on the model for grasping the nature of social life, and so come to grips with practice, or practices; a desire to go beyond the clichés, stereotypes, and classifications of the universally unquestioned *doxa*, and, as a consequence, to make explicit the power relations inscribed in social reality, in a social field. Since undertaking fieldwork in Algeria in the 1960s, Bourdieu has been committed to revealing the underlying modes of class domination in capitalist societies as these appear in all aspects of education and art. His abiding thesis is that the dominant class does not dominate overtly: it does not force the dominated to conform to its will. Nor does it dominate in capitalist society through a conspiracy where the privileged would consciously manipulate reality in accordance with their own self-interest. Rather, the dominant class in capitalist society is, statistically, the beneficiary of economic, social and symbolic power, power which is embodied in economic and cultural capital, and which is imbricated throughout society's institutions and practices and reproduced by these very institutions and practices.

Pierre Bourdieu was born in Dengvin in the south of France, in 1930. He attended the prestigious Parisian Lycée, Louis-Le-Grand in 1950–1, and completed his *agrégation* in philosophy at the Ecole Normale Supérieure. As part of his military service, Bourdieu taught in Algeria, and so experienced French colonialism at first hand. This experience was formative, and the effort to understand it set the philosopher on the path of anthropology and sociology. Later, between 1959 and 1962, Bourdieu taught philosophy at the Sorbonne, and in the mid-1960s, he became director of studies at the Ecole des Hautes Etudes, and the director of European Sociology. In 1982, he was elected to the chair of Sociology at the Collège de France.

In his book, *Homo Academicus*, Bourdieu says that the Ecole des Hautes Etudes in Paris remains one of the rare marginal, yet prestigious, institutions in the French academic system, one which fostered original thought and research. This was important for Bourdieu early in his career, because higher education in France tends to be structured around academically prestigious individuals and institutions (like the Ecole Normale Supérieure – rue d'Ulm). 'Academically prestigious' does not necessarily mean scholarly and intellectually challenging. Rather, it means that academic accolades tend to go to those who know – whether consciously or not – how to work the patronage system, and make best use of any inherited privileges, or cultural capital, they might have. Academic privilege and the institutional power that goes with it are contrasted by Bourdieu with scholarly and intellectual renown. While the latter might entail a certain imagination, originality and critical acuity, the former requires 'the most authentic proof of *obsequium*, unconditional respect for the fundamental principles of the established order'.[1]

The view of the academic milieu as 'fair' and 'competitive' and supposedly charged with 'pushing back the frontiers of knowledge', and selecting 'the best minds' for the task, is the kind of common-sense orthodoxy Bourdieu's sociological research and reflection aims to dispel. Indeed, for Bourdieu, what is self-evident, and taken for granted, goes without saying – our common-sense ideas, or our imprecise unscientific language are founded on a misrecognition (méconnaissance) of unequal power relations and a concomitant *reproduction* of privilege.

To a large extent, Bourdieu's underlying theoretical stance was presented in his early 1970s essay, *An Outline of a Theory of Practice*. There, in the context of ethnographic studies, Bourdieu delineates a three-tiered framework of theoretical knowledge, where the most reflexive level will eventually be employed to classify 'the classifiers', to 'objectify the objectifying subject', and to

judge the very arbiters of taste themselves. The first element of this framework is 'primary experience', or what Bourdieu also calls the 'phenomenological' level. This level is known to all researchers in the field because it is the source of their basic descriptive data about the familiar, everyday world – either of their own society or of another. The second level, almost as familiar, is that of the 'model' or of 'objectivist' knowledge. Here, knowledge 'constructs the objective relations (e.g., economic or linguistic) which structure practice and representations of practice'. Thus at a 'primary' level, the researcher might note that at every wedding, birthday or Christmas people exchange presents. At an objectivist level, the researcher might theorise that, despite what common sense suggests, gift exchange is a means of maintaining prestige and confirming a social hierarchy, and perhaps also an instance of the way exchange as such is a mode of social cohesion. The point Bourdieu emphasises about such knowledge is that it is fundamentally the knowledge of the detached, neutral observer who is engaged in developing a theory of the practice implied in the primary data. When it comes to studying language or gift-exchange in particular, the knowledge of the detached theorist is significantly limited. Clearly, if language is studied only from the position of the listener (often the position of detachment), and not also from the position of speaker, a defective form of knowledge is derived. Bourdieu thus argues that an adequate theory of practice must also have a theory of the major defect of the objectivist approach to practice, which is that it is too rigidly detached from practice. It therefore fails to account for elements integral to practice – such as 'style', 'tact', 'dexterity', '*savoir-faire*', and particularly, 'improvisation'. Similarly, in constructing a model of practice – e.g., exchange of gifts – objectivist knowledge cannot account for 'misfires', or 'strategies' which might undermine the universality of the model. In other words, time is left out of the model along with the notion of 'strategy'. 'Strategy', says Bourdieu, 'allows for individual intervention against the model.' This the structuralist position as enunciated by Lévi-Strauss failed to do. To be sure, relations, and not substances, characterise social and cultural life – as Saussure's theory of language led researchers to see. However, to remain at this level, as Bourdieu claims first-wave structuralism tended to do, is to remain at the level of the model, or objectivist knowledge.

Bourdieu proposes, then, that a theory of objectivist knowledge will, at the same time, be a more rigorous and illuminating theory of practice. He claims that a truly rigorous theory of practice is accomplished by taking up the position of the realisation of practice. A tall order it might well be thought. Bourdieu, though, is not to be denied. And from the position of theory in the *Outline*, he goes on to produce three important works on education and taste – *Homo Academicus*, *Distinction*, and *La Noblesse d'état: Les Grandes Ecoles et esprit de corps* – works in which a number of Bourdieu's key concepts are deployed. '*Habitus*', 'field' and 'cultural capital' are cases in point.

Although sometimes mistaken for specific routines of everyday life, or as a synonym for socialisation, *habitus* is in fact part of Bourdieu's theory of practice as the articulation of dispositions in social space. The space is also a social field in that the positions in it form a system of relations based on stakes (power) that are meaningful and desired by those occupying the positions in social space. *Habitus* is a kind of expression of the (unconscious) investment those in social space have in the power stakes so implied. *Habitus* is a kind of grammar of actions which serves to differentiate one class (e.g., the dominant) from another (e.g., the dominated) in the social field. In *Distinction* Bourdieu refers to *habitus* as a system of schemas for the production of particular practices. Thus if 'good taste' entails that the university professor will have a marked preference for Bach's *Well Tempered Clavier*, while 'middle-brow' manual and clerical workers will prefer *The Blue Danube*, the validity of good taste is only undermined when it is revealed that the professor (especially of law or medicine) is himself the son of a professor who had a private art collection and whose wife was a good amateur musician. For the professor is marked as someone who has not only 'achieved' a certain amount in the field of education, but also as someone who has inherited cultural capital. That is to say that, in particular cases, the family environment can provide a significant amount of knowledge, understanding and 'taste' which is not formally learned, but is unconsciously acquired.

A specific *habitus* becomes evident when a range of variables (occupation, education, income, artistic preferences, taste in food, etc.) are shown, statistically, to correlate with each other. Thus, in contradistinction to the manual worker, the professor of law will tend to have had a private school education, prefer Bach (and more generally, the form of art to its content), have a high income, and will prefer a simple, if elegant, cuisine of lean meats, fresh fruit and vegetables. This correlation is what Bourdieu says constitutes a specific (in this case bourgeois, or dominant) set of dispositions, or a *habitus*. A *habitus* is generative of a set of dispositions common to a class. With the knowledge of a class *habitus*, it is not possible to predict exactly *what* a member of the dominant, or the dominated, class will do at a particular time and in a particular situation. To do so would be to eliminate time and agency and to reaffirm the primacy of the model over practice, the very thing that the *Outline* had criticised in the early 1970s. Bourdieu has also said that *habitus* has to do with a 'sense of one's place' which emerges through processes of differentiation in social space, and that it is a system of schemas for the production of practices, as well as a system of schemas of perception and apperception of these practices. The boundaries between one *habitus* and another are always contested because always fluid – never firm.

Bourdieu has worked hard to refine this key concept of his *oeuvre*, for it is the basis on which he lays claim to originality as a sociologist. Because the economistic approach of Marxism is too reductionist, and because early structuralism was too objectivist, and because, finally, conspiracy theories of class domination give too much weight to primary experience – as exemplified, for instance, in specific, everyday acts of naked self-interest – Bourdieu has worked to refine his theory of practice in order that it may be both scientific and beholden to practice. To be scientific here, is to account for contingency, agency, and time.

The success of Bourdieu's approach is another matter. For it could be argued that any link with theory is bound to freeze practice in its tracks. To be sure, *habitus* might be a disposition, but what exactly is the relationship between this disposition and contingent acts? Statistical regularities, Bourdieu replies. Scientific knowledge, in other words. But of what use (cultural, political, social, etc.) is this knowledge? When it is used by groups for political purposes it risks becoming purely ideological, a dimension of symbolic power: the power to represent.

While it is true that Bourdieu's notion of entering the game of practice without being carried away by it, is suggestive, and while his more tragic image of science as real freedom to the extent that it is the 'knowledge of necessity' offers a possible basis for a deeper understanding of the scientific, and thus sociological, enterprise, Bourdieu's work is still reliant on a fundamental division between theory and practice, or between theory and reality. This division itself needs to be reworked if Bourdieu's work is to encompass the dynamism of Freud's.

Again, in a postscript in his monumental study, *Distinction*, Bourdieu takes to task the 'cultivated' disposition of the philosopher as exemplified even in Jacques Derrida's 'unorthodox' reading of Kant on aesthetics.

To oppose philosophy philosophically is merely to reinforce the privileged status of the 'philosophical field', says Bourdieu. It is still to pay homage to a body of canonical texts which are relatively inaccessible to the outsider. It is still to forget the 'objective conditions' of philosophy, where prestige is awarded to the erudite and denied to the neophyte. It is, moreover, characteristic of intellectuals to have the *habitus* of the privileged, even though they tend to be the dominated fraction of the dominant class.

All this is fine up to a point. The importance of being aware of the social conditions of philosophy – and art – should put a break on any sanctimonious assertion of its autonomy. Nevertheless, Bourdieu himself is clearly a product of a training in philosophy, just as his work also relies on the canon of privileged texts for its inspiration. Bourdieu thus tacitly recognises that this canon is the only one we have at the moment, and that, for better or for worse, we are led to seek inspiration there, even though there can be no absolute confirmation of its truth and legitimacy. Drawing attention to the objective conditions of different kinds of discourse is no doubt Bourdieu's greatest contribution to sociological thought. However, this sociology risks standing still if it does not also develop new theoretical insights in light of this contribution.

Notes

1 Pierre Bourdieu, *Homo Academicus*, trans. Peter Collier, Cambridge, Polity Press, 1988, p. 87.

See also in this book

Derrida, Lévi-Strauss, Saussure, Touraine

Bourdieu's major writings

Sociologie de l'Algérie, Paris, PUF, second edn, 1962

The Inheritors (1964), trans. Richard Nice, Chicago, University of Chicago Press, 1979

'Structuralism and theory of sociological knowledge', *Social Research*, 35, 4 (Winter 1968), pp. 682–706

The Craft of Sociology: Epistemological Preliminaries (1968) (with Jean-Claude Passeron), trans. Richard Nice, New York and Berlin, de Gruyter, 1991

Reproduction in Education, Society and Culture (1970) (with Jean-Claude Passeron), trans. Richard Nice, London, Sage, 1977

An Outline of a Theory of Practice (1972), trans. Richard Nice, Cambridge, London, New York and Melbourne, Cambridge University Press, 1977

Algeria 1960 (1977), Cambridge, Cambridge University Press, 1979

'Sport and social class' (1978) in Chandra Mukerji and Michael Schudson (eds), *Rethinking Popular Culture*, Berkeley, University of California Press, 1991, pp. 367–73

Distinction (1979), trans. Richard Nice, London and New York, Routledge & Kegan Paul, 1986

The Logic of Practice (1980), trans. Richard Nice, Cambridge, Polity Press, 1990

Homo Academicus (1984), trans. Peter Collier, Cambridge, Polity Press, 1988

In Other Words: Essays Toward a Reflexive Sociology (1987), trans. M. Adamson, Cambridge, Polity Press, 1990

The Political Ontology of Martin Heidegger (1988), trans. Peter Collier, Cambridge, Polity Press, 1991

La Noblesse d'état: Les Grandes Ecoles et esprit de corps, Paris, Minuit, 1989

Language and Symbolic Power, ed. John B. Thompson, Cambridge, Polity Press, 1991

An Invitation to Reflexive Sociology (with Loïc J.D. Wacquant), Chicago, University of Chicago Press, 1992

The Field of Cultural Production: Essays on Art and Literature, ed. Randal Johnson, Cambridge, Polity Press, 1993

Further reading

Jenkins, Richard, *Pierre Bourdieu*, London and New York, Routledge, Key Sociologists Series, 1992

Harker, Richard *et al.* (eds), *An Introduction to the Work of Bourdieu: The Practice of Theory*, Basingstoke, Macmillan, 1990

Miller, Don, and Branson, Jan, 'Pierre Bourdieu: culture and praxis' in Diane J. Austin-Broos (ed.), Sydney, Allen & Unwin, 1987, pp. 210–25

Robins, Derek, *The Work of Pierre Bourdieu*, Milton Keynes, Open University Press, 1991

NOAM CHOMSKY

If critical interest and acclaim are any indication, Noam Chomsky would have to be seen as one of the most significant and influential linguists of the twentieth century. Chomsky received his linguistic training under Leonard Bloomfield, whose behaviourist empiricism dominated American linguistics during the 1930s and 1940s, and from Zellig Harris, whose political stances during the 1950s pleased Chomsky more than his version of linguistic structuralism.

Chomsky's contribution to linguistics, and thence to modern thought, has been broadly threefold. In the first place, he moved the emphasis of linguistics from the strictly descriptive and inductive level (the level of the endless cataloguing of utterances from which conclusions about grammar could then be drawn) to the ideal level of competence and 'deep structure', the level which opens up a creative aspect in language. In short, Chomsky showed, within his technical expertise in linguistics, that language was more than its material execution. Second, he brought about a reconsideration of language learning by arguing that language competence is not acquired inductively through a behaviourist stimulus-response conditioning, but is the consequence of an innate cognitive capacity possessed by humans. In other words, linguistic freedom and creativity is not acquired, but always already exists as a governing a priori. Third, the distinction between 'competence' and 'performance' – even when it was poorly understood – has served as a metaphor for structural studies in other disciplines such as philosophy and sociology (cf., Habermas's notion of 'communicative competence', and Bourdieu's notion of '*habitus*' – notions which echo Chomsky's conception of agency).

It is worth noting that Chomsky has also become an outspoken, left-liberal intellectual who vigorously opposed America's involvement in the Vietnam War, and who has written nearly a dozen books dealing with international and domestic political issues of the day. Some of the best known of these are: *American Power and the New Mandarins* (1969); *The Backroom Boys* (1973); *Human Rights and American Foreign Policy* (1978); *The Fateful Triangle: The United States, Israel and the Palestinians* (1983); *Necessary Illusions: Thought Control in Democratic Societies* (1989); and *Deterring Democracy* (1991).

In what seemed like a tremendous lapse of political judgement, Chomsky – himself a Jew (his father was in fact a Hebrew scholar) – wrote a Preface in 1980 to Robert Faurisson's notorious book against the existence of the Nazi gas chambers. Chomsky based his intervention on the (misguided) principle that to be a consistent liberal in politics all shades of opinion have a right to be heard.

Noam Chomsky was born in Philadelphia in 1928. His early education was in an 'experimental progressive school', and at the Central High School, Philadelphia. At the University of Pennsylvania, he studied mathematics and philosophy, as well as linguistics under the influence of Zellig Harris. Although he took out his PhD degree at the University of Pennsylvania, most of the work for it was completed at Harvard University between 1951 and 1955. Since 1955, Chomsky has taught at the Massachusetts Institute of Technology, and he has been an Institute Professor there since 1976.

Through his father – who published *Hebrew: The Eternal Language* (1958) – Chomsky was introduced to historical linguistics. In fact, the son's first major piece of writing is his unpublished Master's thesis – also on Hebrew – entitled 'Morphophonemics of modern Hebrew' (1951). Given Chomsky's parallel interest in logic and mathematics, it was no doubt to be expected that the work of logicians (Goodman, Quine, Kripke, Lakatós, Hintikka) and analytical philosophers (Austin, Wittgenstein) would be of greater interest to him than philoso-phers or linguists from the so-called Continental tradition. Such an interest has at times given Chomsky's writings the sparse style imitative of the putative rigor of the natural sciences. As he himself has put it, like physics, the intellectual interest of linguistics resides less in phenomena (the products of language) and more in the explanatory power of its principles.[1] 'Natural science', says Chomsky, 'as distinct from natural history, is not concerned with the phenomena in themselves, but with the principles and the explanations that they have some bearing on.'[2] Such an approach – also evident in work in logic – entails that a certain style (use of notation), format (use of micro-examples), and method (idealisation) are taken to be axiomatic, and so generally to be beyond critical scrutiny. This has meant that although his work has been taken up elsewhere (e.g., France), Chomsky himself has often been unable to engage in a dialogue with linguists whose presuppositions are inherited from a different tradition.

Chomsky initially set out to explain how an ideal language-user could generate and understand new and unique grammatical sentences without ever having encountered them in practice. As a result, he set out to show that a finite and describable set of transformational rules constituted the 'competence' of the ideal language-user, and that this competence could generate grammatical sentences. 'Performance', which is equivalent to the finite number of grammatical sentences realised by actual language-users, provides evidence (a corpus), Chomsky said, for an investigation of competence, and he added that competence did not imply a conscious appreciation and invocation of generative rules on the part of the language-user; instead, it had to be seen as equivalent to the mode itself of the speaker's being in language. In other words, competence is the very condition of possibility of language: competence is constitutive of the speaker rather than the other way around.

In turning now to aspects of Chomsky's

theory of language, we focus first of all on the notion of 'generative' grammar. Generative grammar is a kind of elementary system of rules that recursively define and give rise to sentence transformations. It is linked to the basic 'competence' of an ideal speaker-hearer, a competence which enables the production of a potentially infinite number of well-formed sentences. 'Generative' evokes the mathematical term, 'generator'. The latter gives rise to a 'generating function' – e.g., $2x + 3y - z$ – which generates an infinite set of values. For his part, Chomsky defines a generative grammar as a set of rules which, in defining a set (of objects), 'may be said to *generate* this set'.[3] And he continues:

[A] (generative) grammar may be said to generate a set of structural descriptions, each of which, ideally, incorporates a deep structure, a surface structure, a semantic interpretation (of the deep structure), and a phonetic interpretation (of the surface structure).[4]

The structure (for this is indeed what it is) of a generative grammar may be – following Chomsky's approach in *Syntactic Structures* – of three basic types (it being remembered that a grammar explains how sentences are generated):

1 *Finite state grammar*: this is linear only, so that sentences are generated by means of simple choices from left to right with each preceding choice limiting the scope of a succeeding choice.

2 *Phrase structure grammar*: this corresponds to parsing (the classification of constituent elements of the 'surface' structure of a sentence), and is concerned with the multiple meanings possible in the same phrase constituents: 'old men and women' (to take the example given by Lyons) can mean '(old men) and women', or, 'old (men and women)'.

3 *Transformational grammar*: this is a way of deriving a new constituent structure (e.g.,

active form into passive form) through a set of rules based both on the horizontal string of the base phrase structure (represented by a phrase-marker) and on the vertical 'tree' resulting when account is taken of how this string was derived.

Chomsky was able to show that both phrase structure grammar and transformational grammar are more powerful (i.e. can do more) than finite state grammar, and that transformational grammar is a more powerful grammar than phrase structure grammar. Transformational grammar is essentially Chomsky's own contribution to a general theory of grammar. The other two grammars – although previously not formalised – existed in linguistics prior to Chomsky's work. Only a transformational grammar can derive the basic rules constitutive of the ideal speaker–hearer of, for example, English. The logic behind transformational grammar is that if every utterance implied a unique rule as a condition of its acceptability, there would be too many rules to deal with. Clearly, the number of rules are not equivalent to the number of utterances; this is what any grammar implies. On the other hand, Chomsky points out that if one cannot show that many sentences – apparently different at a 'surface' level of phrase structure grammar – are in fact transformations of the same rule, the grammar becomes almost infinitely complex and contains little explanatory power. Phrase structure grammar would thus become too complex if it alone were charged with providing all the rules of the ideal speaker-hearer's sentence formation. In sum, then, a transformational grammar is a way of reducing sentence formation to the smallest number of rules possible. From a slightly different angle, the transformational grammar, providing the rules of competence, is equivalent to Chomsky's notion of 'deep structure'.

One further facet of Chomsky's theory of language needs to be considered before we move to a brief assessment of his work. It concerns his attempt to bolster his theory of generative grammar by linking it to a notion of 'cognitive capacity'.[5]

Because he believes that we cannot explain language acquisition and language competence (which presupposes language creativity) inductively, or in terms of any version of stimulus-response theory, Chomsky resorts to the notion of an innate, specifically human, language capacity as a way of explaining the nature of human language. In particular, he has been much taken with the Cartesian view that language and mind are so inextricably linked that a knowledge of language would open up a knowledge of the human mind. For the inventor of generative grammar, therefore, language is fundamentally part of human psychology – psychology to be understood as a theory of the faculties of the human mind. Language competence is thus less linguistic than psychological in origin; or, should we not rather say that the origin of language is the psychological subject? In these views, Chomsky has been particularly influenced by Descartes and the seventeenth-century rationalist, scientific tradition. Instead of giving language autonomous status – as came to be the case in the twentieth century with Saussure's structuralist view of language – seventeenth-century rationalism saw language as an expression of the psychological subject. Apparently, Chomsky believes that only by identifying with this tradition can justice be done to the dynamic and creative essence of language and a relapse into some form of empiricist explanation of it avoided. Indeed, to Chomsky's eyes, Saussure's incipient (or even full-blown) empiricism makes him unacceptable to generative linguistics. According to the Cartesian linguist, Saussure ended up privileging *parole* (speech) over *langue* (grammatical structure).[6]

What, then, are we to make of Chomsky's work? Let it be acknowledged that any profound evaluation of generative grammar will need to take account of Chomsky's considerable technical expertise in linguistics.

That said, some things are clearly debatable, even to the outsider. Thus, even though the theory of generative grammar is undoubtedly one of the intellectual achievements of the twentieth century, it is limited in at least four respects.

The first of these limitations concerns the notion of idealisation. In this regard, we recall that 'competence' refers to the 'competence of the idealised speaker-hearer'. The problem with this does not pertain to the fact that 'competence' is virtual (i.e. is never fully realised empirically), but with the fact that this competence is identified with a non-linguistic component, the ideal 'speaker-hearer', rather than with language itself. Here, idealisation is quite compatible with Chomsky's rationalist view that language is an expression of something else – namely, an individual cognitive capacity inseparable from individual psychology. The question arises as to what language must be for it to be an expression of individual psychology. But is language only an expression of something? That is, is it purely transparent? Modern semiotics and poetics would suggest that the answer is in the negative, for there is also poetic language: language as (relatively) opaque.

Let us suppose that Chomsky were to respond by saying that idealisation is a methodological exigency and is not to be confused with the way language is in itself. The difficulty here is that it is impossible to avoid the sense that idealisation is being linked with the principle of competence *per se* – competence being equivalent to an infinite (= ideal) number of sentences. Still another problem with idealisation is that it fails – as Kristeva has shown – to account for language as a *process* of realisation. Chomsky's level of 'performance' does not alter this. For performance simply focuses on utterances as already realised; it does not account for the *fact* of the process of their realisation: the level of discourse for Benveniste. As a result, Chomsky's is a static, rather than a dynamic view of language.

Still another problem raised by Chomsky's linguistics stems from the emphasis placed on the competence of the native speaker as the model speaker of a language. Two issues (at least) need to be considered here. The first is whether the native speaker (the speaker of a 'mother' tongue) is an adequate model of how language works. Although there may be advantages in relying on the native speaker in assessing grammaticalness, could it not be proposed that, ideally, speakers can acquire native competence in a number, or even many, languages? The fact that they do not cannot necessarily be attributed to the nature of language itself. Second, it could be suggested that an essential aspect of language is the possibility of its being translated. This aspect is necessarily overlooked in Chomsky's focus on the competence of the native speaker.

Finally, Chomsky's rationalism seems to be a vast over-reaction to the behaviourism and empiricism characteristic of the Anglo-American philosophical and linguistic environment in which Chomsky was trained. As a result, he often comes across as the embattled rationalist painfully trying to make some headway against the forces of empiricism. However, the important theoretical debates about language and philosophy today are clearly not limited to those that the rivalry between rationalism and empiricism has thrown up. That Chomsky's theoretical writing does not seem to have registered this is a serious limitation.

Notes

1 Noam Chomsky, *Language and Responsibility, Based on Conversations with Mitsou Ronat*, trans. John Viertel, New York, Pantheon Books, 1979, pp. 58–9.
2 ibid., p. 59.
3 Noam Chomsky, *Language and Mind* (enlarged edn), New York, Harcourt Brace Jovanovich, 1972, p. 126.
4 ibid.
5 See, for example, Noam Chomsky, *Reflections on Language*, London, Temple Smith in association with Fontana Books, 1976 (reprinted 1977), Ch. 1 and *passim*.

6 The irony is that most critics of Saussure (e.g., Bourdieu) tend to argue that he privileged *langue* over *parole*.

See also in this book

Benveniste, Jakobson, Kristeva, Saussure

Chomsky's major writings

Syntactic Structures, The Hague, Paris, Mouton, 1957
Current Issues in Linguistic Theory, The Hague, Paris, Mouton, 1964
Aspects of the Theory of Syntax, Cambridge, Mass., MIT Press, 1965
Cartesian Linguistics: A Chapter in the History of Rationalist Thought, New York, Harper & Row, 1966
The Sound Pattern of English (with Morris Halle), New York, Harper & Row, 1968
Chomsky: Selected Readings, ed. J.P.B. Allen and Paul Van Buren, London and New York, Oxford University Press, 1971
Studies on Semantics in Generative Grammar, The Hague, Paris, Mouton, 1972
Language and Mind, New York, Harcourt Brace Jovanovich, enlarged edition, 1972
Studies on Semantics in Generative Grammar, The Hague, Paris, Mouton, 1972
The Logical Structure of Linguistic Theory, New York, Plenum Press, 1975
Reflections on Language, London, Temple Smith in association with Fontana Books, 1976
Rules and Representations, Oxford, Basil Blackwell, 1980
Language and Problems of Knowledge: The Managua Lectures, Cambridge, Mass., MIT Press, 1988

Further reading

Alexander, George (ed.), *Reflections on Chomsky*, Oxford, Cambridge, Mass., Basil Blackwell, 1990
Botha, Rudolf P., *Challenging Chomsky: The Generative Garden Game*, Oxford and New York, Basil Blackwell, 1989
Lyons, John, *Chomsky*, Hassocks, Harvester Press, second edn, 1977
Modgil, Sohan, and Modgil, Celia (eds), *Noam Chomsky: Consensus and Controversy*, New York, Falmer Press, 1987
Radford, Andrew, *Transformational Syntax: A Student's Guide to Chomsky's Extended Theory*, Cambridge, Cambridge University Press, 1981

GEORGES DUMEZIL

Along with Claude Lévi-Strauss, Georges Dumézil is recognised, in the social sciences, as one of the earliest exponents of a comparative structuralist method. This method, based on a carefully constructed system of classifications and analyses, allowed Dumézil to mark out, in Indo-European 'civilisation', three invariant social functions: sovereignty, war, and production. More precisely, Dumézil sought to demonstrate the nature and connectedness – without denying the differences – of the elements constitutive of Indo-European civilisation. This demonstration takes place through an astonishing foray into Indo-European religion and mythology, as these are rendered manifest in epics, legends, and histories (cf. the founding of Rome). Amongst Dumézil's privileged sources should be mentioned the Indian *Mahabharata*, the Iranian *Avesta* (the sacred book of the Zoroastrians), the Scandinavian *Edda*, and, for Rome, Virgil's *Aeneid*. How did Dumézil come to be the scholar of Indo-European civilisation? And what is it, exactly, that Dumézil calls 'Indo-European civilisation'?

Georges Dumézil was born in Paris in 1898. According to his own account, he first became interested in myth through reading Greek legends as a child. His father had given him the well-known parallel German-French text by Niebuhr. Also read at an early age by the future mythologist were the tales of Perrault.

At the end of his secondary schooling, Dumézil attended the prestigious Parisian *lycée*, Louis-Le-Grand, and entered the Ecole Normale (rue d'Ulm) in 1916. Although his studies were interrupted by the First World War (he was demobilised in 1919), Dumézil passed his *agrégation* in *lettres* in December 1919, and was shortly afterwards named 'professeur' at the Lycée of Beauvais in the north of France, where he taught until October of 1920. Unable to tolerate the life of a secondary school teacher, Dumézil resigned his post in order to devote himself to preparing his *doctorat d'état* – *Le Festin d'immortalité. Etude de mythologie comparée indo-européenne (The Festival of Immortality. A Study of Comparative Indo-European Mythology)* – under the direction of the leading historical linguist of the day, Antoine Meillet. He also thought to look out for a foreign posting and was subsequently named as a reader in French at the University of Warsaw. As living away from France at that time was too painful, Dumézil resigned after six months returning to Paris in the summer of 1921. Three years on a scholarship saw the completion of his thesis, defended in 1924. Soon afterwards, the young scholar left for Turkey to take up a post as professor of the history of religions at the University of Istanbul, a post made possible by the secularising policies of Mustapha Kemal. For six years (1925–31), Dumézil taught in Turkey – 'the best years' of his life, he said in 1986. Dumézil returned to France in 1933 to take up a post as director of studies at the Ecole Pratique des Hautes Etudes, after having spent two years at the University of Uppsala (where he started to learn Scandinavian languages) as a reader in French. In 1949, Dumézil was elected to the Collège de France to the chair of Indo-European civilisation, where he taught until his retirement in 1968. He then spent three years teaching in the United States, and was elected to the French Academy in 1978. He died in October 1986.

Dumézil always insisted on the progressive and provisional character of his *oeuvre*, often comparing his numerous publications to annual reports. As a result many of his books are elaborations of works already published. The various volumes of *Myth et épopée*, for example, have been published in three and four editions, each carefully revised and corrected. In Dumézil's terms, Indo-European civilisation refers to the cultures of India, North Africa (especially

Egypt and Iran), Europe (especially Rome), and Scandinavia. And in his earliest work, *Le Festin d'immortalité* published in 1924, and the result of his doctoral research, Dumézil begins his exploration of the way elements of different cultures within the Indo-European framework, contain within them echoes of others. In the case of *Le Festin d'immortalité*, the concern is to reconstitute the mythology of the sacred drink of Indo-European peoples, and to show how the sacred drink of ambrosia (the drink which permits the gods to be immortal) in the Occident corresponds to the Indian (Sanskrit) *amr̥ta*. Although Dumézil distanced himself from this and other work done before 1938, it contains in embryo the programme of all his future research. As with his *Ouranos-Varuna: Etude de mythologie comparée indo-européenne* (1934) – where the god of Greek mythology (Uranus) is ranged with the Indian god (Varuna) – and *Flamen-Brahman* (1935) – where the Roman god, Flamen is ranged with the Indian Brahman – the comparison is deemed by Dumézil in 1938 not to work.

After 1938, Dumézil is inspired by the idea, derived from his research, that the three functions of sovereignty, war, and production link together the diverse origins of the cultures constitutive of the Indo-Europeans. This tripartition will become the focus of all of Dumézil's subsequent writing. The first two functions (sovereignty and war) are treated in individual studies: in books on sovereignty – such as *Mitra-Varuna: An Essay on Two Indo-European Representations of Sovereignty* (1940) – in books on war – such as *Aspects de la fonction guerrier chez les indo-européens* (1956) (reworked and republished as *Heur et malheur du gerrier* (1969)) – in books, such as *Jupiter, Mars, Quirinus* in relation to Rome, which treat of all three functions both in terms of specific areas, and in terms of the way the three functions occur in the context of the Indo-European mythology as a whole. The latter theme is examined in works such as

L'Idéologie tripartie des indo-européens (1953) (incorporated into *L'Idéologie des trois fonctions dans les épopées des peuples indo-européens* (1968)). The significant absence from this series of studies is any work which specifically analyses the third function: productivity, fertility and the people in general. According to Dumézil, this function resists systemisation and is the most difficult to treat in isolation. What follows now is a brief, and extremely schematic summary of the three functions as these are analysed by Dumézil in relation to a number of different cultures. Before proceeding, however, we note that Dumézil often called the three functions a 'tripartite' (or 'three-party') ideology. By ideology Dumézil means

a conception and an appreciation of the great forces which animate the world and society, and their relations. Often this ideology is implicit and must be deciphered through the analysis of what is said overtly about the gods – and above all about their actions – about theology and, above all, about mythology.[1]

Clearly, if the three functions are an ideology, this means that their presence is not immediately apparent. Later, ideology in Dumézil's writing comes closer to the unconscious structure of society. We shall return to this.

The three functions in Roman myths are Jupiter (representing the priestly class), Mars (representing war), and Quirinus (representing agriculture or productivity). In India, the three functions are represented respectively in the Vedic – the oldest Indian religion – by Mitra-Varuna, Indra, and Nâsatyâ. Similarly the three functions appear in Scandinavian myths as Odin, Thorr, and Freyr. These Scandinavian gods bear a close resemblance to their Germanic counterparts, Thorr, Wodan, and Fricco. From the North African perspective, Iran was historically attached to the Indian world before the Muslim conquest (the name 'Iran' is derived from 'Iran shahr'). Dumézil thus studies Indo-Iranian myths and language prior to the Vedic religion which produced Sanskrit, and he finds parallels between the Indian Mitra (equivalent to the first function: sovereignty) and the Iranian Vohu Manah (also equivalent to the first function). Dumézil shows that in the Vedas, Mitra is accompanied by two gods, Aryaman – protector of the community (second function of war) – and Bhaga in charge of repartition of the goods (the third function of production). In the theology of Zarathustra, Aryaman is replaced by Sroasa, protector of the Zoroastrian community (second function), and Bhaga by Asi, the patron of the just retribution of this world in the other (third function). For each part of the Indo-European domain, Dumézil's work forges links between the gods, heroes, and various mythical and theological figures, so as to demonstrate the presence of the three functions across what became religious, social, and political boundaries. The point for Dumézil is that the tripartite function has its origin in Indo-Iranian culture, and that this tripartite structure progressively spread to every part of the Indo-European 'family' – as Dumézil called it on occasion. This exact division of functions has no counterpart elsewhere in the world. One of the objections against Dumézil's work has been that one is bound to find evidence of such a structure in Indo-European culture because it is basic to the very survival of human society. Dumézil countered by saying that the precise *form* of the tripartite division is not essential: it is quite possible to point to a deity elsewhere in the world in which the functions overlap or are quite different.

Despite the undoubted originality of his scholarship and its links with the structuralist project of the 1960s, Dumézil was, in several important ways, a product of nineteenth-century comparative and historical linguistics. Antoine Meillet, his mentor and the supervisor of his thesis, and Michel Bréal, the first professor of comparative linguistics at the Collège de France in 1864, were both keen students of the founder of historical linguistics, Franz Bopp. Meillet's *L'Aperçu d'une histoire de la langue greque* (*An Overview of the History of the Greek Language*) published in 1913, was a formative influence, while Michel Bréal had translated from the German Bopp's *Grammaire comparée*. Bréal had done much more for the young Dumézil. He had published his *Dictionnaire étymologique du latin* (*Etymological Dictionary of Latin*). Through Bréal's dictionary, Dumézil came to experience the marvels of etymology and to develop his Indo-European passion: 'There, I discovered that in Sanskrit "father" [*père*] would have been "pitar", and mother [*mère*], "matar". That bedazzled me. It's the origin of my Indo-European passion.'[2] Thus, as we shall see shortly, although Dumézil is, methodologically speaking, close to contemporary structuralism, his 'Indo-European passion' – the dream of discovering the origin of, and subsequent kinship between the three functions in Indo-European societies – places at least part of his enterprise squarely within the paradigm of nineteenth-century historical linguistics. On the other hand, Saussure himself (whose importance for structuralist thought is undoubted) also came out of the very same intellectual milieu, and Emile Benveniste, for some time Dumézil's opponent but later his strongest supporter, was also Meillet's student, and one of the inspirations of the contemporary structuralist movement.

Even though fascinated by etymology and the notion of origin, the influence on Dumézil of scholars such as Meillet and Bréal meant that he too – while using science to do so – came to study language as a social rather than as a natural fact. The goal was to detach the science of language from the science of nature. It was a question of studying the nature of social action through rites, myths, and customs.[3]

Although loath to become embroiled in general questions about method, Dumézil was not, as he said, the least enamoured of the 'a priori' approach often taken in the studies of language and of myth. Indeed, Dumézil publicly expressed his repulsion at (in his view) Durkheim's 'a priori' approach both in *The Elementary Forms of Religious Life* and in *The Rules of Sociological Method*. In the former, Dumézil says, facts are made to fit an a priori schema; they are not the material from which schema itself arises. And within the work on method, written early in Durkheim's career, Dumézil mused about how any researcher could produce a text on method before he had actually published a piece of empirically based research. As a result, Frazer's *The Golden Bough*, as well as the writing and teaching of Marcel Mauss, was much more important for Dumézil than anything Durkheim wrote.

Despite his apparent leaning towards an inductive-empirical approach in the social sciences, Dumézil, at the same time, argues strongly against the view that social facts are autonomous and meaningful in themselves. 'Structure' and 'system', and not facts in isolation, are at the heart of Dumézil's approach.

For Dumézil 'structure' and 'system' are interchangeable: structure says in Latin what system says in Greek. Coupled with Dumézil's comparative method, structure becomes the key to the Dumézilian effort to show that each religion, culture or society is an equilibrium. The composition of intrinsically meaningful elements do not come together by chance to form a sort of (possibly) defective whole. Rather, the whole is always already constituted by the relations between the elements themselves – the meaning of the whole being given by the fact of these relations. Here Dumézil is clearly ranged with the structuralist movement in thought. However, as opposed to Lévi-Strauss's search for the universals in human affairs, Dumézil made it clear that he was much more wedded to the particular, to the 'facts', as he called them. To leave the realm of facts is to 'do poetry', to enter a dream-world, Dumézil claimed. Because of his emphasis on facts, on the particular, Dumézil

could not see how one could draw out of his work any kind of broadly based philosophical system, similar to the system of Lévi-Strauss.[4] In addition, Dumézil consciously resisted throughout his life all efforts to place him within a 'school' of thought, desiring – and very keenly – to be his own person in intellectual or scholarly matters. To be the member of a school, he believed, was to lose the autonomy essential to truly original and rigorous scholarship.

Notes

1 Georges Dumézil, *Myths et dieus des indo-européennes* (Selections presented by Hervé Coutau-Bégarie), Paris, Flammarion, 1992, p. 240.
2 *Le Magazine Littéraire*, 229, April, 1986, p. 16. (Interview with François Ewald.)
3 See Jean-Claude Milner, 'Le Programme Dumézilien' in *Le Magazine Littéraire*, 229, April 1986, pp. 22–4.
4 See Georges Dumézil, *Entretiens avec Didier Eribon*, Paris, Gallimard: 'Folio/Essais', 1987, pp. 120–2.

See also in this book

Benveniste, Saussure, Lévi-Strauss

Dumézil's major writings

Le Festin d'immortalité. Etude de mythologie comparée indo-européenne, Paris, Annales de musée Guimet, 1924. (This was Dumézil's doctoral thesis.)
Ouranous-Varuna: étude de mythologie comparée indo-européenne, Paris, Adrien-Maisonneuve, 1934
Flamen-Brahman, Paris, Annales du musée Guimet, petit collection, 1935
Mitra-Varuna: An Essay on Two Indo-European Representations of Sovereignty (1940), trans. Derek Coltman, New York, Zone Books, 1988
Jupiter, Mars, Quirinus, Paris, Gallimard, 1941
The Stakes of the Warrior (a translation of *Heur et malheur du gerrier*) (1956 and 1969), trans. David Weeks, University of California Press, 1983
Les Dieux souverains des indo-européens (1959), Paris, Gallimard, 1977. Partially translated into English as *Gods of the Ancient Northmen*, ed. Einar Haugen, trans. various, Berkeley, University of California Press, 1973

Idées romaines, Paris, Gallimard, 1968
Destiny of a King (partial translation of *Myth et idéologie II*, 1971), trans. Alf Hiltebeitel, Chicago, University of Chicago Press, 1988
Myth et épopée:
  I. *I. L'Idéologie des trois fonctions dans les épopées des peuples indo-européens*, Paris, Gallimard, 1968. Fourth revised edn, 1986
  II. *Types épiques indo-européens: Un héros, un sorcier, un roi*, Paris, Gallimard, 1971, 1986
  III. *Histoires romaines*, Paris, Gallimard, 1973
Fêtes romaines d'été et d'automne, followed by *Dix questions romaines*, 1976
Apollon sonore, et autres essais, Esquisses de mythologie, Paris, Gallimard, 1982

Further reading

Belier, Wouter, *Decayed Gods: Origin and Development on Georges Dumézil's 'idéologie tripartie'*, Leiden, New York, E.J. Brill, 1991
Scott Littleton, C., *New Comparative Mythology: An Anthropological Assessment of the Theories of Georges Dumézil*, Berkeley, University of California Press, 1966

GERARD GENETTE

The work of Gérard Genette is of particular importance to literary theorists and semiologists. The abiding concern in Genette's substantial *oeuvre*, which ranges over the literary spectrum from the Greek Classics to Proust, is to produce a general theory – based on classificatory schemas – of the *singularity* of the literary object. Keen to avoid a procrustean procedure of imposing categories on to literary works from the outside, yet refusing the naivety of literary criticism's empiricism, Genette has endeavoured – by way of a supple 'analytic method' – to produce a knowledge of the 'mystery' of the literary work without thereby destroying that mystery. Inspired by structuralist insights which took formal textual analysis to new heights in the 1960s, Genette has been careful to argue for the autonomy of the literary object. Thus, he says, in the end, Proust's great work, *Remembrance of Things Past*,

taken as whole, is irreducible: it 'illustrates nothing but itself'.[1]

Born in Paris in 1930, and a product of the Ecole Normale Supérieure – where he gained his *agrégation* in *Lettres classiques* in 1954 – Genette is a direct contemporary of Jacques Derrida and Pierre Bourdieu. Derrida's reflections on writing in *Of Grammatology* in particular left their mark on Genette's articles of the 1960s in literary criticism and literary theory. He was one of the first to signal the importance of Derrida's notion of grammatology for a spatial view of literary works.[2] In 1959–60, both Genette and Derrida taught in a *lycée* and prepared students for their entry into the Ecole Normale Supérieure. He then became, in 1963, an *assistant* in French literature at the Sorbonne, then *Maître-assistant*. In 1967, he was appointed to the position of director of studies in aesthetics and poetics at the Ecole des Hautes Etudes en Sciences Sociales.

With Tzvetan Todorov and Hélène Cixous, Genette started, in 1970 at the Editions du Seuil, the very influential journal, *Poétique* as well as the literary collection of the same name. It was *Poétique* in fact which first published Derrida's important essay, 'White mythology: Metaphor in the text of philosophy'.[3]

In the collection of Genette's early articles published in *Figures I* (1966), an intimation of later themes may be observed. There is, for instance, the critique of psychologism, rejected because of its reductive and determinist impulse. A literary text is seen by the theorist to be literary precisely because it cannot be reduced to an author's psychological disposition. Following Blanchot, Genette agrees that the writer's place is a place of anonymity. To write is to hide, to wear a mask. At most the writer's lived experience is refracted – displaced – in the text: it is not reflected, or expressed there. The literary theorist is interested in the process of displacement *per se*, rather than in the psychological condition (if this could ever be established) of the author. Genette thus joins

Foucault, Barthes and others in taking the 'death' of the author as his point of departure.

From *Figures III* (1972) onwards, the issue of the presence/absence of the author gives way to Genette's major concerns of the 1970s and the 1980s. These include: analyses of narrative (culminating in *Nouveau discours du récit* (1983)); the study of the imagination of language in *Mimologiques* (1976); the development of a theory of genres in *Introduction à l'architexte* (1979); to the formation of the notion of 'transtextuality' and 'hypertextuality' in *Palimpsests* (1982), and, finally, a study of the 'paratext' (the title, Foreword, Afterword – elements in, but not of, the main text) in *Seuils* (1987). More recently, Genette has published his reflections on a theme first signalled in *Figures II*, namely, the nature of fiction and the condition of 'literarity' in *Fiction and Diction*. What important insights thus emerge from Genette's writing in these two decades of sustained theorising and reflection?

Genette's contribution to a theory of narrative and the literary (i.e. aesthetically satisfying) object in general resides in the meticulous way he substantially broadens the reader-cum-critic's analytical purview. Many aspects of narrative writing have hitherto been taken for granted. A story 'works' for some reason, but few have asked penetrating questions about how and why this is so. Take narration. Genette shows – particularly with regard to Proust – how numerous aspects and levels constitute a narrative function: it is simply not reducible to a single instance of story-telling. If, for the purposes of illustration, we take the aspect of narrative 'voice', through Genette's analysis we realise that voice alone is constituted by the following elements:

1 *Narrative instance*: this refers to the fact that there is always an enunciative moment or context, in which the narration takes place. As such, the narrative instance is crucial for attributing meaning or significance to what is uttered by the narrating voice. Here we are reminded of Benveniste's insight that to understand fully the way language works we must account for the *act* of stating (*énonciation*) as well as the statement made (*énoncé*). In themselves, narrative utterances (*énoncés*) are often simple and transparent (e.g., Proust's 'For a long time I went to bed early', cited by Genette). Only when the narrative instance is taken into account can the full weight of an utterance's singular narrative meaning be appreciated.

2 *Narrative time*: whereas place, or space, can remain indeterminate in narrative, time cannot – if only because it is inscribed in the tense of the verb and thus in language as a whole. In addition, the narrative instance will have a specific temporal relation to the events recounted. Often narrative succeeds the events, but not inevitably. There are 'predictif' narratives (prophetic, apocalyptic, oracular) which refer to a future moment, as there are also narratives which describe events as they are happening, or which make the act of narration itself (e.g., *A Thousand and One Nights*) the focus of the story. Narrative time inevitably refers to the time of the narrative. One of the clearest examples of this is in the epistolary novel where the act of writing/narrating (e.g., in Rousseau's *La Nouvelle Héloïse*) is itself part of the narration. In this case, the time of the event recounted can be the time of the narration itself. Numerous variations on this theme are possible. For instance, there can be a narration narrated within another narration, as in Homer's *Odyssey*. Or again, in an epistolary novel, a prior letter which played its part in keeping the novel going can become the event narrated in a subsequent letter. Clearly, in order that the time of the story might coincide with the narration, both have to be 'in' the same time. An intriguing possibility flowing from the coincidence of the two times is that the end of narration becomes an event in the story – such as when, at the end of a confession, the narrator is executed.

Since the nineteenth century, the most common form of narration has been the one in the third person and ulterior to the events recounted. As Genette notes, a curious feature of this narration is that it is 'intemporal': there is no index of the time of writing/narration.

3 *Narrative levels*: this refers to the relation between the act of recounting and the event recounted. Every recounted event is deemed to be at a level superior to the event of recounting. Balzac's short story *Sarrasine* exemplifies the possible variations in narrative level. Thus the narrator in the story narrates the events leading to his narration of the story about Sarrasine, then narrates the story of Sarrasine's infatuation with the young La Zambinella, before returning to the point of his narration, as it were. A story within a story, we might say; but for Genette it constitutes an illustration of narrative level.

These, then, are some of the features of 'voice' that Genette brings to light in his discussion of narrative. He also highlights 'metalepse' (narration of the movement from one narrative level to another), 'person' (the difference between the narrator who refers to himself as narrator, and a narration in first person), 'hero' (as narrator and as narrated), 'functions of the narrator' (to tell the story; to facilitate the internal organisation of the text; to ensure the narrative situation of narrator and reader; to ensure the affective, moral or intellectual status of the narrative; to give vent to an ideology), and the 'recipient' (*narrataire*) of the narration as this is marked within the narration itself.

In addition to 'Voice', Genette also defines and discusses four other aspects of narrative:

1 *Order*: the order of events in relation to the order of narration. An event can occur prior to the point of narration (analepse), or an ulterior event might be evoked in advance (prolepse), or again, there might be a discor-dance between the two orders (anachronie).

2 *Duration*: the rhythm at which things happen.

3 *Frequency*: the extent of repetition in a narrative.

4 *Mode*: the point(s) of view, including the 'distance' of the narrator from what is being narrated.

To this point, we have focused on aspects of Genette's theory of narrative. Three terms specify the essential elements of every narrative act: (1) a story (*histoire*); (2) the narrative discourse (*récit*); and (3) the narration (the act of telling the story). Genette comments: 'As a narrative, the narrative discourse lives through its relation to the story it recounts; as discourse, it lives through the narration which proffers it.'[4] Even at a general level, therefore, there is never simply a story which is told, but also a third element (narrative discourse) which, while not separable from the story or the act of its telling, is nevertheless not identical with them. Looked at linguistically, the narrative (*récit*) corresponds to the level of the statement made (*énoncé*), while narration would correspond to the act of stating (*énonciation*).

In discussing the narrative discourse in *Figures II*, Genette refers to the opposition between diagesis and mimesis which appears in Plato's *Republic* and Aristotle's *Poetics*. Diagesis in particular occurs frequently in Genette's discussion of narrative. For the Greeks, diagesis is the purely narrative aspect of fiction (an imperfect mimesis) to be distinguished from mimesis: the imitative or dramatic aspect. Diagesis, then, is the narrative discourse without direct speech or other dramatic effects. Today, the distinction between mimesis and diagesis has been lost to the advantage of diagesis. In Genette's work of the early 1970s, diagesis came to refer specifically to the narration of events. In *Sarrasine*, Genette sees the introduction to the telling of the story of Sarrasine and La Zambinella as 'extradiagetic' – that is, as not being part of the recounting proper of the events of a story. Not only is this a doubtful distinction (the uniqueness of *Sarrasine* is surely that it is a story of two stories), but the point of the notion of diagesis seems minimal in light of the story-narrative-narration trilogy.

In his work of the mid-1970s, *Mimologiques*, Genette sets about reading Plato's enigmatic theory of naming in the *Cratylus*. Unlike the majority of critics and interpreters of Plato, Genette takes seriously Plato's mimologism – that is, the idea that names, in some fundamental way, imitate that to which they refer. Although a structuralist approach emphasises language's conventional nature, Genette embarks on a long and detailed study of writers of the early modern and modern eras who have been influenced by the Platonic principle of 'eponymy'. 'The function of eponymy', says Genette, 'is to give a meaning to a name which is supposed not to have one, that is, to find in it one or two hidden names hypothetically endowed with meaning.'[5] The 'meaning' will inevitably be a form of mimesis.

In *Mimologiques*, Genette studies the witting and unwitting inventiveness of those who have speculated about the origin of language for over a period of three centuries or more, and who have, like Plato, presupposed, according to the principle of eponymy, a mimetic relationship between a name and what is named.

Palimpsests, in the rigour and extent of its analytical purview, is possibly Genette's most accomplished work. In it he classifies and analyses a vast range of ways one text is echoed within another. In Genette's use of the term, the palimpsest is a function; it is literature in the second degree, a 'transtextuality' comprised, in part, of the following aspects: 'intertextuality' – including citation, plagiarism, and allusion; 'metatextuality' – the way one text is united within another without being cited, as when Hegel evokes Diderot's *Le Neveu de Rameau* in the *Phenomenology of Mind*; 'architextu-

ality' – types of discourse, modes of enunciation, literary genres which transcend each individual text, but to which each individual text refers; and 'hypertextuality'. The latter is the main focus of Genette's study, and is defined as: 'every relation uniting a text B . . . to an anterior text A . . . onto which it is grafted in a way that is not that of commentary'.[6] Text B could not exist without text A, but it does not speak of it. An example is Joyce's *Ulysses* which clearly relates to Homer's *Odyssey*. One clear outcome of Genette's study is that it is doubtful as to whether any text really is the singularity it is often presented as being by literary history.

As mentioned at the outset, Genette's *oeuvre* is, for better or for worse, a drive to construct a systematic and rigorous terminology for theorising the 'literarity of literature'. We thus have before us a project which seeks to objectify, and thus render transcendent, every aspect of the production and being of the literary text. Despite Genette's protestation that he also seeks to do justice to the mystery of the singularity of the literary text, it is often difficult not to become weighed down with a terminology that appears concerned above all to leave nothing to chance – that is, to leave nothing to the indeterminacy at the heart of literature, and, more generally, at the heart of the art product.

Notes

1 Gérard Genette, *Figures III*, Paris, Seuil, Poétique, 1972, p. 68.
2 Gérard Genette, *Figures II*, Paris, Seuil, TEL, 1969, p. 17.
3 See Jacques Derrida, 'La mythologie blanche', *Poétique*, 5 (1971).
4 Genette, *Figures III*, p. 74.
5 Gérard Genette, *Mimologiques: voyage en Cratylie*, Paris, Seuil, Poétique, 1976, p. 25.
6 Gérard Genette, *Palimpsests: La littérature au second degré*, Paris, Seuil, Points, 1982, p. 13.

See also in this book

Derrida, Greimas, Todorov

Genette's major writings

Figures I, Paris, Seuil, TEL, 1966
Figures II, Paris, Seuil, TEL, 1969
Figures III, Paris, Seuil, Poétique, 1972
Figures of Literary Discourse (1966–72), trans. Alan Sherdan, New York, Columbia University Press, 1984. Selections from *Figures* (1966–72)
Mimologiques: voyage en Cratylie, Paris, Seuil, Poétique, 1976
The Architext (1979), trans. Jane E. Lewin, Los Angeles, University of California Press, 1992
Palimpsests: La littérature au second degré, Paris, Seuil, Points, 1982
Narrative Discourse Revisited (1983), trans. Jane E. Lewin, New York, Cornell University Press, 1990
Seuils, Paris, Seuil, Poétique, 1987
Paratexte, Paris, Maison des Sciences de l'homme, 1989
Fiction and Diction (1991), trans. Catherine Porter, New York, Cornell University Press, 1993
Narrative Discourse: An Essay in Method, trans. Jane E. Lewin, New York, Cornell University Press, 1979. Translation of *Discours du récit* and part of *Figures III*

Further reading

Mosher, Harold, 'The structuralism of G. Genette', *Poetics*, 5, 1, 1976.
Smith, Barbara H., 'Narrative versions, narrative theories', *Critical Inquiry* (Autumn 1980), pp. 213–36.

ROMAN JAKOBSON

Roman Jakobson was born in Moscow in 1896. He is generally regarded as one of the twentieth century's foremost linguists, and a major proponent of the structuralist approach to language, particularly because of his emphasis on seeing the sound-pattern (Jakobson's first and abiding area of linguistic inquiry) of language as fundamentally relational. The relations between sounds within specific contexts are what come to constitute meaning and significance. Within his very diverse and prolific writings (nearly 500 articles) on poetics, phonology, Slavic languages and folktale, language acquisition,

epistemology and the history of linguistics, Jakobson unflinchingly endeavours to elucidate 'the different levels of linguistic structure' through 'a consistent elicitation and identification of relational invariants amid the multitude of variations'.[1] A strictly relational approach is forced on the linguist because, first, 'every single constituent of any linguistic system is built on an opposition of two logical contradictories: the presence of an attribute ("markedness") in contraposition to its absence ("unmarkedness")';[2] and, second, the 'interplay of invariants and variations proves to be an essential, innermost property of language at each of its levels'.[3]

Here, we can see the extent to which Jakobson influenced Lévi-Strauss's anthropology. For Lévi-Strauss's interest in language is inseparable from his effort to isolate 'marked' and 'unmarked' oppositions, and to analyse society as a relationship between 'invariant' model, and 'variable' history. Such influence was no doubt intensified by the common experience of teaching with Lévi-Strauss in New York during the Second World War at the New School of Social Research set up at Columbia University.

In 1914 Jakobson entered the historico-philological faculty at the University of Moscow, and enrolled in the language section of the Department of Slavic and Russian. The study of language would be the key to understanding literature and folklore as well as culture in general. In 1915, Jakobson founded the linguistic circle of Moscow and became influenced by Husserl, with the result that Husserl's phenomenology became particularly important for helping him to think through the relationship between 'part' and 'whole' in language and culture. The poetic word revealed one of the clearest links between the part and the whole. Poetry comes closest to having a structure where the part is equal to the whole.

By the end of 1920, Jakobson had left Moscow and had taken up residence in

Prague where, from its inception in 1926, he became an influential member of the Prague linguistic circle. It was in Prague that Jakobson became especially interested in the differences between the phonic and prosidic structures of Russian and other Slavic languages. Under the auspices of the Prague circle, Jakobson published, in 1929, his *Remarques sur l'évolution phonologique du russe comparée à celle des autres langues slaves* (*Remarks on the Phonological Evolution of Russian Compared with Other Slavic Languages*).

In the 1930s, Jakobson collaborated with his friend, Nikolai Trubetskoy in research on the sound-pattern of language. A follower of Saussure, it was Trubetskoy who directed Jakobson towards the idea that sounds in language function differentially: they have no intrinsic meaning. This set the way for Jakobson to elaborate his theory of the 'distinctive feature', more of which below.

During the late 1930s with the rise of Nazism and the prospect of war, Jakobson travelled to Sweden and Denmark. In Copenhagen he collaborated with Louis Hjelmslev and the Copenhagen linguistic circle. His pioneering work, *Kindersprache, Aphasie und allgemeine Lautgesetze* (*Child Language, Aphasia and Phonological Universals*) was written in Sweden in 1940–1, just before his departure for New York. Although victim during the 1950s of the prejudices of McCarthyism because of his connection with communist Eastern Europe, Jakobson eventually obtained appointments at Harvard and the Massachusetts Institute of Technology, and he remained in America until his death in Boston in 1982.

Jakobson was one of the very first linguists of the twentieth century to examine seriously both the acquisition of language and the ways in which the language function could break down – as, for example, in aphasia. Of seminal importance here is the emphasis he placed on two basic aspects of language structure represented by the rhetorical figures of metaphor (similarity), and metonymy (contiguity) (Metonymy, Jakobson says, is not to be confused with synecdoche which, like the former, is sometimes defined as the part standing for the whole. However, with synecdoche, one has an internal relation of part to whole (sail for ship), while with metonymy, the relation is external (pen for writer)). To understand the way that various forms of aphasia affect the language function, is to understand how a breakdown occurs in the faculty of selection and substitution – the metaphoric pole – or in combination and contextualisation – the metonymic pole. The first implies an inability at a metalinguistic level; the second, a problem with maintaining the hierarchy of linguistic units. The relation of similarity is lost in the first, and contiguity in the second.

Although he did not invent the term, the 'shifter' is another aspect of language elaborated by Jakobson, and is closely associated with the capacity for contextualisation. The shifter is in operation in personal pronouns (I, you, etc.), and demonstratives like 'this' and 'that', 'here' and 'there'. During language acquisition, the use of shifters – terms applicable to any specific context whatever – is one of the last abilities the child acquires. Shifters are specifically linked to the enunciative function of language: their meaning cannot be grasped independently of the context in which they are used. They constitute what Jakobson calls a 'duplex structure', meaning that their meaning simultaneously invokes the code ('I' is the first-person pronoun) and the message (specifies the actual speaker). Shifters make it possible for each person to use language individually; they thus constitute the place where history enters language. In other words, in order to understand a statement like, *L'état, c'est moi*, an account must be given of the context and the identity of the speaker (i.e. reference must be made to the message) as well as of the meaning of the words used at the level of the code. As Jakobson shows,[4] the situation can be more complex with the message referring to the code (' "I" is a pronoun') and the code referring to the message (' "I" means me, the speaker'). Moreover, code can refer to code (' "Jerry" is the name of the boy called Jerry'), and message can refer to message (He said, 'I am not coming'). More generally, shifters would constitute the link between *'langue'* (structure, or code) and *'parole'* (speech act), so that language would be the constant interaction between *langue* and *parole*.

Because of this duplex structure, Jakobson suggested that far from being more 'primitive' than the denotative, descriptive aspect of language, the use of shifters is one of the last capacities the child masters in the process of language acquisition. In aphasia, this capacity is the first to be lost. Looked at from a slightly different angle, it could be said that the shifter is an empty category – a little like the floating signifier in the work of Mauss as interpreted by Lévi-Strauss. Through shifterisation, the code can be adapted to a wide range of contexts, thus enabling the production of a relatively heterogeneous set of messages, and so becoming language's more or less direct link with history.

Such at least would be the kind of argument adduced by Jakobson when accused of ignoring the social and historical dimensions of language, poetry and art, and of supporting the principle of *l'art pour l'art*. In his own defence, and in defending the Russian formalists (with whom he was aligned in the 1920s) on this point, Jakobson claimed in the 1930s that neither he nor the other Russian formalists had 'ever proclaimed the self-sufficiency of art'.[5] And he went on to say that,

What we have been trying to show is that art is an integral part of the social structure, a component that interacts with all the others and is itself mutable since both the domain of art and its relationship to the other constituents of the social structure are in constant dialectical flux. What we

stand for is not the separation of art but the autonomy of the aesthetic function.[6]

In sum, not poetry, but the poetic function – or *poeticity* – contained in the diversity of spoken and written forms was what interested Jakobson and his colleagues at this time. 'Poeticity' becomes a necessary part of the study of language when it is realised that language and reality – or words and things, sign and referent – do not coincide: that, in short, meaning in language is only minimally linked to referentiality. Very importantly, Jakobson goes on to say here that this fundamental antinomy between language and reality means that 'without contradiction there is no mobility of concepts, no mobility of signs, and the relationship between concept and sign becomes automatized. Activity comes to a halt, and the awareness of reality dies out'.[7]

Although, for Jakobson, as for many others, poetry tends towards the metaphoric pole of linguistic endeavour, it was the sound pattern of poetry – and not the role of metaphor as such – initially illustrated in the differences between the sound patterns of Czech and Russian poetry, which first stimulated Jakobson's original researches in this area. In effect, the difference between Czech and Russian poetry, Jakobson discovered, was in the rhythm. It was out of the study of poetic rhythm that Jakobson's 'phonology' developed. In particular, by focusing on the link between sound and meaning, Jakobson concluded that sound and meaning were mediated by difference – what he came to call the 'distinctive feature'. Or rather, because, in Jakobson's view, language is primarily a system of meanings, speech is not made up of sounds, but of phonemes: 'a set of concurrent sound properties which are used in a given language to distinguish words of unlike meaning'.[8] As this notion of phoneme still focuses on the intrinsic qualities of the linguistic element – although it hints at the differential aspect – Jakobson came to use the term 'distinctive feature', first presented in the work of the linguists, Bloomfield and

Sapir. Distinctive features are 'the simplest sense-discriminating units such as sonority, nasality, etc.'[9] These 'sense-discriminating units' which are only established differentially, become crucial in the constitution of meaning. Prior to Jakobson's work in this area, phonemes were thought to resemble 'atoms' of sound which did not in themselves call for 'opposites'. Further analysis revealed that even if phonemes in themselves did not call for opposites, a distinctive feature always does. Thus the apparently minimal, but ultimately critical, difference between phonemes constitutes the difference in meaning between 'boor' and 'poor'. What distinguishes 'boor' from 'poor' is the difference between /b/ and /p/: /b/ is partially voiced and /p/ is unvoiced. From this example, we can see a distinctive feature constituted by the difference between voiced and unvoiced features. The remaining phonemes of each word become redundant. With the words, 'tome' and 'dome', the distinctive feature is the aspirated /t/ as opposed to the non-aspirated /d/. In sum, whether or not the difference between /p/ and /b/, or between /t/ and /d/, and other phonemes which present a similar potential ambiguity, appear in close proximity in a text, is less important than the fact that they exist within the linguistic universe, and that meaning depends on discriminating successfully between them. Thus when a speaker of American English is confronted with two names 'Bitter' and 'Bidder',[10] the difference between /t/ and /d/ becomes crucial for hearing the names correctly, although when they occur in isolation from each other, the two sounds are often pronounced in the same way.

More controversial with regard to Jakobson's theory of distinctive features is his claim that the same features are present in every language, and that they constitute a category of linguistic invariables: 'The list of distinctive features that exist in the languages of the world is supremely restricted, and the co-existence of features within one language is restrained by implicational laws.'[11] On this basis, distinctive features become one of the invariants of the communication system as such.

The sounds of language, too, form the basis of Jakobson's theory of poetics. Once again, though, the term 'sound' is a misleading one when dealing with Jakobson's approach. Because sound is a purely physical entity, Jakobson rather compares speech to music which 'imposes upon sound matter a graduated scale', while 'language imposes upon it the dichotomous scale which is simply a corollary of the purely differential role played by phonemic entities'.[12]

In his study of poetic practice, Jakobson was a pioneer in pointing to the way that oppositions of all kinds (phonemic oppositions, the opposition between sound and vision, oppositions in pitch and rhythm, etc.) – but especially oppositions between consonants – figured in the production of poetry. He was also one of the first to emphasise the importance of rhythm in the poetry of the Russians Mayakovsky and Khlebnikov. In short, few linguists before or since have analysed poetry with such success in revealing the structures of poetic discourse. In this Jakobson brought together the 'literary' and the 'overall linguistic' dimensions through a notion of structure that united one to the other. Speaking at a conference in 1958, Jakobson affirmed:

> I believe that the poetic incompetence of some bigoted linguists has been mistaken for an inadequacy of the linguistic science itself. All of us here, however, definitely realize that a linguist deaf to the poetic function of language and a literary scholar indifferent to linguistic problems and unconversant with linguistic methods are equally flagrant anachronisms.[13]

For all his innovation, however, Jakobson remained in certain ways locked within the phenomenological framework of language which influenced him in his early years as a linguist. As a result, he never deviated from retaining as the most pertinent model of language the transmission of a message from a sender to a receiver. Even if Jakobson repeatedly emphasised the need to consider the sender's (active) role in the circuit of communication, as well as that of the (passive) receiver, it remains true that the sender and receiver – psychological, rather than linguistic entities – constitute the indispensable givens of the system. The main problem with such a model is that it does not recognise that language, far from being the property of *a* hypothetical sender and *a* hypothetical receiver, is a fundamentally social fact – that is, it can only be understood correctly as a *system*, which, as such, is the pre-condition of individuality.

Moreover, while Jakobson was instrumental in drawing attention to the rhythm and sound of poetry, he did not see these aspects of poetry as being in any way a challenge to the ideal communicability and meaningfulness of the linguistic utterance. Rhythm even reinforced the notion of language as communication. Compared to those such as Barthes and Kristeva, who emphasise polysemy and the semiotic respectively, and for whom the notion of language as uniquely a means of communication is problematic, Jakobson often appears somewhat at odds with his psychologism. The latter sometimes belies Jakobson's effort to analyse linguistic phenomena linguistically.

Notes

1 Roman Jakobson, *Selected Writings – VI: Early Slavic Paths and Crossroads*, ed. Stephen Rudy, The Hague, Paris, Mouton, 1985, p. 85.
2 ibid.
3 ibid.
4 Roman Jakobson, 'Shifters, verbal categories and the Russian verb' in *Selected Writings – II: Word and Language*, ed. Stephen Rudy, The Hague, Paris, Mouton, 1971, pp. 130–1.
5 Roman Jakobson, 'What is poetry?' in *Selected Writings – III: The Poetry of Grammar and the Grammar of Poetry*, ed. Stephen Rudy, The Hague, Paris, Mouton, 1980, p. 749.
6 ibid., pp. 749–50.
7 ibid., p. 750.
8 Roman Jakobson, *Selected Writings – I: Phono-*
9 Roman Jakobson and Krystyna Pomorska, *Dialogues*, Cambridge, Cambridge University Press, 1983, p. 25.
10 See Jakobson, *Selected Writings – I*, p. 462.
11 Jakobson and Pomorska, *Dialogues*, p. 87.
12 Jakobson, *Selected Writings – I*, p. 423.
13 ibid., p. 51.

See also in this book

Barthes, Hjelmslev, Kristeva, Lévi-Strauss, Saussure

Jakobson's major writings

Selected Writings, The Hague, Paris, Mouton, vols I–VI, ed. Stephen Rudy:

   I: *Phonological Studies*, 1971
  II: *Word and Language*, 1971
 III: *The Poetry of Grammar and the Grammar of Poetry*, 1980
 IV: *Slavic Epic Studies*, 1966
  V: *On Verse, Its Masters and Explorers*, 1978
 VI: *Early Slavic Paths and Crossroads*, Pt One and Pt Two, 1985

Six Lectures on Sound and Meaning, Cambridge, Mass., MIT Press, 1978
The Sound Shape of Language (with Linda Waugh), Bloomington, Indiana, Indiana University Press, 1979
The Framework of Language, Ann Arbor, Michigan, Michigan Slavic Publications, 1980

Further reading

Holenstein, Elmar, *Roman Jakobson's Approach to Language*, Bloomington, Indiana, Indiana University Press, 1974
Steiner, Peter, *Russian Formalism: A Metapoetics*, Ithaca, New York, Cornell University Press, 1984
Waugh, Linda, *Roman Jakobson's Science of Language*, Bloomington, Indiana, P. de Ridder, 1976

JACQUES LACAN

Although Jacques Lacan was to change the whole orientation of psychoanalysis in France and elsewhere, his early education and training were quite conventional. Born in Paris of a bourgeois Catholic family in 1901, Lacan undertook – as was normal practice – a medical degree at the Sorbonne before pursuing further training in psychiatry in the 1920s under the celebrated psychiatrist, Gaëtan de Clérambault. From the latter, Lacan learned the art of observation; from the surrealists, he learned the art of a baroque self-presentation. This is beautifully evoked in the words of a historian of psychoanalysis in France, Elisabeth Roudinesco when, in describing Lacan's performance at his seminar, she says:

> he dressed in a manner similar to his baroque syntax. Shortly after the first split, he moved to the amphitheater at Sainte-Anne.... There, over a period of ten years, he held forth in a vacillating voice, alternately faltering and thunderous, laced with sighs and hesitations. He would note down in advance what he would say, and then, in the presence of his audience, improvise like an actor from the Royal Shakespeare Company who might have had Greta Garbo as diction coach and Arturo Toscanini as spiritual guide. Lacan played false because he was speaking true, as though through the rigor of a voice perpetually on the verge of cracking, he was, like some ventriloquist, effecting the resurgence of the secret mirror of the unconscious, the symptom of a mastery endlessly on the brink of collapse. A sorcerer without magic, guru without hypnosis, prophet without god, he fascinated his audience in an admirable language, effecting, in the margins of desire, the revival of a century of enlightenment.[1]

The rhetoric of Lacan's seminar put into practical form the principle, first formulated in the 1950s, that language has the capacity to say something other than what it says. Language, in short, speaks through human beings, as much as they speak it.

The effort to reinterpret Freud – to 'return to Freud', as Lacan preferred – possibly began in the 1930s inspired by Alexandre Kojève's interpretation of Hegel. Certainly, a Hegelian vocabulary is evident in Lacan's writings of the 1950s, as is a Hegelian sensitivity to the intersubjective nuances of Hegel's Master–Slave dialectic.[2] What stands out here is the role of the Other (with a capital 'O' to show that this is not simply the other person) as fundamental in the articulation of human desire. Because it is founded on the loss of the object (the mother in the first instance), desire does not confirm the subject in its identity, but puts it into question: desire, indeed, highlights a division in the subject.

To rework the theory of subjectivity and sexuality as these derive from the Freudian corpus, Lacan re-read Freud so as to clarify and reinvigorate a whole series of concepts – not the least of which being the concept of the unconscious. What had most inhibited a knowledge of the subversiveness and revolutionary nature of Freud's work, Lacan contended in the 1950s, was the view that the ego was of primary importance in understanding human behaviour. The theory of the ego as identical with itself, as homogeneous, and the privileged source of individual identity not only held sway in ego-psychology in America under the influence of Heinze Hartmann, but spilled over into all the disciplines in the social sciences and humanities. In effect, the early post-war period (especially in America and other English-speaking countries) was the era of humanism and the belief that human intention, understanding, and consciousness were fundamental. A certainty reigned in which the ego – for good or ill – was at the centre of human psychical life.

With the structuralist emphasis on language as a system of differences without positive terms, Lacan highlighted the importance of language in Freud's work. But even before the structuralist approach had become generally known, Lacan had, in 1936, developed the theory of the 'Mirror Stage'.[3] The Mirror Stage concerns the emergence, between the ages of 6 to 18 months, of the capacity of the infant (*enfans* = speechless) before it is able to speak, and before it has control over motor skills, to recognise its own image in the mirror. This act of recognition is not self-evident; for the infant has to see the image as being both itself (its own reflection), and not itself (*only* a reflected image). The image is not identical with the infant subject, and to become a human subject (that is, a social being) means coming to terms with this. The child's entry into language is entirely dependent on this recognition. So, too, is the formation of an ego (the centre of consciousness). Language and symbolic (i.e. cultural) elements now become fundamental, whereas before, it was generally held that biological (i.e. natural) factors were the basis of human subjectivity. As Lacan puts it in the 1953 Rome Discourse: 'Man speaks, . . . but it is because the symbol has made him man.'[4]

The Saussurian theory of the arbitrary relation between signifier and signified, together with the notion of language as a system of differences, led Lacan to go on to say in the early 1960s that the subject is the subject of the signifier. Because the signifier is always separated from the signified (as in the bar in the Saussurian algorithm) and has a real autonomy, no signifier ever comes to rest, finally, on any signified. The realm of the signifier is the realm of the Symbolic order – the order of signs, symbols, significations, representations, and images of all kinds. In this order the individual is formed as subject.

Language is also crucial in the psychoanalytic session where the analysand is encouraged to say everything that comes to mind – without exception – as it is crucial to the very constitution of memory. This is why human beings are inevitably traversed by the Symbolic order.

But language is not simply the bearer of thoughts and information; nor is it simply a medium of communication. Rather, Lacan argues that what causes communication to be defective is also significant. Misunderstandings, confusions, poetic resonances, and a whole series of features (such as slips of the tongue, absent-mindedness, the forgetting of names, misreadings, etc. – features analysed in Freud's *The Psychopathology of Everyday Life*) also emerge in and through language. These are the features through which the effects of the unconscious may be perceived. They are features which enabled Lacan in a famous aphorism to link language and the unconscious: 'The unconscious is structured like a language', Lacan said. It is the unconscious, then, which disrupts communicative discourse – not according to chance, but according to a certain structural regularity.

In light of Roman Jakobson's work in linguistics, Lacan linked Freud's concepts of 'condensation' and 'displacement' to Jakobson's concepts of 'metaphor' and 'metonymy'. Metaphor, accordingly, is defined as the 'replacement of one word by another', while metonymy is the 'word-to-word connexion' (contiguity). Such an approach allows Lacan to equate the 'presence' of the unconscious in language with the effects generated by metaphor and metonymy – much as Freud, in *The Interpretation of Dreams*, relates the evidence of the unconscious in the dream to the working of condensation and displacement.

While language, as the privileged part of the Symbolic order, is central to Lacan's psychoanalytic theory, it is but one element in a trilogy of orders constitutive of the subject in psychoanalysis. The other orders in the trilogy are the Imaginary and the Real. While the unconscious decentres the subject because it introduces division, at the level of the Imaginary (that is, in the discourse of everyday life), the effects of the unconscious are not acknowledged. At the level of the Imaginary, the subject believes in the transparency of the Symbolic; it does not recognise the lack of reality in the Symbolic. The Imaginary is not, then, simply the place where images are produced or where the subject engages in the pleasures of the imagination. In effect, the Imaginary is where the subject mis-recognises (*méconnaît*) the nature of the symbolic. The Imaginary is thus the realm of illusion, but of a 'necessary illusion', as Durkheim said of religion.

One formulation of the Real given by Lacan, is that it is always 'in its place'. The Real is always in its place because only what is missing (absent) from its place can be symbolised, and therefore formalised. The Symbolic is a substitute for what is missing from its place. The symbol, word, etc. always entails the absence of the object or referent. This approach to the Real is elaborated in Lacan's essay on Edgar Allan Poe's short story, 'The Purloined Letter'.[5]

However, at the level of the formation of the individual subject as sexed, what is missing is the mother's phallus. The story is that the infant's entry into language parallel's its separation from the mother. Before separation, there is a plenitude based on the union of mother and child. After separation, the mother becomes the child's first object – that is, its first experience of absence, or lack. For the mother, on the other hand, the child is a substitute for the missing phallus: she feels a sense of fulfilment in light of her close bond with the child. Without separation, however, the formation of language is inhibited. The father, for his part, is the element which tends to intervene in the mother–child relationship, so that in identifying with him, the child can come to form an identity of its own. In this scenario – whose metaphorical status should not be neglected – the mother's place (also the place of the feminine) tends to be that of the Real, while the father evokes the Symbolic and the Imaginary can be grasped from the child's place. At a more precise and specific individual level, the child's identity is the outcome of its coming to terms with sexual difference. First and foremost in this process of sexual differentiation is the recognition on the part of the child that its mother does not have a penis: she thus bears the indelible *mark* of difference. From this, Lacan demonstrates that the penis has an irreducibly symbolic status, a status he signals by speaking only of the phallus. The penis is real, but it is the (symbolic) phallus which is a signifier; in fact, the phallus, because of its role in signifying what is missing (or lacking), becomes the signifier of signification.

This experience does not simply derive from a knowledge (on the part of the child) of the mother's real lack of a penis, but derives also from the mother as an intimation of the child's own potential lack in castration. Consequently, the Symbolic, through the role of phallus as symbol *par excellence*, confronts the subject with its own vulnerability and mortality.

In the most general sense, the Symbolic is what gives the world its meaning and its law – if not its order. Indeed, in the 1950s, Lacan spoke about the law as the being embodied in the Name-of-the-Father: it would thus be the Symbolic Order exemplified by the Name-of-the-Father that constitutes society. Or rather, it is in the name of the dead father – following Freud's story in *Totem and Taboo* – that the sons give up their right to possess their father's women. For Lévi-Strauss, whose work was of great interest to Lacan at the time, this is the moment of the institution of the law against incest.

For many feminist writers, a patriarchal system which valorises masculinity and therefore most males is the predominant outcome of Lacan's Freudian anthropology. No doubt Lacan has only reinforced this impression in the eyes of many women with his provocative aphorisms, '*la* femme n'existe pas' [woman does not exist], and 'la femme n'est pas toute' [woman is not whole]. The first statement is meant to indicate that there is no stereotype that captures a female essence; in fact there is no essence of femininity. And this is why sexuality is always a play of masks and disguises. To say that 'woman' does not exist, then, is to say that sexual difference cannot be contained in any essential symbolic form: it cannot be represented. The second statement plays on the notion that the woman does not have a penis, and is thus part of the emergence of the symbolic: the penis becomes a phallus which becomes the signifier of absence. Before saying with too great a haste that this picture of woman is a negative one (one that therefore benefits males), it has to be said that 'man' is no more disposed to accept this figure of woman as castrated than many women might be. Indeed, we need to take account of the resistance to the 'reality' of the myth of castration that emerges constantly in social life. This resistance is not marked in words or images, but precisely in the refusal to try to symbolise the sense of loss engendered by castration. Be this as it may, the question that still must be asked – although it cannot be answered here – is whether this 'story' that the psychoanalyst tells, partly in order to give psychoanalysis its coherence, finally spells oppression for women as social beings. A supplementary question might be: Does the choice have to be between a false symbolic figure of woman (as with the phallic mother), and an inexpressible (woman as) truth?

A further dimension of Lacan's theory, especially evident in his later seminars, such as *Encore*, is the attempt to give psychoanalysis a mathematical basis. Thus if a signifier only takes on meaning in relation to other signifiers, it can be symbolised by an 'x'. A pure signifier, in other words, would be a letter in mathematical language in as far as this signifier is purely formal. Lacan, after the work of Jacques-Alain Miller, argues that the unconscious also was a pure signifier of this type, and is thus able to take on any meaning whatever; that is, it is entirely open to the context in which it is found. Such is the sense Lacan subsequently attaches to the letter in his reading of Edgar Allan Poe's short story, 'The Purloined Letter'. The letter (epistle) which is stolen assumes significance according to whether it is in the possession of the king, the queen, or the minister who stole it. Because the content of the letter is unknown (to the reader) – because it has no essential content – it begins to resemble the letter as the material support of language: a letter

of the alphabet. In this sense, the unconscious becomes a form of writing detached from any natural object. As a mathematical formula, it is also teachable. For the inexpressible unconscious now becomes the object = x. During the 1960s and early 1970s, Lacan's teaching bore the influence of mathematicians, Frege, Russell, Gödel, and Cantor. More and more he moved away from the rhetorical mode that had dominated his teaching of the 1950s. In Roudinesco's view, 'Lacan's recourse to formalization and mathematics was a final attempt to save psychoanalysis from its hypnotic roots, but also, at the other end of the chain, from schooling, in a society where school tends to replace church.'[6]

Notes

1 Elisabeth Roudinesco, *Jacques Lacan and Co. A History of Psychoanalysis in France, 1925–1985*, trans. Jeffrey Mehlman, Chicago, University of Chicago Press, 1990, pp. 295–6.
2 See in particular, Jacques Lacan, 'The subversion of the subject and the dialectic of desire in the Freudian unconscious', in *Ecrits: A Selection*, trans. Alan Sheridan, London, Tavistock, 1977, pp. 294–324.
3 See Jacques Lacan, 'The mirror stage as formative of the function of the I' in *Ecrits: A Selection*, pp. 1–7.
4 Lacan, *Ecrits: A Selection*, p. 65.
5 See Jacques Lacan, 'Seminar on "The Purloined Letter"', trans. Jeffrey Mehlman in *Yale French Studies (French Freud)*, 48 (1972), pp. 38–72.
6 Roudinesco, *Jacques Lacan and Co.*, p. 561.

See also in this book

Freud, Irigaray, Jakobson, Kristeva, Lévi-Strauss, Saussure

Lacan's major writings

Ecrits, Paris, Seuil, 1966
Ecrits: A Selection, trans. Alan Sheridan, London, Tavistock, 1977
Television: A Challenge to the Psychoanalytic Establishment (1973) trans. Denis Hollier, Rosalind Krauss, and Annette Michelson, New York, Norton, 1990

Le Séminaire (The Seminar):

Livre XX, Encore, Paris, Seuil, 1973
*Book I, (1975) Freud's Writings on Technique,
1953–1954*, trans. John Forester and Sylvana
Tomaselli, New York, Norton, 1988
*Livre II, Le moi dans la théorie de Freud et dans la
technique de la psychanalyse*, Paris, Seuil, 1978
Book III, The Psychoses (1981), trans. Russell
Grigg, New York, Norton, 1993
Livre VII, L'ethique de la psychanalyse, Paris,
Seuil, 1986
Livre XVII, L'envers de la psychanalyse, Paris,
Seuil, 1991
Livre VIII, Le transfert, Paris, Seuil, 1991
*Book XI, Four Fundamental Concepts of
Psychoanalysis* (1973), trans. Alan Sheridan,
New York, Norton, 1978

Further reading

Flower MacCannell, Juliet, *Figuring Lacan:
Criticism and the Cultural Unconscious*, London
and Sydney, Croom Helm, 1986
Muller, John P. and Richardson, William J., *Lacan:
A Reader's Guide to* Ecrits, New York,
International Universities Press, 1982
Ragland-Sullivan, Ellie, *Jacques Lacan and the
Philosophy of Psychoanalysis*, Urbana and
Chicago, University of Illinois Press, 1986
Schneiderman, Stuart, *Jacques Lacan: the Death of
an Intellectual Hero*, Cambridge, Mass., Harvard
University Press, 1983

CLAUDE LEVI-STRAUSS

Claude Lévi-Strauss was born into a Belgian Jewish family in 1908. Both his parents were artists, and so while he was learning to read and write, the future anthropologist had a paintbrush or crayon in his hand.

Although he completed an *agrégation* in philosophy at the Sorbonne in the early 1930s, the desire to escape from the philosophical orthodoxies then in vogue in Paris (neo-Kantianism, Bergsonism, phenomenology and, later, existentialism) prompted Lévi-Strauss in 1934 to accept a position as professor of anthropology at the University of Sao Paulo. Later, following military service in France, Lévi-Strauss fled, to escape persecution, to the United States where, from 1941 to 1945 he taught at the New School for Social Research in New York. In 1941, he met Roman Jakobson who was to be a formative influence in the linguistic and structuralist turn in Lévi-Strauss's post-war anthropology.

Not only did Lévi-Strauss distance himself from the French philosophy of his day, he also distanced himself from orthodox interpretations of Durkheim, which played up the positivistic and evolutionist aspects of his thought. However, it was a reinterpretation of the work of Durkheim's disciple, Mauss, which played a major part in defining Lévi-Strauss's early intellectual trajectory.

In his classic work on the link between kinship and exchange – *The Elementary Structures of Kinship* (1949) – Lévi-Strauss describes the following custom. In inexpensive restaurants in the south of France, especially in the wine-growing regions, a meal normally includes a small bottle of wine. The quality and quantity of wine for each diner is the same: one glass of the lowest quality. Instead of pouring wine into his or her own glass, the owner will pour the wine into that of a neighbour. Despite the exchange, the quantity of wine remains the same.[1] The exchange of wine becomes a means of establishing social contact. Even more. In microcosm, the link between exchange and the 'total social fact' is revealed, since it is not what is exchanged that is important, but the *fact* of exchange itself, a fact inseparable from the very constitution of social life.

Two important aspects of Lévi-Strauss's anthropology are introduced here. The first is the principle that social and cultural life cannot be uniquely explained by a version of functionalism: cultural life is not explicable in terms of the intrinsic nature of the phenomena in question. Nor can it be explained empirically by facts deemed to speak for themselves. In short, although empirical research constitutes an important part of his work, Lévi-Strauss is not an empiricist. Rather, he has always maintained that he is first and foremost a structural anthropologist.

Broadly, structural anthropology, inspired by Saussure, focuses on the way elements of a system combine together, rather than on their intrinsic value. 'Difference' and 'relation' are the key notions here. Moreover, the combination of these elements will give rise to oppositions and contradictions which serve to give the social realm its dynamism.

'Scope' is another crucial aspect of Lévi-Strauss's approach. For while many social researchers have limited their interpretations of social life to the specific society in which they have carried out fieldwork, Lévi-Strauss adopts a universalist approach, theorising on the basis of both his own and other anthropologists' data. Of all the general criticisms that have been levelled against Lévi-Strauss, the one which claims that he theorises from an inadequate fieldwork base is probably the most common in English-speaking countries. For these are also the countries with the strongest empiricist tradition.

Generally speaking, the stakes of Lévi-Strauss's work are high. They amount to a demonstration that when all the data are to hand, there is no basis upon which one could draw up a hierarchy of societies – whether this be in terms of scientific progress, or in terms of cultural evolution. Rather, every society or culture exhibits features that are present in a greater or lesser degree in other societies, or in other cultures. Lévi-Strauss argues this way because he is persuaded that the cultural dimension (in which language is predominant), and not nature – or the 'natural' – is constitutive of the human. Symbolic structures of kinship, language, and the exchange of goods become the key to understanding social life, not biology. Indeed, kinship systems keep nature at bay; they are a cultural phenomenon based on the interdiction against incest, and as such are not a natural phenomenon. They make possible the passage from nature into culture, that is, into the sphere of the truly human. To understand this more fully, we turn to Lévi-Strauss's notion of structure.

'Structure' for Lévi-Strauss is not equiva-lent to the empirical structure (whether, by analogy, it is deemed to be skeletal or archi-tectural) of a particular society, as it is in Radcliffe-Brown's work. Thus, structure is not given in observable reality, but is always the outcome of at least three elements, and it is this ternary nature that gives it its dynamism. Having said this, we should acknowledge that in Lévi-Strauss's *oeuvre*, there is in fact an ambivalence between the kind of structuralism which views structure as an abstract model derived from an analy-sis of phenomena seen as a (more or less) static system of differences – that is, the syn-chronic dimension is privileged – and the notion of structure as being fundamentally ternary, containing an inherently dynamic aspect. The third element of the ternary structure would be always empty, ready to take on any meaning whatsoever. It would be the element of diachrony, that is, the element of history and contingency, the aspect which accounts for the perpetuation of social and cultural phenomena. While Lévi-Strauss's own explanation of the 'structural' in struc-tural analysis[2] tends towards focusing on the synchronic dimension, in practice his work clearly leads towards seeing structure as being essentially ternary and dynamic. We can confirm this point through reference to Lévi-Strauss's most important writings on kinship, myth, and art.

Lévi-Strauss's *Introduction to the Work of Marcel Mauss*,[3] published shortly after the appearance of *The Elementary Structures of Kinship*, shows that while exchange in Mauss's *Essay on the Gift* is equivalent to the 'total social fact', Mauss failed to recognise that exchange was also a key to understand-ing the phenomenon of *mana*. Although Mauss had seen that exchange was a concept constructed by the anthropologist and that it did not have an intrinsic content, he treated *mana* differently. Like Durkheim, Mauss attributed to it the meaning it took on in indigenous societies, a meaning that sees *mana* as having an intrinsic, or sacred, content.

Lévi-Strauss, on the other hand, argues that the diversity of contents assumed by *mana* means that it has to be seen as empty, much like an algebraic symbol,[4] and able to take on any number of meanings – like the word 'thing' in English. In short, *mana* is a 'floating', or pure signifier with a symbolic value in itself of zero. And it exists in a general sense (every culture will have examples of floating signifiers) because there is an abundance of signifiers in relation to signified, since language must be thought of as having come into being all at once (it is a system of differences, and therefore fundamentally relational), while knowledge (the signified) only comes into being progressively.

The structural aspect of Lévi-Strauss's approach here is more implicit than explicit. It consists in the fact, first, that emphasis is not placed on the (hypothetical) content of *mana*, but on its potential to assume a multitude of meanings. It is an empty signifier, much as for Lacan the phallus has no intrinsic meaning, but is the signifier of signification. Second, and more importantly perhaps, *mana*, in Lévi-Strauss's interpretation, is a third element intervening between the signifier and the signified, the element which would give language its dynamism and continuity. For if there were a perfect 'fit' between the level of the signifier and the level of the signified, there would be nothing more to be said, language would come to an end. The floating signifier, therefore, is a structural feature of language in general, an element that introduces into it an asymmetrical, generative aspect: the aspect of contingency, time and, in Saussure's terms, the level of *parole*.

Although the title might suggest it, no explicit reference to Saussurian linguistics is to be found in *The Elementary Structures of Kinship*. The reason, no doubt, is that this, the first major work in structural anthropology, was written in New York in the 1940s, and so before the revival of interest in Saussure's work had taken place in Europe

– let alone America. In *The Elementary Structures of Kinship*, marriage (the outcome of the universal interdiction against incest) in non-industrialised cultures is reduced to two basic forms of exchange: restricted exchange, and generalised exchange. The former, may be represented as in Figure 1.

Figure 1 Restricted exchange

$$X \rightarrow Y \quad Y \rightarrow X$$

Here, reciprocity requires that when an X man marries a Y woman a Y man marries an X woman. Similarly, generalised exchange can be represented as in Figure 2.

Figure 2 Generalised exchange

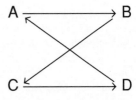

Source: Lévi-Strauss, *The Elementary Structures of Kinship*, p. 178.

Thus, where an A man marries a B woman, a B man marries a C woman; where a C man marries a D woman, a D man marries an A woman. Almost all of *The Elementary Structures of Kinship* is a development of the variants of these two forms of matrimonial exchange.

Even to the untrained observer, what is striking about both forms of exchange is that reciprocity seems to entail a symmetrical structure (the only difference between restricted and generalised exchange being that the latter has twice the number of terms, thereby remaining entirely symmetrical). As Lévi-Strauss later realised, the question arises as to whether a symmetrical structure can be permanent; for after a period of time, groups X and Y in restricted exchange would, through marriage, merge into a single group. Similarly, even with generalised exchange – because of the symmetrical nature of the structure – a single group would eventually emerge. In other words, exchange, set in motion by the interdiction against incest, would encounter an insuperable limit, one that would place at risk the very continuation of social relations.

For exchange to remain viable as an institution, the presence of a third, heterogeneous element is always necessary. Such is indeed the theme of two important articles – one published in 1945[5], the other in 1956[6] – which clarify this point. In the first article, Lévi-Strauss points out that the child is the dynamic, asymmetrical element in the kinship structure:

> we must understand that the child is indispensable in validating the dynamic and teleological character of the initial step, which establishes kinship on the basis of and through marriage. Kinship is not a static phenomenon; it exists only in self-perpetuation. Here we are not thinking of the desire to perpetuate the race, but rather of the fact that in most kinship systems the initial disequilibrium produced in one generation between the group that gives the woman and the group that receives her can be stabilized only by the counter-prestations in following generations.[7]

In the article on dual organisations, Lévi-Strauss points out that every apparent division into two groups in fact implies three elements precisely because of the requirements of self-perpetuation. Any truly dual (i.e. symmetrical) structure leads to the dissolution of the groups involved. There must, then, be a third element – whether real or imagined – which introduces asymmetry and dynamism into the situation. Consequently, institutions having a 'zero value' are an indispensable element in any society. Like

mana, these institutions 'have no intrinsic property other than that of establishing the necessary preconditions for the existence of the social system to which they belong; their presence – in itself devoid of significance – enables the social system to exist as a whole'.[8]

The study of myth led Lévi-Strauss to refine his structuralist approach. A clear enunciation of the principle that the elements of myths gain their meaning from the way they are combined and not from their intrinsic value, leads Lévi-Strauss to the position that myths represent the mind that creates them, and not some external reality. Myths resist history: they are eternal. Even different versions of a myth are not to be thought of as falsifications of some true, authentic version, but as an essential aspect of the structure of myth. On the contrary, different versions are part of the same myth precisely because a myth is not reducible to a single uniform content, but is a dynamic structure. Eventually, all the versions (diachronic aspect) of a myth have to be taken into consideration so as its structure can become apparent. From another perspective, myth is always the result of a contradiction – for instance, 'the belief that mankind is autochthonous', 'while human beings are actually born from the union of man and woman'.[9] In effect, contradiction, as the unassimilable aspect of human society, generates myths. Myth derives from the asymmetry between belief and reality, the one and the multiple, freedom and necessity, identity and difference, etc. Looked at in terms of language, myth, says Lévi-Strauss, is 'language functioning on an especially high level'.[10] Moreover, if langue – the synchronic element of language – is equated with reversible time, and parole with the diachronic, or contingent, historical aspect, myth constitutes a third level of language.[11] Myth is the (impossible) synthesis between the diachronic and the synchronic aspects of language. It is the continual attempt to reconcile the irreconcilable:

since the purpose of myth is to provide a logical model capable of overcoming a contradiction (an impossible achievement if, as it happens, the contradiction is real), a theoretically infinite number of [versions] will be generated, each slightly different from the others.[12]

Myth thus becomes the third dimension of language: in it a continuous attempt is made to reconcile the other two dimensions (*langue* and *parole*) of language. Because complete reconciliation is impossible 'myth grows spiral-wise until the intellectual impulse which has produced it is exhausted'.[13] Myth grows, then, because, structurally, the contradiction – the asymmetry – which gives it life, cannot be resolved.

Like myth, the facial painting of the South American Caduveo Indians, described in Lévi-Strauss's autobiographical work, *Tristes Tropiques*,[14] provide another illustration of structure as a dynamic, ternary phenomenon. There, facial painting designs are asymmetrical arabesques – a ternary structure geared to generate more designs. A purely symmetrical design, as well as being difficult to 'fit' to a real face, would fail to fulfil the purpose assigned to it. This purpose is like that of a figure in European playing cards. Each figure on a playing card must fulfil both a contingent function; it is an element in a specific game between players – and a structural (synchronic) function; it is an element occupying a particular place in the pack, and this place never changes. Caduveo facial painting tries to capture the symmetry of function (status in the group), and the asymmetry of part played (contingency)

> by the adoption of a composition that is symmetrical but set on an oblique axis, thus avoiding the completely asymmetrical formula, which would have met the demands of the role but run counter to those of the function, and the reverse and completely symmetrical formula, which would have had the opposite effect.[15]

The arabesques of the facial painting bring two conceptions of structure into sharp focus. For his part, Lévi-Strauss writes as though his own work were more focused on the static, symmetrical, binary notion of structure, while his actual analyses of social and cultural phenomena suggest that it is the second, ternary view of structure which has far greater explanatory and methodological significance.

Such an ambivalence with regard to the basis of his theoretical framework has led to misunderstandings. In particular, critics have been able to claim that history is neglected in structural anthropology, a fact that has been played up because, no doubt, of Lévi-Strauss's hostility to Sartre's Existentialism, a doctrine in which almost every act is historical (that is, contingent).[16] Furthermore, Lévi-Strauss's insistence on the scientific status of anthropology (admittedly in order to defend the possibility of a social science detached from immediate political debates) sits oddly with his view that science cannot entirely escape being mythical, and the view that cultures are not hermetically sealed off from each other, but constitute an infinite series of transformations. And so while, for instance, science thinks *of* the concrete, native thought thinks *with* the concrete. Again, when Lévi-Strauss says in the 'Overture' to *The Raw and the Cooked*[17] that the book about myth is itself a myth, the very possibility of a detached science in the usual Western sense is brought into question. Lévi-Strauss, however, has often shown himself to be loath to take the consequences of this into account.

Unlike Julia Kristeva, or those inspired by Lacan's reading of Freud, there is little about subjectivity in Lévi-Strauss's *oeuvre*. It is as though he believed that Durkheim's battle to separate psychology from anthropology and sociology were still to be won, and that any concessions to a theory of subjectivity would be equivalent to conceding to the explanatory power of psychology over anthropology. But this battle is not still to be won. And the anthropologist's work suffers from the absence of any attempt to include within it a theory of the subject.

Nevertheless, the significance of Lévi-Strauss's anthropology, as mentioned earlier, cannot be limited to its analytical contents. Much more is at stake. For Lévi-Strauss shows the complexity of non-industrialised cultures which the West – often through its anthropologists (cf. Lévy-Bruhl and Malinowski) – had assumed to be equivalent to the childhood of mankind and who, through that fact, were deemed to be more primitive and more simplistic than the West in their thinking (primitive societies have myth; the West has science and philosophy, etc.). Lévi-Strauss's universalism should thus be understood to mean that transformations of the same myth (as in the Oedipus myth) throughout the world indicate that human beings belong to a single humanity, but that the presence of others is essential if we are to constitute our differences.

Notes

1 Claude Lévi-Strauss, *The Elementary Structures of Kinship*, trans. James Bell and John von Sturmer, Boston, Beacon Press, revised edn, 1969, pp. 58–60.
2 See, for example, Claude Lévi-Strauss, 'Structural analysis in linguistics and anthropology' in *Structural Anthropology*, trans. Claire Jacobson and Brooke Grundfest Schoepf, Harmondsworth, Penguin Books, 1972, pp. 31–54, esp. p. 33.
3 Claude Lévi-Strauss, *Introduction to the Work of Marcel Mauss*, trans. Felicity Baker, Routledge & Kegan Paul, 1987.
4 ibid., p. 55. See pp. 56–66 for the discussion of *mana* as a 'floating' signifier.
5 Lévi-Strauss, 'Structural analysis in linguistics and anthropology', pp. 31–54.
6 Lévi-Strauss, 'Do dual organizations exist?' in *Structural Anthropology*, pp. 132–63.
7 Lévi-Strauss, 'Structural analysis in linguistics and anthropology', p. 47.
8 Lévi-Strauss, 'Do dual organizations exist?', p. 159.
9 Lévi-Strauss, 'The structural study of myth' in *Structural Anthropology*, p. 216.
10 ibid., p. 210.
11 ibid., p. 209.
12 ibid., p. 229.
13 ibid.
14 Claude Lévi-Strauss, *Tristes Tropiques*, trans. John and Doreen Weightman, Atheneum, New York, 1974, pp. 178–97.
15 ibid., p. 194.
16 David Pace, *Claude Lévi-Strauss, The Bearer of Ashes*, Boston, Routledge & Kegan Paul, 1983, pp. 183–4, and Ch. 6.
17 Claude Lévi-Strauss, *Introduction to a Science of Mythology, Volume I: The Raw and the Cooked*, trans. John and Doreen Weightman, New York and Evanston, Harper Torchbooks, 1970, p. 7.

See also in this book

Jakobson, Kristeva, Lacan, Mauss

Lévi-Strauss's major writings

The Elementary Structures of Kinship (1949), trans. J.H. Bell and John von Sturmer, Boston, Beacon Press, 1969
Introduction to the Work of Marcel Mauss (1950), trans. Felicity Baker, Routledge & Kegan Paul, 1987
Tristes Tropiques (1955), trans. John and Doreen Weightman, Atheneum, New York, 1974
Structural Anthropology (1958), trans. Claire Jacobson and Brooke Grundfest Schoepf, New York, Basic Books, 1963
The Savage Mind (1962) (translated from the French), London, Weidenfeld & Nicolson, 1966
Totemism Today (1962), trans. Rodney Needham, Boston, Beacon Press, 1963
Introduction to a Science of Mythology:

Volume I: The Raw and the Cooked (1964), trans. John and Doreen Weightman, London, Jonathan Cape, 1978
Volume II: From Honey to Ashes (1967), trans. John and Doreen Weightman, London, Jonathan Cape, 1973
Volume III: The Origin of Table Manners (1968), trans. John and Doreen Weightman, London, Jonathan Cape, 1978
Volume IV: The Naked Man (1971), trans. John and Doreen Weightman, London, Jonathan Cape, 1981

Structural Anthropology, Volume II (1973) trans. Monique Layton, Harmondsworth, Penguin, 1978
The Way of Masks (1975), trans. Sylvia Modelski, Seattle, University of Washington Press, 1982
The View From Afar (1983), trans. Joachim Neugroschel and Phoebe Hoss, New York, Basic Books, 1985

The Jealous Potter (1985), trans. Bénédicte Chorier, Chicago, Chicago University Press, 1988

Further reading

Badcock, C.R., Lévi-Strauss: Structuralism and Sociological Theory, London, Hutchinson, 1975
Pace, David, Claude Lévi-Strauss, The Bearer of Ashes, Boston, Routledge & Kegan Paul, 1983

CHRISTIAN METZ

Born in 1931 in Béziers in the south of France, Christian Metz died tragically at the end of 1993. Metz opened the way in the 1960s to the establishment of film theory as a new intellectual discipline. Indeed, articles (written between 1964 and 1968) in Metz's *Essais sur la signification au cinéma* (1968) paved the way for the establishment of a department of cinema studies at the University of Vincennes (Paris VIII).

Along with other intellectuals of his generation who were inspired by the structuralist impulse (cf. Bourdieu, Derrida, Genette), Metz attended the Ecole Normale Supérieure (rue d'Ulm) where he obtained an *agrégation* in 'classical letters' (French, Greek, Latin) after also obtaining a degree in German and a *maîtrise* in ancient history. Metz's academic training culminated in a *doctorat d'état* in general linguistics at the Sorbonne.

Parallel to his studies, Metz was engaged in the activities of cinephile and animator of ciné-clubs. Much of his knowledge of film history, and of specific films which often serve as examples for his theoretical work, actually come from these activities. In addition, Metz did translations from German and English, specialising in works on jazz. Strangely, perhaps, contact with such works on music has failed to leave any visible mark on Metz's film theory, music being a neglected aspect of his (and others') film and cinema studies.

To appreciate the significance of Metz's impact, we need to recognise that before the mid-1960s little work had been done on analysing the nature of film (especially as image) or the institution of cinema (especially from the spectator's position). In short, while there was no shortage of film criticism, almost nothing had been done on film as a medium. In response to this, and in accordance with the evolution of his theoretical framework, Metz's work follows two broad lines of inquiry: the semiological study of film, and the psychoanalytic study of the cinema. Consideration of these two lines of inquiry will enable us to get an idea of Metz's work as a whole.

Inspired by his background in linguistics (in light of his *doctorat d'état*, Metz taught a course in general linguistics (1966–9) at the Ecole des Hautes Etudes en Sciences Sociales before teaching film theory), Metz began to investigate film in light of Saussure's work on language – especially in terms of the categories of (in French) *langage* (language in general, or a specific, technical language), *langue* (so-called natural language: French, English), and *parole* (the level of speech or discourse). Just as a Saussurian approach to literary texts took the text's opacity (its status as a linguistic system) as its point of departure, so Metz began by taking the film's opacity as his point of departure. Almost immediately it became clear that such an operation was by no means straightforward; for while the literary analyst had both grammar and poetry as points of departure for investigating the opacity/transparence of literary texts, no such ready-made supports existed for the investigation of film – the medium *par excellence* of transparency. Transparency in film, Metz saw, was intimately tied to its realism – or verisimilitude. Not that film is more real than theatre. Just the opposite. The actors on stage might constitute a real presence for the spectator by contrast with the celluloid image of film, but theatre, in relation to the drama that is enacted, lacks the power of illusion based on verisimilitude which, Metz will come to emphasise, is the mark of film as a medium. At least this is so unless the theatre audience were primarily interested in the presence *per se* of a great actor.

By comparison with theatre, the real power of film derives from its capacity to create an illusion of reality. 'Because the theatre is too real,' says Metz, 'theatrical fictions yield only a weak impression of reality'.[1] Paradoxically, perhaps, the 'realism' of film is only achieved after a threshold of 'irreality' has been crossed. This is tied to the requirement that the spectator suspend his or her disbelief because film as a medium – as a vehicle of representation – is an illusion in relation to the supposedly true reality beyond the representation. Of course 'a film is only a film . . . but all the same': this is the attitude the suspension of disbelief is founded upon.

Metz's early essays thus reflect on the notion that film in general is a specific kind of illusion, one that is undeniably successful in seducing the spectator into suspending disbelief. Once immersed in the film world, once having accepted the principle that film is an illusion, or an 'impression' of reality, the image assumes all its seductive power. To present film largely from the spectator's position, as we have done here, is, however, to move too quickly. For Metz's early essays were less focused on film as experienced by the spectator (this focus would come later with a psychoanalytic study of cinema), and more on the way film signifies. In particular, Metz was interested in the way the film signifier, by comparison with other media – other signifiers – succeeds in presenting a narrative (diagesis), intrigue, description, drama, etc. The key point here concerns the way film as such presents a narrative structure, and not the way specific films unfold and may be interpreted in light of this unfolding. In other words, the point is not to interpret (particular) films (in which case the film signifier becomes incidental), but to analyse film as a structure of signification.

Film in general tends to defy analysis because being an 'impression of reality' is its defining feature. At all times in his early work, Metz keeps in view the fact that the filmic story, or subject-matter, is always realised through the image (the filmic signifier), and that the latter, although an essential element of fascination, is not what a film is about.

How then is it possible for a series of images to present a story which is, however minimally, always narrated (i.e. always presented through a diagesis)? A documentary film can resort to a voice-over in order to give the images presented in time an order and coherence. Some feature films, it is true, resort to the same device; but most do not. What is the basic syntax of the unfolding of the feature film – the film of fiction? Like Greimas's analysis of the basic meaning structure of actions in literary texts, where an attempt is made to construct a universal syntax of actions, Metz is concerned to construct the basic structure, or syntax, of film diagesis as it is realised in images. Neither Greimas nor Metz is interested in interpreting a specific text (they are not, to repeat, working only at the level of the signified), but set out to achieve a much more daunting objective: a description of the basic syntactic order of every possible text – be it of literary or of filmic form. While it is true that some light might be thrown on to the problem of the filmic signifier by way of a detailed analysis of particular films, and while it might be possible to throw light on to the structure of the filmic signifier through a knowledge of a select number of films, Metz's interest is primarily in film in general.

To say that a feature film – a film of fiction – unfolds by way of a narrative structure, is to say that it is a discourse, and thus, as Benveniste said, is an enunciation (*énonciation*) enacted by a subject of enunciation (*sujet de l'énonciation*) – or by, as Metz prefers, a 'narrating agency' (*instance racontante*). In effect, film images are always organised in a specific way; they are never simply given in a raw, descriptive form, although, to be sure, descriptive sequences can occur within the film diagesis. As a discourse, then, film has to be understood in terms of *parole* – or process – rather than *langue* – or system. On the other hand, Metz argues that film images correspond to statements (*énoncés*), or speech acts, rather than to words, precisely because, unlike words, images are of indefinite number and are created by the film-maker/speaker. Furthermore, film is not a language (*langue*) but an art of both connotation (unlike music or architecture) and expressivity (it uses natural objects which do not invoke a code). While 'a concept signifies, a thing is expressive', Metz points out.[2]

Due to its reliance on the presentation of images in time and space, film tends to privilege the syntagmatic, or horizontal axis over the paradigmatic, or vertical axis. Caution leads us to ask exactly why this is so. The answer is that although a page of graphic text might also appear to unfold syntagmatically, a word, as Lacan said, is a knot of (largely conventional) meanings which thus renders fragile the horizontal flow of language. An image (to repeat) is not a word, however. It is produced (in time and space) by the filmic discourse, a discourse that is not only realised through the direction taken by the camera, but also through the procedure of montage – the act of linking one image with another through contiguity. This is not to deny the existence of certain stereotypes (heroic cowboy) in film, nor to deny the use of symbols to create oppositions (e.g., white versus black corresponding to good versus evil). However, Metz, at least in his essays of the 1960s, points out that such paradigmatic features are extremely fragile. Another film-maker can come along and render the stereotype or symbol obsolete by changing the content of the signifying elements (black = good, for example).

Metz in any case chose to base his most rigorous construction of a film syntax on the syntagmatic axis of signification. This construction, which he calls *la grande syntagmatique* (the great syntagmatic chain), we shall now briefly summarise. The great syntagmatic chain is divided into eight autonomous segments. These are:

1 *Autonomous plan*: this is not a syntagm, but a syntagmatic type. It is equivalent to the exposure in isolation of a single episode of the intrigue. Inserts – e.g., a 'non-diagetic insert' (image outside the action of the story) – can also be equivalent to an autonomous plan.

2 *Parallel syntagm*: corresponds to what is often called a 'sequence of parallel montage'. Here, no precise relationship between syntagms is evident. This is an a-chronological syntagm.

3 *Accolade syntagm*: syntagm of evocations. For example, Metz points to the way that eroticism is evoked in Goddard's *Une femme mariée* through references to the 'global signified' of 'modern love'. This syntagm is also a-chronological.

4 *Descriptive syntagm*: here the relation between all the elements presented successively is one of simultaneity. For example, a face, then the person to whom it belongs, then the room or office where the person is located (Metz gives the example of a view of the countryside, bit by bit). A descriptive syntagm is chronological.

5 *Alternating syntagm*: this syntagm corresponds to 'alternating montage', 'parallel montage', etc. Through alternation, the montage presents several series of events which are then understood to be happening simultaneously.

6 *Scene*: the scene properly speaking is equivalent to a continuous flow of images without any diagetic hiatus – one of the oldest cinematic constructions.

7 *Sequence by episodes*: discontinuity becomes a principle of construction. A linear syntagm produces a discontinuity of facts.

Metz calls this 'the sequence properly speaking'.

8 *Ordinary sequence*: disposition of ellipses in dispersed order exemplified by jumping moments deemed to be without interest. The point about any sequence is that it is removed from the 'real conditions of perception'.

By the mid-1970s, Metz had come to see that the semiotic approach to film tended to privilege the level of the structure of film discourse and to neglect the conditions of film reception – the position of the spectator. Furthermore, Metz realised that to account for the dynamics of the spectator's position at the same time entailed accounting for the cinema as an institution; for the cinema would hardly exist if it were not for the spectator's desire to 'go to the cinema'. This shift in focus from signification to film reception coincided with his interest in a psychoanalytical (i.e. Freudian and Lacanian) study of cinema.

Metz thus employs the key Lacanian concepts of the 'imaginary' and the 'symbolic' to explain the logic of the spectator's fascination with the image. Thus through an evocation of Lacan's 'Mirror Stage', Metz sees the spectator's captivation by the image as being equivalent to the child's identification of itself with its image in the mirror. Most importantly, this identification is pleasurable, a factor reinforced by the cinema institution's encouragement of the spectator. Clearly, the cinema institution has a vested interest in ensuring that the spectator experiences any individual film as a – to use Kleinian terms – 'good object': the object of fantasy that often forms the basis of a pleasant day-dream. A 'bad object', by contrast, is what the subject/spectator wants to avoid.

The spectator, then, has assimilated the positive cue associated with going to the cinema institution because he or she is part of that very institution. This is to say that the subject's imaginary is an integral part of the same institution. Film, in effect, becomes integrated into the subject's desire. The screen becomes equivalent to a mirror which offers an image of the subject's own desire. Because the cinema is structured in this way, Metz shows, discourse on the cinema is often part of the cinema institution. Only rarely, therefore, is cinema discourse critical of the cinema institution.

The theorist, by contrast, attempts to take up the position of the symbolic, but this position, as Metz recognises, is precarious, precisely because the theorist's own imaginary (read: desire) is also involved. In other words, film poses in an acute form the problem of distinguishing a judgement of what is good, or objective, from an expression of what is desirable.

In a sustained psychoanalytical study of the cinematographic signifier (that is, the materiality of film, not what it signifies), Metz attempts to compare cinema with the level of the primary process in Freud's theory. This brings the drive aspect into consideration: the way the image fascinates, that way the viewing of film approximates dream, and that way metaphor and metonymy approximate primary process thinking based on condensation and displacement. The drive aspect implies, first of all, that there is a pleasure in perceiving what passes on the screen, and that, furthermore, due to the irreality of film, the spectator's pleasure does not derive from an object properly speaking, but is narcissistic, that is, imaginary. The irreality of the cinematographic signifier invites a comparison between dream and the image in the mirror. Like dream, film has a hallucinatory quality which at the same time calls for interpretation; like the child's proto-typical experience with the mirror as enunciated by Lacan, film images also please. Unlike the mirror, of course, the spectator's own body is not there on the screen. Also, the spectator is quite aware that the image is only an image. Nevertheless, argues Metz, identification is still crucial, only now the spectator '*identifies with himself*, with himself as a pure act of perception'.[3]

In the darkness of the cinema, the spectator acts out a number of Freudian scenarios, scenarios precisely deriving from the very nature of the film signifier's irreality. Scopic passion, voyeurism and fetishism in particular come to the fore. Each of these stimulate the drives which, to a certain extent, do not need a real object for achievement of satisfaction. Voyeurism evokes the primitive scene of the child being present while its parents have intercourse. The voyeuristic position is one of passivity, entailing a gap between eye and object. The fetish is equivalent to a substitute for the penis in castration. It is a way of denying the absence of the penis (= real object) and marvelling at the cinema as a grand technique of illusion. To the point of delusion and hallucination? Metz almost implies as much at certain points, so concerned is he to emphasise the fact that spectator, *qua* spectator, disavows cinematic irreality.

The same might be said of Metz's treatment of dream and cinema as we have just said of the treatment of the spectator as fetishist. The analogy is made to be too complete. For whereas dream and hallucination often lead to a confusion between reality and illusion (this is why Freud called a dream a psychosis[4]), the distinguishing mark of the cinematic signifier, it could be argued, lies precisely in its being experienced *as* an illusion. This is the very same kind of pleasure Lacan attributes to *trompe l'oeil* in painting, which, far from deceiving, gives itself for what it is, namely, *as* a pure appearance, *as* an illusion, in short. Many will feel that this aspect is not given nearly enough emphasis in Metz's analysis. So much is this the case that one writer[5] has observed that Metz has contributed to the confusion in film theory between Foucault's panoptical subject, deluded by an all-too-powerful identification with what passes on the screen (the screen being made the equivalent of a mirror) and Lacan's theory of the subject of the gaze for whom an illusion is always perceived as an illusion (the screen is not the equivalent of a mirror).

Notes

1 Christian Metz, *Film Language: A Semiotics of the Cinema* (a translation of *Essai sur la signification au cinéma* (1968), Volume I), trans. Michael Taylor, New York, Oxford University Press, 1974, p. 10.
2 ibid., p. 78. Translation modified.
3 Christian Metz, *The Imaginary Signifier: Psychoanalysis and the Cinema*, trans. Celia Britton *et al.*, Bloomington, Indiana University Press, 1982, p. 49. Metz's emphasis.
4 Sigmund Freud, *An Outline of Psychoanalysis*, trans. James Strachey, London, The Hogarth Press, 1940, revised edn 1969, p. 29.
5 Joan Copjec, 'The orthopsychic subject: Film theory and the reception of Lacan', *October*, 49 (Summer 1989), pp. 58–9.

See also in this book

Barthes, Benveniste, Lacan, Jakobson, Saussure

Metz's major writings

Film Language: A Semiotics of the Cinema, trans. Michael Taylor, New York, Oxford Universtiy Press, 1974
Essai sur la signification au cinéma, Volume II, Paris, Klincksieck, 1973, second edn, 1976
Essais sémiotiques, Paris, Klincksieck, 1977
The Imaginary Signifier: Psychoanalysis and the Cinema (1977), trans. Celia Britton, *et al.*, Bloomington, Indiana University Press, 1982
Film Language and Cinema (1971 and 1977), trans. J. Donna Uniker-Sebeok, Berlin, Mouton de Gryter, 1974

Further reading

Agis Cozyris, George, *Christian Metz and the Reality of Film*, New York, Arno Press, 1980
Copjec, Joan, 'The orthopsychic subject: Film theory and the reception of Lacan', *October*, 49 (Summer 1989), pp. 53–71
Henderson, Brian, *Classical Film Theory: Eisenstein, Bazin, Godard, and Metz*, Ann Arbor, Mich., University Microfilms International, n.d.
Rose, Jacqueline, 'The imaginary' in *Sexuality in the Field of Vision*, London, Verso, 1986

MICHEL SERRES

Michel Serres is a 'voyager' between the arts and the sciences, and a thinker for whom voyaging is invention. Invention is also called 'translation', 'communication', and 'metaphor'. By way of introduction to Serres's simultaneously philosophical, scientific and poetic work, we refer to a nodal event in the history of science: thermodynamics, and the consequent transcending of the closed system of Newtonian mechanics. To transcend the closed system is, for Serres, to fuel invention.

In 1824, a French army engineer, Sadi Carnot drew attention to the fact that in the steam-engine heat flowed from a high-temperature region (the boiler) to a low-temperature region (the condenser). Although Carnot incorrectly concluded that no energy was lost from the system, he did appreciate that the more efficient the system, the less the energy required for its operation, and that it was the difference in the temperature between the boiler and the condenser which produced energy. Carnot's work ended prematurely when he died at the age of 36. A number of people like Hermann Helmholtz and Rudolph Clausius in Germany, and William Thompson (Lord Kelvin), in Glasgow, further developed Carnot's work, with the result that in 1865, Clausius coined the term 'entropy' for the heat lost from any mechanical system. The era of thermodynamics had arrived. Its first and second laws are, respectively, that 'The energy of the world remains constant', and that 'The entropy of the world tends to a maximum.'[1] Entropy is also the tendency towards disorder in a system.

Of interest here with respect to Serres is the difference between a simple mechanical notion of energy, and that of thermodynamics. In Newton's mechanical model, no energy in principle is lost from the system: the mechanics of the system are reversible. There are in principle no chance effects. 'According to the second law of thermodynamics . . . the unidirectional motion of [a] projectile would be continuously transformed by the frictional resistance of the air into heat, that is, into random, disorderly motions of the molecules of the air and the projectile.'[2]

This randomness or disorder – as in the unstable borders of a cloud, or in the effects of steam, or in the movement of the tides – is only now being taken in charge by chaos theory. Prior to this, stochastics – the theory of randomness – like the theory of probability developed principles aimed at explaining disorderly phenomena.

From this brief outline we note that a Newtonian mechanical system is a system of reversibility: time in it is reversible. With the thermodynamic system, contingency and chance predominate, making it a system of irreversible time. To give a sociological twist to this, we can note that Bourdieu has called the logic of practice the logic of irreversible time.

Serres is ostensibly a philosopher of science. But unlike even his mentor, Gaston Bachelard, he has never accepted that any particular science – let alone natural science – conforms to the positivist determination of a hermetic and homogeneous field of enquiry. In a recent work,[3] Serres has indicated that the shape and nature of knowledge more closely approximates the figure of the harlequin: a composite figure that always has another costume underneath the one removed. The harlequin is a hybrid, hermaphrodite, mongrel figure, a mixture of diverse elements, a challenge to homogeneity, just as chance in thermodynamics opens up the energy system and prevents it from imploding.

Michel Serres was born in 1930 at Agen in France. In 1949, he went to naval college and subsequently, in 1952, to the Ecole Normale Supérieure (rue d'Ulm). In 1955, he obtained an *agrégation* in philosophy, and from 1956 to 1958 he served on a variety of ships as a marine officer for the French national maritime service. His vocation of voyaging is therefore of more than academic import. In 1968, Serres gained a doctorate for a thesis on Leibniz's philosophy. During the 1960s he taught with Michel Foucault at the Universities of Clermont-Ferrand and Vincennes and was later appointed to a chair in the history of science at the Sorbonne, where he still teaches. Serres has also been a full professor at Stanford University since 1984, and he was elected to the French Academy in 1990.

With the recognition of the interrelation between different sciences and different forms of knowledge, as well as between science and different artistic practices, has come Serres's effort to plot the way that different knowledge domains interpenetrate. Even more: Serres has set himself the task of being a means of communication (a medium) between the sciences and the arts – the Hermes of modern scholarship.[4] With the advent of information science, a new figure for representing science becomes possible: this is the 'model' of communication. Accordingly, we have three elements: a message, a channel for transmitting it, and the noise, or interference, that accompanies the transmission. Noise calls for decipherment; it makes a reading of the message more difficult. And yet without it, there would be no message. There is, in short, no message without resistance. What Serres initially finds intriguing about noise (rather than the message) is that it opens up such a fertile avenue of reflection. Instead of remaining pure noise, the latter becomes a means of transport. Thus in the first volume of the Hermes series noise is analysed as the third, empirical element of the message. Ideally, communication must be separated from noise. Noise is what is not communicated; it is just there as a kind of chaos, as the empirical third element of the message, the accidental part, the part of difference that is excluded. Every formalism (mathematics, for example) is founded on the exclusion of the third element of noise. Every formalism is a way of moving from one region of knowledge to another. To communicate is to move within a class of objects that have the same

form. Form has to be extracted from the cacophony of noise; form (communication) is the exclusion of noise, an escape from the domain of the empirical.

In his book, *The Parasite*,[5] Serres recalls that 'parasite' also means noise (in French). A parasite is a noise in a channel. And so when describing the rats' meals in a story from the fables of La Fontaine – the meals of two parasites – Serres also refers to noise: 'The two companions scurry off when they hear a noise at the door. It was only a noise, but it was also a message, a bit of information producing panic: an interruption, a corruption, a rupture of information. Was this noise really a message? Wasn't it, rather, static, a parasite?'[6]

Serres addresses the theme of noise and communication to show that 'noise is part of communication';[7] it cannot be eliminated from the system. Noise in language as in other systems of communication has its equivalent in the very notion of system itself. For, 'we know no system that functions perfectly, that is to say, without losses, flights, wear and tear, errors, accidents, opacity – a system whose return is one for one'.[8]

Serres's interest in 'noise' as the empirical third excluded element in human existence has led him to translate (*traduire*) between apparently heterogeneous domains in an effort to forge 'passages' (e.g., north-west passage) between them – passages not just of communication, but also of non-communication, and static. At one point in his intellectual trajectory, the notion of structure seemed to serve the purposes of translation – and therefore, transport – very well. Indeed, Serres characterises the structuralist method as a method in the 'etymological sense: that is to say, a mode of transfer'.[9] Beginning as part of Serres's mathematical training in algebra and topology, structure is brought to the human sciences where a structural analysis,

examines one or two particular models reduced to a form (or to several): a preestablished, transitive order. Then, analogically, it finds this form or structure in other domains, *et similia tam facilia*. Whence its power of comprehension, of classification and of explication: geometry, arithmetic, mechanics, method, philosophy.[10]

Influenced less by Saussure, than by the Bourbaki group of mathematicians, Serres finds in structural analysis a means of travelling between different domains, and even between different realities. Structural analysis inevitably leads to comparison, and this is why Serres has great respect for Georges Dumézil's work; for Dumézil was able to show, through a comparison of sets of relations, that Indo-European mythology has the same structure, despite the variety of contents. In a very precise formulation Serres says: 'with a given cultural content, whether this be God, a table or a washbasin, an analysis is structural (and is only structural) when it makes this content appear as a model'[11] – a structural model being defined as 'the formal analogon of all the concrete models that it organises'. Rather than 'structural analysis', Serres proposes the term, '*loganalyse*'.

Through its non-referential and comparativist approach to place (no single place constitutes the object of structural analysis), the structuralist place is both 'here and there' at the same time. It is a highly mobile site that is constituted through an enunciation. There is no fixed point, here and now, but a multiplicity of spaces and of times. This implies, too, that there is no punctual empirical subject, but rather a subject as a discontinuous virtuality.

Serres's more recent work has emphasised the importance to him of poetry and the effect of new technologies (such as information technology) on everyday life. Poetry, in a sense, is the noise of science. Without poetry there would be no science. Without science – or at least philosophy – there can be no poeticising and fictionalising. Serres's

reading of Jules Verne, Emile Zola, and the paintings of Turner serve to confirm this point. In Verne, for example, the meaning of coming to grips with non-knowledge is demonstrated. Non-knowledge is the mystery – the noise, we could now say – necessary to the constitution of knowledge as such. Non-knowledge in Verne is the unknown that one must venture into in order to constitute knowledge. The unknown is composed of worlds for which there would be as yet no concept or language. With Zola and Turner, the principle of stochastics is illustrated by their artistic endeavour in presenting steam, smoke, water and a variety of indeterminate phenomena.

For Serres, 'the perception of stochastics replac[ing] the specification of form' is a breakthrough in linking the sciences. *For science is a system, just as poetry is a system.* Rain, sun, ice, steam, fire, turbulence – they all engender chance effects. Modern physics begins here with the realisation that turbulence prevents the implosion of systems. The 'outside' of the system is what prevents implosion.

'What exists', says Serres, 'is the most probable' (i.e. disorder, chance, and the exception). The real is not rational. 'There is only science of the exception, of the rare, and of the miracle' (i.e. of law, order, rule). System in the Classical Age is an equilibrium; in the nineteenth century it is thermodynamics and meteorology becomes a metaphor for knowledge.

In *The Parasite*, Serres asks whether system is a prior set of constraints, or whether, on the other hand, system is the regularity manifest in the various attempts to constitute a system. 'Do these attempts themselves constitute the system?' Serres asks. Noise, we have seen *is* the system. 'In the system, noise and message exchange roles according to the position of the observer and the action of the actor.'[12] Noise is a joker necessary to the system. It can take on any value, and is thus unpredictable so that the system is never stable. Instead, it is non-knowledge. Systems work because they do not work. Dysfunctioning remains essential for functioning. The model, then, is free of parasites, free of static (as in mathematics), while the system is always infected with parasites which give it its irreversible character. The system is a Turner painting. With his representation of the chance effects of clouds, rain, sea, and fog, Turner interprets the second law of thermodynamics – the law made possible by Carnot. Turner translates Carnot. Such is Serres's poetic insight.

Two figures, then, inform Serres's *oeuvre*: Hermes and the Harlequin. Hermes the traveller and the medium allows for the movement in and between diverse regions of social life. The Harlequin is a multi-coloured clown standing in the place of the chaos of life. Two regions of particular interest to the voyager in knowledge are those of the natural sciences and the humanities. Should science really be opened up to poetry and art, or is this simply an idiosyncrasy on Serres's part? Is this his gimmick? The answer is that Serres firmly believes that the very viability and vitality of science depends on the degree to which it is open to its poetical other. Science only moves on if it receives an infusion of something out of the blue, something unpredictable and miraculous. The poetic impulse is the life-blood of natural science, not its nemesis. Poetry is the way of the voyager open to the unexpected and always prepared to make unexpected links between places and things. The form that these links take is of course influenced by technological developments; information technology transforms the senses, for example.

Serres's writing is a challenge for good reason. In his view, not to stimulate the reader to find the coherence in his work – as he has done with others – is to render it sterile and subject to the collapse that inevitably awaits all closed systems. In the history of physics Serres has argued that Lucretius anticipates the framework of modern physics. *De rerum natura* (*On the Nature of Things*) has conventionally been treated as a piece of poetic writing that has little relevance to modern science. But, Serres argues, clearly, turbulence of all kinds is fundamental to Lucretius's system. With the idea of the *clinamen* – of infinite variation in the course of an object's trajectory – Lucretius anticipates the theory of disorder – entropy – of modern physics. More than this, though, Serres endeavours to show that a mathematics can be produced in light of Lucretius's writings of the last century before Christ.

By extension, the history of science itself is subject to turbulence: it is subject to chance connections of all kinds being made between various domains. Against the rigid orderliness of convention, Serres proposes the relative disorder of poetry, that is, of the miracle, chance and the exception. In its own way, Serres's writing is a glimpse of this miracle of poetry in an island of order.

Notes

1 The information on the history of thermodynamics comes from Stephen Mason, *A History of the Sciences*, New York, Collier, new revised edn, 1962, Ch. 39.
2 Mason, *A History of the Sciences*, p. 496.
3 Michel Serres, *Le Tiers-Instruit*, Paris, François Bourin, 1991.
4 cf. the five volumes published under the title of *Hermès*, the Greek messenger god: *I, La communication* (1969); *II, L'interférence* (1972); *III, La traduction* (1974); *IV, La distribution*, (1977); *V, Le passage du nord-ouest* (1980).
5 Michel Serres, *The Parasite*, trans. Lawrence R. Schehr, Baltimore, Johns Hopkins University Press, 1982.
6 ibid., p. 3.
7 ibid., p. 12.
8 ibid., pp. 12–13.
9 Michel Serres, *L'interférence*, Paris, Minuit, 1972, p. 145.
10 Michel Serres, *La communication*, Paris, Minuit, 1969, p. 121.
11 ibid., p. 32.
12 Serres, *The Parasite*, p. 66.

See also in this book

Bachelard, Canguilhem, Cavaillès

Serres's major writings

Le Système de Leibniz et ses mathématiques, 2 vols, Paris, Presses Universitaires de France, 1968 (one vol., 1982)

Hermes: Literature, Science, Philosophy (1969f), trans. Josve Harari and David Bell, Baltimore, Johns Hopkins University Press, 1983

Hermès I. La communication, Paris, Minuit, 1969

Hermès II. L' interférence, Paris, Minuit, 1972

'Turner translates Carnot' (1972), trans. Mike Shortland, *Block*, 6 (1982), pp. 46–55. This article first appeared in 1972 as a review of an exhibition of English and pre-Raphaelite paintings held at the Petit Palais in Paris and was subsequently published in Michel Serres, *Hermès III. La traduction*, Paris, Minuit, 1974, pp. 233–42

Hermès III.La traduction, Paris, Minuit, 1974

Jouvences. Sur Jules Verne, Paris, Minuit, 1974

Feux et signaux de brume. Zola, Paris, Grasset, 1975

Auguste Comte. Leçons de philosophie positive, Vol. 1, Paris, Hermann, 1975

Hermès IV. La distribution, Paris, Minuit, 1977

La Naissance de la physique dans le texte de Lucrèce Fleuves et turbulences, Paris, Minuit, 1977

Hermès V. Le passage du nord-ouest, Paris, Minuit, 1980

The Parasite (1980), trans. Lawrence R. Schehr, Baltimore, Johns Hopkins University Press, 1982

Genèse, Paris, Grasset, 1982

Rome: The Book of Foundations (1983), trans. Felicia McCarren, Stanford University Press, 1991

Detachment (1983) trans. James Geneviere and Raymond Federman, Athens, Ohio University Press, 1989

Les cinq sens, Paris, Grasset, 1985

Statues, Paris, François Bourin, 1987

Le Contrat naturel, Paris, François Bourin, 1990

Further reading

Latour, Bruno, 'Postmodern? No simply Amodern! Steps towards an anthropology of science', *Studies in the History and Philosophy of Science*, 21, 1 (March 1990), pp. 145–71. Review of Serres's *Statues*

STRUCTURAL HISTORY

To speak of 'structural' history is sometimes seen as contradictory. History, it might be supposed, is produced by subjects – understood as sensuous human beings – and structuralists talked about history without a subject. However, through the *Annales* school, led by Fernand Braudel, the notion of history is broadened to include the slower rhythm of geographical history; and change is measured, not simply in relation to an immediate consciousness of events, but in relation to the longer term changes that are always going on despite the consciousness of individuals. History of the long span (*longue durée*), is thus history of fundamental structural changes, but these are only knowable in light of the patterns through which they are realised; structure does not determine these changes.

FERNAND BRAUDEL

With his conception of time as plural – a conception partially evoked by the notion of the *longue durée* (long span) – Fernand Braudel, founder of the post-war version of the *Annales* historical journal, turned towards the spatial dimension of history. Opening history up to space is, in Braudel's hands, to give it a structural aspect, an aspect not immediately available to the consciousness of historical actors. If for the English historian, R.G. Collingwood, history is the actions of men in the past, Braudel effectively added that history is also the effect of the slow, and often imperceptible effects of space, climate and technology on the actions of human beings in the past. As a result, the context, both human and natural, affects actions as much as actions affect context. More than this, however, Braudel temporalises space and aspects like the natural environment; he thus temporalises elements which were largely treated as though they were timeless.

Braudel was born in 1902 in a small French village of 250 inhabitants, Luméville-en-Ornois. At the age of 20, he became an *agrégé* in history. While teaching at a secondary school in Algeria, between 1923 and 1925, he discovered the Mediterranean – the subject of his first major, and possibly most famous work, *The Mediterranean and the Mediterranean World in the Age of Philip II*.[1] In 1925, Braudel completed his military service in the Rhineland, then returned to Algeria until 1932, all the time collecting material for his *doctorat d'état* on the Mediterranean. From 1932 to 1935 he taught in the Paris *lycées* of Pasteur, Condorcet, and Henry IV, after which he left for a three-year appointment at the University of São Paulo. The year Braudel took up this appointment – 1935 – was the year that Lévi-Strauss arrived at the same university in order to begin fieldwork for *The Elementary Structures of Kinship*. Of his experience of a different culture in Brazil, Braudel later said that it was the 'greatest period of his life', a sentiment echoed by other youthful escapees from Metropolitan France, such as Dumézil in Istanbul, and Foucault in Uppsala.

In 1938, Braudel entered the Ecole Pratique des Hautes Etudes as a teacher in the philology of history. At the outbreak of war in 1939, he was called up and subsequently taken prisoner in 1940 for the duration of hostilities. During the period of his captivity, he developed the framework for his doctoral thesis, in particular the notion of three levels of time. His thesis on the Mediterranean was published in 1949, the year that he was elected to the Collège de France upon Lucien Febvre's retirement. In 1947, with Lucien Febvre and Charles Morazé, Baudel founded the famous Sixième Section for 'Economic and social sciences' at the Ecole Pratique des Hautes Etudes. He retired in 1968, and in 1983 was elected to the Académie Française. He died in 1985.

Without doubt, the single most important contribution made by Braudel to the writing of history and, more broadly, to the social sciences, is his theory of the *longue durée*. Although at first emerging intuitively through a desire to capture the rich tapestry of a 'world' interacting with other 'worlds' in his monumental history of the Mediterranean from the sixteenth to the eighteenth century, the *longue durée* progressively became more explicit as Braudel and the *Annales* school of historians reached the height of their influence in the 1960s and 1970s. The *longue durée* has a more global focus than traditional, narrative history; it places emphasis on the diversity of interactions constituting a broadly based unity: 'conjuncture and structure' is Braudel's phrase. As if responding to Nietzsche's notion of perspectivism, Braudel's is history written simultaneously from many different positions or perspectives, and not one based, whether intentionally or not, on a single position or perspective. Moreover, instead of attempting to distinguish – usually at one or more given moments – between degrees of reality, the aim now, as with Foucault's history, is to 'understand how patterns of practice and series of discourses are articulated',[2] and, we might add, to understand patterns of nature as well as patterns of human activity.

Prior to the *Annales* approach, says Braudel, the writing of history was focused on the *courte durée* (short span), or on what is known as *histoire événmentielle* (a history of events). Political and diplomatic history has been the prime example of *histoire événmentielle*, although it does not have to be. With such traditional history made famous in the nineteenth century, not only does history become a painting, or objectification, with the observer left out so that the idea of history as a reconstruction is thereby erased, but the insight that the problem of history is *in* the landscape, 'in life itself', becomes inaccessible.[3] For Braudel, by contrast, there is no unilateral history, as there are no abstract individuals. Instead a 'fleeting spectacle' is always in movement; 'a web of problems' is meshed together able to assume 'a hundred different and contradictory aspects in turn'.[4]

A major difficulty with history that focuses on the very short, or medium term is that it risks becoming pure chronicle and lacking in profundity because it assumes the homogeneity of time and a singularity of perspective. In its use of representation, a short-span history of events tends to use a dramatic mode along with the rhetorical paraphernalia that accompanies it. For example, a society, or even an entire culture, has often been framed by an organic, biological metaphor; thus, like the individual, a society is born, goes through a period of development and dies. Biography thus becomes the basic framework of analysis irrespective of the complexity of the subject matter. Furthermore, a cause and effect logic accompanies the tendency to see events in isolation within a single time, rather than as part of a complex web of forces interacting according to a plurality of times.

By contrast, the *longue durée* is derived from the 'thousand different paces' of social time. It can include the time of the changes in the environment which is, says Braudel, history at its slowest. It tends to be structural in orientation, being derived from the way many events – which may be represented in statistical series – are organised over different time periods. For the *Annales* historian, structure is a construct which can become a prison if the radical plurality of times is not acknowledged. Accepting the *longue durée* entails a readiness to change everything: from one's thinking to a style of writing and presentation, to accepting a time which may be so slow as to border 'on the motionless'. Clearly, although Braudel does not say so in so many words, he pleads for a conception of history that is radically open – history as an open system, where each sub-system, to the extent that it can be distinguished, would be dependent on its environment.

In order to put his aspirations for historical writing into practice, Braudel argued strongly for a radical interdisciplinary approach to be adopted in the social sciences. Disciplines like economics, geography, anthropology and sociology should be brought to bear on problems detected by the historian. No particular discipline has a monopoly of the truth about human or natural existence; but the logic of their respective presentations often implies that each is making a bid for the right to claim that it alone can explain the nature of existence. For his part, Braudel saw that all the social sciences should be mobilised because it was essential that a history based on the *longue durée* be truly multi-faceted.

Even though Braudel's three volume work, *Civilisation matérielle*,[5] has also captured the imagination of scholars and non-historians alike, it is in his study of the Mediterranean that the real innovations of Braudel's historical writing are most clearly in evidence. The innovations Braudel brought to the writing of history are there for all to see.

In the first place, Braudel does not proceed by way of narrative history – at least not by way of a single-view narrative history as this had been bequeathed by the nineteenth century. For Braudel, there is no one focus which would allow a single narrative to be actualised. Rather, there is a multiplicity of views. Consequently, when he studies the Mediterranean Sea, Braudel is quick to point out that for him there is no single sea; rather, there are many seas; indeed a 'vast, complex expanse' which confronts human beings. Life is conducted on the Mediterranean: people travel, fish, fight wars, and drown in the many seas. Again, the sea gives on to plains and islands. Life on the plains is diverse and complex; the poorer south is affected by religious diversity (Catholicism and Islam), as well as by intrusions – both cultural and economic – from the wealthier north. In other words the Mediterranean cannot be understood independently from what is exterior to it. Any rigid adherence to boundaries is a way of falsifying the situation. It is equivalent to giving a 'philosophy of history' instead of writing history itself.[6] The great thing about Braudel's study, then, is that it makes one sharply aware of the effect of dogmatic categorising, and of constituting problematic identities. In this sense, Braudel is probably the first truly postmodern historian.

Braudel expands the scope of the Mediterranean from being a stereotypical individuality with a given character (warm climate and whitewashed houses) to its being a world: that is, to its being a plurality of sub-systems which interact with each other, which flow into one another. Thus the Moslem Ottoman Empire is inextricably bound up with the Mediterranean; Catholic life on the plateaux and hills is enmeshed with the more Moslem life in the mountains; nomadic life is tied up with sedentary existence. Space, in short, is envisaged as the intersection of all sorts of spatial clusters.

Three levels of time organise Braudel's history of the Mediterranean. The first level is that of the environment. It entails slow, almost imperceptible change, a sense of repetition and cycles. Here change may be slow, but change there is. This is Braudel's point. This, then, is geographical time. The second level of time is that of social and cultural history. This is the time of groups and of groupings, of empires and civilisations. Change at this level is much more rapid than that of the environment; however, the span can often be two or three centuries in order to study a particular cluster of phenomena, such as the rise and fall of various aristocracies. The third level of time is that of events (*histoire événmentielle*). This is – or can be – the history of individual men. This, for Braudel, is the time of surfaces and deceptive effects. It is the time of the *courte durée* proper and it is exemplified by Part 3 of *The Mediterranean* which treats of 'events, politics and people'. In addition, there is probably a fourth level of time: the time of the moment, or conjuncture, where a specific situation – the entry and effect of the English into the Mediterranean in the sixteenth century – is studied from a number of different angles. The conjuncture opens out on to social and geographical time. In fact, Braudel's disagreement with sociology was that, as he saw it, sociology focused too much attention on individual time, on the time of the conjuncture for its own sake, without considering the time of the *longue durée*. As a result, sociology risked drawing a superficial picture of humanity.

The Mediterranean, Braudel shows, is a complex of seas. But it is also the desert and the mountains. While the desert might entail a nomadic form of social organisation where the whole community moves, mountain life is sedentary. Before a hard and fast rule can be laid down here, however, a third kind of social organisation based on transhumance needs to be considered. Transhumance (movement from the mountain to the plain, or vice versa in a given season), seems to be a combination of sedentary and nomadic existence. Braudel goes to great lengths here as elsewhere in order to show that a strict adherence to rigid boundaries in this matter is untenable.

From another angle, Braudel uses the motif of snow in order to show how an aspect of the mountain climate becomes intertwined with village life at the edge of the sea. Snow being brought down from the mountain in Italy is the origin of the creation of ice-cream in the hot cities in summer.

Hardly an aspect of existence is neglected. Shipping and its technology; the economy in all its multiplicity, including labour, money, prices, wages, trade, war, classes, banditry and crime; transport and communications. All go to form a rich texture with the part submerged in the whole, but where the unity of the whole is not an individual closed system, but is the unity of a multiplicity. The Mediterranean becomes a complex grid network, a fascinating array of crossroads and intersections of all kinds. Most importantly, to grasp the full significance of Braudel's project, it is necessary to realise that each sub-system moves according to its own rhythm. A rhythmical web is one way of describing what Braudel has made manifest. As he says,

Science, technology, political institutions, conceptual changes, civilizations (to fall back on that useful word) all have their own rhythms of life and growth, and the new history of conjunctures will be complete only when it has made up a whole orchestra of them all.[7]

Instead of eschewing complexity and attempting a single, monographic approach in which variables are more or less controlled, Braudel and the *Annales* school embrace complexity. Thus, rather than give up the category of 'civilization' because it covers too broad a field to be grasped as a whole, Braudel reinstates it to a position of pre-eminence in his historical writing. The notion of a 'world' is also a fundamental one in the Braudelian approach to history.

Predictably, there have been objections to Braudel and his school. From the Marxists has come the claim that his work is in fact a single point of view on the material being analysed whether Braudel likes it or not. A choice of subject-matter and the manner of treating it is unavoidable. Others have argued that there is a more or less unresolvable tension in Braudel's history between a problem orientation – in which as many of the social sciences as possible would participate – and a desire to see the whole picture. Still others have argued that the extensive use of series of statistical data in revealing long-term trends in everything from climatic changes to changes in eating habits turns human beings into objects who are objectified, and thus robbed of their freedom.

Whether or not there is validity in such arguments, it is difficult to see how a heightened readiness to focus on relationships, coupled with the imperative that one kind of history should never be chosen to the exclusion of all others (that one should always be open to new kinds of history) can fail to be a productive starting point for any history worthy of the name.

Notes

1 Fernand Braudel, *The Mediterranean and the Mediterranean World in the Age of Philip II*, 2 vols, trans. Siân Reynolds, Glasgow, William Collins, 1972, Vol. I, 1973, Vol. II; Fontana/Collins, 1975.
2 Roger Chartier, *Cultural History. Between Practices and Representations*, trans. Lydia G. Cochrane, Cambridge, Polity Press, 1988, p. 61.
3 Fernand Braudel, *On History*, trans. Sarah Matthews, Chicago, University of Chicago Press, 1980, p. 9.
4 ibid., p. 10.
5 Fernand Braudel, *Civilisation matérielle, économie et capitalisme (XV–XVIII siècles)*, 3 vols, Paris, Armand Colin, 1980.
6 Braudel, *The Mediterranean*, Vol. I, p. 18.
7 ibid., p. 30.

See also in this book

Foucault, Lévi-Strauss

Braudel's major writings

The Mediterranean and the Mediterranean World in the Age of Philip II (1949 and 1966), 2 vols, trans. Siân Reynolds, Glasgow, William Collins, 1972, Vol. I, 1973, Vol. II; Fontana/Collins, 1975

On History (1969), trans. Sarah Matthews, Chicago, University of Chicago Press, 1980

Civilisation matérielle, économie et capitalisme (XV–XVIII siècles), 3 vols, Paris, Armand Colin, 1980. In English as *Capitalism and Material Life, 1400–1800*, trans. Miriam Kochan, Glasgow, Fontana/Collins, 1974

L'Ere industrielle et la société d'aujourd'hui: le siècle 1880–1980, 3 vols, Paris, PUF, 1982

The Identity of France, Volume I: History and Environment (1986), trans. Siân Reynolds, HarperCollins, 1990

The Identity of France, Volume II: People and Production (1990), trans. Siân Reynolds, HarperCollins, 1992

Further reading

Bintliff, John (ed.), *Annales School and Archaeology*, Leicester, Leicester University Press, 1991

Knapp, A. Bernard (ed.), *Archaeology, Annales and Ethnohistory*, Cambridge, Cambridge University Press, 1992

Burke, Peter, *French Historical Revolution: The Annales School, 1929–89*, Stanford, California, Stanford University Press, 1990

POST-STRUCTURALIST THOUGHT

Often associated with the work of Jacques Derrida, post-structuralist thought examines the notion of difference in all its facets and discovers that Saussure had left intact certain (metaphysical) presuppositions about subjectivity and language (for example, the privileging of speech over writing) – vestiges of the historicist framework with which Saussure himself was dissatisfied. Post-structuralist thought examines writing as the paradoxical source of subjectivity and culture, whereas once it was thought to be secondary. Most importantly, post-structuralism is an investigation as to how this is so.

A further aspect of post-structural thought involves a radical questioning of otherness (Levinas, Bataille), and of the subject–object relation. In Deleuze's work, inspired by Nietzsche, the 'tree' (search for origins) of the 'subject–object' relation is compared to the 'rhizome' of horizontal thought, thought always in movement.

GEORGES BATAILLE

It is appropriate to begin an explication of Georges Bataille's work with biographical fragments for in an important sense Bataille's writing stands at the crossroads of fiction and biography.

Bataille was born at Billon in France in 1897. His father had gone blind before the birth of his son, and he became partially paralysed in 1900 when Georges was not yet 3 years old. Bataille claims in his autobiographical fragments that his father's condition was the result of syphilis. However, this was contested by his brother. Whatever the truth of the matter, Bataille claims to have retained from his childhood experience images of horror which he used in his fictional writing. In particular, there is the memory of the blank whites of the father's eyes, open wide while he urinated. This memory served, Bataille said, as a basis of imaginative transposition. Thus, in *Story of the Eye by Lord Auch*, the whites of the eye are transformed into egg whites and bull's testicles, and become associated with urination and death – specifically, the death of a matador, Granero, who was gored through the eye.

The horror which so often emerges in Bataille's fiction has its origin in the childhood memory of the slow and painful death of his father, and the periodic insanity of his mother. Whether this is true or not, Bataille's writing, both fictional and scientific, is often focused on horror and obscenity. In his book, *Eroticism*, for example, Bataille emphasises how the erotic is fundamentally a violation of the pure self; it is thus (unconsciously) linked with death. Similarly, in *The Tears of Eros* Bataille argues that the history of art shows that art has always been linked to horror. This is why it originated in caves, such as those discovered at Lascaux in France.

For some, Bataille's focus on, or even obsession with, horror and obscenity in his fiction and, to a lesser extent, in some of his key theoretical works, seems to echo a certain mental instability. This, at any rate, appears to have been the view of André Breton in the *Second Surrealist Manifesto* when he referred to Bataille as a 'case'.[1] And it is true that during 1927, and perhaps for longer, Bataille was in analysis with the liberal psychoanalyst, Dr Adrien Borel. Borel encouraged Bataille to put his obsessions on paper, and thereby gave a fillip to the writing career of his analysand.

Whether or not Bataille remained on the edge of insanity for much of his life – whether or not he was obsessed by horror and death – he has left an *oeuvre* which, it is now generally agreed, is of great theoretical profundity and intensity. For Bataille was indeed able to theorise the central themes of his obsessions; he was also able to bring his training in numismatics to bear in his intellectual enterprises – one of these being the creation of the ethnographic and art journal, *Documents*, edited by Bataille from 1929 to 1930. In 1946, Bataille established what was to become one of France's best-known journals: *Critique*. *Critique* presented the early work of Blanchot, Barthes, Foucault and Derrida to a wider audience.

Intellectually, Bataille attended the Reims Lycée. In 1913 he left to become a border at Epernay College where, in 1914, he gained his first *baccalauréat*. In 1915 he passed his second *baccalauréat*, and after being demobilised from military service in 1917, was admitted to the Ecole des Chartes in Paris, to study to be a Mediaevalist, from where he graduated in second place in 1922. In the same year, Bataille travelled to Madrid to attend the Ecole des Hautes Etudes Hispaniques. In 1923, he read Nietzsche and Freud for the first time, and in 1924 was appointed as a librarian to the Cabinet des Médailles at the Bibliothèque Nationale in Paris.

For Bataille, Nietzsche is a writer as much as a philosopher, first, because he does not exclude autobiography (whether fictive or not) from his philosophical writings, and second, because in refusing to lend his voice to any cause, he condemns himself to solitude. Nietzsche's philosophy becomes a cry in the wilderness. The very notion of 'cry', along with tears, anguish and laughter assumes a fundamental place in Bataille's own philosophical outlook. The cry is part of a series of terms which mark the presence of the horizontal axis (the axis of difference) in Bataille's thought. Bataille's own explanation of the horizontal axis is to be found in his 1930 essay, 'The pineal eye'. Vegetation, Bataille says there, occupies a position exclusively on the vertical axis, while animal life tends towards the horizontal axis, although animals strive to raise themselves up and so assume a certain literal verticality.

To capture the full force of the complex interaction between the horizontal and the vertical in Bataille's thought, we must consider Hegel's influence. Like a number of other important thinkers, Bataille learned his Hegel from Alexandre Kojève's idiosyncratic lectures on the *Phenomenology of Mind*, which he intermittently attended from 1933 to 1939. For Bataille, Hegel's system of Absolute knowledge, where even death is appropriated by consciousness, represents the end point of a kind of delirium of reason. The extreme point of illumination is so illuminating that it opens the way to a certain blindness, just as one can be blinded by looking directly into the sun, even though the sun is the source of illumination. Bataille's approach to Hegel had no doubt been anticipated in his 1930s article on Picasso, 'The rotten sun', where the myth of Icarus (who fell to the earth after flying so high because the sun had melted the wax of his wings) is used to illustrate the danger of too much enlightenment (illumination). Hegel, with his great idealist system, flies high, like Icarus. His philosophy would thus be the incarnation of the vertical axis, its most extreme manifestation, perhaps. But, Bataille says, there is a point of blindness in the Hegelian system: it is that total illumination hides the very real obscurity of non-knowledge, of a base materialism, of the madness that Hegel himself

feared was at hand in 1800 after the death of his father. What Hegel's system cannot state, let alone integrate, is that element in it which is equivalent to its own blindness, a blindness that foreshadows the fall of the all-seeing philosopher. Another way of putting it is to say that the Hegelian system, as the embodiment of the transcendental vertical axis, makes no room for horizontality. Just as the obelisk from Egypt, erected at Place de la Concorde in Paris in 1836, marks the place of the Revolutionary instrument of death – the guillotine – so Hegel's homogenising philosophical system hides a heterogeneous, material baseness.

A great deal of Bataille's writing is concerned with 'material baseness' – manifest in obscenity, in the case of his fiction, and in a series of practices, in the case of his theoretical writings. These practices open up the horizontal axis as the axis of sacrifice, loss, chance, and eroticism. We will briefly examine each of these in turn.

Bataille's concern to show how highly intellectual productions often conceal an unassimilable base element, led him to ethnographies of societies whose social bond seemed to be founded on practices quite horrific to a modern Western sensibility. Thus, in *The Accursed Share*,[2] the theorist of expenditure as excess argues that the magnificence of Aztec cultural artifacts has to be understood in conjunction with the practice of human sacrifice: the beautiful has to be linked to baseness. Wars provided the victims for the bloody ritual, where the priest would plunge an obsidian knife into the chest of the victim and pull out the still pulsating heart, which he would then offer to the sun, the supreme god of the Aztecs. Without in the least condoning Aztec sacrifice, Bataille shows that it does conform to a certain logic. In the first place, human sacrifice is a way of introducing disequilibrium into a society dominated by utilitarian exchange values. The degradation of utilitarian relations is embodied in slavery, where the slave is nothing but an object to be used by free people. The victim of Aztec sacrifice, by contrast, was often treated humanely, and even given special treatment; for there was an intimate link between the victim and captor. The victim in fact dies in the place of the executioner. He or she is their experience of death, an experience manifest in anguish as the executioners identify with the suffering of the victim. Sacrifice 'restores to the sacred world that which servile use has degraded, rendered profane'.[3] The sacred, then, lies beyond exchange-value; it has no equivalent: nothing, as a result, can be a substitute for the sacrificial act. In a society where exchange value has almost completely taken over, sacrifice cannot be understood. However, it still has an echo in bodily mutilation (such as Van Gogh's), where the act ruptures the homogeneity of self, and introduces heterogeneity into social life.

By a somewhat paradoxical turn, the rupture of sacrifice and mutilation turns into a moment of continuity. For the witness who experiences the anguish of identification with the victim also communicates this to others, and so establishes a continuity with others. As a result, 'the sacred is only a privileged moment of communal unity, a convulsive form of what is ordinarily stifled'.[4]

Closely linked with sacrifice and the sacred is the notion of loss. For Bataille, Marcel Mauss's theory of potlatch does not show that exchange is essentially a system of reciprocity. Rather, potlatch should be seen as an instance of the general economy where excess and luxury are the central aspects. The general economy is an economy of loss, disequilibrium, and expenditure without return. It cannot be analysed in terms of what Bataille calls the 'restricted' economy of production, equilibrium and balanced books: the economy of 'classical utility'. All forms of excess – which, by definition, do not have any equivalent – fall within the general economy. Excess and loss have no obvious function in social life; they stand for necessarily dysfunctional, heterogeneous elements.

In two texts in particular, Bataille discusses chance.[5] However, chance is more than a concept in his writing; it is also part of a practice. Thus Bataille's text on Nietzsche is also an analogue of chance, in the same way that Surrealism often aimed to be an analogue of madness.[6] The element of chance has to be included in any analysis of Bataille's practice of writing; for it is as a practice that chance fully assumes its place on the horizontal axis. To appreciate chance in Bataille's theoretical writings, we recall that, since Laplace, chance has often been thought of as a symptom of the limitedness of human knowledge. Chance, in short, would be subjective rather than objective in nature. Moreover, causality, and the accompanying notion of determination, has been assumed to be the very basis of scientific explanation. Knowledge has always made chance an exception. Only since quantum mechanics emerged in the 1920s has this view been superseded.

Three of Bataille's most important books – *Inner Experience*, *Guilty*, and *On Nietzsche* – were written between 1941 and 1944, that is, during the Occupation in France. Chance figures, first and foremost, analogically in each one. Each has the air of a journal – the air of contingency that comes from the admixture of a transcription of day-to-day events, and personal recollection. Thus the 'shape' of each text is fortuitous rather than predetermined. In his introduction to *Guilty*, Denis Hollier reiterates that what he is introducing is not really a book, 'Bataille isn't concerned with giving thoughts a systematic form or developing a story'.[7] There is, though, a certain logic informing Bataille's writing here, one based on a desire to indulge in a kind of play which would enable a glimpse of chance. In *On Nietzsche* this is made clearer: the book is partly a day-to-day narrative of 'dice throws'. Chance then becomes the truth of life; it is equivalent to the disequilibrium brought to the vertical axis. More strongly, chance is explicitly linked to anguish. Anguish, like chance, is an impossible obscurity. 'Anguish says: "impossible": the impossible remains at the *mercy of chance*.'[8] Furthermore: 'Anguish alone defines chance entirely: chance is what the anguish in me regards as impossible. Anguish is the contestation of chance.'[9] The cry, laughter, tears, excrement (the waste products of the system), poetry – all these give rise to chance. Chance cannot be integrated into any system, for it is the 'other' of system. This is why chance does not exist for Hegel. Chance is Nietzsche's *amor fati* (love of fate) which is opposed to the grand equilibrium of the Hegelian edifice. Chance is linked to sacrifice, because like the latter, it is also a rupture with identity and the utilitarian experience based on the determination of events.

In eroticism, human sexuality obtains its zenith as a (regulated) transgression of taboos.[10] Eroticism becomes, in Bataille's theory, a way to the continuity of being in death. As an individual, each person is discontinuous. Eroticism, as a violation of this discontinuity, is a fundamental source of anguish; for this is also the violation, or transgression, of interdictions; the interdiction is made known by the transgression. Eroticism thus confirms the rupture of boundaries and frontiers, and leads to a fusion of beings, a fusion giving rise to the communication of anguish based on a loss of integrity. The erotic impulse has, for this reason, been appropriated for religious ends. And so, instead of being the very antithesis of the sacred, eroticism – as an opening up to otherness – is its very foundation. Through tears, wounds, and the violation of boundaries, human beings are united. Eroticism, clearly, is located on the horizontal axis; however, a system of interdictions – the vertical axis – is the condition of possibility of this horizontality.

The thesis that progressively emerges from a reading of Bataille is that blindness is an essential element in knowledge – that the great heights of enlightenment are the correlate of the depths of non-knowledge and

obscene laughter. Seeing – theory – cannot grasp its other, as Denis Hollier has rightly suggested.[11] Bataille shows that seeing, and all theoretical work, entails a vital component: the intellectual energy needed to sustain it. Thus the exhaustion and fatigue to which Bataille's texts constantly refer finds its analogue in the relatively fragmentary nature of the *oeuvre*: in the bursts of poetry, the prolific number of occasional pieces, and the essay style. These indices of an expenditure of energy are perhaps the closest a reader can get to an analogue of his or her own blindness.

Notes

1 André Breton, *Second Surrealist Manifesto* in *Manifestoes of Surrealism*, trans. Richard Seaver and Helen R. Lane, Ann Arbor, University of Michigan Press, 1972, p. 184.
2 Georges Bataille, *The Accursed Share*, Vol. I, trans. Robert Hurley, New York, Zone Books, 1988.
3 ibid., p. 55.
4 Georges Bataille, 'The sacred' in *Visions of Excess. Selected Writings, 1927–1939*, trans. Allan Stoekl, Minneapolis, University of Minnesota Press, second printing 1986, p. 242.
5 See Georges Bataille, *Guilty*, trans. Bruce Boone, Venice, the Lapis Press, 1988, pp. 69–86, *On Nietzsche*, trans. Bruce Boone, New York, Paragon Press, 1992, *passim*.
6 See Elisabeth Roudinesco, *Jacques Lacan & Co. A History of Psychoanalysis in France, 1925–1985*, trans. Jeffrey Mehlman, Chicago, University of Chicago Press, 1990, p. 26.
7 Denis Hollier, 'A tale of unsatisfied desire', Introduction to Bataille, *Guilty*, p. vii.
8 Georges Bataille, 'Sur Nietzsche', *Oeuvres Complètes, VI*, Paris, Gallimard, 1973, p. 134. Bataille's emphasis. *On Nietzsche*, p. 114.
9 ibid.
10 See Georges Bataille, *Eroticism*, trans. Mary Dalwood, London and New York, Marion Boyars, 1987, reprinted 1990, pp. 63–70.
11 Denis Hollier, *Against Architecture: The Writings of Georges Bataille*, trans. Betsy Wing, Cambridge, Mass., MIT Press, 1989, pp. 87–8.

See also in this book

Baudrillard, Kristeva, Lévi-Strauss, Mauss

Bataille's major writings

Story of the Eye by Lord Auch (1928), trans. Joachim Neugroschal, Harmondsworth, Penguin Books, 1982. Reprinted 1986

Inner Experience (1943), trans. Leslie Anne Boldt, Albany, State University of New York Press, 1988

Guilty (1944), trans. Bruce Boone, Venice, The Lapis Press, 1988

On Nietzsche (1945), trans. Bruce Boone, New York, Paragon Press, 1992

The Impossible. A Story of Rats followed by Dianus and by The Oresteia (1947–62), trans. Robert Hurley, San Francisco, City Lights Books, 1991

The Accursed Share (1949), Vol. I, trans. Robert Hurley, New York, Zone Books, 1988

L'Abbé C (1950), Paris, Minuit, 1950

Blue of Noon (1957), trans. Harry Mathews, New York, Marion Boyars, 1986. Reprinted 1991

Eroticism (1957), trans. Mary Dalwood, London and New York, Marion Boyars, 1987 (reprinted 1990)

Literature and Evil (1957), trans. Alastair Hamilton, London, Marion Boyars, 1986

The Tears of Eros (1961), trans. Peter Connor, San Francisco, City Lights Books, 1989 (second printing 1990)

The Trail of Gilles de Rais (1965), documents presented by Georges Bataille, trans. Richard Robinson, Los Angeles, Amok, 1991

My Mother, Madame Edwarda, The Dead Man (1966, 1967) (three novels), trans. Astryn Wainhouse, New York, Marion Boyars, 1988

Visions of Excess. Selected Writings, 1927–1939, ed. Allan Stoekl, trans. Allan Stoekl, Carl R. Lovitt and Donald M. Leslie, Jr., Minneapolis, University of Minnesota Press, 1985. Second printing 1986

The College of Sociology, 1937–39, ed. Denis Hollier, trans. Betsy Wing, Minneapolis, University of Minnesota Press, 1988. Contains texts by Bataille and other participants in the College

Theory of Religion, trans. Robert Hurley, New York, 1989

Further reading

Gill, Carolyn (ed.), *Georges Bataille: Writing and the Sacred*, London and New York, Routledge, 1994

Hollier, Denis, *Against Architecture: The Writings of Georges Bataille*, trans. Betsy Wing, Cambridge, Mass., MIT Press, 1989

Lechte, John, 'Introduction to Bataille. The impossible as (a practice of) writing', *Textual Practice*, 7, 2 (Summer, 1993), pp. 173–94

Pefanis, Julian, *Heterology and the Postmodern: Bataille, Baudrillard, and Lyotard*, Sydney, Allen & Unwin, 1991

Plotnitsky, Arkady, *Reconfigurations: Critical Theory and General Economy*, Florida, University Press of Florida, 1993

Richman, Michèle, *Reading Georges Bataille: Beyond the Gift*, Baltimore, Johns Hopkins University Press, 1982

Stoekl, Allan, 'On Bataille', *Yale French Studies*, 78 (1990). Collection of articles on Bataille

GILLES DELEUZE

As Jean-Jacques Lecercle notes in his excellent book on philosophy and *délire*,[1] Gilles Deleuze's philosophical writing has progressed from works in the history of philosophy (works respectively on Hume, Nietzsche, Kant, Bergson, Spinoza), to works in critical philosophy and 'unconventional' literary criticism (*Différence et répétition*, *Logique du sens*, and, with Félix Guattari, two volumes of *Capitalism and Schizophrenia*, *Kafka*, and 'Rhizome'). Lecercle also remarks that Deleuze is, 'on the French philosophical scene, an outsider'[2] whose work has received little critical attention in France, largely because he 'has remained aloof from the master-disciple relationships in which so many of his colleagues are involved'.[3]

In English-speaking countries, by contrast, Deleuze, along with Michel Foucault and Jacques Derrida, is possibly one of the most cited of all contemporary French thinkers. This is all the more remarkable given that, unlike his counterparts, Deleuze has rarely travelled outside France to present his ideas. While it is true that he has rejected 'master-disciple relationships', Nietzsche's role in Deleuze's philosophical trajectory must also be acknowledged: if, like Nietzsche, Deleuze has few, if any, imitators, there is, nevertheless, a definite logic to this inimitable bearing: the logic of a thinker whose thought is radically horizontal.

Deleuze was born in 1925. He attended

the Lycée Carnot in Paris, and studied philosophy at the Sorbonne between 1944 and 1948, where he knew, among others, Michel Butor, Michel Tournier, and François Châtelet. His main teachers were Ferdinand Aliquié (Descartes specialist, and explicator of the philosophy of Surrealism), Georges Canguilhem (Foucault's supervisor), and Jean Hyppolite (Hegel specialist). After gaining his *agrégation* in philosophy in 1948, Deleuze taught philosophy, until 1957, in various *lycées*. From 1957 until 1960, he taught the history of philosophy at the Sorbonne, and for four years from 1960 he was a researcher with the Centre National de Recherche Scientifique (CNRS). From 1964 until his appointment in 1969, at the behest of Michel Foucault, as professor of philosophy at Vincennes, Deleuze taught at the University of Lyon. Also in 1969, Deleuze defended his major thesis, *Différence et répétition* and his minor thesis, *Spinoza et le problème de l'expression*. He retired from teaching in 1987.

Broadly speaking, the argument of *Différence et répétition* rests on the view that, in the contemporary era, the play of repetition and difference has supplanted that of the Same and representation. Difference and repetition are, in effect, indices of a move towards non-representational, and radically horizontal, thought; and Deleuze is the supreme practitioner of such thought. As we shall see, Deleuze's reading of Nietzsche offers a way into the labyrinth of horizontality. But before proceeding to this, let us note what is implied in saying that Deleuze's thought is radically horizontal. Although the terms 'horizontal' or 'vertical', or their variants (the Deleuzian term, 'rhizome' already evokes horizontality, but the latter is broader in scope), do not actually figure largely in any explicit sense in Deleuze's *oeuvre*, but that they tend to illuminate its structure, and thus have a certain explanatory power.

Radically horizontal thought can only be compared to other forms of thought with difficulty; for the means of translation are difficult to formulate. Such thought operates largely according to its own norms and concepts. Deleuze, significantly, has never, for this reason, embraced the history of philosophy as it has been conventionally defined by the discipline in France. For him, a philosopher who thinks (i.e. one who creates an event in thought), separates him or herself from the history of philosophy – enters the desert, in Nietzsche's terms. This radical horizontality, perhaps paradoxically, does not lead to an order of sameness (everyone on the same level), but to the instability of differences. Radical horizontality, then, is the quasi-order of radical difference, where a basis of comparison becomes problematic. Again, the horizontal axis does not entail the firming of boundaries between identities, as is the case with representational thought based on the Same, but leads instead to the permeability of all boundaries and barriers. This is why horizontal thought by-passes (it does not oppose) the vertical thought of everyday, bureaucratic hierarchy – the thought which entails the consolidation of identities.

In light of radical horizontality how then does Deleuze read Nietzsche? Does not the fact that he indeed reads Nietzsche (a philosopher of the canon, so to speak) mean that the idea of his being outside the history of philosophy is suspect? Two points of clarification need to be made here. First, Deleuze counts himself as a philosopher, and works with the material provided by the history (canon) of philosophy. To be a philosopher is to relate to the work of other philosophers. Second, Nietzsche is tangential to the history of philosophy, and Deleuze reads him in a particular way, emphasising the importance of the Nietzschean concepts of 'eternal return' and the 'will to power'.

While Deleuze's reading of Nietzsche is too complex to be fully explicated here, a number of points stand out. First among these is the fact that for Nietzsche – unlike for Hegel – 'origin' means a plurality of differences. This idea links up with Nietzsche's use of the notion of genealogy. A genealogy is the positing of forebears at a given moment in an effort to separate oneself from them. Thus Plato's idealism, Kant's critiques, and Hegel's dialectic are important for Nietzsche to the extent that his philosophy is a positive distancing from all of them, one achieved by means of a re-evaluation. More than an interpretation, then, genealogy for Nietzsche, Deleuze shows, is fundamentally an evaluation. Evaluation entails a distancing; distancing is the element of difference. Nietzsche needs the philosophers of the past only in the sense that a warrior needs a worthy enemy to confirm his prowess; there is thus nothing reverential about his use of the past. Deleuze argues that Nietzsche's thought is resolutely anti-dialectical and suspicious of all identities. The object against which the philosopher of difference pits himself is 'the hierarchy of forces' – or intensities – which express it. This hierarchy of forces is the object's value.[4] If the object for Nietzsche is always a play of forces, this means that in reality it is another subject – or rather: Nietzsche's philosophy begins to make the very distinction between subject and object problematic. Indeed, subject and object are metaphysical categories; they presuppose the notions of unity and identity. They are categories of a 'vertical' philosophy (like Hegel's). The singular aspect of all vertical philosophy is the separation in it of the truth of the concept from the reality to which it refers. Thus for Plato the concept 'good' is distinct from any material manifestation of the good; the world of appearance is deemed to be separate and distinct from the world of essence, or reality. By contrast, Deleuze's Nietzsche refuses these distinctions. For him, good and bad are values; there is no objective good, only subjective values – or, more rigorously, there are only values, that is, differences; the apparent, 'subjective' world is the only world there is. The vertical axis of objective truth is thus overturned by Nietzsche in favour of the horizontal axis of values. Deleuze is greatly attracted to this.

Horizontality in thought, inaugurated in the modern era by Nietzsche, opens the way to thought as creative, as a form of poetry, perhaps. And indeed, Nietzsche is not only a great stylist, but makes an excess of style a part of his philosophy. Deleuze notes that the great philosophers have always been great stylists. Style confirms the incomparable nature of the philosopher of difference. Style, too, turns philosophy into a practice, in the sense that there is no transcendental, philosopher-subject over and above the products of his philosophy – as there is no actor separate from his acts, or any cause separate from its effects. 'Subject', 'actor', and 'cause' are metaphysical notions characteristic of the vertical axis. The latter axis embodies what is entrenched and relatively unchanging, whereas the horizontal axis is always in movement.

Deleuze makes substantial use of the principle of horizontality in his readings of Spinoza, Proust, Leibniz, and Lewis Carroll. Thus for Spinoza 'expression' is not an appearance through which an essence is expressed. Nor is morality a set of ideals to which one might aspire. Expression is rather a way of being and acting in the world, while morality is 'an ethics of joy' which enhances the power of acting.[5] With Proust, the focus is on signs – not on signs as representations of objects, meanings, or truth, or – as one might have thought in the case of *Remembrance of Things Past* – on signs as vehicles for memory, but on signs as entities which teach something. In Proust's writing, to interpret signs is to go through a fundamental learning process, which, in the case of the work of art, shows that signs are linked to essences, and that essences are constituted through differences (they are not unities, but singular qualities) within which subjects are implicated. Again, Deleuze shows that when Leibniz invented the concept of the 'fold' in philosophy – a concept inspired by the

Baroque period in the history of art – he opened the way to a new practice of philosophy as the constitution of disjunctive figures. The fold is the mode of unity of these figures (e.g., the monad). More precisely, the fold is the relationship of difference with itself. Finally, the horizontal emerges in the reading of Lewis Carroll in a book – *The Logic of Sense* – constructed (or assembled) in series. Series can, by definition, proliferate; and, as Lecercle points out, 'proliferation is always a threat to order'.[6] The horizontal would thus be equivalent to the proliferation of series.

In his collaborative work with Felix Guattari, the principle of horizontality which marks Deleuze's own philosophy is strikingly evident in the critique of Freud and psychoanalysis. For Deleuze and Guattari, Freud's theory of the Oedipus complex serves to confirm the dominance of hierarchical and 'tree-like' thought. The Oedipus principle, they say, inevitably leads to the notion of an original event, or trauma, which the authors of *Anti-Oedipus* find unimaginatively reductive. Unlike Lacan, Deleuze and Guattari refuse the theory of desire founded on lack and, in effect, also reject Freud's concept of repression. For Freud, the very possibility of the distinction between subject and object depends on the notion of repression. Repression occurs in the process of the child's separation from the mother and its entry (as Lacan sees it) into the symbolic order – the order of the Law and the Name-of-the-Father. This 'father principle' – the principle of the origin as identity – is firmly rejected by our authors. For them, there is no distinction between the individual – defined by desire – and the collectivity – defined by the law; rather, there is only a social desire. As a result, desire is always in movement, always made up of different elements depending on the situation; it is machine-like, rather than an Oedipal theatre of representation. The phrases, 'desiring machines' and 'body without organs' reinforce the theory's horizontality. We have seen that desire is not

a desire based on lack – which is negative – but is always in movement and reforming itself: it is an affirmative process of flows and lines of flight. The 'body without organs' (the term is borrowed from Antonin Artaud) is, perhaps predictably, not at all an organic body (a body with organs, 'the body of Oedipal reduction'), but a body like the body politic, one that is always in the process of formation and deformation. The body without organs is produced in a connective synthesis, and is neither an image of the body, nor a projection. In short, the body without organs is 'rhizomatic' and not engendered, or tree-like.

Overall, there is no doubt that Deleuze is one of the most self-consciously creative philosophers of the contemporary era. Although he does in fact write from the position of someone who is steeped in the history of philosophy, his philosophy seems to have struck a democratic chord in many English-speaking countries. One wonders, though, whether the very radical pursuit of horizontality inspired by Nietzsche might not harbour its own kind of purity. For we seem to have, at least in Deleuze's more overtly political writings, a Nietzscheanism without reserve: Nietzsche's 'yes' is raised to the 'nth' degree, and 'no' is erased. In the rush to avoid repression and the negative in the interest of unfettered creativity, it is important to ask whether, as some psychoanalysts have suggested, the result of this creativity might be a decrease in war (organised vertically) but with an increase in the potential for violence. The very importance of Deleuze's philosophy demands that such an issue be fully investigated.

Notes

1 Jean-Jacques Lecercle, *Philosophy through the Looking-Glass: Language, Nonsense, Desire*, La Salle, Illinois, Open Court, 1985, p. 90.
2 ibid, p. 91.
3 ibid.
4 Gilles Deleuze, *Nietzsche and Philosophy*, trans. Hugh Tomlinson, New York, Columbia University Press, 1983, p. 8.

5 Gilles Deleuze, *Spinoza: Practical Philosophy*, trans. Robert Hurley, San Francisco, City Lights Books, 1988, p. 28.
6 Lecercle, *Philosophy through the Looking Glass*, p. 95.

See also in this book

Bataille, Freud, Lacan, Nietzsche

Deleuze's major writings

Empiricism and Subjectivity: An Essay on Hume's Theory of Human Nature (1953), trans. Constantin V. Boundas, New York, Columbia University Press, 1991
Nietzsche and Philosophy (1962), trans. Hugh Tomlinson, New York, Columbia University Press, 1983
Kant's Critical Philosophy: The Doctrine of the Faculties (1963) trans. Hugh Tomlinson and Barbara Habberjam, Minneapolis, University of Minnesota Press, 1984
Proust and Signs (1964 and 1970), trans. Richard Howard, New York, G. Braziller, 1972
Bergsonism (1966), trans. Hugh Tomlinson and Barbara Habberjam, New York, Zone Books, 1988
Expressionism in Philosophy: Spinoza (1968), trans. Martin Joughin, New York, Zone Books, 1990
Difference and Repetition (1969), trans. Paul Patton, London, The Athlone Press, 1994
The Logic of Sense (1969), trans. Mark Lester, edited by C.V. Boundas, New York, Columbia University Press, 1990
Anti-Oedipus: Capitalism and Schizophrenia (1972) (with Felix Guattari), trans. Robert Hurley, M. Seem and H.R. Lane, New York, Viking Press/A Richard Sever Book, 1977
Kafka: Toward a Minor Literature (1975) (with Felix Guattari), trans. Dana Polan, Minneapolis, University of Minnesota Press, 1986
Dialogues (1977) (with Claire Parnet), trans. Hugh Tomlinson and Barbara Habberjam, New York, Columbia University Press, 1987
A Thousand Plateaus: Capitalism and Schizophrenia (1980) (with Felix Guattari), trans. Brian Massumi, Minneapolis, University of Minnesota Press, 1987
Francis Bacon: The Logic of Sensation (1981), 2 vols, trans. Daniel Smith, Cambridge, Mass., MIT Press, 1992
Spinoza: Practical Philosophy (1981), trans. Robert Hurley, San Francisco, City Lights Books, 1988
Cinema 1: The Movement-Image (1983), trans. Hugh Tomlinson and Barbara Habberjam, Minneapolis, University of Minnesota Press, 1986
Cinema 2: The Time-Image (1985), trans. Hugh Tomlinson and Roberts Galeta, Minneapolis, University of Minnesota Press, 1989
The Fold: Leibniz and the Baroque (1988), trans. Tom Conley, Minneapolis, University of Minnesota Press, 1992
Interviews, 1972–1990 (1990), New York, Columbia University Press, 1994
Qu'est-ce que la philosophie? (with Felix Guattari), Paris, Minuit, 1991
Critique et clinique, Paris, Minuit, 1993
Constantin Boundas (ed.), *The Deleuze Reader* (contains, among others, selections from *Nietzsche and Philosophy*, *Difference and Repetition*, *Anti-Oedipus*, *A Thousand Plateaus*, *The Logic of Sense*, *Kafka*, as well as an excellent bibliography of Deleuze's works), New York, Columbia University Press, 1993

Further reading

Bogue, Ronald, *Deleuze and Guattari*, London and New York, Routledge, 1989
Boundas, C.V. and Olkowski, D. (eds), *Deleuze and the Theatre of Philosophy*, New York, Routledge, 1993
Burchell, Graham, 'Introduction to Deleuze', *Economy and Society*, 13 (1984), pp. 43–51
Hardt, Michael, *Gilles Deleuze: An Apprenticeship in Philosophy*, Minneapolis, University of Minnesota Press, 1993
Lecercle, Jean-Jacques, *Philosophy through the Looking Glass*, La Salle, Illinois, Open Court, 1985, pp. 86–117, and 160–97
Patton, Paul, 'Conceptual politics and the war-machine in *Mille Plateaux*', *Substance* (1984), 44/5, Vol. XIII, Nos 3–4, pp. 61–80

JACQUES DERRIDA

Recently, Jacques Derrida has added another edge to his work with a book on Marx. His deconstructive philosophy, he has said, has never been anti-Marxist in any simple sense. Thus many are now waiting, perhaps wrongly, in anticipation to see if there is indeed a political element in Derrida's grammatology.

Son of an Algerian Jewish family, Jacques Derrida was born in 1930 in Algeria and came to France in 1959. Educated at the Ecole Normale Supérieure (rue d'Ulm) in Paris, Derrida first came to the attention of a wider public at the end of 1965 when he published two long review articles on books on the history and nature of writing, in the Parisian journal, *Critique*.[1] These pieces formed the basis of Derrida's most important and possibly best-known book, *Of Grammatology*.

A number of important tendencies underlie Derrida's approach to philosophy, and, more specifically, to the Western tradition of thought. These are, first, a concern to reflect upon and undermine this tradition's dependence on the logic of identity. The logic of identity derives particularly from Aristotle and, in Bertrand Russell's words, comprises the following key features:

(1) *The law of identity*: 'Whatever is, is.'
(2) *The law of contradiction*: 'Nothing can both be and not be.'
(3) *The law of excluded middle*: 'Everything must either be or not be.'[2]

These 'laws' of thought not only presuppose logical coherence, they also allude to something equally profound and characteristic of the tradition in question, namely, that there is an essential reality – an origin – to which these laws refer. To sustain logical coherence, this origin must be 'simple' (i.e. free of contradiction), homogeneous (of the same substance, or order), present to, or the same as itself (i.e. separate and distinct from any mediation, conscious of itself without any gap between the origin and consciousness). Clearly, these 'laws' imply the exclusion of certain features, to wit: complexity, mediation, and difference – in short, features evoking 'impurity', or complexity. This process of exclusion takes place at a general, metaphysical level, one, moreover, at which a whole system of concepts (sensible–intelligible; ideal–real; internal–external; fiction–truth; nature–culture; speech–writing, activity–passivity, etc.) governing the operation of thought in the West, come to be instituted.

Through the approach called 'deconstruction', Derrida has begun a fundamental investigation into the nature of the Western metaphysical tradition and its basis in the law of identity. Superficially, the results of this investigation seem to reveal a tradition riddled with paradox and logical aporias – such as the following one from Rousseau's philosophy.

Rousseau argues at one point that the voice of nature alone should be listened to. This nature is identical to itself, a plenitude to which nothing can be added or subtracted. But he also draws our attention to the fact that nature is in truth sometimes lacking – such as when a mother cannot produce enough milk for the infant at her breast. Lack now comes to be seen as common in nature, if it is not one of its most significant characteristics. Thus self-sufficient nature, Derrida shows,[3] is, according to Rousseau, *also* lacking. Lack in fact endangers nature's self-sufficiency – that is, its identity, or, as Derrida prefers, its self-presence. Nature's self-sufficiency can only be maintained if the lack is supplemented. However, in keeping with the logic of identity, if nature requires a supplement it cannot also be self-sufficient (identical with itself); for self-sufficiency and lack are opposites: one or other can be the basis of an identity, but not both if contradiction is to be avoided. This example is not an exception. The impurity of this identity, or the undermining of self-presence is in fact inescapable. For more generally, every apparently 'simple' origin has, as its very condition of possibility, a non-origin. Human beings require the mediation of consciousness, or the mirror of language, in order to know themselves and the world; but this mediation or mirror (these impurities) have to be excluded from the process of knowledge; they make knowledge possible, and yet are not included in the knowledge process. Or if they are, as in the philosophy of the phenomenologists, they themselves (consciousness, subjectivity, language) become equivalent to a kind of self-identical presence.

The process of 'deconstruction' which investigates the fundamentals of Western thought, does not do so in the hope that it will be able to remove these paradoxes or these contradictions; nor does it claim to be able to escape the exigencies of this tradition and set up a system on its own account. Rather, it recognises that it is forced to use the very concepts it sees as being unsustainable in terms of the claims made for them. In short, it, too, must (at least provisionally) sustain these claims.

The impetus of deconstruction is not simply to show that, philosophically, the 'laws' of thought are found to be wanting. Rather, the tendency evident in Derrida's *oeuvre* is a concern to generate effects, to open up the philosophical terrain so that it might continue to be the site of creativity and invention. The notion of difference, or *différance*, perhaps leads to the second most clearly discernible tendency in Derrida's work – one closely aligned with the desire to maintain the creativeness of philosophy.

Différance is a term Derrida coined in 1968 in light of his researches into the Saussurian and structuralist theory of language. While Saussure had gone to great pains to show that language in its most general form could be understood as a system of differences, 'without positive terms', Derrida noted that the full implications of such a conception were not appreciated by either latter-day structuralists, or Saussure himself. Difference without positive terms implies that this dimension in language must always remain unperceived, for strictly speaking, it is unconceptualisable. With Derrida, difference becomes the proto-type of what remains outside the scope of Western metaphysical thought because it is the latter's very condition of possibility. Of course, in everyday life people readily speak about difference and differences. We say, for instance, that 'x' (having a specific quality) is different from 'y' (which has another specific quality), and we usually mean that it is possible to enumerate the qualities which make up this difference.

This, however, is to give difference *positive* terms – implying that it can have a phenomenal form – so it cannot be the difference Saussure announced, one that is effectively unconceptualisable. The first reason for Derrida's neologism thus becomes apparent: he wants to distinguish the conceptualisable difference of common sense from a difference that is not brought back into the order of the same and, through a concept, given an identity. Difference is not an identity; nor is it the difference between two identities. Difference is difference deferred (in French the same verb (*différer*) means both 'to differ' and 'to defer'). *Différance* alerts us to a series of terms given prominence in Derrida's work whose structure is inexorably double: pharmakon (both poison and antidote); supplement (both surplus and necessary addition); hymen (both inside and outside).

Another justification for Derrida's neologism also derives from Saussure's theory of language. Writing, Saussure had said, is secondary to the speech *spoken* by the members of the linguistic community. Writing for Saussure is even a deformation of language in the sense that it is (through grammar) taken to be a true representation of it, whereas, in fact, the essence of language is only contained, Saussure claimed, in *living* speech, which is always changing. Derrida interrogates this distinction. As with difference, he notices that both Saussure and the structuralists (cf. Lévi-Strauss) operate with a colloquial notion of writing, one that attempts to evacuate all complexities. Thus writing is assumed to be purely graphic, an aid to memory perhaps, but secondary to speech; it is deemed to be fundamentally phonetic, and so represents the sounds of language. Speech, for its part, is assumed to be closer to thought, and thus to the emotions, ideas, and intentions of the speaker. Speech as primary and more original thus contrasts with the secondary, representative status of writing. Derrida, the grammalogist (theorist of writing), endeavours to show that this distinction is unsustainable. The very term *différance*, for example, has an irreducibly graphic element which cannot be detected at the level of the voice. In addition, the claim that phonetic writing is entirely phonetic, or that speech is entirely auditory becomes suspect as soon as the exclusively graphic nature of punctuation becomes apparent, together with the unpresentable silences (spaces) of speech.

One way or another, the whole of Derrida's *oeuvre* is an exploration of the nature of writing in the broadest sense as *différance*. To the extent that writing always includes pictographic, ideographic, and phonetic elements, it is not identical with itself. Writing, then, is always impure and, as such, challenges the notion of identity, and ultimately the notion of the origin as 'simple'. It is neither entirely present nor absent, but is the trace resulting from its own erasure in the drive towards transparency. More than this, writing is in a sense more 'original' than the phenomenal forms it supposedly evokes. Writing as trace, mark, grapheme becomes the precondition of all phenomenal forms. This is the sense implicit in the chapter in *Of Grammatology* entitled 'The end of the book and the beginning of writing'. Writing in the strictest sense, this chapter shows, is virtual, not phenomenal; it is not what is produced, but what makes production possible. It evokes the whole field of cybernetics, theoretical mathematics and information theory.[4]

In meditations on themes from literature, art and psychoanalysis, as well as from the history of philosophy, part of Derrida's strategy is to make visible the 'impurity' of writing (and any identity). That is to say, Derrida often demonstrates what he is attempting to confirm philosophically by employing rhetorical, graphic, and poetic strategies (as, for example, in *Glas* or *The Post Card: From Socrates to Freud and Beyond*) so that the reader might become alerted to the blurring of boundaries between disciplines (such as philosophy and litera-

ture), and subject-matter (as with writing/philosophy and autobiography). At the first extended presentation of *différance* at the Sorbonne in 1968, an astute listener remarked, albeit with some regret, that, 'In your work, the expression is so important that the attention of the listener is constantly divided and directed, on the one hand, to your way of talking, and on the other, to what you want to say.'

Derrida responded by saying, 'I try to place myself at a certain point at which . . . the thing signified is no longer easily separable from the signifier.'[5]

The demonstration that it is impossible rigorously to separate the poetic-cum-rhetorical dimension of the text (the level of the signifier) from the 'content', message or meaning (the level of the signified) is the most necessary and yet controversial move in the whole Derridean enterprise. While a significant number of American literary critics seem to have been highly enamoured of this strategy, one may indeed wonder about the extent to which such a strategy *can* be under the (conscious) control of the philosopher. If discipline and genre boundaries *are* conventions with quite specific histories – that is, by implication, if they are only set up on the basis of a kind of trust – it becomes possible to subvert them. What is then being subverted is in fact a relatively fragile working principle, and not a deeply entrenched, essential truth of some kind. With the work of Laclau (who has been inspired by Derrida) in political theory, it is exactly this fragility of identity that is seen to give a new fillip to politics. Because identities are constructed and not essential, they are inevitably fragile, but no less important for all that.

From another angle, Derrida's work opens up a new creativity, a sense in which the concern for writing as grammatology has *practical* effects. Here, we recall that Derrida shows that eternal, metaphysical principles have an extremely fragile and ultimately ambiguous basis. What is right and 'proper' (like the proper noun) because it has a fixed identity, in the end gives rise to a deconstruction of the 'proper' (for instance, a name does not simply refer to a simple, 'real' or phenomenal object or person; for it also has a rhetorical dimension, one that punning makes visible). When a proper name is shown to be 'im'-proper writing in Derrida's sense emerges. The name of the French poet, F. Ponge (which, in a well-known essay, Derrida makes into *éponge* (sponge)), provides an admirable source of creative philosophical and critical writing. In English, one only need think of *Word*sworth and the 'joy' in Joyce for a whole series of 'improper' associations to begin. Through pun, anagram, etymology, or any number of diacritical features (recall the 'joy' of Joyce), a proper name can be connected to one or more different systems of concepts, ideas, or words (including those of other languages). Derrida has in fact also connected the proper name to varying series of images and sounds so that, from one point of view, the reference text appears to have a very tangential relationship to the critical text (see the treatment of the work of Jean Genet in *Glas*; or the essay, *Signéponge* 'on' the work of Francis Ponge). Indeed, whereas the traditional literary critic might tend to search for the truth (whether semantic, poetic or ideological) of the literary text written by another, and then adopt a respectful, secondary role before the 'primacy' of this text, Derrida turns the 'primary' text into a source of new inspiration and creativity. Now the critic/reader no longer simply interprets (which was never entirely the case anyway), but becomes a writer in his or her own right.

Again, while common sense tends to assume that iterability is a more or less accidental quality of language, so that words, phrases, sentences, etc. can be repeated in different contexts, it is in fact the very quality which Derrida says irrevocably detaches the level of the signifier from the signified. Thus, if meaning is related to context, there is, with respect to the very structure of language, no proper context to provide proof of a final meaning. Context is unbounded, as Jonathan Culler has said. Derrida's debate, with the American philosopher, John R. Searl, about J.L. Austin's theory of 'performatives', turns precisely on this point. While Austin tried to make a felicitous performative (doing by saying – as when making a promise) depend upon its being realized in the proper context by the proper person, an infelicitous performative – as when somebody says, 'I do' outside the marriage ceremony, or when the wrong person opens a meeting – cannot be eliminated from language. This is so, Derrida notes, because infelicity is embedded in the performative's very structure: the quality of iterability means that language – including signatures – can be taken over by anyone at any time. Iterability thus entails the possibility of forged signatures.

In sum, Derrida's philosophical enterprise claims to deconstruct pervasive shibboleths as these occur in both academic work and in the language of everyday life. Everyday language is not neutral; it bears within it the presuppositions and cultural assumptions of a whole tradition. At the same time, the critical reworking of the philosophical basis of the tradition in question results, perhaps unexpectedly, in a new emphasis on the individual autonomy and creativeness of the researcher/philosopher/reader. Maybe this anti-populist yet anti-Platonic element in grammatology is Derrida's most important contribution to the thought of the post-war era.

Notes

1 See Jacques Derrida, 'De la grammatologie (I)', *Critique*, 223 (December 1965), pp. 1016–42; and 'De la grammatologie (II)', *Critique*, 224 (January 1966), pp. 23–53.

2 Bertrand Russell, *The Problems of Philosophy*, London, New York, Oxford University Press, reprinted 1973, p. 40.

3 Jacques Derrida, *Of Grammatology*, trans. Gayatri Chakravorty Spivak, Baltimore and London, Johns Hopkins University Press, 1976, p. 145.

4 ibid., p. 9.
5 David Wood and Robert Bernasconi (eds),
   Derrida and 'Différance' Evanston,
   Northwestern University Press, 1988, p. 88.

See also in this book

Joyce, Laclau, Lévi-Strauss, Saussure

Derrida's major writings

Speech and Phenomena and Other Essays on Husserl's Theory of Signs (1967), trans. David B. Allison, Evanston, Northwestern University Press, 1973

Of Grammatology (1967), trans. Gayatri Chakravorty Spivak, Baltimore and London, Johns Hopkins University Press, 1976

Writing and Difference (1967), trans. Alan Bass, Chicago, University of Chicago Press, 1978

Positions (1972), trans. Alan Bass, Chicago, Chicago University Press, Phoenix edition, 1982

Dissemination (1972), trans. Barbara Johnson, Chicago, Chicago University Press, 1981

Margins of Philosophy (1972), trans. Alan Bass, Chicago, Chicago University Press, 1982

Glas (1974), trans. John P. Leavey Jr and Richard Rand, Lincoln, University of Nebraska Press, 1986

The Truth in Painting (1978), trans. Geoff Bennington and Ian McLeod, Chicago, Chicago University Press, 1987

Spurs: Nietzsche's Styles = Eperons, Les styles de Nietzsche (1978) (English and French), trans. Barbara Harlow, Chicago, University of Chicago Press, 1979

The Post Card: From Socrates to Freud and Beyond (1980), trans. Alan Bass, Chicago, University of Chicago Press, 1987

Signéponge = Signsponge (English and French), trans. Richard Rand, New York, Columbia University Press, 1984

Psyché: inventions de l'autre, Paris, Galilée, 1987

'Some statements and truisms . . .' in David Carroll (ed.), *The States of Theory*, New York, Columbia University Press, 1989

Heidegger et la question, Paris, Flammarion: Champs, 1990

L'autre cap, Paris, Minuit, 1991

Spectres de Marx. L'Etat de la dette, le travail du deuil et la nouvelle internationale, Paris, Galilée, 1993

Further reading

Bennington, Geoffrey (with Jacques Derrida), *Jacques Derrida*, Paris, Seuil, 1991. English translation by Geoffrey Bennington, Chicago, Chicago University Press, 1993

Gasché, Rodolphe, *Tain of the Mirror: Derrida and the Philosophy of Reflection*, Cambridge, Mass., Harvard University Press, 1986

Norris, Christopher, *Derrida*, London, Fontana, 1987

Ulmer, Gregory, *Applied Grammatology: Post(e)-Pedagogy from Jacques Derrida to Joseph Beuys*, Baltimore and London, Johns Hopkins University Press, 1985

MICHEL FOUCAULT

Born in Poitiers in 1926, Michel Foucault was awarded his *agrégation* at the age of 25, and in 1952 obtained a diploma in psychology. During the 1950s, he worked in a psychiatric hospital, and in 1955 taught at the University of Uppsala in Sweden. His first major book, *Folie et déraison: Histoire de la folie à l'âge classique* (Madness and Unreason: History of Madness in the Classical Age) was published in 1961 after having been presented as a *doctorat d'état*, supervised by Georges Canguilhem, in 1959. He died from an AIDS-related illness in 1984.

In April 1970, Foucault was elected to the chair of 'history of systems of thought' at the Collège de France. The résumé of his first course called 'The will to truth' – professed there in 1970–1 – speaks of 'discursive practices', and says, *inter alia*:

Now these groups of regularities [in discursive practices] do not coincide with individual works. Even if they appear through them, even if they happen to become evident for the first time in one of them, they extend substantially beyond them and often unite a considerable number. But they do not necessarily coincide either with what we habitually call sciences or disciplines, although their boundaries can sometimes be provisionally the same.[1]

Foucault's explanation illustrates the innovative and often strikingly individual character of his work. Thus in the passage quoted, he alludes to the thesis presented in *The Archaeology of Knowledge* that we cannot reduce 'discursive practices' to the familiar categories of individual *oeuvre*, or academic discipline. Rather, a discursive practice is the regularity emerging in the very fact of its articulation: it is not prior to this articulation. The systematicity of discursive practices is neither of a logical nor linguistic type. The regularity of discourse is unconscious and occurs at the level of Saussure's *parole*, and not at the level of a pre-existing *langue*.

Rather than study movements in thought in the manner of the History of Ideas – where the ideas would be prior to the material being studied – or the way ideologies or theories *express* material conditions, Foucault analyses 'regimes of practices'. Or, because the line between saying and doing – as between seeing and speaking – is always unstable (the division itself always changing), 'regimes of practices' cannot be reduced to an ahistorical form of doing, or practice, any more than saying can be reduced to the realm of theory. Put another way, Foucault's histories, inspired by Nietzsche's anti-idealism, endeavour to avoid 'projecting "meaning" into history'.[2] And in this regard, even the notion of cause is suspect – like the actor behind the act. The famous last paragraph of *The Order of Things: An Archaeology of the Human Sciences* confirms this point by speaking of man, the actor, being erased, 'like a face drawn in sand at the edge of the sea'.[3] All we have are material effects and material acts; there is no essential meaning to things – no essential subject behind action; nor is there an essential order to history. Rather, order is the writing of history itself. Foucault's books, *The Order of Things*, and *The Archaeology of Knowledge* are the outcome of just such a Nietzschean approach to the history of knowledge. A new map is drawn up: practices become modes of thought with 'their logic, their strategy, their evidence, their reason'.

Before giving a brief review of some of Foucault's major works, it is important, for a fuller appreciation of Foucault's originality, to clarify five interconnected, key terms. These are: the present, genealogy, epistemology, discontinuity, and technology (technique).

Because, as Nietzsche showed, there is no intrinsically important area or problem in history, but only areas of material interest, the historian is always taken up by what is of interest at the present moment, at a given conjuncture. History, therefore, is always written from the perspective of the present; history fulfils a need of the present. The present offers up problems to be studied historically – the rise of structuralism in the 1960s, or the disturbances in prisons in the early 1970s, are cases in point, and gave rise, respectively, to Foucault's *The Order of Things* (1966) and *Discipline and Punish: The Birth of the Prison* (1975).

If the present determines the historian's themes of interest, will there not be a danger of the past becoming a more or less inevitable lead up to the present? Foucault's response is that this is a danger exacerbated by idealism. History is only a lead up to the present if the notion of cause is allowed to predominate over (material) effect, and if continuity is allowed to override the discontinuities that the level of practices reveal. In addition, however, the fact that the present is always in a process of transformation means that the past must be continually re-evaluated; to write a history of the past is to see it anew, just as the analysand sees anew events of his or her individual biography in light of the experience of psychoanalysis. The past, in short, takes on new meanings in light of new events. This precludes the possibility of any simple relationship of causality being proposed between past and present. The danger of historicism recedes when it is realised that no past era can be understood purely in its own terms, given that history is, in a sense, always a history of the present.

Closely connected to the notion of the

present and the continual re-evaluation of the past is the notion of genealogy. Genealogy is the history written in light of current concerns. Genealogy is history written in accordance with a commitment to the issues of the present moment, and as such it intervenes in the present moment. Genealogy, in short, is 'effective history' (Nietzsche) written as a current intervention.

Inspired by Bachelard, Canguilhem and Cavaillès, Foucault recognises that if history is always genealogy and an intervention, frameworks of knowledge and modes of understanding are themselves always changing. Epistemology studies these changes as the 'grammar' of knowledge production and is revealed by the practice of science, philosophy, art, and literature. Epistemology is also a way of connecting material events to thought or ideas. That a particular practice embodies an idea is not self-evident; the connection has to be made evident within the practice of epistemology. Even in Foucault's later work this remains important, as the following passage from his history of sexuality demonstrates:

Thought, ... is not, then, to be sought only in theoretical formulations such as those of philosophy or science; it can and must be analysed in every manner of speaking, doing, or behaving in which the individual appears and acts as subject of learning, as ethical or juridical subject, as subject conscious of himself and others.[4]

With regard to technology or technique, so important in Foucault's later work, inspiration seems to have been derived from Mauss, although there is hardly a specific reference to Mauss in Foucault's writings. For Mauss, there was virtually no form of human action that was not embodied in a framework of repetition. Even spitting, Mauss showed, was, in this sense, a technique. Mauss thus gave precedence to technique over contingency in understanding human action, and he called techniques of the body a 'technology without instruments'.

A regularity of actions can emerge as a technique which is so much taken for granted that it seems not to have been learned. Foucault, in his analyses of power in particular, is concerned to reveal the unacknowledged regularity of actions which is the mark of a technique. And, towards the end of his life, he moved on to talk about the 'technologies of the self'. As a technology, techniques can be transferred across different sets of practices, as forms of bodily discipline demonstrate. Let us now turn to a review of some of Foucault's most important texts.

The title of Foucault's major thesis, *Folie et déraison: Histoire de la folie à l'âge classique*, defended in May 1961, is a reminder that the Classical Age – the age of Descartes – is also the Age of Reason. For his part, Foucault endeavours to show how Descartes, in the 'First Meditation', excludes madness from hyperbolic doubt: Descartes can doubt everything except his own sanity. Foucault wants to find out what madness and unreason could be in the age of Descartes, and why the difference between them was such an issue. Or, as a much later formulation would have it, he wanted to study the way the division between madness and reason is established. Reason and madness are thus presented as the outcome of historical processes; they do not exist as universally objective categories. For some, such an approach appears too relativistic. By the same token, it also provides the opportunity to come to grips with a much more complex and subtle approach to historical events.

More specifically, Foucault proceeds to map the way that the mad person, who was not confined in any institution before 1600, comes to assume, by the middle of the seventeenth century, the status of excluded person *par excellence* – the position previously occupied by the leper. In the fifteenth century mad people were wanderers, as immortalised in Sébastian Brant's poem, *Stulifera navis* ('Ship of Fools', 1497) and in Hieronymous Bosch's painting of the same name inspired by Brant's poem. Moreover, the theme of madness emerged generally in literature and iconography because the mad person was seen as a source of truth, wisdom, and criticism of the existing political situation. In the Renaissance, madness occupies a grand place: it is 'an experience in the field of language, an experience where man was confronted with his moral truth, with the rules proper to his nature and his truth'.[5] Madness here has its own form of reason and is seen as a general characteristic of human beings. Unreasonable reason, and reasonable unreason could exist side by side.

With the Classical Age (the seventeenth and eighteenth centuries), madness is reduced to silence; or rather, it has no voice of its own but exists confusedly in supposedly anti-social figures such as the libertine, the homosexual, the debauched person, the dissipater, or the magician. These are the people confined in hospitals, workhouses, and prisons. Similarly, seventeenth- and eighteenth-century thought defines fury – which includes both criminal and insane behaviour – as 'unreason'. Not only does the figure of madness change between the Renaissance and the Classical Age, but so too do society's strategies for dealing with it. We are still a long way from anything like a medical conception of madness. Until the nineteenth century, madness, or insanity, was more a police matter than a medical matter. Mad people were not judged to be ill. Thus there is no basis, Foucault argues, for researching the antecedents of the treatment of the mentally ill in the history of psychiatry or, more generally, in the history of medicine. Rather, historical discontinuities are revealed – first, between the Renaissance view of madness and the view of the Classical Age, which reduced it to unreason and so to silence; and, second, between the Classical Age and the nineteenth-century medicalisation of madness as mental illness. Discontinuity (between eras) thus predominates in the history of madness.

Although mad people were confined from the beginning of the seventeenth century (the formation of the *Hôpital général* in 1656 being a key event here), and although medicine in the modern era gradually moved into the asylum to treat the mentally ill, the asylum had fundamentally changed by the time Tuke and Pinel came to carry out their reforms at the end of the eighteenth century. Medicine and internment thus came closer to each other, not because of some great medical discovery, but because of two indirectly related factors: a greater concern for individual rights in the wake of the French Revolution, and the transformation of the asylum into a space of therapeutic practices, instead of being a uniquely punitive institution.

As the wave of structuralist enthusiasm began to subside in the 1970s, discourse began to figure less prominently in Foucault's work and 'technology' in relation to power and the body began to take its place. Two aspects of Foucault's theory of power become evident in his two major books of the 1970s. These are: power as it relates to knowledge and the body in punishment and sexuality, and power understood as being distinct from the philosophico-juridical framework of the Enlightenment, and its emphasis on representative government. Briefly: power ceases to have any substantive content; rather than being possessed and centralised, it comes to be seen as a technology.

Discipline and Punish presents two images of the body of the condemned: the tortured and publicly mutilated body of the would-be regicide, Damiens, and the disciplined body of the prisoner in his cell, a prisoner secretly under the threat of constant surveillance. As with the history of madness, Foucault argues that it is not possible to separate the birth of the prison as the main form of legal punishment in the nineteenth century, from the history of a range of institutions – such as the army, the factory and the school – which emphasised the disciplining of the body through techniques of real or perceived surveillance. Not the good will and humanity of reformers and changes to the criminal law, but the emergence of a disciplinary society and a consequent new articulation of power gave rise to the prison.

The figure which most accurately captures the structure of the post-eighteenth-century articulation of power is, says Foucault, Jeremy Bentham's Panoptican. It allows for the invisible surveillance of a large number of people by a relatively small number. Like madness, legal punishment has a varied and unstable history which depends not only on perceptions of the criminal, but also on the changes engendered by the emergence of institutions dealing with the formation of a knowledge of individuals. Knowledge is thus linked to power, and the prison becomes a tool of knowledge.

More theoretically, perhaps, the first volume of the history of sexuality again analyses the link between power and knowledge. There, the juridico-philosophical conception – which sees power as essentially repressive, and thus as essentially negative and to be avoided – is presented as belonging to the era of the Enlightenment. Now, says Foucault, power is dispersed throughout society (it is not possessed by anyone) and it has positive effects. The persistence of the juridical definition of power as centralised and possessed, means that the king's head is still to be cut off. Just as power has no substantive content, sex has not been repressed. Instead, historical research shows that there has been a veritable explosion in discourses about sexuality and sexual activity. Thus, theories claiming to explain historical events are to be distinguished from actual events. Again, a meticulous genealogical approach discovers that theories – rather than explaining practices – are themselves part of practices situated in a specific historical era.

Foucault's last works on the history of sexuality turned to Ancient Greece and the way that sexuality there was part of a whole network of practices (moral, political, economic) fundamental to the production, government and care of the self. Here, the history of subjectivity is Foucault's explicit

concern; but the approach adopted – the meticulous analysis of texts – recalls *The Order of Things* where subjectivity is the outcome of discursive practices. *The Use of Pleasure* shows how pleasure (sexual and other), although a legitimate part of the Greek social system, is, nevertheless, a source of tension – especially in the play of social relations between superiors and inferiors. The greatest amount of pleasure derives from the full realisation of one's social position in sexuality; pleasure is thus not the outcome of transgression, or illicit conduct, as it was to become in Christianity, but is realisable in marriage.

The Greeks also linked pleasure and individual freedom to the control over the self in one's regulated relations with others. In *The Care of the Self*, Foucault analyses the notion of self-control and outlines the way that the Greeks devoted much effort to developing various systems of rules to be applied to a great variety of conducts – not the least of these being sexual conduct. Without carrying out work upon the self – leading to ever greater self-control – access to both pleasure and truth become quite limited. For a life dominated by the care of the self, excess, rather than deviance, is the danger; not sex outside marriage, but too much inside it, is the problem.

Foucault's history thus presents another face of pleasure: pleasure through regulation and self-discipline instead of through libertine, or permissive conduct. With regard to sexuality, the Greek world is now discontinuous with the Christian world, and another received idea is shattered.

Notes

1 Michel Foucault, *Résumé des cours, 1970–1982*, Paris, Julliard, 1989, p. 10.
2 Friedrich Nietzsche, *The Will to Power*, trans. Walter Kaufmann, New York, Vintage Books, 1968, sect. 1011, p. 523.
3 Michel Foucault, *The Order of Things: An Archaeology of the Human Sciences*, trans. from the French, New York, Vintage Books, 1973, p. 387.

4 Michel Foucault, Preface to *The History of Sexuality*, Vol. II, trans. William Smock in Paul Rabinow (ed.), *Foucault Reader*, New York, Pantheon Books, 1984, pp. 334–5. This is clearly a translation of an earlier version of what would become the Introduction to *The History of Sexuality*, Vol. II.

5 Michel Foucault, *Histoire de la folie à l'âge classique* (1961), Paris, Gallimard: TEL, 1972, p. 39.

See also in this book

Bachelard, Braudel, Canguilhem, Cavaillès, Mauss, Nietzsche, Saussure

Foucault's major writings

Mental Illness and Psychology (1954 and 1962), trans. Alan Sheridan, New York, Harper & Row, 1976

Folie et déraison. Histoire de la folie à l'âge classique, Paris, Plon, 1961

Histoire de la folie à l'âge classique, Paris, Gallimard: TEL, 1972

Madness and Civilization: A History of Insanity in the Age of Reason (1961) (abridged), trans. Richard Howard, New York, Vintage/Random House, 1973

The Birth of the Clinic: An Archaeology of Medical Perception (1963), trans. A.M. Sheridan-Smith, New York, Vintage Books, 1975

Raymond Roussel, Paris, Gallimard, 1963

The Order of Things: An Archaeology of the Human Sciences (1966), trans. from the French, New York, Vintage, 1973

The Archaeology of Knowledge (1969), trans. A.M. Sheridan-Smith, London, Tavistock, 1974

'Orders of discourse' (1971), *Social Science Information*, 10, 2 (April 1971)

Discipline and Punish: The Birth of the Prison (1975), trans. Alan Sheridan, London, Allen Lane, 1977

The History of Sexuality, Volume 1: An Introduction (1976), trans. Robert Hurley, London, Allen Lane, 1979

The History of Sexuality, Volume 2: The Use of Pleasure (1984), trans. Robert Hurley, New York, Pantheon, 1985

The History of Sexuality, Volume 3: The Care of the Self (1984), trans. Robert Hurley, New York, Pantheon, 1986

Further reading

Cousins, Mark and Hussain, Althar, *Michel Foucault*, London, Macmillan, 1984 (reprinted 1990)

Dreyfus, Hubert L., and Rabinow, Paul, *Michel Foucault: Beyond Structuralism and Hermeneutics*, Brighton, Harvester Press, 1982

Martin, Luther H., Gutman, Huck and Hutton, Patrick H., *Technologies of the Self: A Seminar with Michel Foucault*, London, Tavistock, 1988

Morris, Meaghan and Patton, Paul, *Michel Foucault: Power, Truth, Strategy*, Sydney, Feral Publications, 1979

O'Farrell, Clare, *Foucault*, Basingstoke, Macmillan, 1990

EMMANUEL LEVINAS

In her biography of Jean-Paul Sartre, Annie Cohen-Solal relates that because the subject of her book had, by 1930, developed a kinship with phenomenology, 'he bought a recent book by Emmanuel Levinas, *Théorie de l'intuition dans la phénoménologie de Husserl*, eagerly leafed through it, constantly recognizing his own thoughts in its pages'.[1] Such would be the way that the person to become one of France's most influential philosophers was himself indebted to the scholar of phenomenology, Emmanuel Levinas. Of equal importance is the way Levinas has also influenced a later generation of thinkers – people such as Blanchot, Derrida, Irigaray, and Lyotard. Of particular interest to the later generation has been Levinas's rethinking of the concept and reality of the Other (*Autrui*). In ethics, as we shall see, Levinas has said that he is concerned with the Other, 'prior to any act'.[2]

Levinas was born into a Jewish family in Kovno in Lithuania in 1906. As his parents saw their future belonging to the Russian language and literature rather than to the Lithuanian language, the young Emmanuel came to read both Russian and Hebrew. Lithuania was, in the early twentieth century, a centre of Talmudic studies, and this has also left its mark on Levinas's *oeuvre* in the form of his own Talmudic readings and other writings in Jewish theology. As an avid reader of Dostoyevsky, Tolstoy, Pushkin, and Gogol,

Levinas became absorbed by the ethical issues raised by these writers, particularly the issue of responsibility for the Other in Dostoyevsky. Dostoyevsky and the great Russian writers, were, to Levinas's mind, a good preparation for reading Plato and Kant.

His reading of the Russian writers mentioned led Levinas, in 1923, to Strasbourg in France to study philosophy under Charles Blondel and Maurice Pradines. At the time, Bergson's philosophy was making an impact. For Levinas this meant being greatly affected by Bergson's theory of duration. While at Strasbourg, Levinas also made friends with Maurice Blanchot who introduced him to Proust and Valéry. A collection of Levinas's writings on Blanchot was published in 1975.

In 1928–9, Levinas attended Husserl's lectures in Freiburg, and he also read Heidegger's *Being and Time*. The book of his *doctorat de troisième cycle* thesis on Husserl appeared in 1930 – the same book that was to captivate Sartre. In the same year that his thesis was published, Levinas received French citizenship. He was thus eligible, at the outbreak of the Second World War, to be mobilised, and served as an interpreter in Russian and German until he was made a prisoner of war in 1940. Almost all of Levinas's family remaining in Lithuania were killed by the Nazis. During his captivity in Germany, Levinas began his book, *Existence and Existents*, which was published in 1947.

After the war, Levinas became director of the Ecole Normale Israélite Orientale. In 1961, his doctoral thesis, *Totalité et infini*, was published and led to his appointment as professor of philosophy at the University of Poitiers. He was subsequently appointed to the University of Paris-Nanterre in 1967, and then to a chair in philosophy at the Sorbonne in 1973. He retired from the Sorbonne in 1976.

Levinas's intimate acquaintance with Husserl's phenomenology provided the basis for a detailed consideration of the 'givenness' of existence, as embodied, for example, in the impersonal (in English) form of the verb to be: 'there is', or its French equivalent, *il y a*, or again (in German), *es gibt*. Levinas gives this most everyday of everyday expressions a powerful twist by linking it with horror. 'There is' is impersonal and given; it is neither exterior nor interior; it is, says Levinas, the 'sheer fact of being'.[3] 'There is' – the givenness (cf. *es gibt*) of Being – is the equivalent of the night, of ambiguity, of indeterminateness. 'There is' comes to thought, confronts it before revelation or the concept orders it in any way; it slips through transcendence and indeed defies the ego, and all personal forms of the symbolic. As such, Levinas argues, 'The rustling of the *there is* . . . is horror.' And he continues by noting the way 'it insinuates itself in the night, as an undetermined menace of space itself disengaged from its function as a receptacle for objects, as a means of access to beings'.[4] Although Levinas would refuse the vaguest hint of a psychoanalytic explanation, it is as though the 'there is' as horror were a trauma for consciousness, and an impossibility for symbolic processes. However, we should also remember that horror here is always already given: it is thus unavoidable, as being is unavoidable. It is not to be understood, then, as equivalent to the Heideggerian anxiety before the acknowledgement of nothingness. 'To be conscious is to be torn away from the *there is*.'[5] This is because consciousness has to form itself into a subjectivity constructed by a certain framework of rationality. Levinas is interested in the underside of this rationality which is not simply the irrational, or the unspeakable void, but is a positive force that cannot be excluded. Put another way: subjectivity forms itself according to the universal principles of Western philosophy; the 'there is', by comparison, is contingency – the particular which eludes the universal. The 'haunting spectre' as seen in Shakespeare's *Macbeth*, is Being as the 'there is', and it is this, precisely, which horrifies Macbeth. Night, crime, phantom and horror here come together to give the shadow of being.

What exactly is at stake in the Levinasian project if, as Levinas proposes, neither a phenomenological nor a psychoanalytical framework can do justice to horror as Being as an Otherness? To answer this question, we note that from the time of his lectures given at the College of Philosophy in 1946–7 on time and the Other, to his later work on God and the idea, otherness – alterity – has been at issue. Thus, time as alterity, existence as alterity, the other person (*autrui*) as alterity, language as alterity, and God as alterity – these words point to a project of great subtlety and determination. For Levinas effectively wants to bypass thought in philosophy. His trajectory leads, he argues, away from ontology, epistemology, or reason, to a point where alterity is confronted in all its 'nudity' (to use a term dear to Levinas) – a point where its irreducibility can be acknowledged.

The transcendence of Western philosophy is against this enterprise if by transcendence we mean that which can be conceptualised, theorised, visualised, objectified – universalised. Levinas, by contrast, uses transcendence in the sense of rupture, and opening up to the Other, as opposed to the Western tradition's reduction of the Other to the Same in its drive to objectify and universalise. The dominance of the Same makes the universal the goal of thought. The universal is, by definition, independent of any given set of concrete circumstances. It is thus disembodied and idealist. In keeping with the tenor of the phenomenological project, the aim is to reduce the gap between thought and embodiment – or, as in the case of Heidegger, between Being and existence.

In attributing a kind of primacy to alterity, rather than to the thinking subject, Levinas has, of course, met the objection which says that, in the end, whether one likes it or not, the Other of the universal – the alterity which calls to us – is inevitably the Other of Western thought itself, an Other waiting to be put into conceptual form and universalised, an Other which Western thought needs. This Other of Western thought would be inescapably another version of the Same – ultimately a formal Other (the Other of negation) and not true alterity at all. Feminists meet a similar objection when they argue, like Irigaray does, that the feminine is an alterity which must be thought of independently of the patriarchal order of identity (= the Same). Interestingly, in an interview given in 1985, Levinas points out that when he wrote his lectures published as *Time and the Other* in 1948, he thought that femininity was the modality of alterity that he was looking for.[6] Knowledge, too, Levinas recognises, reiterates the relationship of the Same to the Other in which the Other is reduced to the order of the Same.[7] Despite this, Levinas is still searching for a way of presenting the irreducible Other in philosophy, an Other that is indeed foreign to the order of the Same. No doubt one should pause on the resonances of the notion of 'search' here; for what Levinas may in fact be presenting is the trace of his search for a way of rendering the Other intelligible without resorting to the language of idealism.

For his own part Levinas has never ceased to emphasise that the Other arises in relation to others and not immediately in relation to the universality of the law. This relation is the unique relation of ethical responsibility. Ethics is the practical relation of one to an other – a relation which is prior to ontology. The Absolutely Other is the other person (*autrui*). The Other, Levinas continues, is a 'nudity'. This is not the nudity emerging in light of an unveiling; rather, says Levinas, true nudity is the face (of the Other) as an epiphany which solicits us; it is that face which comes to us from the exterior. 'The face *is* by itself and not by reference to a system.'[8] The Other is also the infinite in me to the extent that he or she brings about a rupture in the self as an entity identical with itself. The self even poses itself *for the other* rather than for itself. The nudity of the other as a practical exterior unassimilable to ontology entails that the relationship between Self and Other is dissymmetrical; in other words, it bypasses the symmetry of intersubjectivity so forcefully outlined in idealism. Levinas likens this dissymmetry to irreversible time – the time that cannot be represented by clocks, but which corresponds to the internal experience of time captured in Bergson's notion of 'duration'.

The dimension of time that interests Levinas more than any other is the future. Unlike the past, the future cannot so easily be assimilated to another present. Instead, the future is the present's difference with itself: this is the future as absolutely new, and so absolutely Other. The future is time without a concept.

An intriguing aspect of Levinas's philosophy of alterity concerns language. While it could have been expected that Levinas would see language as largely dominated by idealism and the order of the Same, he in fact finds that language is the basis of the ethical because it enables links to be made between people. The signifier here is never a complete presence. As such, the signifier becomes an opening-up to the Other. Although language is a formal structure, it can be defined, according to Levinas, as a potential break with representation and the totalising impulse of the order of the Same. To stress this point, Levinas defines signification in general as infinity – that is, as the existence of alterity. The interest of Levinas's approach here comes in part from his insight that language cannot be reduced to a system of logic or representation. Like the future, the infinite, and the face, language becomes an extended epiphany. It is the astonishment of the Other speaking in me – the Other speaking in me which enables me to become a self in language; in other words, through language, the Other enables me to have an identity.

Through the face of alterity, Levinas says, God is reached:

The face 'signifies' beyond, neither as an index nor as symbol, but precisely and irreducibly as a face that *summons me*. It signifies *to-God (à Dieu)*, not as sign, but as the questioning of myself, as if I were summoned or called, that is to say, awakened or cited as myself.[9]

In his later work, Levinas is more insistent in equating God with the infinite. It is almost as though theology comes to take the place of a Western philosophical outlook in order to ensure that alterity once again finds its place in thought – a place beyond ontology.

With his emphasis on the practical importance of ethics as being distinct from ontology, Levinas opens up a new vista within philosophy. Within philosophy? This is perhaps the question that needs to be posed to the one who has revealed the solipsism of reason, and who has shown that previous philosophies of the subject have reduced alterity to the order of the Same. Another question which arises is: how is Levinas, the interpreter of Husserl and Heidegger, to be understood given that he speaks clearly within the history of philosophy, but endeavours to escape from it – although, it is true, his writing clearly gestures towards theology? For Levinas, to speak within the history of philosophy would seem to imply that the very tradition he challenges might have within it a hitherto unsuspected suppleness – much as Levinas himself shows that language is vested with hitherto unsuspected possibilities. In other words, Levinas may well have shown that philosophy is in fact not reducible to ontology.

Notes

1 Annie Cohen-Solal, *Sartre: A Life*, trans. Anna Cancogni, New York, Pantheon Books, 1987, p. 91.
2 Emmanuel Levinas, 'Ethics and politics' (Levinas in discussion with Alain Finkielkraut), trans. Jonathan Romney in Sean Hand (ed.), *The Levinas Reader*, Oxford, Basil Blackwell, 1989, p. 290.
3 Emmanuel Levinas, 'There is: Existence without existents', trans. Alphonso Lingis in Hand (ed.), *The Levinas Reader*, p. 31.
4 ibid., p. 32.
5 ibid.
6 Emmanuel Levinas, 'Intretien' [realised in February 1985] in Jean-Christophe Aeschli-

mann (ed.), *Répondre d'autrui Emmanuel Lévinas*, Neuchâtel, Editions de la Baconnière, Collection, *Langages*, 1989, p. 10.
7   Emmanuel Levinas, *Transcendance et intelligibilité*, Genève, Labor et Fides, 1984, p. 12.
8   Emmanuel Levinas, *Totalité et infini: essai sur l'extériorité*, La Haye, Martinus Nijhoff, 1961, p. 47.
9   Emmanuel Levinas, 'Beyond intentionality', trans. Kathleen McLaughlin in Alan Montefiore (ed.), *Philosophy in France in France Today*, Cambridge, Cambridge University Press, 1983, p. 112.

See also in this book

Blanchot, Derrida, Irigaray, Lyotard

Levinas's major writings

The Theory of Intuition in Husserl's Phenomenology (1930) (Studies in Existential Philosophy), trans. Andre Orianne, Evanston, Northwestern University, 1985
Existence and Existents (1947), trans. A. Lingis, Kluwer Academic Publishers, 1978
Time and the Other (1948), trans. Richard Cohen, Pittsburgh, Duquesne University Press, 1990
Totality and Infinity (1961), trans. A. Lingis, Pittsburgh, Duquesne University Press, 1987
Difficult Freedom: Essays on Judaism (1963), trans. Sean Hand, Baltimore and London, Johns Hopkins University Press, 1991
Otherwise than Being, or Beyond Essence (1974), trans. Alphonso Lingis, Kluwer Academic Publishers, Martinus Nijhoff Philosophy texts, 1981
Sur Maurice Blanchot, Montpellier, Fata Morgana, 1975
Nine Talmudic Readings by Emmanuel Levinas (1977), trans. Annette Aronowicz, Bloomington, Indiana University Press, 1990
Ethics and Infinity (1982), trans. Richard Cohen, Pittsburgh, Duquesne University Press, 1985
Transcendance et intelligibilité, Genève, Labor et Fides, 1984
Collected Philosophical Papers, ed. A. Lingis, Kluwer Academic Publishers, 1987
Outside the Subject (1987), Stanford, California, Stanford University Press, 1993
The Levinas Reader, ed. Sean Hand, Oxford, Basil Blackwell, 1989. Contains Levinas's writings on existence, ethics, aesthetics, religion and politics

Further reading

Bernasconi, Robert, 'Levinas face to face – with Hegel', *Journal of the British Society for Phenomenology*, 13, 3 (1982), pp. 267–76
Gans, Steven, 'Ethics or ontology?', *Philosophy Today*, 16, 2 (1972), pp. 117–21
Libertson, Joseph, *Proximity, Levinas, Blanchot, Bataille and Communication*, The Hague, Paris, Martinus Nijhoff, 1982
Lingis, Alphonso, *Libido: the French Existential Theories*, Bloomington, Illinois, Indiana University Press, 1985, pp. 58–73 and 103–20
Lyotard, Jean-François, 'Jewish Oedipus' in *Driftworks*, New York, Semiotext(e), 1984, pp. 35–55

SEMIOTICS

Semiotics is the theory and analysis of signs and significations. A semiotician like the early Barthes sees social and cultural life in terms of signification, and therefore in terms of the non-essential nature of objects. Jean Baudrillard brings home this point in his book, *The System of Objects*. Through a semiotic approach, based on a Saussurian linguistic framework, social life becomes a struggle for prestige and status; or rather, it becomes a sign of this struggle. Semiotics also studies the *way* that signs signify – in conventional literary texts and legal documents, or in advertisements and bodily conduct.

ROLAND BARTHES

Roland Barthes was born at Cherbourg in 1915. Barely a year later, his father died in naval combat in the North Sea, so that the son was brought up by the mother and, periodically, by his grandparents. Before completing his later primary and secondary schooling in Paris, Barthes spent his childhood at Bayonne in south-west France. Between 1934 and 1947, he suffered various bouts of tuberculosis. And it was during the periods of enforced convalescence that he read omnivorously and published his first articles on André Gide. After teaching in Rumania and in Egypt, where he met A.J. Greimas, then at the Ecole des Hautes Etudes en Sciences Sociales, Barthes was appointed to the Collège de France in 1977. He died in 1980.

Such elementary facts of biography have often provided the psycho-critic with material for explaining underlying (unconscious) aspects of the writer's *oeuvre*. Barthes, however, takes them in hand and uses them as the raw material of his own writing, and even of his style. This is so in two books he wrote towards the end of his life: *Roland Barthes by Roland Barthes*, and *Camera Lucida: Reflections on Photography*. Here, the status of raw material is the key; for Barthes in no sense becomes a conventional autobiographer. Instead, he fictionalises his life through using the third person when (conventionally) referring to himself, as he – like Joyce – reveals the profundities of life in the 'bread' of everyday experience. He writes, for example, of a photograph of his mother in the above-cited essay on photography, that he had found his mother's face – that face he had loved – in the photograph: 'The photograph was very old. The corners were blunted from having been pasted into an album, the sepia print had faded.'[1] Eventually, he says, 'I studied the little girl and at last rediscovered my mother.'[2] Godard's disenchanting words then ring in his ears: ' "Not a just

image, just an image".'[3] In his grief, Barthes wants a just image.

This 'personalised' style, characteristic of the later Barthes, confirmed the semiotician and literary critic as a writer in his own right. Barthes writes 'the novelistic without the novel', as he himself put it. Indeed, this is arguably the true basis of his originality, over and above his theories of writing and signification. Thus in *A Lover's Discourse*, Barthes says that 'we do not know who is speaking; the text speaks that is all'.[4] Today, a lover's discourse can only be one of solitude; it has no specific subject but may be invoked by 'thousands of subjects'. The lover's discourse, as the equivalent of the novelistic, becomes the discourse of the construction of a lover's discourse: a pure weaving of voices spelling out what one would say and could say were the narrative to be enacted.

Roland Barthes's work embodies a significant diversity. It ranges between semiotic theory, critical literary essays, the presentation of Jules Michelet's historical writing in terms of its obsessions, a psycho-biographical study of Racine, which outraged certain sectors of the French literary establishment, as well as the more 'personalised' works on the pleasure of the text, love, and photography.

Although a certain refinement in style is already visible, the early Barthes aimed to analyse and criticise bourgeois culture and society. *Mythologies* (1957) is the clearest statement of this. There, the everyday images and messages of advertising, entertainment, literary and popular culture, consumer goods, are subjected to a reflexive scrutiny quite unique in its application and results. Sometimes Barthes's prose in *Mythologies* is, in its capacity to combine a sense of delicacy and carefulness with critical acuity, reminiscent of Walter Benjamin's. Unlike Benjamin, though, Barthes is neither essentially a Marxist philosopher nor a religiously-inspired cultural critic. He is, in the 1950s and 1960s, a semiotician: one who views language modelled on Saussure's theory of the sign as the basis for understanding the structure of social and cultural life.

The nascent semiotician formulates a theory of myth that serves to underpin the writings in *Mythologies*. Myth today, Barthes says, is a message – not a concept, idea, or object. More specifically, myth is defined 'by the way it utters its message'; it is thus a product of 'speech' (*parole*), rather than of 'language' (*langue*). With ideology, what is said is crucial, and it hides. With myth, how it says what it says is crucial, and it distorts. In fact, myth 'is neither a lie nor a confession: it is an inflexion'.[5] Consequently, in the example of the Negro soldier saluting the French flag, taken by Barthes from the front cover of *Paris-Match*, the Negro becomes, for the myth reader, 'the very *presence* of French imperiality'. Barthes's claim is that because myth hides nothing its effectiveness is assured: its revelatory power is the very means of distortion. It is as though myth were the scandal occurring in the full light of day. To be a reader of myths – as opposed to a producer of myths, or a mythologist who deciphers them – is to accept the message entirely at face value. Or rather, the message of the myth is that there is no distinction between signifier (the Negro soldier saluting the French flag) and the signified (French imperiality). In short, the message of the myth is that it does not need to be deciphered, interpreted, or demystified. As Barthes explains, to read the picture as a (transparent) symbol is to renounce its reality as a picture; if the ideology of the myth is obvious, then it does not work as myth. On the contrary for the myth to work as myth it must seem entirely natural.

Despite this clarification of the status of myth, the difficulties in appreciating its profundity derive from the ambitiousness of the project of distinguishing myth from both ideology and a system of signs calling for interpretation. While, on the one hand, the subtlety of giving myth a *sui generis* status of naturalised speech has often been missed by Barthes's commentators, the issue is still to know what the import of this might be, other than the insight that the successful working of myth entails its being unanalysable as myth.

The analysis and practice of writing which begins in *Writing Degree Zero* (1953) gives a further clue about the concerns implicit in *Mythologies*. These centre on the recognition that language is a relatively autonomous system, and that the literary text, instead of being the transmitter of an ideology, or the sign of a political commitment, or again, the expression of social values, or, finally, a vehicle of communication, is opaque, and not natural. For Barthes, what defines the bourgeois era, culturally speaking, is its denial of the opacity of language and the installation of an ideology centred on the notion that true art is verisimilitude. By contrast, the zero degree of writing is that form which, in its (stylistic) neutrality, ends up by drawing attention to itself. Certainly, *Nouveau Roman* writing (originally inspired by Camus) exemplifies this form; however, this neutrality of style quickly reveals itself, Barthes suggests, as a style of neutrality. That is, it serves, at a given historical moment (post-Second World War Europe), as a means of showing the dominance of style in all writing; style proves that writing is not natural, that naturalism is an ideology. Thus if myth is the mode of naturalisation *par excellence*, as *Mythologies* proposes, myth, in the end, does hide something: its ultimately ideological basis.

Barthes's influential study of narrative in 1964[6] continues the semiotician's mission of unmasking the codes of the natural, evident between the lines in the works of the 1950s. Taking a James Bond story as the tutor text, Barthes analyses the elements which are structurally necessary (the language, function, actions, narration, of narrative) if narrative is to unfold as though it were *not* the result of codes of convention. Characteristically, bourgeois society denies the presence of the code; it wants 'signs which do not look like signs'. A structural analysis of texts, however, implies a degree of formalisation that Barthes began to reject. Unlike theorists such as Greimas, the reader is nearly always struck by the degree of freedom and informality in his writing. Although linguistic notation, diagrams, and figures appear in works like *The Fashion System*, Barthes was unhappy with this foray into 'scientificity' and only published his book on fashion (originally intended as a doctoral thesis) at the behest of friends and colleagues. It is in *The Fashion System*, however, that Barthes clarifies a number of aspects of the structural, or semiotic, approach to the analysis of social phenomena. Semiology, it turns out, examines collective representations rather than the reality to which these might refer, as sociology does. A structural approach, for its part, attempts to reduce the diversity of phenomena to a general function. Semiology – inspired by Saussure – is always alive to the signifying aspect of things. Indeed, it is often charged with revealing the language (*langue*) of a field such as fashion. Barthes therefore mobilises all the resources of linguistic theory – especially language as a system of differences – in order to identify the language (*langue*) of fashion in his study of fashion.

Much of *The Fashion System*, however, is a discourse on method because fashion is not equivalent to any real object which can be described and spoken about independently. Rather, fashion is implicit in objects, or in the way that these objects are described. To facilitate the analysis, Barthes narrows the field: his corpus will consist of the written signs of women's clothing fashion as these appear in two fashion magazines between June 1958 and June 1959. The complication is that there, fashion is never directly written about, only connoted. For the fashion system always implies that things (clothing) are naturally, or functionally, given: thus some shoes are 'ideal for walking', whereas others are made 'for that special occasion . . .'. Fashion writing, then, refers to items of clothing, and not to fashion. If fashion writing has

a signified (the item), it is now clear that this is not fashion. In fact, the language of fashion only becomes evident when the relationship between signifier and signifier is taken into account, and not the (arbitrary) relationship between signifier and signified. The signifier–signifier relation constitutes the clothing sign. Barthes orients his study along a number of different axes all of which have to do with the nature of signification. After methodological considerations, he looks at the structure of the clothing code in terms of: the fashion signifier – where meaning derives from the relationship between object (e.g., cardigan), support (e.g., collar), and variant (open-necked) – and the fashion signified: the external context of the fashion object (e.g., 'tusser = summer'). The fashion sign, however, is not the simple combination of signifier and signified because fashion is always connoted and never denoted. The sign of fashion is the fashion writing itself, which, as Barthes says, 'is "tautological", since fashion is only ever the *fashionable* garment'.[7]

In the third section of *The Fashion System*, Barthes examines the rhetorical system of fashion. This system captures 'the entirety of the clothing code'. As with the clothing code, so with the rhetorical system, the nature of the signifier, signified, and sign are examined. The rhetoric of the signifier of the clothing code opens up a poetic dimension, since a garment described has no demonstrably productive value. The rhetoric of the signified concerns the world of fashion – a kind of imaginary 'novelistic' world. Finally, the rhetoric of the sign is equivalent to the rationalisations of fashion: the transformation of the description of the fashion garment into something necessary because it naturally fulfils its purpose (e.g., evening wear), and naturally fulfils its purpose because it is necessary.

Barthes's later book, *S/Z*, analyses Balzac's short story 'Sarrasine', and is an attempt to make explicit the narrative codes at work in a realist text. 'Sarrasine', Barthes argues, is woven of codes of naturalisation, a

125

process similar to that seen in the rhetoric of the fashion sign. The five codes Barthes works with here are: the hermeneutic code (presentation of an enigma); the semic code (connotative meaning); the symbolic code; the proairetic code (the logic of actions), and the gnomic, or cultural code which evokes a particular body of knowledge. Barthes's reading aims less to construct a highly formal system of classification of the narrative elements, than to show that the most plausible actions, the most convincing details, or the most intriguing enigmas, are the products of artifice, rather than an imitation of reality.

After analysing Sade, Fourier, and Loyola as 'Logothetes' and founders of 'languages' in *Sade, Fourier, Loyola* – an exercise recalling the 'language' (*langue*) of fashion – Barthes writes about pleasure and reading in *The Pleasure of the Text*. The latter marks a foretaste of the more fragmentary, personalised, and semi-fictional style of the writings to come. The pleasure of the text 'is bound up with the consistency of the self, of the subject which is confident in its values of comfort, of expansiveness, of satisfaction'.[8] This pleasure, which is typical of the readable text, contrasts with the text of *jouissance* (the text of enjoyment, bliss, loss of self). The text of pleasure is often of a supreme delicacy and refinement, in contrast to the often unreadable, poetic text of *jouissance*. Barthes's texts themselves, especially from 1973 onwards, can be accurately described in terms of this conception of pleasure. Thus after distilling the language (*langue*) of others, Barthes, as a writer of pleasure, then came to give vent to his own, singular language. From a point where he became a critic for fear of not being able to write (fictions in particular), Barthes not only became a great writer, he also blurred the distinction between criticism and (poetic) writing.

Notes

1 Roland Barthes, *Camera Lucida: Reflections on Photography*, trans. Richard Howard, London, Vintage, 1993, p. 67.

2 ibid., p. 69.

3 ibid., p. 70.

4 Roland Barthes, *A Lover's Discourse*, trans. Richard Howard, New York, Hill & Wang, 1978 (sixth printing 1984), p. 112.

5 Roland Barthes, *Mythologies*, trans. Annette Lavers, St Albans, Herts, Paladin, 1973, p. 129.

6 Roland Barthes, 'Introduction à l'analyse structurale des récits', *Communications*, 8 (1966), pp. 1–27. In English as 'Introduction to the structural analysis of narratives' (1964) in *Image-Music-Text*, trans. Stephen Heath, Glasgow, Fontana/Collins, second impression 1979, pp. 79–124.

7 Roland Barthes, *The Fashion System*, trans. Matthew Ward & Richard Howard, New York, Hill and Wang, 1983 (second printing 1984), p. 220 n.16.

8 Roland Barthes, *The Grain of the Voice. Interviews 1962–1980*, trans. Linda Coverdale, New York, Hill & Wang, 1985, p. 206. Translation modified.

See also in this book

Benjamin, Eco, Genette, Greimas, Saussure, Todorov

Barthes's major writings

Writing Degree Zero (1953), trans. Annette Lavers and Colin Smith, New York, Hill & Wang, second printing, 1977

Michelet (1954), trans. Richard Howard, Oxford, Basil Blackwell, 1987

Mythologies (1957), trans. Annette Lavers, St Albans, Herts, Paladin, 1973

Critical Essays (1964), trans. Richard Howard, Evanston, Ill., Northwestern University Press, 1972

'Introduction to the structural analysis of narratives' (1964) in *Image-Music-Text*, trans. Stephen Heath, Glasgow, Fontana/Collins, second impression 1979

Elements of Semiology (1964), trans. Annette Lavers and Colin Smith, New York, Hill & Wang, second printing, 1977

Criticism and Truth (1966), trans. Katrine Pilcher Keuneman, Minneapolis, University of Minnesota Press, 1987

The Fashion System (1967), trans. Matthew Ward and Richard Howard, New York, Hill & Wang, 1983, second printing, 1984

S/Z (1970), trans. Richard Miller, New York, Hill & Wang, 1974

The Empire of Signs (1970), trans. Richard Howard, New York, Hill & Wang, fourth printing, 1986

Sade, Fourier, Loyola (1971), trans. Richard Howard, New York, Hill & Wang, 1976

The Pleasure of the Text (1973), trans. Richard Miller, New York, Hill & Wang, 1975

Roland Barthes by Roland Barthes (1975), trans. Richard Howard, New York, Hill & Wang, 1977

A Lover's Discourse: Fragments (1977), trans. Richard Howard, New York, Hill & Wang, sixth printing, 1984

Camera Lucida: Reflections on Photography (1980), trans. Richard Howard, London, Vintage, 1993

The Grain of the Voice: Interviews 1962–1980 (1981), trans. Linda Coverdale, New York, Hill & Wang, 1985

The Responsibility of Forms (1982), trans. Richard Howard, New York, Hill & Wang, 1985

Further reading

Culler, Jonathan, *Roland Barthes*, New York, Oxford University Press, 1983

Lavers, Annette, *Roland Barthes: Structuralism and After*, Harvard, Harvard University Press, 1982

Moriarty, Michael, *Roland Barthes*, Cambridge, Polity Press, 1991

UMBERTO ECO

Umberto Eco is known to a world-wide audience for his two novels, *The Name of the Rose*,[1] and *Foucault's Pendulum*.[2] Both works allude to aspects of past and present theories of signs, as well as to a vast array of scholarly (those of the Middle Ages in particular) and other texts (Sherlock Holmes in the *Name of the Rose*, and the *Corpus Hermeticum* in *Foucault's Pendulum*).

Eco was born in 1932 in Piedmont, Italy. Before becoming a semiotician, he studied philosophy specialising in the philosophical and aesthetic theories of the Middle Ages. His thesis at the University of Turin on the aesthetics of Thomas Aquinas was published in 1956 when he was 24. Three years later, Eco contributed a chapter called 'Sviluppo dell'estetica medievale' ('The development of Medieval aesthetics') to a four-volume handbook on the history of aesthetics. In 1986, the lengthy chapter came in an English translation under the title of *Art and Beauty in the Middle Ages*. This erudition, we have noted, has been put to good effect in Eco's fiction, but does it have any real connection with his work in semiotics? One can answer in the affirmative here for two reasons. First, as Todorov and others have shown, the age of Thomas Aquinas is also a chapter in the history of sign theory. The Aristotle who so influenced the 'Angelic Doctor' has also left his mark, Eco recognises, on more contemporary semiotics – such as in the theory of metaphor.[3] Second, as a medievalist, Eco became fascinated by the writings of James Joyce where one finds liberal references to Aquinas, Aristotle, Dante, Medieval bestiaries, and rhetoric.

His interest in Joyce has to be seen in the context of Eco's 'curiosity' and 'wonder' about the modern world, and about modernity as a cultural and historical phenomenon. Joyce thus bridges a gap between Eco's scholarly passion for a time now past (although it may be returning[4]) and the empirical world of the here and now – a world of complexity and diversity: a polyphonic and open world. The two poles of Eco's intellectual field can be appreciated through the knowledge that in the year that he published his chapter on Medieval aesthetics, an article under Eco's name appeared entitled, 'L'opera in movimento e la coscienza dell' epoca' ('The poetics of the open work'), which considered the way modern music (Stockhausen, Berio, Boulez), modern writing (Mallarmé, Joyce), modern art (Calder, Pousseur) in relation to modern science (Einstein, Bohr, Heisenberg) now produce 'works in movement' and 'open works' – works whereby the addressee becomes an active element in bringing a work to provisional completion, or where the work itself brings openness to the fore. From this starting point, Eco develops that theme of his intellectual trajectory which is concerned with 'the role of the reader'.

In a recent statement on reading and interpretation,[5] Eco has stressed that the 'anything goes' version of postmodern criticism is not what is implied in the notion of an open work. Rather, every literary work can be said to propose a model reader corresponding to real and justifiable possibilities set by the text. For Eco, to propose that an infinite number of readings is possible for *any* text is a wholly empty gesture. This does not mean, on the other hand, that an empirical author should be able to adjudicate on the validity of interpretation in light of his or her intentions. It is a question of pointing to evidence that could lead to a pertinent and coherent interpretation, whether or not this be in spite of the empirical author. In this regard, Eco is fond of quoting the line from *Finnegans Wake* which refers to 'that ideal reader suffering from an ideal insomnia' (*FW* 120: 13–14). The ideal reader is not so much a perfect reader as one who represents the range of possible readings justified in terms of the structure of the text itself – the reader who is *awake* to these possibilities.

The other dimension constitutive of Eco's intellectual and scholarly trajectory is semiotics. Since 1975, Eco has held the chair of semiotics at the University of Bologna, and he has written in English two key books which develop his theory of signs and signification. These are *A Theory of Semiotics* (1976) and *Semiotics and the Philosophy of Language* (1984).

Although *A Theory of Semiotics* explicitly deals with a theory of codes and of sign production, its underlying point of departure is Peirce's notion of 'unlimited semiosis'. Unlimited semiosis refers, in Eco's hands, to the kind of middle position in relation to the position of the reader. Although unlimited semiosis is the result of the fact that signs in language always refer to other signs and that a text always offers the prospect of infinite interpretations, Eco wants to avoid the extremes of univocal meaning on the one hand opposing infinite meanings on the other. Unlimited semiosis rather corresponds to Peirce's 'interpretant' where meaning is established with reference to conditions of possibility.

In light of unlimited semiosis, how does Eco explain the nature of a code? To speak generally, codes can be of two types. They can be of a univocal, Morse code type, where a given set of signals (dots and dashes) corresponds to a given set of signs – in this case the letters of the alphabet. A code of this type – where one system of elements is translated into another system – has extremely wide application, so that the relationship between DNA and RNA in biology can be analysed in terms of a code.

Although Eco gives a number of technical examples of this type of code, his main interest is in language as composed of *langue* (where code = grammar, syntax, system) and *parole* (language act). Here, code corresponds to the structure of the language. Or, to use Hjelmslev's terms as Eco often does: the code correlates the expression plane of language with the content plane. Eco uses the term 's-code' to designate a code used in this sense. Put another way: the s-code of language is equivalent to the specific organisation of the elements of *parole*. Without a code, the sounds/graphic marks have no meaning, and this in the most radical sense of not functioning linguistically. S-codes can be either 'denotative' (when a statement is understood literally), or connotative (when another code is detected – e.g., code of courtesy – within the same statement). None of this is really foreign to Saussure's work, but Eco wants to introduce an understanding of an s-code which is more dynamic than that found in Saussure's theory, and in much of current linguistics besides. He does this by developing what he calls, after Quillian, a 'Model Q' – a model of the code which accounts for unlimited semiosis. First, however, Eco has to show that the meaning of a 'sign-vehicle' (e.g., a word or image) is independent of a supposedly real object. In other words, it is necessary to avoid the 'referential fallacy'. Thus the sign-vehicle /dog/ is not equivalent to any particular dog (= real object), but has to stand for all dogs, both living and dead. A clearer example perhaps is the fact that /nevertheless/ does not have a referent; rather, it is a pure product of the code. Second, Eco recognises that codes do have a context. This context is social and cultural life. 'Cultural units', then, 'are signs that social life has put at our disposal: images interpreting books, appropriate responses interpreting ambiguous questions, words interpreting definitions and vice-versa.' What somebody does in response to a particular sign-vehicle (e.g., /your shout/ in Australia results in someone buying all the drinks) gives us, Eco points out, 'information about the cultural unit' in question.[6] As a result of taking into account the sign's status as a cultural unit, a theory of codes is able to explain how signs can take on a multiplicity of meanings, how meaning is derived from the competence of the user of language or sign system, and how, as a result, new meanings can be created. *Langue* as a code thus becomes equivalent to the competence of the language-user. This is so even with the case in which the speaker of language might use the code incompetently. For 'incompetence' (e.g., that snow is peanut butter, to cite Eco) is still semiotically interesting. Laughter is a possible response to this incompetence, laughter which has to be excluded from a notion of language viewed as a semantics based on the truth-value of propositions. Indeed, laughter, lying, tragedy are fundamental to understanding the code viewed semiotically.

The semantic field is rather involved 'in multiple shiftings' which render inadequate the notion of the code as the equivalence of the elements of two systems. In fact, says Eco, every major linguistic code is 'a *complex network of subcodes*'.[7] To put it in its most succinct form: Eco's model Q 'is a model of linguistic creativity'. As he confirms: 'In effect the model Q supposes that the system can be nourished by fresh information and that further data can be inferred from incomplete data.'[8] With model Q, therefore,

the code is modified in accordance with the changing competencies of language users, instead of being determined by the code.

The other side of a theory of codes is a theory of sign production. In his discussion of sign production, Eco focuses again on the tension between elements that can be easily assimilated, or foreseen, by the code (cf. symbols in Peirce's terminology), and those that cannot be easily assimilated (cf. Peirce's notion of icon). Elements of the former category, Eco designates as *ratio facilis* and those of the second, *ratio difficilis*.[9] The closer one comes to *ratio difficilis*, the more the sign of the object is 'motivated' by the nature of the object itself. Icons are the category of sign which bring this out most clearly. Eco is, however, concerned to show that even the most strongly motivated signs (e.g., image of the Virgin) have conventional elements. And even where there appears to be a clear case of an object, or behaviour, which seems to exist outside any conventionalised format (i.e. beyond the code), such instances rapidly become conventionalised. The most telling illustrations of this are Gombrich's examples (referred to by Eco) of what passed for realism in painting at various points in art history (e.g., the drawings of Dürer). Even a photograph can be shown to have conventional aspects: for instance, the development of the negative offers the possibility of a certain conventionalisation on the part of the photographer. Again, if a photograph is considered from the perspective of its analogical status (how much it looks like its object), Eco reminds us that digitalisation, as a certain form of codification, implies new possibilities of reproduction. In summary, the key elements of Eco's typology of modes of sign production are as follows:

1 *Physical labour*: effort required to produce the sign.

2 *Recognition*: object or event is recognised as expression of a sign content, as with imprints, symptoms, or clues.

3 *Ostension*: an object or act is shown to be the exemplar of a class of objects or acts.

4 *Replica*: tends towards *ratio difficilis* in principle, but takes on features of codification through stylisation. Examples are emblems, musical types, mathematical signs.

5 *Invention*: the clearest case of *ratio difficilis*. Unforeseen by the existing code; is the basis of a new material continuum.

What Eco proposes via his model Q and via the invention of sign production – and what conventional semiotics has tended to neglect (Kristeva's work being a notable exception) – is the need to account for the language system's capacity for renewal and revitalisation. Instead of being closed and static, Eco's argues that the sign system is open and dynamic.

A comparable motivation is evident in Eco's discussion of signs and signification in *Semiotics and the Philosophy of Language*. There, Eco argues that a sign is not only something which stands for something else (and therefore has a dictionary meaning), but must also be interpreted. As we have noted above, the view of interpretation in operation here is that of Peirce's 'interpretant', which gives rise to unlimited semiosis.

The key theme in *Semiotics and the Philosophy of Language* concerns the difference between the structure of the dictionary and the encyclopedia. Although he does not explain it in precisely these terms, for Eco, the dictionary, as the hierarchical 'Porphyrian tree' ('that model of definition, structured by genera, species, and differentiae'[10]), corresponds to a view of language as the static and closed system of conventional linguistics. The dictionary model of language would thus fail to account for unlimited semiosis. By contrast, the encyclopedia would correspond to a network without a centre, to a labyrinth from which there is no exit, or to an infinite, inferential model that is open to new elements. Where the dictionary suffers from the aporia of being either meaningful but limited in its scope, or of being unlimited in scope but incapable of providing a specific meaning, the encyclopedia corresponds to a 'rhizomatic' network of local descriptions; its structure is thus map-like, rather than tree-like and hierarchical. In fact, to function properly as a network of words allowing for the possibility of new meanings, a dictionary has to be like an encyclopedia. It is in fact 'a disguised encyclopaedia', says Eco. Thus the encyclopedia can become a general model of language, a way of talking about it without forcing upon it an artificial and finite globality.

Perhaps, finally, then, Eco's most enduring contribution to a theory of semiotics is to show that language is like the encyclopedia, invented by the *philosophes* in the eighteenth century. Could it be that Eco is showing us that the Enlightenment, at least in this respect, is also postmodern?

Notes

1 Umberto Eco, *The Name of the Rose*, trans. William Weaver, New York, Harcourt Brace Jovanovich, 1983. British edition by Secker & Warburg, 1983.

2 Umberto Eco, *Foucault's Pendulum*, trans. William Weaver, London, Secker & Warburg, 1989.

3 See, for example, Eco's discussion in *Semiotics and the Philosophy of Language*, London, Macmillan, 1984, pp. 91–103.

4 See Umberto Eco, 'The return of the Middle Ages' in *Travels in Hyperreality*, trans. William Weaver, San Diego, Harcourt Brace Jovanovich, 1986, pp. 59–85.

5 See Umberto Eco, 'Between author and text' in Stefan Collini (ed.) with Richard Rorty, Jonathan Culler and Christine Brooke-Rose, *Interpretation and Overinterpretation*, Cambridge, Cambridge University Press, 1992, pp. 67–88.

6 Umberto Eco, *A Theory of Semiotics*, Bloomington, Indiana University Press, 1976 (first Midland Book edn, 1979), p. 71.

7 ibid., p. 125. Eco's emphasis.

8 ibid., p. 124.

9 See ibid., pp. 183–4.

10 Eco, *Semiotics and the Philosophy of Language*, p. 46.

See also in this book

Eco's major writings

A Theory of Semiotics, Bloomington, Indiana University Press, 1976
Art and Beauty in the Middle Ages (1959), trans. Hugh Bredin, New Haven, Yale University Press, 1986
The Role of the Reader: Explorations in the Semiotics of Texts, London, Hutchinson, 1981. Reprinted 1985
The Name of the Rose, trans. William Weaver, New York, Harcourt Brace Jovanovich, 1983. British edition by Secker & Warburg
Semiotics and the Philosophy of Language, London, Macmillan, 1984
Foucault's Pendulum, trans. William Weaver, London, Secker & Warburg, 1989
'Between author and text' in Stefan Collini (ed.) with Richard Rorty, Jonathan Culler and Christine Brooke-Rose, *Interpretation and Overinterpretation*, Cambridge, Cambridge University Press, 1992

Further reading

Fry, Virginia, 'A juxtaposition of two abductions for studying communication and culture', *American Journal of Semiotics*, 5, 1 (1987), pp. 81–93

ALGIRDAS JULIEN GREIMAS

In a revealing statement written in 1975 about the relationship between his work and Vladamir Propp's, A.J. Greimas writes:

Today, though its heuristic value is diminished somewhat and even though this stance is not very original, we are still tempted to follow Propp's example and, by virtue of the principle of proceeding from the known to the unknown, from the simpler to the more complex, move from oral literature to written literature, from folktale to the literary tale, in our quest to confirm the partial theoretical models at hand and even to recalcitrant facts which

would enable us to increase our knowledge about narrative and discursive organization.[1]

At least two things are of interest in this statement. The first is that 'Propp's example' in developing a model of the Russian folktale – despite its notorious rigidity – still influences the work of the scientistically-inspired semiotician in the mid-1970s; and, second, the reader notices references to metaphysical notions: the movement from 'the known to the unknown', from 'the simpler to the more complex', and even the movement from 'oral to written literature' (cf. the work of Derrida). These seem to derive from a certain philosophical predisposition which would give Greimas's semiology its momentum, but which, at the same time, he has striven to avoid or transform. In Greimas's own terms, the implicit reliance on a metaphysical framework or set of assumptions would amount to confusing semiotic being with the sphere of ontology – or being as such.

Perhaps from the moment when linguistics sought to separate the linguistic sphere from the extra-linguistic difficulties of a conceptual and even empirical nature were bound to arise. As we shall see, although Greimas does not escape from the problems thus engendered, he has probably gone further than any other semiotician, both in developing a strictly semiotic (read: descriptive) theory of discourse, and in recognising the real difficulties involved in doing so. In the end, reading Greimas repays the effort – even if his relentless push to render semiotics scientific at times risks being positivistic.

Algirdas Julien Greimas was born in Lithuania in 1917. He first came to France in 1936 to study law at the University of Grenoble. While he was there, he developed a taste for the culture of the Middle Ages. After completing his *licence ès lettres* in 1939, Greimas began studies of the franco-provençale dialect. He returned to Lithuania in 1940, only to see his homeland successively invaded by the Soviets and the Germans. Upon returning to France in 1944, he enrolled in the doctoral studies which culminated in his thesis on fashion: 'Le mode en 1830. Essai de description du vocabulaire vestimentaire d'après les journaux de mode de l'époque' (1948) ('Fashion in 1830: A descriptive essay of the vestimentary vocabulary in the newspapers of the time'). There are in this title, echoes of Roland Barthes's *The Fashion System*, which also began as a doctorate.

In 1956, Greimas published an influential and timely article on the work of Saussure, one which made use of the work of two other important influences, Maurice Merleau-Ponty and Claude Lévi-Strauss. Ten years later, in the halcyon year of structuralism of 1966, Greimas founded, with R. Barthes, J. Dubois and others, the journal, *Langages*, and also published his seminal work in structural semantics, *Sémantique structurale* (*Structural Semantics*). With Todorov, Kristeva, Genette, Metz and others, Greimas was also a member of Lévi-Strauss's semiotic research group at the Collège de France. He died in 1992.

Greimas's intellectual trajectory is the result of an effort to analyse and formalise every aspect of discourse. As well as narrative discourse, discourse includes the discourses of the social and human sciences. Greimas has written on legal discourse, specifically on the French law relating to commercial companies, pointing out that 'as far as its form is concerned, every legal discourse is produced by a *legal grammar* that is distinct from the grammar of the natural language in which this discourse appears'.[2] The presence of recurring units that are distinct from conventional linguistic units is one of the indices that a more or less formalisable grammar of units exists, and that the possibility that a model of the relations between these units thus also exists. Like Saussure, Greimas recognises the importance of system: a single sign does not signify.

Unlike Saussure, however, Greimas places emphasis on language as an 'assemblage of structures of signification' which entails that the system is not given in advance, but must be articulated, or produced. The way that language works is thus the focus of Greimas's research; and in this we can see the influence of Merleau-Ponty. And so even though Greimas studies the relations between elements of a discourse – most often narrative discourse – rather than the substantive qualities of these elements, he also distances himself from the idealist persuasion of the 'father' of general linguistics.

Greimas follows Hjelmslev in developing a veritable grid of terms – a whole vocabulary in fact – for describing and analysing – semiotically – the domain of discourse. At a more or less auxiliary level, we have: the 'seme' (minimal meaning unit), the 'sememe' (the semic nucleus plus contextual semes which corresponds to the 'particular meaning of a word'), the 'classeme' (or contextual semes), the 'anaphora' (what serves to link utterances, or paragraphs) and so on.[3] While such a vocabulary differs from the terminology of conventional linguistics because its unit of analysis is not the sentence, but discourse, Greimas none the less often shows himself to be indebted to conventional linguistics in both the technical twist he gives to current terms, like 'inventory', 'presupposition', or 'practical', and in the way linguistics is, in Greimas's own words, 'the most developed of the semiotic disciplines', the one 'recognised as having the greatest claim to the status of science'.[4] The scientific, and putative rigour of linguistics, makes it the necessary point of departure for a researcher who values this rigour in intellectual work almost above all else, and who began his academic career in lexicography. In 1969, Greimas published his *Dictionnaire de l'ancien français* (*Dictionary of Old French*).

Structural semantics, however, breaks away from a conventional linguistic conception of meaning by focusing on neither the word nor the sentence out of context, but on the network of relations in which meaning emerges. As we have seen above, because, for Greimas, the notion of a 'network of relations' goes hand in hand with the enactment of language, a structural semantics becomes a structural semiotics when meaning is transposed into units of analysis *describing* the production of meaning in a given context. In short, structural semiotics describes the meaning of meaning. This meaning will be neither intentional (related to the psychological subject), nor hermeneutic (a meaning existing prior to the enactment of language). In sum, Greimas seeks to study the production of meaning in discourse: meaning as a process of signification.

By discourse, Greimas means what Benveniste meant: 'language as taken on by the person who is speaking'. Discourse is thus language as it is *enacted*. Understood in this way, it becomes clear that Greimas is interested in the first instance in the '*parole*'-side of the '*langue/parole*' equation. However, *langue*, or 'system' is not forgotten; for if a semiotic 'grammar' of meaning production is to be constructed, utterances have to be understood as being organised in some specific way; they are not simply contingent and arbitrary. For this reason, Greimas's structural semiotics of action, like Bourdieu's ethnography, is focused on strategies rather than on rules. Rules presuppose an actor behind the actions who conforms to these rules. The notion of rule dominates much of the work of early structuralism, with the consequent privileging of the actor behind the action. For Greimas, by contrast, there are only 'actants' – entities produced by the very configuration of discursive actions. Similarly, for a structural semiotics of the Greimasian kind, there is no subject behind discourse; only the subject produced by the discursive instance itself. Or rather, there may be an ultimate subject, but this is the concern of ontology not semiotics. Greimas thus says that the 'syntactic actant' is not 'the *person* who is speaking' – the ontological subject – but 'the *person who is speaking*'

– the virtual person constituted by virtue of his speaking.[5] In addition, Greimas – like other structuralist thinkers – is keen to avoid psychologising the discursive subject. One actant could be equivalent to two psychological actors – e.g., a husband and wife who together constitute a bundle of functions pertinent to the unfolding of a narrative. Or again, a city could be an actant, as is Paris in Greimas's analysis of 'Two Friends' by Maupassant.[6]

In order to describe the way that actants function, particularly in narrative discourse, Greimas has developed a number of key terms which need to be understood fully if what he has done is to be appreciated, or, for that matter, opposed.

The first key term is 'modality'. In linguistics this term originally referred to 'what modifies the predicate of an utterance'.[7] Thus with the statement, 'John had to write the letter' the predicate is in the mode of obligation. In logic, modality refers to the *way* in which something is, or is not, the case, is true or false; for example, to say that 'he was ill in 1930' is to attribute a temporal modality to the fact of being ill. Greimas's use of modality is perhaps closer to the logical sense than to the linguistic sense because he wants to give this notion an axiomatic status. Modalisation, then, is what characterises and limits any actantial situation. Indeed it is what is always *given* in any such situation. Thus 'wanting-to', 'having-to', 'knowing', 'being-able-to', 'doing' and 'being', etc., constitute fundamental modal values corresponding to specific levels of existence of the autonomous, semiotic micro-universe: 'wanting-to' and 'being-able-to' correspond to the virtual level of existence of modal values, 'knowing' and 'being-able-to' correspond to the level of actuality, while 'doing' and 'being' belong to the level of realisation. In sum, modalisation is a 'positing' in the form of an 'axiomatic declaration'; it is based on 'a hypothetico-deductive procedure' rather than on induction.

Modalisations overdetermine the action

of actants – the subjects in narrative discourse. Because they are related specifically to actions, they are necessarily discontinuous. They are therefore unable to account for continuous states relating, for example, to passion and emotion, to dispositions – or 'modalizations of the state of the subject'[8] – rather than to doing. Furthermore, if modalisations result from an axiomatics which gives rise to an order and a system, the passions introduce disorder, inchoateness, intertwining, undulations, and instabilities – processes which are precisely very difficult to systematise. To cope with this, the term 'aspectuality' was introduced in Greimas's semiotic study of passions. There, aspectuality is seen to be predominant in Paul Eluard's poem, *Capital de la douleur*, because of the poem's focus on inchoateness rather than on the 'semantic value of the objects yearned for'. Thus: 'love is acceptable only at its beginning; the gaze, when eyelids open on awakening; the day, at the moment it breaks with darkness; human life in infancy'. Eluard's poem, in short, valorises inchoateness. A key point about aspectuality is the important place assumed in it by the body in relation to passions and the subject's disposition, something that is a welcome initiative in a body of research that has the appearance of being incredibly abstract and cerebral.

'Isotopy' is another fundamental term in Greimas's semiotic vocabulary. As has been pointed out by Ronald Schleifer in his Introduction to the English translation of *Sémantique structurale*, Greimas, through the notion of isotopy, was able to shift the focus of semiotics from the sentence to discourse. Borrowed from chemistry (Greimas borrows frequently from the natural sciences), isotopy refers to parallel levels of meaning within a single, homogeneous discourse. It differs from the hierarchical 'surface/latent' opposition, which it renders redundant, and is more akin to the structure of the pun. Isotopy enables different elements (meanings, actions, utterances) to be related to the same discourse. In his study of Maupassant's short

story, 'Two Friends', Greimas shows that an isotopy can be: *actorial* – when passages describing separate actions are seen, ultimately, to refer to the actor, 'Paris'; *discursive* – when independently realised sentences are seen to refer to the same subject; *figurative* – when the text becomes the vehicle for several different allegories, or parables; and *thematic* – when the text implies a knowledge extending beyond narrative knowledge (in the case in point, about fishing and friendship). With 'isotopy', Greimas believes he has rendered invalid Freud's distinction, in the *Interpretation of Dreams*, between the 'manifest' and the 'latent' content of the dream.[9] Without denying either the possible insightfulness of 'isotopy' or the complexities of the matter, we should perhaps recall that while Greimas investigates the way an already-homogeneous text (e.g., 'Two Friends') is homogeneous, Freud was most often dealing with a radically heterogeneous set of elements from which a homogeneous text had to be constructed. As a result, the notions of 'manifest' and 'latent' are likely to differ in the two cases.

Let us now briefly attempt an assessment of Greimas's enterprise, first, in terms of the issue concerning the separation of the semiotic and the metaphysical, raised at the outset and, second, in terms of Greimas's analysis of the final part of his semiotic study of Maupassant's story, already referred to, 'Two Friends'.

As regards the separation of the semiotic from the metaphysical, or the ontological, we might simply ask the following question: is this separation really feasible, given that natural language, containing many metaphysical encrustations (cf. Derrida), has to be the vehicle of the science of semiotics itself? The evidence presented by Greimas's own language would seem to confirm the real difficulty involved.

With regard to Greimas's study of Maupassant's 'Two Friends', it is no doubt methodologically suspect to examine a commentary on the end of the story in isolation from what has preceded it. Despite this, the following point is a general one, and does try to take into account Greimas's enterprise as a whole.

First, we note that the tutor text – 'Two Friends' – comprises barely six pages, while the analytical text is nearly 250 pages long. Such a disparity, which is typical of the enterprise,[10] would seem to bring into question the practical possibility of analysing, not only a longer text, but also a more complex one. Above all, the reader begins to wonder whether Greimas has *really* left behind the linguistic fastidiousness characteristic of studies of the sentence.

More importantly, the way his analysis treats the dénouement of the story raises some doubts about the clear-sightedness of Greimas's enterprise. After being caught by the Prussians (it is the time of the Franco-Prussian War) while enjoying a day's fishing, the two friends are shot as French spies, their bodies weighted and dumped into the river from whence came their fish. The execution completed, the Prussian officer who ordered it then orders the live fish to be cooked. Immediately after, the final line reads: 'Then he began to smoke his pipe again.'

Here, the reader is struck with great force by the sharp contrast between the final line and the events immediately preceding it. This final line, we might suggest, because it is so out of place – or better, because it seems so arbitrary – holds the key to the story's emotional charge, a charge provoked by a sense of the callous indifference of the Prussian officer. Despite his references – through the use of isotopy – to Christian and other symbolism, Greimas nowhere treats of this key aspect of the story. This is what Greimas writes in the segment dealing with the final lines of the story: ' "To smoke a pipe" is without doubt the figurative representation of a state of *calm*, characterized by the absence of either somatic or noological disturbances.'[11] For Greimas, the final line is an element contributing to part of the grammar of narrative discourse he is trying

to construct. In this light he is seeking to reveal the structure of what determines the possibilities of narrative discourse as these are constituted by modalities, istotopes, cognitive and pragmatic doing, etc. This grammar would be the system implicit in the narrative processes. It, very laudably, gives precedence to strategy over rules. Nevertheless, in a fundamental way, it still seems to be exterior to the processes it isolates; it still dominates the tutor text and seems to have this as its key objective, coupled with the avoidance of being dominated (i.e. mystified) by it.

That said, the scientific aspiration behind Greimas's project entails an openness to the modifying of theory in light of difficulties encountered. In principle, therefore, the emotional charge of the text could perhaps eventually be accounted for, even if it poses the biggest challenge yet to structural semiotics.

Notes

1 A.J. Greimas, *Maupassant: The Semiotics of the Text*, trans. Paul Perron, Amsterdam and Philadelphia, John Benjamins, 1988, p. xxiv.

2 A.J. Greimas, *Narrative Semiotics and Cognitive Discourses*, trans. Paul Perron and Frank Collins, London, Pinter Publications 1990, p. 108.

3 The reader will find an excellent, elaborated inventory of all the pertinent terms in Greimas's *oeuvre* in A.J. Greimas and J. Courtés, *Semiotics and Language: An Analytic Dictionary*, trans. Larry Crist, et al., Bloomington, Indiana University Press, 1982.

4 Greimas, *Narrative Semiotics and Cognitive Discourses*, p. 12.

5 ibid., Greimas's emphasis.

6 Greimas, *Maupassant: The Semiotics of the Text*, p. 3.

7 Greimas and Courtés, *Semiotics and Language*, p. 193.

8 A.J. Greimas and Jacques Fontanille, *The Semiotics of Passion* (1991), trans. Paul Perron and Frank Collins, Minneapolis and London, University of Minnesota Press, 1991, p. 5.

9 A.J. Greimas, *Structural Semantics: An Attempt at a Method*, trans. Daniele McDowell, Ronald Schleifer and Alan Velie, Lincoln, University of Nebraska Press, 1983, p. 112.

10 See Greimas, 'On chance occurrences in what we call the human sciences: Analysis of text by Georges Dumézil' in *Narrative Semiotics and Cognitive Discourses*, pp. 59–91.
11 Greimas, *Maupassant: The Semiotics of Text*, p. 243.

See also in this book

Benveniste, Eco, Jakobson, Hjelmslev, Lévi-Strauss, Merleau-Ponty, Saussure

Greimas's major writings

Structural Semantics: An Attempt at a Method (1966), trans. Daniele McDowell, Ronald Schleifer, and Alan Velie, Lincoln, University of Nebraska Press, 1983
On Meaning: Selected Writings in Semiotic Theory (1970), trans. Paul Perron and Frank Collins, Minneapolis, University of Minnesota Press, 1987
Maupassant: The Semiotics of the Text (1976), trans. Paul Perron, Amsterdam and Philadelphia, John Benjamins, 1988
The Social Sciences, a Semiotic View (1976), trans. Paul Perron and Frank Collins, Minneapolis, University of Minnesota Press, 1990
A.J. Greimas and J. Courtés, *Semiotics and Language: An Analytic Dictionary* (1979), trans. Larry Crist, *et al.*, Bloomington, Indiana University Press, 1982
Du Sens II: Essais Semiotiques, Paris, Seuil, 1983
Narrative Semiotics and Cognitive Discourses, trans. (from the German) Paul Perron and Frank Collins, London, Pinter Publications, 1990
Of Gods and Men: Studies in Lithuanian Mythology (1985), trans. Milda Newman, Bloomington, Indiana University Press, 1992
The Semiotics of Passion (1991) (with Jacques Fontanille), trans. Paul Perron and Frank Collins, Minneapolis and London, University of Minneapolis Press, 1991

Further reading

Schleifer, Ronald, *A.J. Greimas and the Nature of Meaning: Linguistic Semiotics and Discourse Theory*, Lincoln, University of Nebraska Press, London, Croom Helm, 1987
Sorensen, Dolf, *Theory Formation and the Study of Literature*, Amsterdam, Rodopi, 1987

LOUIS HJELMSLEV

The Danish linguist and semiotician, Louis Hjelmslev, was born in 1899 and died in 1966. Hjelmslev attempted to render more rigorous and clear Saussure's general theory of language and semiotics. In particular, Hjelmslev is remembered as the inventor of 'glossematics' (see below), and for having given a new rigour to the notion of connotation.

Like Saussure, Hjelmslev starts from the position that language is a supra-individual institution which must be studied and analysed in its own right, rather than be viewed as the vehicle, or instrument, of knowledge, thought, emotion – or, more generally, as a means of contact with what is external to it. In short, the transcendental approach (language as a means) should give way to an immanent approach (the study of language in itself).[1] To this end, Hjelmslev developed what he thought of as a simple and rigorous system of concepts and terms which would both clarify, at the highest level of generality, the nature of language, and also render more proficient the study of its realisations.

For the Hjelmslev of the *Prolegomena to a Theory of Language* – his best-known work – language is both a sign system and a process of realisation (for Saussure, the comparable terminology is, respectively, '*langue*' and '*parole*'). Like Saussure, Hjelmslev also considers language to be a system of signs, and so it is important to be clear about the nature of the sign. First of all, we note that no sign exists by itself in isolation; rather, signs are always in a context in relation to other signs. To mark this fact, Hjelmslev speaks not about a sign as such, but about a sign function. A function he defines as 'a dependence that fulfils the conditions for an analysis'.[2] Just as there is a function between a class and its components, so there is a function between a sign and its components, 'expression' and 'content'. A sign, in short, is not some mark, or gesture with intrinsic qualities (an arrow might not always be a sign), but is what functions as a sign in a given context. For a sign function to exist, then, there must be – again, in Hjelmslev's terminology – an 'expression' and a 'content'. A sign function thus exists between these 'absolutely inseparable' 'terminals'. For the terminals constituting a sign function – the 'sign-expression' and the 'sign-content' – Hjelmslev gives the technical name of 'functives'. The sign-function depends on the mutual correlation of the functives in order to be what it is. Hjelmslev's point here is that a sign is not any physical or non-physical entity that can just be assumed and taken for granted by the linguist or the semiologist. Indeed, there is no actual realisation of a sign which would be identical to the sign-function. Saussure's comparable terminology of 'sign', 'signifier' and 'signified' suggests that this could be so.

To construct signs, language contains various kinds of non-signs (letters of the alphabet, for example) which make up the raw material necessary for the formation of new signs. These not-yet-signs, as it were, Hjelmslev calls 'figurae'. Figurae evoke the notion of the 'floating signifier' Lévi-Strauss discovers in Mauss's work. They suggest that language is always an open-ended totality, and not a system as such, where the elements would constitute a self-contained whole. It must be said, however, that, like Mauss, there is no explicit acknowledgement of this implication in Hjelmslev's own analysis. Even for Hjelmslev, who is intensely absorbed with working out a rigorous, simple, and exhaustive formalisation of language, language must be seen to have a fundamental link to meaning, and/or to thought.[3] Whether it is meaning or thought that is at stake is not quite clear; in any case, Hjelmslev prefers to say that language is linked to 'purport', which is, as he puts it in one formulation, 'the factor that is common . . . to all languages', namely, 'the amorphous "thought-mass" '[4] which to a certain extent is external to language as such. As we shall see, 'purport' is the most problematical factor in the whole of Hjelmslev's theory. For the moment, we note that purport is inseparable from language – language would cease to have any *raison d'être* without it – and yet, in some sense, purport is external to language. 'In itself', Hjelmslev says, 'purport is unformed, not in itself subjected to formation but simply susceptible to formation.'[5] Thus, like Saussure,[6] Hjelmslev says that the most distinctive feature of language in general is its being form in relation to substance (purport). On the other hand, the situation is more complicated for Hjelmslev in that for him, there is both expression-purport and content-purport – and yet, in general, purport is 'inaccessible to knowledge' in so far as knowledge is a 'formation'.[7] To clarify this, it is necessary to explain what Hjelmslev means by 'expression' and 'content'.

As a preliminary to understanding the full import of 'expression' and 'content', we see first of all that Hjelmslev considers language in terms of two different, but interconnected planes: that of 'system' – which corresponds to the underlying, always already realised structure of language – and that of 'process', also called 'text', which is always virtual. Process (text) is not, as one might expect, the realisation of language (system); so while it is impossible to have a text without a language, it is possible to have a language without a text.[8] Because Hjelmslev confuses 'virtual', 'real' and 'concrete', a clearer way of putting it would be to say that language is realised, but remains virtual, while process is concrete but is only ever partially realised. System (grammar, syntax, vocabulary), then, makes possible the production of an innumerable number of texts, while a multitude of texts will only ever imply one system, or language. The relationship between 'expression' and 'content' is thus analysed by Hjelmslev in terms of both the axes mentioned.

'Expression' and 'content', we find, are also the two inseparable functives of the sign-function. Expression can occur in a variety of ways: through speech, writing, gesture (sign language) – each medium itself being realisable in numerous other media (books, television, radio, newspapers, pamphlets, telephone, Morse code, semaphore, stone tablets, inscriptions of all kinds (on walls, floors, tombstones), film, posters, art-works, everyday conversation and writing). In other words, expression takes a particular form (e.g., in the words 'I love Ron'), and it exists in a substance (e.g., the human voice, or as marks carved on a wall). Consequently, there is both an expression-form (the words), and an expression-substance (the material of the words). On the content side, too, there is both 'form' and 'substance'. Content can be defined generally as the form in which a meaning is articulated. Hjelmslev prefers the term, 'content', instead of 'meaning', because the same meaning can often be articulated by different contents – the contents of a natural language. Hjelmslev illustrates this point with the example shown in Figure 3, where the content varies in relation to the same semantic area (area of purport).

Figure 3 Hjelmslev's content–meaning interchange

Danish	German	French
trae	Baum	arbre
skov	Holz	bois
	Wald	forêt

Source: Hjelmslev, *Prolegomena*, p. 57.

Here we see that in Danish, *trae* covers all of the German *Baum* and the French *arbre*, and partly covers the German *Holz* and less of the French, *bois*. Similarly, *skov* partly translates the German *Holz* and *Wald*, as well as most of the French, *bois*, and some of the French, *forêt*. Hjelmslev comments that this 'incongruence within one and the same zone of purport turns up everywhere'.[9] Illustrated

in the example from the perspective of the system plane is the level of the content-form of the sign-function. It is as though language, in its different articulations, divided up the same meaning area (purport) in ways specific to these different articulations (content). The purport is thus given form by the content-form, and the meaning as such is the content-substance. One way of understanding this, according to one of Hjelmslev's interpreters, is to say that 'both forms [expression-form, and content-form] manifest themselves in a "substance" '.[10] The key term here is not 'substance', but 'manifest' – rendered visible, revealed, perceivable, made public, etc. Philosophically of course, substance, in the thirteenth century, was equivalent to essence – precisely what was not *manifest* (Hjelmslev decries so-called non-linguistic usage of terms, and yet it seems that it is precisely a feature of language to evoke a number of different contexts simultaneously). Even in connection to the more modern form of 'substantive', the sense is less to do with what is revealed, and more to do with what is hidden. Not that this would necessarily be a problem for Hjelmslev's theory if the term 'substance' could be consistently translated as what is manifest. However, when purport is also said to be substance,[11] confusion can only result.

Variations in content-form (different meanings attached to the same area of purport, so that languages are not directly translatable), Hjelmslev equates with the system of content, whereas constancy in the content-form (same idea expressed in different languages, so that expressions are directly translatable), Hjelmslev equates with the process of the content. Similarly, when – to take another of Hjelmslev's examples – speakers of different languages are trying to pronounce 'Berlin', the expression purport will vary (due to accent), while the content-purport will remain the same. Again, the same pronunciation (expression-purport) in different languages might be the same (*got*, *Gott* ('God' in German), *godt* ('well' in

Danish)), while the content-purport differs. Both examples come from the plane of process, according to Hjelmslev.

The reason for this elaboration of the sign-function, says our author, is to demonstrate that the sign is not simply a label for a pre-existing thing. It also means avoiding the artificial divisions in linguistics between 'phonetics, morphology, syntax, lexicography, and semantics'. Indeed, so concerned is Hjelmslev to get the study of language on to a new footing that he invoked the name of 'glossematics' (from the Greek *glossa*, meaning 'language') to signal the innovative nature of his approach.

Glossematics would be 'an algebra of language operating with unnamed entities',[12] a science having the 'immanent algebra of language'[13] as its object. The reason for this new approach stems from the point made at the outset to the effect that for too long, according to Hjelmslev, linguistics has studied language from a transcendent point of view, meaning that non-linguistic features have been used to explain language. Glossematics, then, endeavours to provide a rigorous, simple and exhaustive framework and terminology for explaining language reality and language usage. To this end, Hjelmslev devoted his energies to developing and refining a technical vocabulary that we shall not go into here. From a more general, semiotic perspective, however, Hjelmslev's theory of 'denotation' and 'connotation' should be explained. Denotation, as the term implies, is the area of expression which refers to a content – for example, the sentence, 'The cat sat on the mat' denotes a cat sitting on a mat. The same sentence looked at from the perspective of connotation, might evoke the context of young children, or again, a kind of 'typical' example used as an example. More formally, connotation refers to the fact that the expression and content taken together become another expression referring to another content. Diagrammatically, this may be expressed as in Figure 4.

Figure 4 Expression and content in Eco's thought

EXPRESSION		CONTENT
EXPRESSION	CONTENT	

Source: Eco, *A Theory of Semiotics*, p. 55.

For his part, Hjelmslev says that a denotative semiotic is 'a semiotic none of whose planes is a semiotic', whereas a connotative semiotic is a semiotic 'whose expression plane is a semiotic'.[14] Not only this, however. For the content plane, too, can be a semiotic, and this Hjelmslev calls a 'metasemiotics'. Linguistics, says Hjelmslev, is an example of a metasemiotic: the study of language which is itself an example of language. Writers such as Barthes, Todorov, and Eco have made use of the notions of denotative and connotative semiotics, but they have been more circumspect about the viability of the notion of metasemiotics.

It remains to give a brief assessment of Hjelmslev's theory of language and semiotics. Clearly, Hjelmslev's project opens up a wide range of issues, and the rigour introduced into semiotics reveals how easy it is to take the notion of sign for granted, so that it becomes a simple vehicle of meaning, regardless of the language involved. On the other hand, Hjelmslev's own elaboration of his theory of language often goes against the strictures of coherence and simplicity. Similarly, while Saussure's notions of 'form' and 'substance' do indeed call for clarification, it is precisely on this point that Hjelmslev, too, very nearly runs aground. Indeed, a close reading of the *Prolegomena* in terms of its coherence, leaves the reader entirely uncertain as to how 'purport' – the *inaccessible* amorphous mass outside the sign system – can be linked to 'expression' and to 'content' in the expressions, 'expression-purport' and 'content-purport'; for in order to be implicated in either of the two sign funcitves, purport has to take on a specific form, which, by definition, it cannot have. What we have are two different purports that are what they are in being distinguished from each other. The very fact of its being distinguished brings purport into the semiotic sphere, so that it ceases to be either external to language or amorphous.

There is, however, a further problem regarding purport. It is that, even if one were to overlook Hjelmslev's inconsistent use of the term, the author of the *Prolegomena* is forced to have recourse to an extra-linguistic or semiotic dimension to facilitate the development of an 'immanent' linguistics. In other words, purport is Hjelmslev's inadvertent way of giving his theory a transcendental element, the very thing he strove not to do. It is for this reason that Julia Kristeva is able to argue that Hjelmslev's theory remained rooted in the influential phenomenological framework that has dominated linguistics to this very day.[15]

More positively Hjelmslev has made progress in clarifying Saussure's distinction between *langue* and *parole*. For Saussure erred in privileging the spoken word at the level of *parole*, and Hjelmslev's use of 'text', or 'process' adds to the rigour of the description. On the other hand, by defining 'system' (Saussure's *langue*) as being independent of 'text', Hjelmslev seems to be saying that language is essentially a system – for while a language without a text is 'imaginable', a text without a language is not. The risk comes in reducing language as such to a linguistic model of it, instead of recognising that the two levels (model and usage) are inseparable from one another.

Although, as Eco acknowledges, Hjelmslev's theory often strikes the reader as being of 'apparently Byzantine complexity',[16] Hjelmslev's determination to offer a strictly 'immanent' theory of language and semiotics has provided the inspiration for others, such as Eco and Derrida,[17] who have embarked upon a project of setting out a semiotic framework that begins to destabilise the metaphysical edifice at the heart of a

transcendental theory of signs and sign systems.

Notes

1 See Louis Hjelmslev, *Prolegomena to a Theory of Language*, trans. Francis J. Whitfield, Madison, University of Wisconsin Press, revised English edn, reprinted 1963, pp. 4–5.
2 ibid., p. 33.
3 In the French translation of Hjelmslev's *Prolegomena*, 'purport' – a translation of the Danish word, *mening* – is rendered as '*sens*' (meaning).
4 Hjelmslev, *Prolegomena*, p. 52.
5 ibid., p. 76.
6 See F. de Saussure, *Cours de linguistique générale*, Paris, Payot, 1972, pp. 155–6.
7 Hjelmslev, *Prolegomena*, p. 76.
8 ibid., pp. 39–40.
9 ibid., p. 54.
10 B. Siertsema, *A Study of Glossematics. A Critical Survey of its Fundamental Concepts*, The Hague, Paris, Martinus Nijhoff, 1955, p. 17.
11 Hjelmslev, *Prolegomena*, p. 52 and p. 80.
12 ibid., p. 79.
13 ibid., p. 80.
14 ibid., p. 114.
15 Julia Kristeva, *Revolution in Poetic Language*, trans. Margaret Waller, New York, Columbia University Press, 1984, pp. 38–40.
16 Umberto Eco, *A Theory of Semiotics*, Bloomington, Indiana University Press, 1979, p. 52.
17 See Jacques Derrida, *Of Grammatology*, trans. Gayatri Chakravorty Spivak, Baltimore, Johns Hopkins University Press, 1976, pp. 57–60.

See also in this book

Derrida, Eco, Greimas, Kristeva, Saussure

Hjelmslev's major writings

Prolegomena to a Theory of Language (1943), trans. Francis J. Whitfield, Madison, University of Wisconsin Press, 1963
Language. An Introduction, trans. Francis J. Whitfield, Madison, University of Wisconsin Press, 1970

Further reading

Siertsema, B., *A Study of Glossematics: Critical Survey of its Fundamental Concepts*, The Hague, Paris, Martinus Nijhoff, 1955

JULIA KRISTEVA

For some, Julia Kristeva is best known as a feminist theorist. And while it is true that the psychoanalytic orientation of her work has led her to reflect upon the nature of the feminine (which she sees as the source of the unnameable and inexpressible), she has always maintained a clear interest in the nature of language and its manifestations. Indeed Kristeva has now demonstrated this interest in 1990 in a very practical way by publishing a *roman à clé* called, *Les Samouraïs*. Like de Beauvoir's *Mandarins*, which Kristeva's title recalls, *Les Samouraïs*, too, is ostensibly a vivisection of the lives and loves of the Parisian intellectual avant-garde. This time it is Kristeva's own generation – the one coming after Sartre – who are the focus of attention.

Julia Kristeva was born in 1941 and, as a student, came to Paris from Bulgaria in 1965. She immediately became immersed in Parisian intellectual life, attending the seminars of Roland Barthes and becoming involved with the writers and intellectuals centred around the avant-garde literary journal, *Tel Quel*, edited by Philippe Sollers. *Tel Quel* at the end of the 1960s quickly became a leading force in the critique of representation – in writing as much as in politics – and this influence has been a lasting one for Kristeva.

The predominant feature of Kristeva's work is its concern to analyse the unanalysable: the inexpressible, heterogeneous, radical otherness of individual and cultural life. Although this could open the way to mysticism, Kristeva demonstrates an equal concern for the symbolic appropriation of this unanalysable domain. Her later writing, in particular, clearly alludes to the folly of any complete abandonment to otherness.

Kristeva first came into prominence in the late 1960s as the interpreter of the work of the Russian formalist Mikhail Bakhtin.[1] In this regard, she highlighted Bakhtin's theory of the 'dialogical' novel, as well as his notion of 'carnival'. Soon after, Kristeva established herself as an important theorist of language and literature in her own right with the concept of 'semanalysis'.[2] Semanalysis, Kristeva sought to show, focuses on the materiality of language (its sounds, rhythms and graphic disposition), rather than simply on its communicative function. While the logic of the latter can quite readily be included within conventional scientific procedures which, in particular, work to eliminate contradiction, the material base of language cannot be explained within the framework of such a conventional scientific logic. Poetic language, as the embodiment of language's materiality, cannot be formalised using this framework, but requires one that is much more supple and sophisticated. Because of its fundamentally heterogeneous nature, poetic language (as in the works of Joyce or Mallarmé) challenges the homogeneous, commonly accepted form of language as being uniquely a vehicle of meaning and communication. Poetic language disrupts meaning, or at least opens the way to a range of new meanings, and even to new ways of understanding. Not to be able, intially, to understand poetic language, is thus the first perceptible index of its very real effects.

Kristeva's interest in trying to analyse the heterogeneous nature of poetic language while she was still a student in Paris in the late 1960s and early 1970s, distinguished her from other semioticians who were more interested in formalising the conventional workings of language. It gave her a taste for grasping language in its dynamic, transgressive and practical forms, rather than in the form of a static instrument, as the analyses of many linguists implied. The static view of language, Kristeva claimed, is tied to the notion that language is reducible to those dimensions (such as logical propositions) that can be apprehended by consciousness, to the exclusion of the material, heterogeneous and unconscious dimension. Concern for the unconscious leads Kristeva to develop her theory of the subject as a subject in process. This is to say that the subject is never simply the static, punctual subject of consciousness: it is never simply the static phenomenon captured in an imaginary form of one kind or another – one that may be communicated to others; it is also its unspeakable, unnameable, repressed form which is only knowable through its effects.

Concern for the connection between language and its importance in the formation of the subject led Kristeva, in 1974, to develop a theory of the 'semiotic' (le sémiotique) in her doctoral thesis, La révolution du langage poétique [Revolution in Poetic Language]. Here, she distinguishes le sémiotique from both la sémiotique (conventional semiotics) and the 'symbolic' – the sphere of representations, images, and all forms of fully articulated language. At the explicitly textual level, the semiotic and the symbolic correspond respectively to what are called the 'genotext' and the 'phenotext'. The genotext, Kristeva says, 'is not linguistic' 'it is rather a process'.[3] It is language's foundation. The 'phenotext', by contrast, corresponds to the language of communication. It is the level at which we normally read when searching for the meaning of words. Neither the genotext nor the phenotext exists in isolation, however. They always exist together in what Kristeva calls 'the signifying process'.

In her magnum opus, La révolution du langage poétique, Kristeva not only shows how the semiotic basis of language (its sounds and rhythms, and multiple bases of enunciation) is exploited by nineteenth-century avant-garde writers such as Mallarmé and Lautréamont, but she also demonstrates how poetic language has effects within a specific historical and economic formation, namely, the France of the Third Republic. In this work, too, Kristeva continues her development of a theory of the subject as a subject in process; but now she calls quite explicitly on Lacanian psychoanalytic theory. The semiotic thus becomes equated with the feminine chora, which is

roughly the unrepresentable place of the mother. It is a kind of origin, but not one that is nameable; for that place it would place it squarely within the symbolic realm and give us a false notion of it. Like the feminine in general, the chora is on the side of the material, poetic dimension of language.

While the semiotic disposition of language may be observed in the work of poets like Mallarmé, it is important to recognise that what the artist makes explicit is also manifest during the child's acquisition of language. Thus in cries, singing, and gestures, in rhythm, prosody and word-plays, or in laughter, the child presents the raw material to be used by the avant-garde poet. This is an extra-linguistic dimension linked to a signifying practice: that is, a practice capable of shaking an existing, perhaps ossified, form of the symbolic, so that a new form may evolve.

Kristeva has written many often complex and elaborate essays and articles on the themes discussed above, and in 1977 these were published in a collection called Polylogue. But in 1980, the tenor of Kristeva's work changed. Gone were the very elaborate attempts to develop a general theory of the subject and language, and in their place emerged a concern to analyse specific personal and artistic experiences (whether these be her own or those of her analysands), experiences which might, at the same time, offer a deeper understanding of social and cultural life. Thus in Powers of Horror: An Essay on Abjection Kristeva shows how the abject, as a point of ambiguity beyond what can be consciously coped with by either the individual or society, is evoked in an individual's vomiting because of the dislike of certain foods, or in social rituals dealing with pollution, or in works of art which either attempt to express, or repress the abject as horror and ambiguity.

Subsequently, Kristeva has produced studies on love (Tales of Love), melancholy and depression (Black Sun), and on the history and experience of being a foreigner (Strangers to Ourselves). In contrast to her earlier work, the importance for the individual subject of a successful entry into the symbolic predominates. Love, for example, is impossible without the capacity for idealisation and identification. This capacity is the precondition of identity formation and depends on the successful separation of the child from the mother: that is, on the successful assumption of individual autonomy. Given a more religious disposition, it would be easier for us to appreciate the role the notion of God as love (*agape*) once played in the formation of subjectivity. *Agape* is the power coming from the 'outside', the first tentative source of identification, the first tentative movement of separation from the mother. Without *agape*, *eros* becomes a blind impulse on the road to destruction. Kristeva calls the equivalent of *agape* in her psychoanalytic theory of the subject, 'the father of individual prehistory': the most elementary and indispensable basis of identity formation. The message here, perhaps, is not that identity is everything – as some of the early semioticians seemed to imply – but that a kind of harmony needs to be achieved between identity and the heterogeneous, potentially poetic elements capable of tearing it apart. In contrast to love, melancholy is equivalent to a severe impediment to the formation of symbolic and imaginary capacities. Typically, the one severely afflicted by melancholia is unable to love because unable to construct the necessary idealisations. Melancholics and depressives live in a kind of perpetual mourning for the mother. As Kristeva says: 'the speech of the depressed is to them like an alien skin; melancholy persons are foreigners in their maternal tongue'.[4]

Kristeva's work over the last decade can be seen as a series of specific elaborations of a theory of the subject. There can be no *final* elaboration. For Kristeva presents a subject which is never entirely analysable, but rather one always incomplete: the subject as the impetus for an infinite series of elaborations.

The space in which the dynamics of subjectivity are seen by Kristeva to be played out is the artistic space. The sense in which this is so is important; for it differentiates Kristeva from many other critics and semioticians. Thus while any artistic work must exhibit indications of human control and order for it to be identified as such, there is no complete subject prior to the work. Rather, artistic endeavour constitutes the subject as much as the subject constitutes the work of art. Moreover, because of the intimate link between art and the formation of subjectivity, Kristeva has always found art to be a particularly fruitful basis for analysis. Thus Mallarmé's poetry puts the 'semiotic disposition' in evidence, while *Romeo and Juliet* indicates the dynamics of love, and Dostoyevsky the structure of suffering and forgiveness in relation to a melancholic disposition. Given an open disposition, the recipients of the artistic message, or artistic effects, may have their symbolic and imaginary capacities expanded: that is, a work of art may become the basis of an authentic experience capable of opening the way to a change in personality. The problem today, Kristeva's work suggests, is that social life is increasingly characterised by subjects closed off from the qualities of works of art which do not conform to pre-conceptions and stereotypes. Or else people are simply fascinated and seduced by the play of images or acts – by the object – without being able to develop new symbolic capacities which would enable the object to be a new ingredient in social life. The aim, then, is to bring about a situation where subjectivity is an 'open system', or a 'work in progress', a becoming 'open to the other' which at the same time can bring about a revised form of one's own identity.

In this, Kristeva shows herself still to be wedded to an avant-garde theory of art and society. She is avant-garde because she is calling for new identities to be formed, not for the destruction of identity – something which can, she believes, lead to grave social consequences in the form of insidious violence and an incapacity of people to separate themselves, individually and autonomously, from their environment. Instead, individuals would risk becoming totally subsumed by their environment. The point is not, let it be emphasised, to retreat back into a static view of the individual self as prior to social relations, but rather a view of that which reminds us of the need to ensure that the symbolic itself is not destroyed when it is necessarily transformed.

Notes

1 See Julia Kristeva, 'Word, dialogue, novel' in Toril Moi (ed.), *The Kristeva Reader*, Oxford, Basil Blackwell, 1986, pp. 34–61.
2 See Julia Kristeva, *Séméiotiké. Recherches pour une sémanalyse*, Paris, Seuil, 1969; and Julia Kristeva, 'The system and the speaking subject' in Moi (ed.), *The Kristeva Reader*, pp. 24–33.
3 Julia Kristeva, *Revolution in Poetic Language*, trans. Margaret Waller, New York, Columbia University Press, 1984, p. 87.
4 Julia Kristeva, *Black Sun*, trans. Leon S. Roudiez, New York, Columbia University Press, 1989, p. 53.

See also in this book

Bakhtin, Barthes, Joyce, Lacan, Mallarmé

Kristeva's major writings

Séméiotiké. Recherches pour une sémanalyse, Paris, Seuil, 1969
Le Texte du roman. Approche sémiologique d'une structure discursive transformationnelle, The Hague, Paris, Mouton, 1970
About Chinese Women (1974), trans. Anita Barrows, New York and London, Marion Boyars, paperback edn, 1986
Revolution in Poetic Language (1974), trans. Margaret Waller, New York, Columbia University Press, 1984
Polylogue, Paris, Seuil, 1977. Eight of the twenty essays are in English in *Desire in Language. A Semiotic Approach to Literature and Art*, trans. Thomas S. Gora, Alice Jardine, and Leon S. Roudiez, Oxford, Basil Blackwell, reprinted 1984
Powers of Horror. An Essay on Abjection (1980), trans. Leon S. Roudiez, New York, Columbia University Press, 1982
Tales of Love (1983), trans. Leon S. Roudiez, New York, Columbia University Press, 1987
Black Sun (1987), trans. Leon S. Roudiez, New York, Columbia University Press, 1989
Strangers to Ourselves (1988), trans. Leon S. Roudiez, New York, Columbia University Press, 1991

Further reading

Grosz, Elizabeth, *Sexual Subversions. Three French Feminists: Julia Kristeva, Luce Irigaray, Michèle Le Doeuff*, Sydney, Allen & Unwin, 1989
Fletcher, John, and Benjamin, Andrew (eds), *Abjection, Melancholia and Love: The Work of Julia Kristeva*, London and New York, Routledge: Warwick Studies in Philosophy and Literature, 1990
Lechte, John, *Julia Kristeva*, London and New York, Routledge, 1990
Oliver, Kelly, *Reading Kristeva*, Bloomington, Indiana University Press, 1993

CHARLES SANDERS PEIRCE

Charles Sanders Peirce was born into an intellectual family in 1839 (his father, Benjamin, was a professor of mathematics at Harvard), and in the years 1859, 1862, and 1863, respectively, he received the degrees of BA, MA, and BSc from Harvard. For more than thirty years (1859–60, 1861–91), Peirce did mainly astronomical and geodetic work for the United States Coast Survey. From 1879 to 1884, he was a part-time lecturer in logic at the Johns Hopkins University.

Such qualifications and experience do not really convey the classical erudition that comes through in Peirce's writings. Not only did he translate the now familiar term 'semiotic' from the Ancient Greek, he was also a scholar of both Kant and Hegel whom he read in the German, and he had a particular affinity for the philosophy of John Duns Scotus, especially Scotus's term, *haecceity*, meaning 'thisness'.[1] *Haecceity* is also evocative of singularity.

It has often been remarked that Peirce was an original mind who, as well as being the reputed founder of pragmatism, made significant contributions in philosophical and mathematical logic, and, in particular, founded semiotics. Less often remarked upon is the fact that Peirce saw his semiotic theory – his work on signs – as being inseparable from his work on logic. In fact, according to him, logic, in its broadest sense, is 'thought always taking place by means of signs', equivalent to a 'general semeiotic [sic], treating not merely of truth, but also of the general conditions of signs being signs' (1.444). Briefly, signs are connected with logic because signs are the vehicles for thought as the articulation of logical forms. Even more pertinently, Peirce shows in a paper published in 1868, when he was 29, that: 'The only thought, then, which can possibly be cognized is thought in signs. But thought which cannot be cognized does not exist. All thought, therefore, must necessarily be in signs' (5.251). Consequently, for Peirce, philosophy in general is inseparable from the articulation and interpretation of signs. Be this as it may, our interest here is in Peirce's theory of signs; our focus will thus be on Peirce the semiotician.

Although Peirce published more than ten thousand printed pages, he never published a book-length study on any of his cherished subjects. The result is that, with regard to his work on signs, Peirce's thought has to be treated as being always in process and subject to modification and further elaboration. More than this, Peirce often gives the impression that he found it necessary to begin again at each new meditation on a question, as though, on each occasion, a new audience was envisaged (hence the repetition), and as though a previous formulation on the topic was defective (hence the alterations and elaboration). There is, in sum, no systematic and definitive Peircean document on the nature of signs; only successive reworkings which repeat as much as innovate. What, then, are the essential aspects of this material on signs?

Within the domain of semiotics it has often been repeated[2] that, in the most general sense, a sign, according to Peirce, is what represents something for someone (cf. 2.228). The simplicity of this formulation belies the fact that there is a sign function: sign A denotes a fact (or object) B, for an interpretant, C. A sign is thus never an isolated entity, but always has these three aspects. A sign itself, Peirce says, is an instance of Firstness, its object, an instance of Secondness, and the interpretant – the mediating element – an instance of Thirdness. Peirce, indeed, sought out ternary structures wherever they might occur. Thirdness in the context of sign production also gives rise to unlimited semiosis, in as far as an interpretant (idea), which reads the sign as a sign of something (i.e. as the representation of a meaning or a referent), can always be grasped by another interpretant. The interpretant is the indispensable element needed in order to link the sign to its object (induction, deduction, and abduction (hypothesis) constitute three – again, three – important types of interpretant). A sign, to exist as a sign, must be interpreted (and so have an interpretant). The word, 'S-T-O-P' on a red background at a traffic intersection means that one must come to a halt at the intersection. The sign is /stop/; the object is 'coming to a halt', and the interpretant is the idea joining the sign to that particular object. The sign could also indicate the presence of a main road, or a heavily populated area. A process of unlimited semiosis is set in train through the function of the interpretant. That is, as Eco says, the interpretant is another interpretation.[3]

Like the sign function, sign-types also have a basic triadic form. The three fundamental elements of this form are icon, index, and symbol. Put most simply, an iconic sign is one which is, in one or more respects, the same as the object signified. In other words, the 'significant virtue' of an icon is its quality. A portrait then is iconic to the extent that the qualities of the representation are deemed to be similar to the qualities of the subject represented. While Peirce acknowledges that icons may contain conventional elements, Eco has argued that a mirror-image is an 'absolute icon'.[4] An index, for its part, is a sign physically linked to, or affected by, its object. Examples given by Peirce are a weathercock, a barometer, a sundial. Demonstrative pronouns (this, that), a cry of 'Help!' as indicative of someone in need, or a knock on the door indicating that there is someone at the door, are also examples of signs serving as indices. Unlike the icon, an index has a 'dynamical' relation to what it signifies. 'Symbol', as Peirce reminds us, originally meant something 'thrown together' making a contract or convention (2.297). In a contemporary setting, a symbol for Peirce (who differs from Saussure on this point), refers to conventional signs used, for instance, in speaking and writing. 'A genuine symbol', Peirce writes, 'is a symbol that has a general meaning' (2.293). Peirce's notion of symbol hints at Saussure's conception of the arbitrary relationship between signifier and signified. For a symbol's relation to its object is of an 'imputed' character. With the notion of symbol, the force of the notion of interpretant also becomes clearer. For no symbol, given its imputed, or unmotivated relation to its object, could be a symbol without being interpreted. Speech utterances determine corresponding signs (= interpretants) in the mind of the listener. Thus symbol and interpretant are inseparable.

Peirce continued to analyse this fundamental division of signs throughout his life. In light of these analyses he realised that the purity of his basic sign forms of icon, index, and symbol was problematic. Any given instance of an icon (e.g., a portrait) could be seen to have conventional elements. And if the portrait were a photograph, both iconic and indexical features come together. Although the basic, trichotomous sign division mentioned above is his most well-known one, Peirce also distinguished signs in terms of two further trichotomies, perhaps in an effort to add a degree of suppleness to his classifications, but maybe, unconsciously, because he was driven to see things in terms of ternary structures. Whatever the case, Peirce constructed a plethora of trichotomies – to the point where, in the case of sign divisions, he produced (as in the following Table 1) a basic trichotomy of trichotomies.

With the first and third trichotomies, Peirce adds refinement to his division of signs, making it capable of analysing an ever greater diversity and complexity of sign

Table 1 Summary of Peirce's three trichotomies of signs

1 *Qualisign* [= a quality which is a sign.]	*Sinsign* ['sin' = 'only once': an event which is a sign.]	*Legisign* [= a law which is a sign. Every conventional sign is a legisign.]
2 *Icon* [= a sign which has the quality of the object it denotes.]	*Index* [= a sign which denotes an object by being affected by that object.]	*Symbol* [= a conventional sign.]
3 *Rheme* [= a sign of a qualitative possibility, i.e. it represents a possible object.]	*Dicent sign* [= a sign of the actual existence of an object.]	*Argument* [= a sign of a law.]

Source: Based on Peirce, 2.243–53.

production. Having this nucleus of three trichotomies as his point of departure, Peirce went even further towards constructing an analytical nomenclature for distinguishing between different signs by proposing ten classes of signs. These ten classes are made up of combinations of the founding trichotomies. To take but one example – often favoured by Peirce – that of a weathercock: it is a 'Dicent Sinsign' (a classification derived from trichotomies 1 and 3). Of such a sign, Peirce writes that it

> is any object of direct experience, in so far as it is a sign, and, as such affords information concerning its Object. This it can only do by being really affected by its Object; so that it is necessarily an Index. The only information it can afford is of actual fact. Such a sign must involve an Iconic Sinsign to embody information and a Rhematic Indexical Sinsign to indicate the Object to which the information refers. But the mode of combination, or *Syntax*, of these two must also be significant (2.257).

Demonstrated here is the fact that no single, material instance of a sign exactly corresponds to a given classification. Only through continually refining the nomenclature will analytical profundity be attained. By this strategy, Peirce aims to do justice to the very real complexity of sign production. In a sense, there is no Peircean theory of signs, only an ever more supple table of sign classification.

Two crucial issues arise from Peirce's approach to signs. The first concerns the fact that Peirce rarely moves much beyond his attempt to develop and refine a table of sign categories. Like every table of categories it is supposed to be exhaustive. One can wonder, however, as to whether a (relatively) static table does justice to the very real dynamism of sign production. Furthermore, the fact that each sign seems to have a relative autonomy *vis-à-vis* other signs only heightens the sense that, in the end, Peirce's system is rather

Newtonian in character. Unlike Saussure, Peirce seemed to be much more taken with the physical aspect of material signs in themselves than in signs as elements in a system of discourse. The latter would come under Peirce's category of the symbol; and while the nature of the symbol is not neglected by Peirce, his interest is clearly centred on the essentially physical iconic and indexical signs.

While giving due recognition to Peirce's achievement in making sign distinctions, Eco has nevertheless been able to render suspect the very possibility of a truly natural property so necessary for the viability of the Peircean icon or index.[5] According to Eco, the iconic sign is always culturally coded without being entirely arbitrary. And it would seem that it has to be if it is to exemplify Peirce's principle of unlimited semiosis. Unlimited semiosis – perhaps Peirce's most original contribution to semiotics – implies that a sign must be translatable into other signs via an interpretant. Now clearly, if an icon qua sign were to be distinguished from other signs by virtue of its having the same qualities as the object signified, the principle of unlimited semiosis would seem to be placed in jeopardy.

For Eco, a possible way out is to recognise that as far as a sign structure is concerned, so-called physical qualities are in fact embedded in a perceptual structure and are therefore coded. Because it is coded (i.e. because it is not identical with the *perceptum*) a perception can be reproduced, or translated into other signs. Eco thus proposes that 'iconic signs do not possess the "same" physical properties as their objects, but they rely on the same perceptual structure, or the same system of relations'.[6] On the other hand, Eco also suggests that an iconic sign is difficult to analyse precisely because it puts the existing code in question. It is a case of *ratio difficilis* which has the potential to challenge the existing code and thereby render it more subtle.

To some extent Peirce himself anticipated the limitations that Eco and others have detected in his writings on signs. And this not only in the sense of a positivist scientist ready to cede his place in history to a new generation of researchers, but also in the sense of one who saw himself as a 'pioneer, or rather a backwoodsman' engaged in 'clearing and opening up' the '*semiotic*, that is, the doctrine of the essential nature and fundamental varieties of possible semiosis'(5.488). And as though anticipating Bakhtin's reading of Dostoyevsky, Peirce also argued, not only that all thinking is necessarily in signs, but that 'all thinking is dialogic in form' (6.338), even if this dialogue be only with oneself. This dynamic thread in Peirce's theory of signs makes him the father of a non-positivist semiotics.

Notes

1 See *Collected Papers of Charles Sanders Peirce*, 8 vols, ed. Charles Hartshorne and Paul Weiss (vols 1–6) and Arthur Burks (vols 7–8), Cambridge Mass., The Belknap Press of Harvard University Press, 1931–58, Vols 1 and 2 in one volume, 1965, Vol. 1, paragraph 341. Hereafter, the volume and paragraph number will be given in the body of the text.
2 cf. Umberto Eco, *A Theory of Semiotics*, Bloomington, Indiana University Press, (Midland Book edn) 1979; Julia Kristeva, *Language, The Unknown: An Initiation into Linguistics*, trans. Anne Menke, New York, Columbia University Press, 1989.
3 Eco, *A Theory of Semiotics*, p. 68.
4 Umberto Eco, *Semiotics and the Philosophy of Language*, London, Macmillan, 1984, p. 212.
5 See Eco, *A Theory of Semiotics*, pp. 191–201.
6 ibid., p. 193.

See also in this book

Bakhtin, Eco, Kristeva, Saussure

Peirce's major writings

Collected Papers of Charles Sanders Peirce, 8 vols, ed. Charles Hartshorne and Paul Weiss (vols 1–6) and Arthur Burks (vols 7–8), Cambridge Mass., The Belknap Press of Harvard University Press, 1931–58
Peirce on Signs: Writings on Semiotics by Charles Sanders Peirce, ed. James Hope, Chapel Hill and London, University of North Carolina Press, 1991

Further reading

Eco, Umberto, *A Theory of Semiotics*, Bloomington, Indiana University Press, 1979, pp. 68–72 and 195–200
Fisch, Max, 'Peirce's general theory of signs' in Kenneth Laine Ketner and Christian J.W. Kloesel (eds), *Peirce, Semeiotic and Pragmatism: Essays by Max H. Fisch*, Bloomington, Indiana University Press, 1986, pp. 321–55
Kristeva, Julia, *Language and the Unknown: An Initiation into Linguistics*, trans. Anne Menke, New York, Columbia University Press, 1989
Hookway, Christopher, *Peirce*, London, Routledge & Kegan Paul, 1985
Savan, David, *An Introduction to C.S. Peirce's Semiotics*, Toronto, Toronto Semiotic Circle, 1988

FERDINAND DE SAUSSURE

Before 1960, few people in academic circles or outside had heard the name of Ferdinand de Saussure. But after 1968, European intellectual life was a buzz with references to the father of both linguistics and structuralism. That Saussure was as much a catalyst as an intellectual innovator is confirmed by the fact that the work – the *Course in General Linguistics* – for which he is now famous outside linguistics was compiled from three sets of students' lecture notes for the years of the Course in General Linguistics given at the University of Geneva in 1907, 1908–09, and 1910–11. That Saussure, a linguist and, to the wider academic community and general public, an obscure specialist in Sanskrit and Indo-European languages, should become the source of intellectual innovation in the social sciences and humanities, is also cause for thought. It suggests that something quite unique had occurred in the historical epoch of the twentieth century, so that a new model of language based on Saussure's structural approach emerged to become the model for theorising social and cultural life. Saussurian theory has its basis in the history of linguistics, and its implications extend to the whole of the social sciences. We thus need to consider both these aspects.

Saussure was born in Geneva in 1857, to one of the best-known families of the city, one famous for its scientific accomplishments. He was thus a direct contemporary of both Emile Durkheim and Sigmund Freud, although there is little evidence of his ever having had contact with either of them. After an unsatisfactory year at the University of Geneva studying physics and chemistry in 1875, Saussure went to the University of Leipzig to study languages. Then, in the wake of eighteen months studying Sanskrit in Berlin, he published, at the age of 21, his much acclaimed *mémoire* entitled, *Mémoire sur le système primitif des voyelles dans les langues indo-européennes* (*Mémoire on the Primitive System of Vowels in Indo-European Languages*). Fifty years after Saussure's death, the renowned French linguist, Emile Benveniste, would say of this work that it presaged the whole of Saussure's future research on the nature of language inspired by the theory of the arbitrary nature of the sign.

In 1880, after defending his thesis on the absolute genitive case in Sanskrit, Saussure moved to Paris, and in 1881, at the age of 24, he was named lecturer in Gothic and Old High German at the Ecole Pratique des Hautes Etudes. For just over a decade Saussure taught in Paris until he was appointed professor of Sanskrit and Indo-European languages at the University of Geneva.

Although acclaimed by his colleagues, and although devoted to the study of language, Saussure's published output began to dwindle as the years wore on. As he put it, he was dissatisfied with the nature of linguistics as a discipline – with its lack of reflexiveness, as with its terminology[1] – and yet he was unable to write the book which would revamp the discipline and enable him to continue his work in philology.

The work now famous, *Course in General Linguistics*, composed from some of Saussure's lecture notes along with the notes of his students, could be seen perhaps to be a partial fulfilment of Saussure's belief that language as such needed to be re-examined if linguistics was to move on to a sounder footing.

Within the history of linguistics, Saussure's approach, as exemplified in the *Course*, is generally thought to have opposed two influential contemporary views of language. The first is that established in 1660 by Lancelot and Arnauld's *Grammaire de Port-Royal*, where language is seen as a mirror of thoughts and based on a universal logic. For the Port-Royal grammarians, language is fundamentally rational. The second view, is that of nineteenth-century linguistics, where the history of a particular language is deemed to explain the current state of that language. In the latter case, Sanskrit, the sacred language of ancient India, believed to be the oldest of languages, was also believed to function as the connecting link between all languages, so that, ultimately, language and its history would become one with each other. Franz Bopp's Neogrammarian (as the movement was called) thesis on the conjugation system of Sanskrit as compared with other languages (*Über das Konjugationssystem der Sanskritsprache* (*The Conjugation System of the Sanskrit Language*)) inaugurated historical linguistics, and Saussure's early teaching and research did not contradict the Neogrammarian position on the fundamental importance of history for understanding the nature of language. However, the aspect of the *Mémoire* highlighted by Benveniste on the fiftieth anniversary of Saussure's death – the role of arbitrariness in language – makes itself felt with a vengeance in the *Course*.

The historical approach to language and, to a lesser extent, the rationalist approach, assumes that language is essentially a naming process – attaching words to things, whether or not these be imaginary – and that there is some kind of intrinsic link between the name and its object. Why a particular name came to be attached to a particular object or idea, could, it was believed, be determined historically – or even prehistorically. The further back in history one went the closer one was supposed to come to a coincidence between the name and its object. As Saussure put it, such a perspective assumes that language is essentially a nomenclature: a collection of names for objects and ideas.

What, then, are the key elements of Saussure's theory as manifest in the *Course*? To begin with, Saussure shifts the focus of study from the history of language in general, to a consideration of the present configuration of a particular natural language like English or French. Now, a history of language becomes the history of languages, without there being an a priori link between them, as nineteenth-century linguists had assumed.

To focus on the present configuration of (a) language is, automatically, to focus on the relationship between the elements of that language and not on their intrinsic value. Language, Saussure says, is always organised in a specific way. It is a system, or a structure, where any individual element is meaningless outside the confines of that structure. In a strong and insistent passage in the *Course*, Saussure says: '*in language [langue] there are only differences*. Even more important: a difference generally implies positive terms between which the difference is set up; but in language, there are only differences *without positive terms*'.[2] The point is not only that value, or significance, is established through the relation between one term and another in the language system – so that, in the example used by Saussure, 't' can be written in a variety of ways and still be understood – but that the very terms of the system itself are the product of difference: there are no positive terms prior to the system. This implies that a language exists as a kind of totality, or it does not exist at all. Saussure uses the image of the chess game to illustrate the differential nature of language. For in chess, not only is the present configuration of pieces on the board all that matters to the newcomer to the game (no further insight would be gained from knowing how the pieces came to be arranged in this way), but any number of items could be substituted for the pieces on the board (a button for a king, etc.) because what constitutes the game's viability is the differential relationship between the pieces, and not their intrinsic value. To see language as being like a chess game, where the position of the pieces at a given moment is what counts, is to see it from a *synchronic* perspective. To give the historical approach precedence – as the nineteenth century did – is, by contrast, to view language from a *diachronic* perspective. In the *Course*, Saussure privileges the synchronic over the diachronic aspect because it provides a clearer picture of the factors present in any state of language.

Of equal importance for grasping the distinctiveness of Saussure's theory is the principle that language is a system of signs, and that each sign is composed of two parts: a signifier (*signifiant*) (word, or sound-pattern), and a signified (*signifié*) (concept). In contrast to the tradition within which he was brought up, therefore, Saussure does not accept that the essential bond in language is between word and thing. Instead, Saussure's concept of the sign points to the relative autonomy of language in relation to reality. Even more fundamentally, however, Saussure comes to enunciate what has become for a modern audience the most influential principle of his linguistic theory: that the relationship between the signifier and the signified is arbitrary. In light of this principle, the basic structure of language is no longer assumed to be revealed by etymology and philology, but can best be grasped by understanding how language states (that is, specific linguistic configurations or totalities) change. The 'nomenclaturist' position thus becomes an entirely inadequate basis for linguistics.

Perhaps the terms which have caused more conceptual difficulties and drawn more criticism of Saussure's theory than any others, are *langue* (individual natural language viewed as a structure, or system), and *parole* (individual speech acts, or acts of language as a process). This conceptual couple introduces the distinction between language as it exists as a more or less coherent structure of differences, and language as it is practised by the community of speakers. While Saussure proposed in the *Course* that a specific linguistic structure is distinct from speech, and while he argued that the basis of language, as a social fact, is to be grasped exclusively at the level of structure, it is also true that nothing enters into the realm of the linguistic structure without first becoming manifest in individual speech acts. More significantly, the very extent of the totality of the structure could only be known with certainty if the totality of speech acts were also known. In this sense, the domain of the structure always remains, for Saussure, more hypothetical than the domain of speech. However, much depends here on whether one looks at speech from an individual, psychological perspective, or whether one focuses on the whole community of speakers. In the first case, to view language through the speech of the individual qua individual is one thing; to view it through the speech acts of the whole community is quite another. Saussure's point is that language is fundamentally a social institution, and that, therefore, the individualist approach is inadequate for the linguist.

Language is always changing. But it does not change at the behest of individuals; it changes over time independently of the speakers' wills. Indeed through a Saussurian optic, individuals are as much formed by language as it is they who form language, and the question arises as to whether such a vision might have implications for other disciplines in the social sciences. In fact, this was the case for those theorists working under the rubric of 'structuralism' in the 1960s.

With the emergence of the Saussurian model in the human sciences, the researcher's attention was turned away from documenting historical events, or recording the facts of human behaviour, and towards the notion of human action as a system of meaning. Such was the result of emphasising, at the broader societal level, the arbitrary nature of the sign and the corresponding idea of language as a system of conventions. Whereas a search for intrinsic facts and their effects had hitherto been made (as exemplified when the historian supposed that human beings need food to survive, just as they need language to communicate with each other – *therefore* events turned out this way), now the socio-cultural system at a given moment in history, becomes the object of study. This is a system within which the researcher is also inscribed, much as the linguist is inscribed in language. A greater concern to be more reflexive thus also becomes the order of the day.

For many, like the anthropologist Claude Lévi-Strauss, or the sociologist Pierre Bourdieu, or the psychoanalyst Jacques Lacan, as for Roland Barthes in literary criticism and semiotics, Saussurian insights initially paved the way for a more rigorous and systematic approach to human sciences – an approach that would genuinely attempt to take seriously the primacy of the socio-cultural domain for human beings. Just as Saussure had emphasised the importance of not studying speech acts in isolation from the system of conventions which gave them currency, so it was deemed inadequate to study social and cultural facts independently of the social or cultural system which gave *them* currency. Society or culture at a given state of development, and not discrete individual human actions in the past or present, became the focus of study. Whereas the generation before (the generation of Sartre) had sought to discover the natural (intrinsic) basis of human society in history – much as nineteenth-century linguists had sought to reveal the natural elements of language – the structuralist generation's effort was directed towards showing how the differential relations of the elements in the system – whether the latter be a series of texts, a kinship system, or the milieu of fashion photography – produced a meaning, or meanings, and thus had to be 'read' and interpreted. In other words, the study of socio-cultural life is seen to entail deciphering signs through focusing on their differential value, and not on their putative substantive value (often equated with the 'natural'), and also paying attention to the symptomatic level of signification, as well as to the explicit level.

Structure, as inspired by Saussure's theory of language, can thus refer to the 'value' of elements in a system, or context, and not to their mere physical, or natural existence. Now it has become clear that the physical existence of an entity is complicated by the effects of the linguistic and cultural milieu. Structure, then, is a reminder that nothing social or cultural (and this includes, of course, the individual) exists as a 'positive', essential element outside it in isolation from all other elements. Such an approach reverses the one taken in the political philosophy of the eighteenth and nineteenth centuries, where the biological individual is placed at the origin of social life. And just as this philosophy saw no society as existing prior to the individual, so it also denied the relative autonomy of language.

Probably the main objection that can be raised against the translation of Saussure's emphasis on structure into the study of social and cultural life, is that it does not make sufficient allowance for the role of practice and individual autonomy. Seeing human freedom as a product of social life, rather than as the origin, or cause, of social life, has made it seem, in the eyes of some observers, to be quite limited. A conservative bias, denying the possibility of change, would thus be the consequence of structure. While this problem is still unresolved, it is perhaps important to recognise the difference between the freedom of the hypothetical individual (whose very *social* existence would be equivalent to a limit on freedom), and a society of free individuals, where freedom would be the result of social life understood as a structure of differences. Or, rather, we could say that perhaps researchers should begin to explore the idea that, to paraphrase Saussure: Society is a system of freedoms *without positive terms*. On this reading, there would be no *essential*, or substantial freedom – no freedom incarnate in the individual in a state of nature.

Notes

1 Cf. 'I am more and more aware of the immense amount of work required to show the linguist *what he is doing*. . . . The utter inadequacy of current terminology, the need to reform it and, in order to do that, to demonstrate what sort of object language is, continually spoil my pleasure in philology' – Ferdinand de Saussure, Letter of 4 January 1894, in 'Lettres de F. de Saussure à Antoine Meillet', *Cahiers Ferdinand de Saussure*, 21 (1964), p. 95, cited in Jonathan Culler, *Ferdinand de Saussure*, Ithaca, New York, Cornell University Press, 1986, p. 24.
2 Ferdinand de Saussure, *Cours de linguistique générale*, ed. Tullio de Mauro, Paris, Payot, 1976, p. 166. In English as *Course in General Linguistics*, trans. Wade Baskin, Glasgow, Fontana/Collins, 1974, p. 120.

See also in this book

Barthes, Benveniste, Bourdieu, Derrida, Jakobson, Kristeva, Lacan, Lévi-Strauss

Saussure's major writings

Course in General Linguistics, trans. Wade Baskin with an introduction by Jonathan Culler, Glasgow, Fontana/Collins, 1974. New trans., Roy Harris, London, Duckworth, 1983
Cours de linguistique générale, critical edn Tullio de Mauro (Paris, Payot, 1976)
Cours de linguistique générale, 2 vols, critical edn by Rudolf Engler, Wiesbaden, O. Harrassowitz, 1967–74

Further reading

Benveniste, Emile, 'Saussure after half a century' in *Problems in General Linguistics*, trans. Mary

E. Meek, Miami Linguistics Series No. 8, Coral Gables, Florida, University of Miami Press, 1971, pp. 29–40

Culler, Jonathan, *Ferdinand de Saussure*, Ithaca, New York, Cornell University Press, 1986

Gadet, Françoise, *Saussure and Contemporary Culture*, trans. George Elliott, London, Hutchinson Radius, 1989

Harris, Roy, *Reading Saussure: A Critical Commentary on the Cours de linguistique générale*, London, Duckworth, 1987

Holdcroft, David, *Saussure: Signs, System and Arbitrariness*, Cambridge, Cambridge University Press, 1991

TZVETAN TODOROV

Like Julia Kristeva, Tzvetan Todorov was born in Bulgaria and came to Paris in 1963. Having completed a first degree in Bulgaria, and armed with a recommendation from the university in Sofia, Todorov's first insight into the conservative nature of the pre-1968 Sorbonne occurred when he enquired at the faculty letters there about doing research in literary theory. The dean of the faculty responded 'coldly' informing Todorov that 'literary theory was not done in his faculty and there was no question of it being done'.[1] Not to be daunted, the young Todorov began reading in the Sorbonne library, and through one of the library staff eventually made contact with Gérard Genette who suggested that Todorov attend Roland Barthes's seminar at the Ecole des Hautes Etudes en Sciences Sociales.

Contact with Barthes – with whom he completed a *doctorat de toisième cycle* in 1966 – enabled Todorov to contribute articles to the influential interdisciplinary semiotics journal, *Communications*. Two early contributions stand out. One, entitled 'La description de la signification en littérature' elaborates the various levels of structural analysis and emphasises that the form of the literary object takes precedence in a structural analysis over the substance of the content, which relates to semantics.[2] At that time, Todorov, like other structuralist theorists (e.g., Barthes and Genette), associated the study of meaning with a hermeneutic (and thus humanist) framework. Not until the work of A.J. Greimas became better known did a distinctly structuralist paradigm become associated with the field of semantics.

The other important early article of Todorov's – one showing the influence of the Russian Formalists – was 'Les catégories du récit littéraire'.[3] Here, Todorov reiterates that 'a description of the work aims at the meaning of the literary elements; the literary critic looks to give them an interpretation'.[4] The meaning of the elements, following the Saussurian principle, will reside in the relations between them. If, however, this is so, what about the meaning (*sens*) of the work as a whole? To say that meaning is relational is to say that the elements of meaning form a system: they are ordered in a particular way and are not simply an *ad hoc* aggregate. Does the work as a whole escape this principle, so that its meaning would be specific to it in its singularity and autonomy? No, says Todorov. The meaning of a work (as opposed to its interpretation), derives from its relation to other works in literary history. 'The meaning of *Madame Bovary* is to be opposed to romantic literature.'[5]

Echoing Genette's work on the narrative (*récit*), Todorov goes on, in the article in question, to analyse the levels of 'story' (*histoire*) and discourse. This approach leads into the kind of study carried out in *Littérature et signification* – the book based on Todorov's doctoral thesis which took Laclos's eighteenth century epistolary novel, *Les Liaisons dangereuses* as its tutor text. In any narrative story there are actions or events. But these do not occur according to an ideal chronology. Rather, they constitute an often complex network of threads which only come together at a given point. Only by studying the levels of action and personages can light be thrown on the nature of the logic of this network of threads. Using *Les*

Liaisons dangereuses as an example, Todorov shows that: (1) actions in a narrative are not arbitrary, but obey a certain logic; (2) a narrative can have more than one structure which is revealed when two different models can work equally well in the analysis of it; and (3) it may not be possible to isolate for analysis the level of action when the 'action' of the narrative is equivalent to the vicissitudes of the psychological state of the personages – as is the case in *Les Liaisons dangereuses*.

Generally speaking, Todorov aims to bring to light the various processes (*procédés*) by which a narrative is realised. These processes must remain relatively invisible to the reader if the narrative is to succeed as the bearer of a story with an intrigue. These processes are also equivalent to the functions, or meanings (*sens*), of each element in the narrative as a whole. Like Genette, Todorov, too, is interested in analysing, in a given text, time, narration, subjectivity (or the context or process of narration), and objectivity (or the narration as a citation or completed linguistic act).

In his book, *Littérature et signification* (1967), Todorov expands on the analysis of *Les Liaisons dangereuses* begun in the 1966 article. Central to the argument there is that even a genre based as much for its success on verisimilitude through mimesis as the epistolary novel will be founded on a range of processes internal to the structure of the novel as both an act of language (*énonciation*) – in which style and subjectivity are visible – and as a story (*énoncé*). What, however, is the story of any novel? It is, says Todorov, the story of the novel's own creation. In summarising his own position in *Littérature et signification*, Todorov summarises the position of many a structuralist theorist of the sixties generation. Thus, he writes that: 'Every work, every novel recounts, through a series of events, the story of its own creation, of its own story.'[6] The search for a final meaning is in vain because 'the meaning of a work is to

pronounce itself – to speak to us of its own existence'.[7] In effect, a novel begins where it ends: 'for the very existence of a novel is the last link in the chain of its intrigue'. The point is neatly caught in the last letter in *Les Liaisons dangereuses* which explains how the collection of letters constitutive of the novel came to be published. At one level, the fact of a fictive work is not a fiction; yet the difference between fiction and non-fiction would seem to become problematic when a fictive work itself is viewed as the process of its own creation. For now the *fact* of fiction (i.e. non-fiction) seems to become the essential trait of fiction.

When Todorov speaks of the search for a final meaning of any work outside of the work itself – i.e. a search for meaning beyond the *existence* of the work – he is implicitly distancing himself from a hermeneutic approach to the text, the approach that has often aimed to capture the final message (often ideological) of the text. Interestingly, after writing influential works on the *Decameron*, on structuralism, and on literature of the fantastic – all based on the notion of the relative autonomy of the literary text – the direction of Todorov's *oeuvre* began to change with a study on the history of the theory of the symbol. Todorov argues that, even in the structuralist era, the influence of Romanticism is inescapable.

In 1981, Todorov returned again to his Russian formalist mentors – this time not so much to assimilate their formalist methods as to give an interpretation of their thought. His re-reading of Bakhtin's *oeuvre* in this light, marks a turning point in his entire approach to literary theory. Whereas in the 1960s Todorov had embraced formalism through structuralism as a way of rejecting the ideologically correct approach of socialist realism, in the early 1980s Todorov began to work out a more interpretative framework aimed at combating what he saw as the excessively apolitical approach of a formal textual analysis. What Todorov comes to value most in Bakhtin's work is a 'philosophical anthropology' which is concerned with the question of 'otherness'.[8] For Todorov, the 'other' in Bakhtin's articulation of the dialogical principle comes to assume prime importance. He thus argues that Bakhtin's fundamental insight was to realise that no artistic work, worthy of the name, after Dostoyevsky, could fail to come to grips with otherness: 'The renunciation of the unity of the "I" has its counterpart in the assertion of a new status for the "thou" of the other.'[9] Thus, the other ceases to be an object and becomes a subject. Dostoyevsky teaches Todorov this insight through Bakhtin's later writing. 'But', Todorov asks, 'isn't it the essential characteristic of knowledge in the human sciences, as Bakhtin describes it, not to deal with the mute "object" of the natural sciences, and to transform it into a dialogue of texts, knowing and to be known?'[10]

Beginning from the proposition that the researcher has to be seen as implicated in the object of study – has to enter into a dialogue with it – Todorov began a series of works which looked at the way French and European history and culture has engaged – or not engaged – with the other. Two texts in particular stand out: *The Conquest of America* (1982), and *Nous et les autres* (1989).

In *The Conquest of America* Todorov analyses and interprets documents of and about Columbus's discovery of America in 1492. This is a committed study – the study by a moralist concerned about the relations between European and Indian, self and other, identity and difference. If, as Todorov abundantly demonstrates, Columbus had, at both a conscious and an unconscious level, a very specific and fixed way of understanding life (including a view of what he would find on the other side of the world), the point is to know how this impinged upon his actual contact with the peoples of central America. At one level, it means that Columbus behaved rather predictably: he encountered the other through the blinkers of his own cultural (including religious)

prejudices. The Indians are seen and treated as beasts, fit only to be the slaves of the Europeans. Or rather, the Indian is violated – treated as a 'dirty dog' – in the real encounter, while being idealised from a distance as the noble savage, just as the scriptures had ordained. 'Human alterity', says Todorov, 'is at once revealed and refused' by the Europeans.[11]

Todorov wants two aspects of the conquest of America to come through: first of all, he wants to show the way that signs and their interpretation – language and communication – played an immense part in the contact between the Spaniards and the Aztecs in the sixteenth century – the century of conquest. Here, Todorov argues that the Spaniards won the war of conquest through the auspices of Hernando Cortés largely because the conquistador was able to act upon the knowledge derived from observations: that is, Cortés made an effort to inform himself about – and so came to understand – many of the ways of the people he was fighting. Moctezoma and the Aztecs, by contrast, were hamstrung by a vision of the world that depended on an inflexible reading of the present through the prism of the past. Indeed the Aztecs relied on prophecy and the notion of destiny that was inextricably linked to it. The Aztecs, for instance, saw the arrival of the Europeans as a bad omen, and assumed a (negative) psychological disposition in keeping with it. Although influenced by Christian beliefs, Cortés, by contrast to the Aztecs, attempted to learn the language of the other in more than one way. For not only did he pay attention to the information supplied to him by informants, he also made use of Aztec myths in a strategem geared to deceive the enemy. Thus Cortés fostered the Aztec illusion that he was a god, and at one point deceived the inhabitants of what are now the Bahamas into thinking they were going to the promised land of their ancestors when, in fact, they were to be exploited as labourers. Cortés, in sum, recognised the importance of the language and knowledge of Aztec culture, and he used it to manipulate the situation to his advantage.[12]

Despite his genuine understanding of the culture of the other (and this is the second major point to make about the conquest), Cortés nevertheless participated in the destruction of Aztec culture. For the Spaniards – Cortés included – were only interested in objects, particularly gold, and failed to recognise their opponents as human beings. The true horror of this reaches its full height during the course of Spanish colonialism when between 1500 and 1600 not only were the people enslaved, but, according to reliable estimates, a population of 80 million for the whole of South America was reduced to one million at a time when the population of the globe was around 400 million. Despite his capacity to understand the 'other', Cortés's enterprise led to the destruction of Aztec civilisation.

In his conclusion Todorov reaffirms his commitment to Bakhtin's principle of dialogue. Only in a true dialogue, where the voice of the other is rendered audible neither at the expense of one's own voice, nor through the effacement of the other's voice, is real equality possible. Dialogue is the affirmation of Rimbaud's principle that 'I is an other', where 'I' and 'you' would be present simultaneously. Dialogue implies another quality: the more it is realised, the more it produces a capacity for improvisation – for confronting a situation as it is, and acting accordingly. What is contestable about Todorov's stand, however, is that he names Western civilisation (read: Europe) as the *origin* of dialogue, and of writing, and, at least by implication, at the origin of the capacity for improvisation that writing also brings with it. While the intention of our author is clearly not to claim any intrinsic superiority for European culture over any other, it is not clear whether this intention has been realised.

In a subsequent work – *Nous et les autres* (*Ourselves and Others*) – on the self–other dialogue, Todorov examines the themes of race, nation, the universal and the exotic in the writings of a variety of authors – Lévi-Strauss, Montaigne, Gobineau, Renan, Tocqueville, Chateaubriand, Autaud, and others. What most interests Todorov here is the way that certain authors mark a vacillation in the French reflection on human diversity between an all-embracing ethnocentrism (the other as mere object), to an all-embracing relativism (the other as everything and self as nothing). Renan and Barrès would represent the former position, while Lévi-Strauss, for Todorov, would represent the latter. While Todorov is characteristically careful not to make hasty judgements about racism, colonialism or universalism, he appears much less comfortable in tackling philosophical and moral issues than in doing semiotic analysis of texts. For instance, in discussing his view of 'a well tempered humanism', he relies, without acknowledgement, on the a priori notion that the freedom of humanity as a species, is essentially an individual matter: 'it is said that liberty is the distinctive trait of the human species. It is certain that my milieu pushes me to reproduce the behaviour it valorises; but the possibility of uprooting myself from it also exists'.[13] Todorov begs many questions here: can one speak about freedom in relation to humanity as a species being without falling into biologism? What is the exact relationship between humanity and individual? If freedom is uniquely individual, does this not imply that individuals constitute their freedom against humanity? But most pressingly: is freedom inevitably opposed to determination, as Todorov states? Might there not be, for example, a sense in which an individual chooses to embrace existing community values? Is this not precisely the nature of a conservative moral or political choice? In sum, the point is not that Todorov does not raise important issues in *Nous et les autres*, but that the answers he often gives to enormously complex philosophical questions remain alarmingly unelaborated in a book with the stated aim of expanding the understanding in contemporary experience of the interaction between self and other.

Between *The Conquest of America* and *Nous et les autres*, Todorov continued to publish on the nature of literature and criticism with works such as *Critique de la critique* (1984) and *La Notion de la littérature* (1987). These works may in part be contrasted with the more overtly committed texts of *Frêle bonheur: essai sur Rousseau* (1985), which searches to capture the intensity of Rousseau's thought, and *Face à l'extrême* (1991) on Nazi and communist totalitarianism.

In general, Todorov's *oeuvre* is interesting and important for the tension it presents between the rigour of structural analysis, and the writing of moral commitment – the writing of Todorov's post-structuralist phase, as it were. A final question would be to know whether or not this tension is inevitable.

Notes

1 François Dosse, *Histoire du structuralisme, I: le champ du sign, 1945–1966*, Paris, La Découverte, 1991, p. 240.
2 Tzvetan Todorov, 'La description de la signification en littérature', *Communications*, 4, 1964.
3 Tzvetan Todorov, 'Les catégories du récit littéraire', *Communications*, 8 (1966), pp. 125–51.
4 ibid., p. 126.
5 ibid.
6 ibid., p. 49.
7 ibid.
8 Tzvetan Todorov, *Mikhail Bakhtin: The Dialogical Principle*, trans. Wlad Godzich, Manchester, Manchester University Press, 1984, p. 94.
9 ibid., p. 104.
10 ibid., p. 107.
11 Tzvetan Todorov, *The Conquest of America: The Question of the Other*, trans. Richard Howard, New York, Harper & Row, 1984, pp. 49–50.
12 See ibid., pp. 98–123.
13 Tzvetan Todorov, *Nous et les autres. La réflexion française sur la diversité humaine*, Paris, Seuil, 1989, p. 428.

See also in this book

Bakhtin, Kristeva, Genette, Greimas

Todorov's major writings

Grammaire du Décaméron, The Hague, Paris, Mouton, 1969
The Fantastic: A Structural Approach to a Literary Genre (1970), trans. Richard Howard, Ithaca, New York, Cornell University Press, 1975
Genres of Discourse (1978), trans. Catherine Porter, Cambridge, Cambridge University Press, 1990
An Introduction to Poetics, trans. Richard Howard, Minneapolis, University of Minnesota Press, 1981
The Conquest of America: The Question of the Other (1982) (translation of *La conquête de l'Amérique: La question de l'autre*), trans. Richard Howard, New York, Harper & Row, 1984
Mikhail Bakhtin: The Dialogical Principle (1981), trans. Wlad Godzich, Manchester, Manchester University Press, 1984
Literature and its Theorists: A Personal View of Twentieth Century Criticism (1984), trans. Catherine Porter, London, Routledge & Kegan Paul, 1988
Frêle bonheur: essai sur Rousseau, Paris, Hachette, 1985
La Notion de la littérature et autres essais, Paris, Seuil, 1987
On Human Diversity: Nationalism, Racism and Exoticism in French Thought (1989), (translation of *Nous et les autres: La reflexion française sur la diversité humaine*) trans. Catherine Porter, Cambridge, Mass., Harvard University Press, 1993
Les Immorales de l'histoire, Paris, Grasset, 1991
Face à l'extrême, Paris, Seuil, 1991

Further reading

Bann, Stephen, 'Structuralism and the revival of rhetoric', *Sociological Review Monograph*, 25, (August 1977), pp. 68–84
Bottomley, Gill and Lechte, John, 'Nation and diversity in France', *Journal of Intercultural Studies*, 11, 1 (1990), pp. 49–63

SECOND GENERATION FEMINISM

Second generation feminism questions more than the social inequalities experienced by women; it looks also at the deep-seated ideological structures which inevitably place women at a disadvantage in relation to men. Patriarchy is one such structure, and the Social Contract – so influential in justifying Western political institutions – is another. Often inspired by the insights of Lacanian psychoanalysis, which shows that consciousness, or the ego, is not the centre of subjectivity, second generation feminism challenges the gender bias in language, law and philosophy. It argues that women should not just aim to be like men (as is often the case in the battle over social equality), but should aim to develop a new, specifically feminine, language, law and mythology.

LUCE IRIGARAY

Luce Irigaray was trained as a linguist and Lacanian analyst. Her early publications explored the language of those suffering from dementia. In her researches, Irigaray discovered that the language of the schizophrenic tends to be a private language, or an ideolect. But above all, she proposed that what was often taken to be incomprehensible delirium (*délire*) was in fact subject to rules of linguistic structure, even if these rules were continually broken. As Irigaray has subsequently become involved in constructing feminine forms of symbolisation and language – forms based on aspects of female experience deemed to be outside conventional modes of expression (like the ideolect of the schizophrenic) – we should keep this early work in mind in considering her endeavours as one of the leading exponents of philosophical feminism.

In 1974, Irigaray published *Speculum of the Other Woman*, which, in re-examining the notion of femininity – including the mother–daughter relationship – in Freud and psychoanalysis, sought to develop a specifically feminine writing (*écriture féminine*) – a writing that would subvert the hegemony of a male imaginary which condemns women to silence as women.

Although in fierce opposition to many of its aspects, Irigaray's philosophy of the feminine begins with the Lacanian theory of the Real, the Symbolic and the Imaginary – the Real as the place of the mother and death, the Symbolic as the domain of law founded on the Name-of-the-Father, and the Imaginary as the effect of the Symbolic in consciousness and imagination. As Irigaray reads the situation, Lacan's symbolic order – the condition of language – is fundamentally masculine and patriarchal; it speaks the imaginary of men and is organised according to the law of the symbolic order which subtends it. Anything outside the domain of the symbolic order effectively has to be translated into its terms; in other words, its other as symbolised is really the same as itself. Or else, the other (like death, or the feminine) is so radically different that no symbolic means are available for it to be communicated. This is especially evident in the field of sexuality. And sexuality, as Freud showed, affects almost every sphere of intellectual and cultural life. At the moment, the supposedly neutral subject of science, or the neutral subject in language (the third person) are, for Irigaray, both gendered male. To put it in a nutshell: Irigaray's critique of the institutions of psychoanalysis, language and culture is radical in that she sees even ostensibly egalitarian gestures as being compromised from the start; for they will inevitably presuppose that women are on the deficit side of the leger, that they 'lack' something (whether in social or sexual terms) which men have and which women, in all justice, deserve too (social status, a public life, autonomy and independence, a separate identity).

Sexually, the egalitarian gesture which attributes to the vagina a status equal to the penis unwittingly gives in to Freud's notion of penis envy. For the penis is still the benchmark. Why should it be, Irigaray leads us to ask? When Lacan seems to go even further than Freud in saying that the whole of the symbolic order is phallic (that the phallus is the signifier of all signification, that the subject is a signifier) and that it is via the symbolic order that the drama of sexual difference of fullness (the masculine) and lack (the feminine) is played out – Irigaray calls on women to note that this is a masculine view of things. In effect, 'Female sexuality has always been conceptualised on the basis of masculine parameters.'[1] Again, woman's lot, Irigaray confirms 'is that of "lack", "atrophy" (of the sexual organ), and "penis envy", the penis being the only organ of recognized value'.[2] Here, Freud's theory of castration is at issue. He is seen to argue that the presence or absence of the penis is what is crucial to the sexual development of both sexes. As there is no immediate access to the real body, the presence or absence of the penis is understood by Lacan as the presence or absence of the phallus which signifies sexual difference. For Irigaray, on the other hand, the phallus symbolises lack in the woman as other because a woman is effectively a castrated man.

If language (for Lacan) is irreducibly phallic, the only way women can speak or communicate at all is by appropriating the masculine instrument. One way or another, the woman has to 'have' the phallus she lacks; the deficit has to be made up. In order to speak clearly, to communicate and to forge links with others – to be social – the woman must speak like a man. Not to do so is to risk psychosis: a falling back into an ideolect, and the putting asunder of the social bond. Lacan's version (which he calls the *père-version*) of language is, for Irigaray, repeated in most psychoanalytic theories of language and sexuality. If women are to have an identity of their own, the phallic version of the symbolic to which they have been subjected for so long must be subverted. For the symbolic has been the source of women's oppression.

As Irigaray presents it, then, women have a disturbing and oppressively paradoxical status as subjects; for in order to speak, they must speak like men; in order to know their sexuality at all they must compare it to the male version: they must 'be' the lack of a penis. While men can readily invoke the symbolic order (mediation) in knowing and loving themselves, and therefore in representing themselves to others in the social world, women, by contrast, are in a position of what Irigaray calls a condition of 'dereliction'[3] – that is, of not being able to know or to love themselves, because mediation (the symbolic order) is foreign to them. 'Women lack mediation for the work of sublimation', she says.[4] As a result they cannot objectify themselves – or at least they find objectification difficult. Men, on the other hand, not only pose themselves as objects, but are able to objectify women as well. Correlatively,

women are refused access to society and culture in direct proportion that men are of society and culture. Effectively, women's condition here, is, for Irigaray, reminiscent of Marx's view of the proletariat: the proletariat, Marx said, are *in* society, but they are not *of* society. Socially speaking, women – at least from a traditional perspective – must be attached to a man in order to have a social persona; a woman thus does not have her own identity. For her part, Irigaray argues that to have an identity which is not one's own – to be a 'sex which is not one' (i.e. which is not whole because it is lacking – is not unified in itself, but dependent) – is to be excluded from the fullness of being: it is to be left precisely in a condition of 'dereliction'.

Women *as* women are therefore excluded from the social contract. And an important contributing factor here is the difficulty (read: present impossibility) of symbolising the mother–daughter relationship. While psychoanalysis has made much, in talking of the entry of the human into the realm of language, of the separation of the child from its mother, less has been made of the fact that this child has been understood as the son. The son, then, has to separate himself from the mother via the intervention of language, or the Name-of-the-Father. The son is not only a potential father; he is also a subject: a man. The daughter, by contrast, is only a potential mother. Her womanhood thus has to be gleaned from the experience of motherhood.

The son's first lesson, so to speak, is to be able to objectify the mother through the symbolic order so as to comply with the interdiction against incest. The daughter, however, is largely bereft of means for achieving this separation, due to her impoverished relationship to the symbolic. She thus runs a greater risk of psychosis and melancholia – or rather, her language will tend to be dominated by the drives, as Irigaray found in her studies of delirium. Perhaps, Irigaray ponders, delirium has the potential for providing the basis of a woman's language – of providing a way that might enable women to communicate among themselves, just as men have communicated among themselves.

Irigaray has worked continuously since the mid-1970s to perfect the symbolic means equivalent to the mother–daughter relationship. This work has led her to investigate those hitherto repressed and excluded aspects of Western culture which have been particularly related to the condition of the feminine in society: the divine feminine, witchcraft, and sorcery – to cite some examples. As Margaret Whitford has pointed out,[5] the logic of Irigaray's project here is not to valorise an incommunicable mystical state, or an essential woman, but to overcome the deficit of woman unsymbolised as woman. Not mysticism, then, but bringing woman into the symbolic order on her own terms is the aim. Women need to be able to represent themselves to themselves (but in a way quite different from men) in order to constitute themselves as truly social beings who can form positive relationships with each other.

All of this has led to experimentation with different linguistic strategies in Irigaray's own writing, and in the evocation of experiences and cultural figures which have been excluded from social and cultural life because they have been so closely associated with what was thought to be essentially feminine. Regarding style, Elizabeth Grosz has written of Irigaray that: 'Her writing, her "styles", involve new forms of discourse, new ways of speaking, a "poetry" which is necessarily innovative and evocative of new conceptions of women and femininity.'[6] Exemplary experiments of style in this sense are: *Marine Lover of Friedrich Nietzsche*,[7] *Passions élémentaires*,[8] and *L'Oubli de l'air chez Martin Heidegger*.[9] In these readings of figures in the history of philosophy, Irigaray is attentive to the repressed elements which are passed over in silence – elements of pertinence to feminists, such as the body, and the elements: water, earth, fire, air.

Similarly, Irigaray has reflected on the theological tradition in order to find in it a positive notion of the divine (the infinite) appropriate to women. Because the God of Christianity, as the exemplar of the masculine imaginary, excludes women's experience as a point of reference, Irigaray believes it necessary to find a figure able to exemplify the feminine imaginary. The feminine god would be one to give form to multiplicity, difference, becoming, flows, rhythms, and to 'the splendor of the body' – in other words, to those things which cannot receive a viable image within a patriarchal religious experience. 'A *feminine* god', Irigaray admits, 'is yet to come'.[10] And no doubt this is the point: the 'yet to come' of the feminine god is the god of becoming – the god of fluidity and transient boundaries, of the amorphous elements of fire, air, earth and water. 'How could our [women's] God be imagined?' Irigaray asks. 'Or our god?', she continues. 'Is there a quality pertaining to us which could reverse the order and put the predicate in subject position?'[11]

The search for a god that is distinctively feminine is a search for a position – a reference point – that nevertheless would not replicate the positionality of patriarchy. In current terms, such a position would have to be one which in some sense elides all positionality. For the logic of identity this is an untenable position. And the question remains as to whether it is at all sustainable. Clearly, Irigaray is convinced of the necessity and the viability of the project; but what if she were wrong? Women themselves are beginning to ask this question.

Irigaray's philosophical project also concerns the investigation of ethics in light of Emmanuel Levinas's notion of ethical obligation. Like Irigaray in relation to women, Levinas has been concerned to lay bare the repressed elements of the Judaic tradition within Christianity. For Levinas, the moral imperative is focused, not on the status of the self – where the other would only have relevance for confirming the self's own moral worth – but on the other as an exteriority or alterity which calls to the self, and which, in a sense, the self becomes. In short, the other is not reducible to a representation indebted, as all representations are, to the order of the Same. What attracts Irigaray to Levinas, is the emphasis he places on the material encounter in his theory of alterity. Indeed only at a material, corporeal level is real alterity articulated; only the truly material encounter with the other can be surprising and astonishing. For Irigaray, then, the feminine is the prototype of this alterity.

Given the care Irigaray has brought to articulate a new vision of the feminine, it seems surprising that some basic difficulties remain, of which three in particular call for attention. In the first place, there is a debt to Lacanian psychoanalysis. Here – Levinas not withstanding – it is difficult to avoid the sense that Irigaray's work is another anti-Oedipus project, and that, as a result, it is governed by the logic it seeks to subvert. In effect, the Lacanian Real, Symbolic, and Imaginary enables Irigaray to point to the inadequacy of both 'egalitarian feminism', and feminism that defines the feminine in terms of lack, and unrepresentable otherness.

A second, and more troubling point, is the way the terms, 'woman' and 'women', 'man' and 'men' are used to designate apparently homogeneous realities: that is, men must be men and women must be women. Politically, this has led to the proposition that a man (e.g., Derrida) cannot be a feminist.[12] It would seem, however, that the view that men cannot be feminist can only be maintained if the very homogeneous categories of identity (man, woman) which Irigaray intends to subvert are maintained. That is, without the logic of identity in dominance, women would not necessarily be women; the feminine would not necessarily be feminist. The risk – the very grave risk – is a possible form of racism based on an insidious mode of classification from which no one can escape.

The third point concerns elements of the feminine (female god, the elements of fire, air, earth, and water, female language and festivals), rendered visible by Irigaray's

work. On one level, this approach touches on the most creative aspect of her style of feminism. Boundaries have been shaken and new ways of imagining have been opened up. However, there is a strong impression coming through that such imaginings require devotees if the desired political effect is to be achieved. The question that needs to be asked now is whether an individual could be truly feminist in Irigaray's terms and *not* subscribe to her version of the feminine. Irigaray felt a great joy – as a woman – upon seeing a female Jesus in a museum on Torcello island.[13] But could not one *not* be moved, either as a woman, or as an individual – or as both – by such a scene? An affirmative answer would seem to render problematic the very link Irigaray is trying to make between an iconography of the feminine and a sense of becoming a female subject.

Notes

1 Luce Irigaray, *This Sex Which is Not One*, trans. Catherine Porter with Carolyn Burke, Ithaca, New York, Cornell University Press, fourth printing 1988, p. 23.
2 ibid.
3 Luce Irigaray, *Ethique de la différence sexuelle*, Paris, Minuit, 1984, p. 70.
4 ibid.
5 Margaret Whitford, *Luce Irigaray: Philosophy in the Feminine*, London and New York, Routledge, 1991, pp. 84–5.
6 Elizabeth Grosz, *Sexual Subversions. Three French Feminists: Julia Kristeva, Luce Irigaray, Michèle Le Doeuff*, Sydney, Allen & Unwin, 1989, p. 101.
7 Luce Irigaray, *Marine Lover of Friedrich Nietzsche*, trans. Gillian C. Gill, New York, Columbia University Press, 1991.
8 Luce Irigaray, *Passions élémentaires*, Paris, Minuit, 1982.
9 Luce Irigaray, *L'Oubli de l'air chez Martin Heidegger*, Paris, Minuit, 1983.
10 Luce Irigaray, *Divine Women*, trans. Stephen Muecke, Sydney, Local Consumption, 1986, p. 8.
11 ibid.
12 For a more complete and subtle account of why this is so within the economy of Irigaray's philosophy as regards a figure like Derrida, see Margaret Whitford, 'Identity and violence'

in *Luce Irigaray: Philosophy in the Feminine*, pp. 123–47.

13 Luce Irigaray, *Je, tu, nous. Toward a Culture of Difference*, trans. Alison Martin, New York, London, Routledge, 1993, p. 25.

See also in this book

Freud, Kristeva, Lacan, Le Doeuff, Levinas, Pateman

Irigaray's major writings

Le Langage des déments, The Hague, Paris, Mouton: Approaches to Semiotics, 1973

Speculum of the Other Woman (1974), trans. Gillian C. Gill, New York, Cornell, 1985

This Sex Which is Not One (1977), trans. Catherine Porter with Carolyn Burke, Ithaca, New York, Cornell University Press, fourth printing 1988

Marine Lover of Friedrich Nietzsche (1980), trans. Gillian C. Gill, New York, Columbia University Press, 1991

Elemental Passions (1982), ed. Joanne Collier and Judith Still, New York, Routledge, 1992

L'Oubli de l'air chez Martin Heidegger, Paris, Minuit, 1983

An Ethics of Sexual Difference (1984), trans. Carolyn Burke and Gillian C. Gill, New York, Cornell University Press, 1993

Divine Women, trans. Stephen Muecke, Sydney, Local Consumption, 1986

Je, tu, nous. Toward a Culture of Difference (1990), trans. Alison Martin, New York, London, Routledge, 1993

Culture of Difference (1990), trans. Alison Martin, New York, Routledge, 1992

Further reading

Allen, Jeffner and Young, Iris Marion, *The Thinking Muse: Feminism and Modern French Philosophy*, Bloomington, Indiana University Press, 1989

Grosz, Elizabeth, *Sexual Subversions. Three French Feminists: Julia Kristeva, Luce Irigaray, Michèle Le Doeuff*, Sydney, Allen & Unwin, 1989

Whitford, Margaret, *Luce Irigaray: Philosophy in the Feminine*, London and New York, Routledge, 1991

MICHÈLE LE DOEUFF

Michèle Le Doeuff is professor of philosophy at the Ecole normale supérieure at Fontenay in France. She became interested in philosophy not through reading the great thinkers, but through identifying with the Fool in Shakespeare's plays. For the Fool is given to subversive speech, a vocation Le Doeuff initially found to be intrinsic to philosophy, which, unlike the Fool, exists in real life.

In her book, *Hipparchia's Choice*,[1] Michèle Le Doeuff explains that she found it possible to begin her own philosophical project by proving 'that there is in philosophy an imaginary level which has not been imported from elsewhere but is specific to philosophy and sets the conditions of what can be constructed as rationality within it'. Such is the way that Le Doeuff describes the trajectory for the book for which she has become best known outside France, *The Philosophical Imaginary*.[2] There, the author shows, *inter alia*, that Kant, in the first paragraph of the section of the *Critique of Pure Reason* dealing with the distinction between phenomena and noumena, refers to the understanding as a 'territory' that the preceding section of the book has 'explored'.[3] There is more than this image of a territory, however; for Kant goes on to say that the 'domain' of the understanding

is an island, enclosed by nature itself within unalterable limits. It is the land of truth – enchanting name! – surrounded by a wide and stormy ocean, the native home of illusion, where many a fog bank and many a swiftly melting iceberg give the deceptive appearance of farther shores, deluding the adventurous seafarer ever anew with empty hopes, and engaging him in enterprises which he can never hope to abandon and yet is unable to carry to completion.[4]

For Le Doeuff, such images (island, fog, iceberg, stormy sea, etc.) in a philosophical text cannot simply be interpreted metaphorically.

Rather, their effect is to close the text off from further scrutiny – to make it self-contained, much as the understanding as an 'island' of truth is self-contained.

More generally, Le Doeuff says that images in philosophy have been explained within philosophy's meta-discourse about itself in two ways: either they have been seen as a mark of the resurgence of a more primitive, or childlike form of thought; or, they have been seen as possessing an intuitive, and self-evident clarity, as though the image could speak directly the thought the philosopher desired to communicate. The latter quality would make images an efficacious way of transmitting thought to an uncultivated, or an untrained interlocutor. In Le Doeuff's eyes, both explanations only serve to hide the real effect of the image in philosophy. Through images, 'every philosophy can engage in a straightforward dogmatization, and decree a "that's the way it is" without fear of counter-argument, since it is understood that a good reader will by-pass such "illustrations" '.[5] Images, therefore, are a means whereby philosophy can be unphilosophical by closing off the image from scrutiny and discussion. For Le Doeuff, closing the image off from scrutiny is equivalent to the closure of philosophy itself.

Le Doeuff's work in philosophy has often been linked to that of the feminists, Luce Irigaray and Hélène Cixous, and, to a lesser extent, Julia Kristeva. Unlike Irigaray, who treats the language of philosophy with great suspicion because of, as she sees it, its masculinist, rationalist and patriarchal status – a status which deprives women of their own voice – Le Doeuff argues that reason and rationality are not essentially masculine. The fact that there is a plurality of rationalities alone tends to belie the notion of a hegemonic, masculine reason. Moreover, Le Doeuff adds that there have always been women in philosophy throughout its history – although, it is true, without the same advantages as men – so that it becomes counterproductive to repeatedly ask why there have

been few women in philosophy. Le Doeuff pushes this point even further by saying that today, in contrast to the past, 'Nothing prevents a young woman from studying philosophy and then producing philosophical works.' And so she asks, 'What is the point, therefore, in going over and over an outdated question and talking about what happened the day before yesterday?'[6]

On the other hand, the way philosophy has been practised has undoubtedly tended to make it more difficult for women to be professional philosophers, just as it is also true that the way women have been characterised almost exclusively by their sex constitutes another largely unacknowledged element (like the image) of non-philosophy within the history of philosophy. There is a fundamental sexism in philosophy; but to combat it Le Doeuff calls upon the resources of philosophy itself (its concern for openness, and its effort to reflect upon its own presuppositions), even if it must also be admitted that philosophy dreams of being its own founding principle and means of legitimation, as it also dreams of being the basis and founding principle of all other disciplines. In short, philosophy's dream of its own omnipotence and autonomy is one of its most powerful myths. When all is said and done, however, Le Doeuff opposes the sexism of philosophy in the name of philosophy. Not philosophy *per se*, then, but the historical practice of philosophy is what is at stake. This practice has misrecognised the effect of images; has emphasised abstraction and universalisation at the expense of pertinence; has refused the idea of the 'wandering' of thought; has seen 'women' as its other; has been inflexible regarding style so that the place of enunciation has, in principle, remained invisible. All these aspects of philosophical practice have contributed to women's alienation in philosophy.

Similarly, women have often been positioned as devotees and disciples of great male philosophers rather than – as has been the rule for creative work – thinking on their own account. In effect, what marks a man as a philosopher above all, is being an independent and a creative thinker to whom others defer. Those men who have not quite made it have often had a woman there to satisfy the male philosopher's 'ontological lack'. Indeed, despite his success, Sartre tended to depend on de Beauvoir in just such a way. In a detailed treatment of the de Beauvoir–Sartre relation in *Hipparchia's Choice*, Le Doeuff analyses the use de Beauvoir makes of Sartre's existential philosophy (i.e. of her discipleship) in *The Second Sex* in order that she (de Beauvoir) might, surreptitiously, turn the stick in the other direction. The sexism of Sartre's philosophy is not directly challenged by de Beauvoir. Rather, says Le Doeuff, Sartre's categories 'are remodelled "in the heat of the moment" '.[7] De Beauvoir takes the framework of existentialism as given (she herself is not constructing a philosophical system) and uses it in order to present a 'point of view', a perspective on the here and now. She refers to concrete examples and cites ethnographic data not in order to demonstrate a philosophical framework, but because they exist as examples of the way people live. In addition, de Beauvoir does not take a 'collection of "theoretical positions" ' from existentialism, but a set of values. 'So Simone de Beauvoir's choice is first and foremost one of morality.'[8] As a result, although Le Doeuff still finds much that is problematic in *The Second Sex*, she has not, unlike other feminists, built her feminism on a complete rejection of de Beauvoir. And Le Doeuff, in the end, finds de Beauvoir significant precisely because the Sartrian 'phantasmagoria' – which rejected the idea that exteriority (the other) was in any way philosophically or morally determinate – disappears when 'de Beauvoir takes up the same philosophy'. When all is said and done, as it were, Le Doeuff finds de Beauvoir attractive because, although beginning with existentialism, she comes to speak in her own voice. In short, she ceases to be a devotee.

Her view of philosophy as a potentially liberating practice has led some to see in Le Doeuff's approach an implicit reverence for the eighteenth-century *philosophes*. Feminist critics like Elizabeth Grosz have suggested that because of this reverence and propriety in her readings it is 'almost as if she were to claim that if philosophy is misogynist, this can be confined to those imaginary elements she has been concerned to reveal'.[9] According to Meaghan Morris, Le Doeuff's acceptance of philosophy as a globally positive force as far as women are concerned might merely be 'a salvage operation to rescue philosophy from the more damaging charges of feminist critics'.[10]

While acknowledging that the situation is complex, Le Doeuff's response to such a criticism is to say that, whether we like it or not, philosophy offers the model of autonomy and independence of thought that women as feminists can well aspire to. Maybe this does amount to a salvage operation of sorts; but it is one that seeks to salvage philosophy from the closure it has been subject to in the hands of men. If, historically, men have limited philosophy, this does not mean that philosophy is limited in itself.

Even if one were to argue that the possibility of independence of thought offered by philosophy is illusory, it is hard to see how one can escape thinking philosophically in arriving at such a conclusion. For Le Doeuff, however, the historical limitations of philosophy can be turned to account when we recognise that, through such limitations, paradoxical as it might seem, philosophy demonstrates its pertinence. Although this link must be thought through carefully to avoid sounding glib, it is philosophy's failure to be universal, and the reality of its historical limits which makes it pertinent. In other words, historical limits mean being tied up with issues of the day.

A final, but nevertheless fundamental, reason as to why women should not eschew philosophy is that it is, historically, through being designated as unphilosophical that women have been defined as women. This has resulted in the prejudice that the man is philosophical (i.e. not determined by his sex) and the woman is only her sex. In her chapter, 'Pierre Roussel's Chiasmus', in *The Philosophical Imaginary*, Le Doeuff is able to give an example of the lengths to which scientists have gone in order to reduce women to their sex. As if inspired by Book V of Rousseau's *Emile* (where Rousseau says that abstract truths are not for women), Pierre Roussel, in his treatise of 1777 on woman,[11] says, in effect, that women are not suited to theorising because their first impulse, in their natural roles as wives and mothers, is to be practical, to have an over-active imagination which does not allow them to retain ideas, but which enables them to identify with the suffering of others because of their own weakness. Among other things, Le Doeuff makes two general points about a Rousselesque image of woman. The first is that ideas which explain women's capacities by their sex, and, what is more, which see this sex as constant over time and in space, are still prevalent today in certain areas of biology, psychoanalysis and philosophy. The second point is that the argument which presents such views is so specious, so ideological in the end, that its very existence in a supposedly philosophical environment constitutes a limit to philosophy, as images constitute a limit.

One of the abiding images that Le Doeuff analyses in *The Philosophical Imaginary* and elsewhere is Utopia. Thus in an article published in English in 1982,[12] she discusses the way Utopia, in the famous works of More, Bacon, and Campanella, amounts to 'a defense and illustration of socialized intellectual life'.[13] True, Utopia is a reverie of a land of the good life; but because it is also a critique of life in the here and now, it implies both a specific quality of life, and a specific means of obtaining it. Inevitably, the good life is one produced through pedagogical reforms; it requires philosophers to imagine it and educators to teach the uninformed majority about its virtues. Thus, because

Utopias are brought about by way of the school, they are specific to societies based on the ideas of scholars for the school. Where Bachelard had seen a scholarly Utopia as being one form of Utopia, Le Doeuff argues that Utopia is essentially scholarly, essentially a society existing for the school. This scenario is given a contemporary twist when Le Doeuff argues that the modern critique of the power of the intellectual master – as proposed by the New Philosophers – presupposes that an intellectualist Utopia were already realised. These 'ideologues', are, says Le Doeuff, 'actually following the dreams of the first utopias'.[14] Through the image of Utopia, the fantasy of the philosopher would produce a world where the intellectual master already has absolute power. The real Utopia, then, is announced by the fantasy that society is already for the school.

Through a style that evokes the place of enunciation, through a philosophy that shows that 'there is no thinking which does not wander', that does not proceed by digressions, and through a sense of engagement that is supple and reflexive, Michèle Le Doeuff has begun to give philosophy a new face. What would give her work even greater interest, perhaps, is if she engaged more fully with the hidden face (the images, etc.) of the philosophy canon. For although the work of a Pierre Roussel is no doubt significant in gauging how science has defined 'woman', Roussel would hardly qualify as a philosopher: certainly not substantively, because so many of his notions are unexamined, nor formally, for he was an eighteenth-century doctor. Le Doeuff has already shown the way in her commentaries on Descartes, Kant, Rousseau and Sartre where she has opened up new terrain. The point is to go further – much further – if philosophy is to remain open.

Notes

1 Michèle Le Doeuff, *Hipparchia's Choice. An Essay Concerning Women, Philosophy, etc.,*

trans. Trista Selous, Oxford, Basil Blackwell, 1989, p. 23.
2 Michèle Le Doeuff, *The Philosophical Imaginary*, trans. Colin Gordon, Stanford, Stanford University Press, 1989.
3 Immanuel Kant, *Critique of Pure Reason*, trans. Norman Kemp-Smith, London and Basingstoke, Macmillan, reprinted 1970, p. 257.
4 ibid.
5 Le Doeuff, *The Philosophical Imaginary*, p. 12.
6 Le Doeuff, *Hipparchia's Choice*, p. 5.
7 ibid., p. 88.
8 ibid., p. 90.
9 Elizabeth Grosz, *Sexual Subversions. Three French Feminists: Julia Kristeva, Luce Irigaray, Michèle Le Doeuff*, Sydney, Allen & Unwin, 1989, p. 212.
10 Meaghan Morris, 'Operative reasoning: Michèle Le Doeuff, philosophy and feminism', *Ideology and Consciousness*, 9 (1981/2), p. 77, cited in Grosz, *Sexual Subversions*, p. 212.
11 Pierre Roussel, *Système physique et moral de la femme* (1777).
12 Michèle Le Doeuff, 'Utopias: Scholarly', trans. Susan Rotenstreich, *Social Research*, 49, 2 (1982), pp. 441–66.
13 ibid., p. 446.
14 ibid., p. 462.

See also in this book

Le Doeuff's major writings

'Women and philosophy', *Radical Philosophy*, 17 (1977)
The Philosophical Imaginary (1980), trans. Colin Gordon, Stanford, Stanford University Press, 1989
'Utopias: Scholarly', trans. Susan Rotenstreich, *Social Research*, 49, 2 (1982)
Hipparchia's Choice. An Essay Concerning Women, Philosophy, etc., trans. Trista Selous, Oxford, Basil Blackwell, 1989

Further reading

Grosz, Elizabeth, *Sexual Subversions. Three French Feminists: Julia Kristeva, Luce Irigaray, Michèle Le Doeuff*, Sydney, Allen & Unwin, 1989, Ch. 6
Morris, Meaghan, 'Operative reasoning: Michèle Le Doeuff, philosophy and feminism', *Ideology and Consciousness*, 9 (1981/2)

CAROLE PATEMAN

Carole Pateman is a contemporary political theorist. Although her work is well known for its feminist critique of the patriarchal bias in liberal democratic theory, she is also concerned with the way political theory in general might lead to a more democratic and therefore more active and participatory form of politics – in the West as elsewhere. For this to occur, however, Pateman believes that it is necessary to develop a truly general theory of the political, and not just one that, either *de facto* or *de jure*, unjustifiably disqualifies certain categories of person from being full political subjects – a disqualification indeed borne by women, at least up until the appearance of the feminist movement.

Carole Pateman was born in Sussex, England, in 1940. She won a scholarship to go to a grammar school, but left school at the age of 16 to become a clerical worker. In 1963, she entered Ruskin College, and later attended Lady Margaret Hall, Oxford University, where she read politics, philosophy and economics, and completed a doctorate in political theory. In 1970, while still a graduate student, Pateman published her first book on political theory, *Participation and Democratic Theory*. In 1972, she was appointed lecturer in political theory at the University of Sydney. After becoming a reader in politics at Sydney, she was, in 1990, appointed to a chair in political science at the University of California.

A key aspect of Pateman's theory of modern democracy relies on a re-reading of the classical theorists of liberal democracy, such as Hobbes, Locke, Rousseau, and Mill. Two issues in particular have absorbed her attention. The first centres around the question of legitimate political obligation; the second centres on the nature of political society, and includes consideration of the significance of the difference between the private and public spheres in modern society.

Because the starting point of classical

political theory (as Marx said) is the isolated individual in a state of nature, the problem of the legitimacy of authority has to be addressed. If the individual is the essence of political society, how is it that he was induced to give up the freedom of the state of nature in order to come into society and be subject to laws? The somewhat mythical – if not fanciful – answer has been that, being rational (i.e. knowing what was in his own self-interest) the individual consents to form a quasi-legal pact with his fellows, and this pact, or Social Contract, thus becomes the basis of society. Whether men are ultimately as free under the Contract as they were in a state of nature – as Rousseau suggests – or whether their loss of freedom is at least compensated for by the security they receive from a strong state – as Hobbes argued – Pateman believes that a profound explanation for political authority based on consent is lacking. And if the conditions of consent are lacking the idea of free subjects under the law is rendered suspect. According to Pateman, when it comes to the point and we ask why any particular individual should obey the law (i.e. when the basis of the law's legitimacy is interrogated) liberal democratic theory has no real answer. All it can say is that the free individual voluntarily accepts the principle of representative government. But, says Pateman, it is necessary to find an answer to the key question of *'how and why any free and equal individual could legitimately be governed by anyone else at all'*.[1]

While examining the notion of political obligation, Pateman became aware of the problematic way the nature of the political sphere itself was defined in liberal theory. Not only does the existence of a hierarchy of authority stretch the credibility of the hypothesis of 'free and equal individuals', but the fact that the political has been largely defined in terms of the public sphere – or civil society – can be seen to have definite negative repercussions for the political rights of women. Thus in spite of all the talk about individuals leaving the state of nature in

order to enter society, nature is still, paradoxically, in evidence in society in the form of the private or domestic sphere. Following Rousseau in particular, the domestic sphere is deemed to be the exclusive province of women; for the private, or domestic, sphere is more or less defined by the predominance in it of biological reproduction and motherhood, of emotional ties and kin relations: it is, in short, the sphere of the body and particular interests. The public sphere, by contrast, is the sphere of reason and universal freedom, of autonomy and creativity, the sphere of education and rational debate. Given that women are subject to their biological functions largely related to reproduction, and given that they are in general tied to nature their entry into the public sphere becomes highly problematic.

For Rousseau, for example, the existence of women in the public sphere is not only unnatural in the broadest sense, but even constitutes a danger to the orderly running of society. Being unable to sublimate their natural passions and desires, women have no sense of justice; they will therefore always prefer to support and protect their own kith and kin rather than accept the principle of equality before the law. As a result, Pateman is able to demonstrate that the free and equal, abstract individual of liberal democratic theory is in fact a man. Even contemporary theorists of justice, such as John Rawls, have continued to speak of the abstract individual without addressing the problem of how the associating of women with nature can be avoided. In other words, any rigorous theory of justice needs to explain how women, too, can be included in the just and free society.

Current political theory is thus dogged with the opposition between free, universal men, and natural (therefore, unfree), particular women. Again, Pateman points out that political theory only admits parts of the texts of the canon to be studied: sections dealing with sexual difference, or the relationship between the public and private spheres are excluded. The model of politics followed is that of an idealised version of the Greek polis, where politics is freed from the (private) realm of necessity. Similarly, current theory ignores empirical evidence concerning women in social and political life and tends to repeat standard readings of canonical texts. Feminism, or critiques of liberal theory that claim that some are systematically excluded from the political process, are not seen to raise any problems of principle. Rather, political theory claims that, in principle – de jour – all individuals can be included within the liberal polity; existing inequalities are only de facto, and are thus rectifiable. For Pateman, however, 'feminism does not, as is often supposed, merely add something to existing theories and modes of argument. Rather, feminism challenges the patriarchal construction of modern political theory'.[2]

Myths about the origin of political society (including versions of the Social Contract) see women as being unable to transcend their natures. Or, if they do transcend their natures, this can only be with the aid of a man. Both Freud and Rousseau, says Pateman, see anatomy as destiny for women. The myths that Freud and Rousseau support (the primal horde, where the brothers form society after killing the father, in the case of Freud, and the natural place of women as being in the home, in the case of Rousseau) tend to confirm that the social bond that is talked about, if not the one that is implemented, is a *fraternal* social bond. The social bond is what subtends the public sphere – the sphere of freedom, formally speaking. The private realm – the conjugal world where women reside – is completely separate from the public sphere. In fact, Pateman says, the very transition from tradition to modernity, as understood in political theory, can be equated with the opposition between the private and the public spheres. Thus the 'civil body politic is fashioned after the image of the male "individual" who is constituted through the separation of civil society from women'.[3] To grant citizenship to women thus raises the problem of whether, as citizens – as members of the public sphere – women must assume a male identity and speak the language of masculine reason. Pateman's view is that, indeed, the only way that women can be allowed into the public sphere is if they imitate men; for they cannot be different and citizens at the same time. Publicly, therefore, the difference between men and women is the *same* as the difference deemed to exist between individual men. In the language of Irigaray or Levinas (although Pateman does not refer to them), women in public life are effectively reduced to the order of the Same. They must, in particular, disavow their bodies. The only way to make any headway in resolving the difficulties here, Pateman urges, is to start from scratch and produce a new theory of the body politic, one that is a genuine general theory. The aim of such a theory would be to ensure that both masculine and feminine individuality is incorporated into political life.

Given the problem of obligation in the liberal theory and the masculinist bias of the public sphere, it is impossible to be sure about the meaning of consent in general, and in relation to women in particular. Women cannot be said to have consented to the status quo; as a result, the Social Contract cannot be said to have been fully realised. At best it is still in the process of formation. Similarly, with regard to the marriage contract, women cannot be said to have given their consent to enter into an unequal power relationship; the idea that rape or violence could be in any sense consented to thus renders any contract null and void – that is, if marriage is indeed a legal contract. Up until recently, however, the marriage contract was a contract in name only and in fact allowed the husband to dominate the wife in an unequal relationship, for in law, husband and wife had the same legal identity. In the private sphere, then, right paradoxically was allowed to flow from (potential or real) might.

Feminists, Pateman insists, deny that

171

the existing form of the private–public dichotomy is in any sense a natural one. The problem, though, is to know how a private sphere that is not subject to law (except in extreme cases) can even be retained in a fully modern, democratic society. At best one can imagine that the private sphere will be the sphere of the individual, and not that of the family as it has been in the past. A truly general theory of political society will thus have to address the problem of the nature of the private–public dichotomy.

Despite the innovative nature of Pateman's analysis of political society, it does seem to be dogged by a number of limitations. The first is that she clearly speaks within the tradition of liberal democratic theory she is seeking to transform. The very concepts of her analysis (public–private, freedom, citizen, etc.) derive from this tradition. The terms of the debate are thus still set by this tradition. The question is: How can this tradition be totally transformed *from within*? It is not that a form of radical reformism is necessarily impossible; it is rather that Pateman does not give any indication as to how it could be accomplished.

Second, the tenor of Pateman's critique is dependent upon the notion of the abstract individual even if this individual is gendered male. Here implicit questions are as follows: Why should *an* individual allow himself to be governed? Why should *a* woman not be able to attain equal rights in the polity? Such questions presuppose the use of a notion of identity which is being opposed. It also presupposes that, being identical with him or herself, the individual is able to keep non-identity (difference) at bay. The multicultural experience of contemporary societies sharpens these questions still further. For while the theory of the Social Contract produces the identity of the collectivity by raising the 'I' (individual) to the power of a homogeneous 'we', a multicultural experience challenges this by effectively proposing an 'identity' that is not just logically based, but is empirically based – something that

would be equivalent to the subject in psychoanalysis.

Third, and finally, Pateman's intense focus on the framework of classical liberal theory makes it difficult – despite her intentions – not to look for a solution to the exclusion of women from full political participation in terms other than those of citizenship and the public sphere. The body still seems to be problematic. The overly ideal nature of the public sphere, with its focus on universality, makes a more materialist approach eminently appropriate, especially as thinkers like Julia Kristeva and Luce Irigaray have already been moving in that direction. As Kristeva has argued in using another aspect of Freud,[4] a certain foreignness is inevitable and necessary in the modern polity. This foreignness does not simply come from the outside, but is what constitutes the cosmopolitan subject of the late twentieth century. It is a foreignness which can be the basis of a reinvigoration of the West's eighteenth-century political heritage.

Notes

1 Carole Pateman, *The Problem of Political Obligation: A Critique of Liberal Theory*, (1979), Cambridge, Polity Press, Blackwell, 1985, p. 13. Pateman's emphasis.
2 Carole Pateman, *The Disorder of Women*, Cambridge, Polity Press in association with Basil Blackwell, 1989, p. 14.
3 ibid., p. 46.
4 See Julia Kristeva, *Strangers to Ourselves*, trans. Leon S. Roudiez, New York, Columbia University Press, 1991.

See also in this book

Irigaray, Kristeva

Pateman's major writings

Participation and Democratic Theory, Cambridge, Cambridge University Press, 1970
The Problem of Political Obligation: A Critique of Liberal Theory, (1979), Cambridge, Polity Press in association with Basil Blackwell, 1985
The Sexual Contract, Cambridge, Polity Press, 1988

The Disorder of Women: Democracy, Feminism and Political Theory, Cambridge, Polity Press in association with Basil Blackwell, 1989

Further reading

Dean, Mitchell, 'Pateman's dilemma: Women and citizenship', *Theory and Society*, 21, 1 (February 1992), pp. 121–30
Yeatman, Anna, 'Carole Pateman's *The Sexual Contract*', *Thesis Eleven*, 26, (1990), pp. 151–60

POST-MARXISM

Post-Marxism questions the reductive, and anti-democratic nature of Marxism, and of any political movement which explains changes in history in terms of the role of a specific class, or privileged agency. Post-Marxism accepts the inspiration deriving from Marx's political involvement, but denies the Marxist emphasis on the economy as determinate, or on the idea that there is a universal class – the proletariat – which will usher in the era of socialism. Post-Marxists now argue for radical democracy. In Hannah Arendt's work, the theme of democracy is explored in relation to freedom, community and human rights.

THEODOR ADORNO

Adorno was born Theodor Wiesengrund Adorno in 1903. According to Martin Jay he may have dropped the Wiesengrund when he joined the Institute for Social Research in New York in 1938 because of its sounding Jewish. Between 1918 and 1919, at the age of 15, Adorno studied under Siegfried Kracauer. After completing his Gymnasium period, he attended the University of Frankfurt where he studied philosophy, sociology, psychology, and music. He received a doctorate in philosophy in 1924. In 1925, Adorno went to Vienna to study composition under Alban Berg, and at the same time he began to publish articles on music, especially on the work of Schönberg. After becoming disillusioned with the 'irrationalism' of the Vienna circle, he returned to Frankfurt in 1926 and began a *Habilitationschrift* on Kant and Freud, entitled 'The concept of the unconscious in the transcendental theory of mind'. This thesis was rejected, but in 1931, he completed another: *Kierkegaard: The Construction of the Aesthetic*, which was published in 1933 on the day of Hitler's rise to power. Once his thesis was accepted, Adorno joined the Frankfurt Institute for Social Research after Max Horkheimer became director. To escape from Nazism, the Institute moved to Zürich in 1934, and Adorno moved to England.

In 1938, Adorno rejoined the Institute, which was now located in New York, and worked on the Princeton Radio Research Project, headed by Paul Larzarsfeld. While in America he worked on a number of different projects, including one with Thomas Mann on *Doktor Faustus*. With Max Horkheimer, Adorno sounded a pessimistic note about Enlightenment reason in the *Dialectic of Enlightenment* which was first published in 1947. In 1953, at the age of 50, Adorno left the United States and returned to Frankfurt to take up a position with the Institute, and in 1959 he became its director following the retirement of Horkheimer. By the end of the following decade Adorno became embroiled in a conflict with the students who occupied the Institute's offices. Adorno died in 1969 in Switzerland while writing what many believe to be his most important work, *Aesthetic Theory*.

Current debate[1] on Adorno's work has, in part, centred on the extent to which he anticipates aspects of postmodern and post-structuralist thought. Particular attention is often given here to Adorno's critique of 'identity-thinking' in his *Negative Dialectics*.[2] While it is necessary to understand what Adorno means here, we should also bear in mind a number of points which clearly separate his project from those inspired by nominally French thought.

Let us begin with science. While Julia Kristeva has said that structuralist-inspired semiotics must take its cue from developments in quantum physics, and while Jacques Derrida cites Gödel directly in formulating his philosophical notion of 'undecidability'[3] – that is, while semiotics and post-structuralism in France have forged bonds between the natural and the human sciences – Adorno, like other members of the Frankfurt School, saw modern science as inherently positivist. As Adorno aimed to produce a dialectical thought which did not 'positivise' in any way, science in general was treated with the greatest suspicion, if not contempt. Science in Adorno's philosophy would even be the form of thought he most opposed given that, like positivism in general, it is seen to be absolutely dependent on the logic of identity. Philosophy has allowed itself to be terrorised by science, Adorno claims.[4] But philosophical truth does not equal scientific truth, and philosophy should not shy away from this. In sum, 'Philosophy is neither a science nor the "cogitative poetry" to which positivists would degrade it in a stupid oxymoron'.[5]

Second, Adorno retains – albeit more in his works of cultural criticism than his philosophy – the distinction between 'essence' and 'appearance' (a distinction rejected by contemporary French thought of post-structuralist inspiration) in order roundly to reject the superficial nature of appearance in modern capitalist society. For Adorno, the world of appearance, as for Plato before him, is a world of images and mere semblances, a world of relativism and, most of all, of reification. On this reading, reification and commodities in the capitalist world are almost identical; commodities take on a life of their own independently of the conditions of their production. Commodities hide the truth of their illusory nature. They serve to titillate 'the reified consciousness' which is 'a moment in the totality of the reified world'.[6]

Moreover, by contrast with recent French thought, ideology still plays an important part in Adorno's analyses of social conditions, even if, as he shows in *Prisms*,[7] the analysis of ideology can no longer rely on the 'transcendent' method, where the critic claims to be detached from the milieu being analysed. The difference between 'essence' and 'appearance' entails the ideological effect of reification. For behind the reified appearances, lies the truth of the 'phantasmagoria' of commodity production. This truth is that human beings, despite what they might think, are unfree; they have restrictive forms of thought and action imposed upon them by the existing social conditions of capitalist production; they live in 'the open-air prison which the world is becoming'.[8] People adapt to these conditions rather than oppose them. Consequently, the freedom that Simmel talks about in the same context is a myth. 'In a state of unfreedom', says Adorno, 'no one, of course, has a liberated consciousness.'[9]

Finally, Adorno places far more weight on the role of consciousness than is the case with comparable French thinkers such as Lacan or Foucault. Although he spent time developing ways of escaping a reductive view of the individual as 'socialised', and although his position here is in other respects complex, Adorno's view of the unconscious is extremely simple. First of all, the unconscious (like Freud's work in general) receives little elaboration in Adorno's philosophy. On one of the rare occasions in which he actually refers explicitly to the unconscious in *Negative Dialectics*, he says:

> When the doctrine of the unconscious reduces the individual to a small number of recurring constants and conflicts it does reveal a misanthropic disinterest in the concretely unfolded ego; and yet it reminds the ego of the shakiness of its definitions compared with those of the id, and thus of its tenuous and ephemeral nature.[10]

Even if 'shakiness', 'tenuous', and 'ephemeral' suggest a movement away from the primacy of consciousness, there is little evidence that the unconscious poses a real obstacle to philosophy or to thought.

In other words, Adorno still seems to be far more beholden to a logic of identity than some of his more recent readers suggest. On the other hand, it is also true that his aspirations are in the direction of a thought that is not wholly and solely indebted to the logic of identity. Thus when he begins to rethink the nature of philosophy in *Negative Dialectics*, Adorno makes two key points: first, that philosophy 'lives on' after the Marxist attempt to discredit it for being too idealist had failed; and, second, that philosophy needs a sense of its own impotence before the materiality of the world in order that it might remain creative and open to the new. The materiality of the world is philosophy's inexpressible side. The essential character of philosophy thus consists in being only too well aware of the limitedness of the concepts with which it works. 'Disenchantment of the concept is the antidote of philosophy.'[11] In effect, a truly creative philosophy – which, for Adorno *is* philosophy – seeks out those things which are a challenge to thought itself. These things can be generally designated by the terms 'heterogeneity', or more pointedly, by 'non-identity'.

Unlike Hegel's system in which the heterogeneous element would be reclaimed dialectically through the principle of the 'negation of the negation', Adorno announces the principle of 'negative dialectics', a principle which refuses any kind of affirmation, or positivity, a principle of thorough-going negativity. Thus negative dialectics is nonidentity. This key element in Adorno's thought has a number of synonyms in addition to the ones we have given above – for instance: 'contradiction', 'dissonance', 'freedom', 'the divergent', and 'the inexpressible'. Despite the importance of nonidentity, Adorno also says that no thought can in fact express nonidentity: for 'to think is to identify'. Identity thinking can only think contradiction as pure, that is, as another identity. Where, and how, then, does nonidentity thinking actually leave its mark on thought? In short, what is the material basis of negative dialectics in thought?

To begin with, the material aspect is not philosophy as poetry, or as art. For philosophy as art is equivalent of the erasure of philosophy. Nor is philosophy permitted, according to Adorno, to give in to an aesthetic impulse. This does not of course preclude experimenting in the presentation of new concepts, a process which may lead to poetry, just as the most avant-garde art might be an immanent conceptualisation. Nevertheless, philosophy must 'void its aestheticism'. 'Its affinity to art does not entitle it to borrow from art,' and here Adorno continues the point in a tone for which he has become notorious '. . . least of all by virtue of the intuitions which barbarians take for the prerogatives of art.'[12] All that philosophy can do in such circumstances is continue as philosophy. To give up in light of the impossibility of expressing nonidentity would imply that philosophy had misunderstood the heterogeneous, dissonant nature of nonidentity; in other words, to give up in this sense is to misunderstand that nonidentity is impure – not even a pure contradiction. 'Thoughts intended to think the inexpressible by abandoning thought falsify the inexpressible.'[13] Nonidentity is possibly philosophy's hidden, negative *telos*. It was thus Marx's mistake to think of the end of philosophy in precisely these terms.

The other sense in which philosophy might come to an end is if it took the form (as in Hegel) of Absolute knowledge. Then every problem confronting philosophy – especially its relationship with the material world – would be resolved through the affirmative principle of the negation of the negation which produces an affirmation.

By a surprising series of reversals, Adorno turns philosophy's potential limitations into a philosophical gesture whose implications are perhaps now only beginning to be appreciated. 'In principle', Adorno confirms, 'philosophy can always go astray, which is the sole reason why it can go forward.'[14] Philosophy, therefore, is a negative dialectics in the strongest sense; it is itself the very nonidentity it seeks to conceptualise. In this, the role of language becomes crucial because language is equivalent to the presentation of philosophy's 'unfreedom' as equivalent to the impossibility of conceptualising nonidentity. Were language to cease to be important in philosophy, the latter would 'resemble science'.

Adorno's declarative statements in *Negative Dialectics* need to be read in conjunction with his work in aesthetics and literary criticism. In this regard, *Minima Moralia: Reflections on a Damaged Life*, written during the Second World War in an aphoristic style counters, like Kierkegaard (on whom Adorno also wrote), Hegel's dialectical theory which 'abhorring anything isolated, cannot admit aphorisms as such'.[15] In his reflections on a diversity of topics, Adorno seeks – practically, we may assume – to make a philosophical statement, one that takes up the place of the heterogeneity of human experience.

Similarly, Adorno's attraction to avant-garde music and art, particularly the music of Schönberg, Webern, and Berg, was strongly motivated by a desire to see avant-garde works defy the homogenising effects of the commercialisation (read: reification) of art, where art objects would be reduced to exchange-value. Subjectivity is reduced to the status of a 'mere object' by exchange-value. There is thus a desire in Adorno to preserve the sanctity, as it were, of subjectivity embodied in the art object, against the onslaught of the market where value is equated with price. Through a paratactic style (juxtaposition of statement with the link between them being made explicit), and other devices, Adorno's presentation of his theory of aesthetics in *Aesthetic Theory* participates in an effort to by-pass the reduction of art and thought to the culture industry. Unlike his French counterparts who tend to engage with exchange-value in order to subvert it from the inside, Adorno lauds difficult art and philosophy; for, as he sees it, only through a *struggle* to understand can value be given its true rights here. Modernism, as the movement embodying the renewal of value, would thus be essentially avant-garde where the work of art – 'even the simplest' – becomes a complex *tour de force*.[16] This avant-garde strategy is the point of resistance to reappropriation by the market system.

Some (e.g., Lyotard) have come to see Adorno's approach as a last-ditch attempt to maintain a boundary between high art and popular culture just at a time when the logic and social basis of such a boundary is becoming untenable in the name of the very political values (e.g., opposition to conventional Marxism) to which Adorno himself subscribed. Furthermore, in light of Bataille's work, it is clear that exchange-value can be subverted as much by the very 'low' elements (obscenity) in social life, as by the highest and most spiritually charged products of the avant-garde. Both can entail the distancing necessary to counter the ephemeral immediacy of consumer pleasure. Perhaps the 'low' even more than the 'high'; for ultimately 'high' art depends on the judgement of

criticism as to its nature and quality; it is thereby incorporated into the play of concepts. In other words, avant-garde art and philosophy become interdependent and all the more so – if an analogy with *Negative Dialectics* holds – to the extent that the art object becomes inseparable from its materiality (nonidentity). Grasping the force and significance of avant-garde art requires the use of concepts which can never do a work justice; for the materiality of the work constitutes its uniqueness, and this defies conceptualisation. As Peter Osborne has remarked, 'It is out of this critique of identity-thinking that Adorno's basic conception of aesthetic experience, as the experience of the "non-identical", arises.'[17]

Overall, Adorno's *Aesthetic Theory* struggles to reach an accommodation between avant-garde art that risks being 'normalised' and reified in capitalist society, and the essentially radical autonomy of art objects which qua art objects are singularly out of harmony with the social conditions (including criticism) which enable them to speak at all. There is another aspect to the question, however, one that perhaps Adorno forgets. It is that the conceptualising facility itself could become impoverished through a continual rejection of its worth and efficacity. While the detail of art which defies the system because it defies conceptualisation is no doubt fundamental, conceptualisation might well be also. In other words, what Adorno does not readily acknowledge is that a certain degree of identity philosophy is as essential as material nonidentity.

Notes

1 See, for example, chapters by Peter Dews and Peter Osborne in Andrew Benjamin (ed.), *The Problems of Modernity: Adorno and Benjamin*, London, Routledge, 1991.
2 Theodor W. Adorno, *Negative Dialectics*, trans. E.B. Ashton, London, Routledge, 1973 (reprinted in paperback 1990).
3 See Jacques Derrida, *Dissemination*, trans. Barbara Johnson, Chicago, University of Chicago Press, 1981, p. 219.

4 Adorno, *Negative Dialectics*, p. 109.
5 ibid.
6 Adorno, *Negative Dialectics*, p. 95.
7 Theodor Adorno, *Prisms*, trans. Samuel Weber, Cambridge, Mass., MIT Press, 1981 (fourth printing 1988), pp. 30–4.
8 ibid., p. 34.
9 Adorno, *Negative Dialectics*, p. 95.
10 ibid., p. 352.
11 ibid., p. 13.
12 ibid., p. 15.
13 ibid., p. 110.
14 ibid., p. 14.
15 Theodor Adorno, *Minima Moralia*, trans. E.F.N. Jephcott, London, Verso, 1978 (third impression 1985), p. 16.
16 Theodor Adorno, *Aesthetic Theory*, trans. C. Lenhardt, London, Routledge & Kegan Paul, 1984, p. 155.
17 Peter Osborne, 'Adorno and the metaphysics of modernism: The problem of a "postmodern" art' in Andrew Benjamin (ed.) *The Problems of Modernity: Adorno and Benjamin*, London, Routledge, Paperback edition, 1991, p. 28.

See also in this book

Benjamin, Derrida, Habermas

Adorno's major writings

The Dialectic of Enlightenment (1947) (with Max Horkheimer), trans. John Cumming, New York, Continuum, 1972

The Authoritarian Personality (1950) (with E. Frenkel-Brunswik, *et al.*), New York, Norton, 1969

Minima Moralia. Reflections on a Damaged Life (1951), trans. E.F.N. Jephcott, London, Verso, 1978 (third impression 1985).

Notes to Literature (1958, 1961) 2 vols, trans. Shierry Weber Nicholsen, New York, Columbia University Press, 1991

Introduction to the Sociology of Music (1962), trans. E.B. Ashton, New York, Continuum, 1989

Kierkegaard: The Construction of the Aesthetic (1962), trans. Robert Hullot-Kentor, Minneapolis, University of Minnesota Press, 1989

The Jargon of Authenticity (1964), trans. Knut Tarnowski, London and Henley, Routledge & Kegan Paul, 1973 (paperback edn 1986)

Negative Dialectics (1966), trans. E.B. Ashton, London, Routledge, 1973 (reprinted in paperback 1990)

Prisms (1967), trans. Samuel and Shierry Weber, Cambridge, Mass., MIT Press, 1981 (fourth printing 1988)

Aesthetic Theory (1970), trans. C. Lenhardt, London, Routledge & Kegan Paul, 1984

The Culture Industry. Selected Essays on Mass Culture, London, Routledge, 1991

The Philosophy of Modern Music, trans. A. Mitchell and W. Blomster, New York, Seabury Press, 1973

Quasi una Fantasia: Essays on Modern Music, trans. Rodney Livingston, London, Verso, 1992

Further reading

Buck-Morss, Susan, *The Origins of Negative Dialectics*, Sussex, Harvester Press, 1977

Jameson, Frederick, *Late Marxism, or the Persistence of the Dialectic*, London, Verso, 1990

Rose, Gillian, *The Melancholy Science*, London, Macmillan, 1985

HANNAH ARENDT

Hannah Arendt was an intensely controversial political theorist who showed great courage and intelligence. She was passionately concerned to analyse the nature of politics and society in the 'modern age' in light of key events in the 'modern world' – the world of space travel, the theory of uncertainty, the world of the Holocaust and Stalinist death camps. By 'modern age' Arendt means the era of great geographic and scientific discovery – beginning with Columbus and Copernicus – and the period of the twentieth century, which brought the modern age to a close. In the beginning of her great work, *The Human Condition*, Arendt writes that, 'politically, the modern world, in which we live today, was born with the first atomic explosions'.[1] While Arendt hardly remained true in her political writings to her claim to focus more on the modern age than on the modern world, it is true that her most systematic and revered works – *The Origins of Totalitarianism*, *The Human Condition*, and *On Revolution* – all include important historical references to the period, 1600–1900, as well as to Classical Greece and Rome. As we shall see, two themes in particular are present in Arendt's *oeuvre* to an almost obsessive degree: those of freedom and necessity, and the relationship of the exception to the norm. The profound twist Arendt manages to give to these time-honoured themes – one that does not result in Hegelian political theory in any simple sense – makes her work compelling reading in a postmodern age where all idealisms (all considerations of ends) have been put on notice.

Hannah Arendt was born in 1906 in Hanover. At the age of 3, her parents returned to the quiet Baltic town of their childhood, Königsberg (where Kant was also born). When Hannah was 7, her father died of a syphilitic condition apparently contracted before his marriage. In the same year, 1913, her paternal grandfather, who had been like a second father to her, also died. Through her mother, Hannah became familiar with the political developments of the day, including the fortunes of the Sparticist faction of the Social Democratic Party and its leaders, Rosa Luxemburg and Karl Liebknecht – both murdered after the Spartacist inspired workers' uprising of 1919.

In 1924, Arendt went to the University of Marburg to study philosophy under Martin Heidegger, with whom she had an affair. Heidegger's influence in Arendt's work can be seen not only in her valorisation of the Greeks, but also in the etymological method she often employs to establish the exact meaning of key concepts – like 'labour', for example. After the break-up of her relationship with Heidegger in 1925, Arendt became a student of the *Existenz* philosopher, Karl Jaspers. Under Jaspers's supervision, Arendt, in 1929, completed her doctorate, 'The Concept of Love in Augustine'. In the same year, she married Günther Stern in Paris, and later, in 1932, began writing a biography of a nineteenth-century Jewish woman, and well-known Berlin figure, Rahel Varnhagen. With the rise of Nazism in 1933, Arendt and her husband were forced to flee to Paris, where they had met up with Walter

Benjamin and other German Jewish emigrés. With the fall of France in 1940, Arendt managed to escape to America and to establish herself in New York where she taught (mainly at the New School for Social Research) and wrote until her death in 1975.

Arendt's first important book after the publication of her thesis – the one which made her famous and established her reputation as an important scholar and intellectual – was *The Origins of Totalitarianism*, published in 1951. Clearly inspired by the terrible events of the Holocaust, only the last third of the first edition directly analyses the rise of Nazism and Stalinism. The first two-thirds of the work outline what Arendt sees as the historical precedents to the totalitarian mode of political behaviour, especially as these apply to the Jewish people as a historically pariah cast. In the second section of the book, Arendt analyses the way that imperialism introduced an administrative structure in which efficiency alone – independently of the ends to be achieved – became the most important element – more important, certainly, than the lives and welfare of the colonised peoples. The horrific mix of racism and administrative massacre come together in aspects of imperialism.

Stateless people, Arendt shows, posed insuperable problems for the nation-state in the period between the wars. Once deprived of citizenship, and thus of a legal identity, stateless people become potential victims of arbitrary police action, action which is outside the rule of law. Order, rather than law becomes the sought-after goal. Here, Arendt begins to show that an essential feature of what she will define as totalitarianism is its concerted effort to deprive its victims of every semblance of identity, both civil and psychological. Thus more important than glorifying the rights of people within a legally constituted state, Arendt suggests, is the fight to save people from being legal anomalies, together with the fight against the wielding of arbitrary power that this often solicits. In effect, although the law is not good in itself, to be deprived of it is such an unspeakable indignity that the status of a criminal is often preferable because it does constitute a legal status, however minimal. The loss of human rights as a stateless person is thus equivalent to the loss of legality – 'of *all* rights'.[2] For Arendt, another consequence of the deprivation of a civil status is less the loss of freedom and the right to think, than the loss of the right to action and to opinion, and this, because action and opinion are essentially public engagements requiring the recognition of fellow human beings as the *condition sine qua non* of their realisation. This point foreshadows the long discussion and analysis of action as essentially political in Arendt's next book, *The Human Condition* (1958).

In sum, what Arendt calls the 'calamity of the rightless', entails not just a loss of specific human rights (the right to liberty, to equality, to happiness, to life, etc.) – for these have meaning only within a specific community; but the loss of law *per se*, of community *per se*: 'Not the loss of specific rights, then, but the loss of a community willing and able to guarantee any rights whatsoever, has been the calamity which has befallen ever-increasing numbers of people.'[3] Thus abstract human rights, Arendt acknowledges with Edmund Burke, rights deemed to exist independently of any community, are in fact no rights at all.

When she comes to consider the Holocaust and the Stalinist death camps as quintessential instances of the totalitarian form of politics, Arendt thus points to the way that whole communities of people – but particularly the Jews – were systematically deprived of their human rights – were systematically deprived of their humanity, in short. Of course, the question that is there, woven into the fabric of all that she is saying is: What was it that happened? The unbridgeable gap between the horror of genocide and its representation is indeed at issue. The horror of genocide is no doubt made all the more acute by the fact that the observers who come after it, and the victims who survived it might be forced to concede that it was the result of a totally evil human project. An intimation almost as dark as the evil itself now descends: the two genocides in question might just be understandable as the ultimate in evil-doing, powered by a kind of heroism, however perverted, but heroism, nevertheless: the heroism of those who will not stop at the worst excesses, and who undeniably mark themselves out in some way as a result. Thus, not only can we not remember the victims, but we cannot *forget* Hitler.

Arendt tries to meet this enormous difficulty head-on. And so, rather than making judgements about Nazism or Stalinism, she begins to analyse, systematically, the way that totalitarianism works. Totalitarianism is not, then, equivalent to despotism, where the ruler tries to force the community to conform to his own image: in that case, the despot is the one who makes everyone else into a real or potential enemy. Totalitarianism does not have enemies; it has victims: totally innocent people who, like the Jews, are often perfectly integrated community members. Only the innocent, Arendt points out, can have their juridical status expunged so completely; the true enemy of the state is always someone with at least a semblance of a legal status. Again, the totalitarian regime perpetrates terror against a 'completely subdued population'; but most of all, it murders the moral and psychological person, so that death becomes anonymous. The totalitarian state is like a 'secret society in broad daylight', Arendt says; it uses the state and the secret police in its normal operations; it is not founded on anything but the myth that it produces of itself. The totalitarian state is essentially founded on propaganda and is quite impervious to material reality. Through propaganda the very difference between crime and virtue, persecutor and persecuted, reality and fantasy is erased. The Jews, Arendt points out, were forced into complicity with those in charge of the death camps.

Numerous commentators have remarked that the *coup de grâce* of *The Origins of*

Totalitarianism is not to be found in that work, but rather in articles on the trial of Adolf Eichmann, Arendt wrote for the *New Yorker* in February and March 1963, subsequently published as *Eichmann in Jerusalem*. What struck Arendt most at the trial was the difference between the image of Eichmann the monster, and Jew-hater, and the real, innocuous individual, a man without spirit and without emotion, a mere cog in the Nazi machine and too limited in imagination to be anything but absolutely content with his unexceptional status. Eichmann's demeanour and the facts about what he had done in sending vast numbers of Jews to their deaths confirmed for Arendt that Nazi genocide resulted from the most banal, most systematic, efficient, and bureaucratically inspired motives: 'the banality of evil', is Arendt's famous phrase. In light of her effort to demystify totalitarianism, Eichmann became indispensable; for he was the embodiment of the shallowness and ordinariness of the Nazi enterprise. The latter could now clearly be seen as the outcome of unquestioning obedience, regardless of the ends to be achieved, regardless of the cost in human life. Whether Eichmann, and the regime in general, aimed to improve the rail services or exterminate millions of human beings made no difference; the point was to devise the most efficient and effective means for achieving the end and to follow orders. The real horror of totalitarianism, then, is in the banality and utter servility of its agents, not in any deep psychological explanation, or in any vertiginous political will. This is the real basis of its truly abject status.

If Arendt's study of totalitarianism is derived from the need to come to terms with the most terrible events of the twentieth century, her book, *The Human Condition*, seeks to develop a theory of politics very much alive in Classical Greece, but since lost in the modern age. The motivating factor for her inquiry is the perception that politics as the sphere of freedom – of action – among equals no longer exists in a general sense in the modern world, since the social sphere (or what is equivalent to the household (*oikia*) in Classical Greece – the sphere of necessity (housekeeping)) and the satisfaction of needs has all but completely dominated what is nevertheless still called political life. For Arendt, this is equivalent to the banalisation of politics (the evocation of totalitarianism is no doubt not accidental), where utilitarianism reigns and action, having ceased to be creative and an end in itself, has become a mere means to action. Conformity and necessity have squeezed the political dimension out of human life, and an essential aspect of the human condition is thereby stunted: the aspect of creativity. Schematically, Arendt in fact makes a general distinction between the *vita activa* – which is comprised of labour, work, and action – and the *vita contempletiva*, the realm of thought, or more precisely, the realm of the contemplation of the eternal. While the main focus of Arendt's analysis here is on the *vita activa*, she argues that there is complete equality between the two realms.

Both labour and work in the *vita activa* – the one concerned directly with necessity and the satisfaction of immediate biological needs, the other concerned with utility and the world of durable objects – are activities of means; they are not essentially ends in themselves. A person's life should not only consist of labour and work – the tragedy of modern democratic societies being that so many lives are indeed so limited. The realm of action is where individuals act in complete equality with others – freedom only being realisable in association with others. In general, the social has come to dominate what was once the dichotomy between the private realm of necessity and the public, political realm of politics. And the most influential political thinkers such as Locke and Marx only confirm the importance of necessity. Marx's position is acutely paradoxical here. For while on the one hand he extols labour power (and not work) as the creator of all wealth and the 'essence' of man, he also says that with the communist society and the 'withering away of the state', no one will be forced to labour out of necessity, each having the freedom to be a hunter in the morning and a critic at night, without anyone being essentially a hunter or a critic. This conception of labour approaches what Arendt is alluding to with the realm of politics as pure creativity, the realm of the beautiful deed.

The human condition (which is never fixed) can have the realm of freedom restored to it, now, in the modern world, says Arendt, because developments in technology have rendered the 'social question' (about needs and how to satisfy them) redundant. The main activity in the lives of those in privileged societies need no longer simply be governed by necessity, as occurred before in history.

Arendt returns to the 'social question' in her study of the French and American revolutions in her book, *On Revolution* (1963). There, she argues that while the first, Girondist, part of the French Revolution emphasised human rights and so was an important event in political history, the Jacobin terror of 1793 reduced the potential freedom of the Revolution to a concern with necessity. The urgency of solving the 'social question' and ameliorating suffering led to a disregard for 'the Rights of Man' inaugurated by 1789. The Revolution thus turned decidedly inward, and failed to realise its universalist potential. The American Revolution, by contrast, saw a flurry of constitution-making after independence from Britain had been won. Through this gesture the Americans placed rights and freedom above the 'social question' and (although this is rarely acknowledged) they thereby presented a more progressive revolution to the world. For Arendt, the Americans thus came closer than the French to instituting the realm of politics and freedom.

Perhaps, predictably, Arendt's distinction between action and labour and work, has often been sharply criticised. In particular, critics have not failed to ask how Arendt can claim (as she does) that action which contributes to ameliorating social conditions, or which is based on a choice of helping others, can be considered a lesser form of life.

Notes

1 Hannah Arendt, *The Human Condition*, Chicago, University of Chicago Press, 1958, p. 6.
2 Hannah Arendt, *The Origins of Totalitarianism*, New York, Harcourt Brace and World, 1951, p. 292.
3 ibid., p. 294.

See also in this book

Laclau, Touraine

Arendt's major writings

The Origins of Totalitarianism, New York, Harcourt Brace and World, 1951
The Human Condition, Chicago, University of Chicago Press, 1958
Rahel Varnhagen: The Life of a Jewish Woman, London, East and West Library, 1958
Eichmann in Jerusalem: A Report on the Banality of Evil, New York, Viking; London, Faber & Faber, 1963
On Revolution, New York, Viking Press; London, Faber & Faber, 1963
On Violence, New York, Harcourt Brace and World, 1970
The Life of the Mind, New York, Harcourt Brace and World, 1978
Lectures on Kant's Political Philosophy, London, Harvester Press, 1982

Further reading

Bernaver, James (ed.), *Amor mundi: Explorations in the Faith and Thought of Hannah Arendt*, Boston, Nijhoff, 1987
Bowen-Moore, Patricia, *Hannah Arendt's Philosophy of Natality*, Basingstoke, Macmillan, 1989
Canovan, Margaret, *Hannah Arendt: A Reinterpretation of her Political Thought*, Cambridge, Cambridge University Press, 1992
Kaplan, Giesela and Kessler, Clive, *Hannah Arendt. Thinking, Judging, Freedom*, Sydney, Allen & Unwin, 1989

Kateb, George, *Hannah Arendt: Politics, Conscience, Evil*, Oxford, Martin Robertson, 1984

May, Derwent, *Hannah Arendt*, Harmondsworth, Penguin, 1986

Parekh, Bhikhr, *Hannah Arendt and the Search for a New Political Philosophy*, Atlantic Highlands, Humanities Press, 1981

Schurmann, Reiner (ed.), *Public Realm: Essays on Discursive Types in Political Philosophy*, Albany, State University of New York Press, 1989

Tlaba, Gabriel Masooane, *Politics and Freedom: Human Will and Action in the Thought of Hannah Arendt*, Lanham, University Press of America, 1987

Whitfield, S.J., *Into the Dark. Hannah Arendt and Totalitarianism*, Philadelphia, Temple University Press, 1980

Young-Bruehl, Elizabeth, *Hannah Arendt. For Love of the World*, New Haven and London, Yale University Press, 1982

JÜRGEN HABERMAS

Jürgen Habermas is the most renowned member of the second generation of the Frankfurt School of Social Research. Born in 1929 in Düsseldorf, Habermas wrote his PhD dissertation (published in 1954) on the conflict between the Absolute and history in Schelling's thought. Between 1956 and 1959, he was assistant to Theodor Adorno in Frankfurt. He has subsequently been professor of philosophy and the director of the Max Planck Institute in Starberg.

Like other members of the Frankfurt School, Habermas has been strongly influenced by the writings of Hegel and Marx. Unlike Adorno and Horkheimer, however, Habermas rejects Marx's theory of value, as well as the cultural pessimism of the first generation of the School. As with Weber, Habermas also believes that the first generation of the Frankfurt School erred in confusing 'system rationality' and 'action rationality', a confusion which parallels another: the 'uncoupling of system and life-world'.[1] The result, says Habermas, is that the system (e.g., the economy) is seen to dominate the whole of society at the expense of what Habermas, after Husserl and Schutz, calls the 'lifeworld', which is the immediate milieu of the individual social actor.

On the other hand, like the early Frankfurt School, Habermas's writing also bears the marks of Hegel's abiding influence. Thus he begins his lectures in the mid-1980s on modernity by arguing that, philosophically at least, modernity begins with Hegel: 'Hegel was the first philosopher to develop a clear concept of modernity,' Habermas claims.[2] Although these lectures subsequently treat the work of thinkers like Bataille, Derrida and Foucault – that is, thinkers whose work has problematised Marx and Hegel's social theory – the theorist of communicative action shows his allegiance to the tradition that he has always held dear by using it to point up the inadequacies of the so-called 'radical critique of reason' found in the thought of 'postmodern' thinkers.

Characteristic of Habermas's work in the 1960s was its anti-positivism. In particular, he rejected the positivism of Marx's later writings and sought to turn the early work into a more effective springboard of an immanent critique of capitalist society by emphasising its hermeneutic aspect. This critique had the following features. First of all, Habermas argued that science, and even aspects of philosophy, had ceased to have a critical role in determining the worth of the ends to be pursued, and had instead become the slave of 'instrumental', or 'purposive' rationality (Weber's *zweckrationalität*). Science thus contributed to the technical rationality which enabled capitalism to develop more diverse and complex commodity forms, as well as sophisticated weaponry; it was, however, incapable of producing a creditable justification of the capitalist system itself. In short, the technical understanding of science was positivistic, and therefore ultimately ideological. For it denied the hermeneutic component in science as it was practised. As a result,

Habermas saw science and rationality in the capitalist era being turned against human beings – impoverishing their cultural lives, and exacerbating pathological forms – instead of being used for them. Critical theory was needed to combat this negative form of positivistic science and turn it into an emancipatory activity concerned with political and social reform.

Unlike Adorno and Horkheimer's pessimistic account of reason in the *Dialectic of Enlightenment*, Habermas seeks to turn the tide against such a negative conception and works to 'complete the project of modernity' begun in the Enlightenment. Again, this goal necessitates a critique of the purely instrumentalist view of science dominant in post-war capitalism.

Habermas's early work also aimed to show how the modern state was an outcome of, and contributed to, capitalism's very survival. At one point in the 1970s, Habermas argued – in light of the work of certain political economists – that the state would not be able to cushion people from the worst excesses of the crises in the capitalist economy because its capacity to collect the revenue necessary to support welfare programmes was limited. This, according to Habermas, entailed a limit to the state's legitimacy. For the more it became incapable of protecting people from economic crises, the less its legitimacy could be guaranteed.

In keeping with the German idealist tradition, Habermas uses Marx to develop a strategy of critique which would be, as he sees it, essentially emancipatory. Thus while Marx emphasised the self-formative role of practical labour, Habermas, with a nod to Hegel, sees labour as critique – one particularly aimed against the numbing force of instrumental reason. By showing what had been achieved in a practical sense by the German hermeneutic tradition – in which Habermas includes Freud – the way is opened for a much greater emphasis to be placed on symbolic forms of interaction than Marx had ever envisaged.

In this light, the early 1970s sees Habermas formulating the first elements of a theory of language, communication and the evolution of society intended to provide the basis of a normative framework within which an emancipatory interest could be realised. This work culminated in the massive volumes of *The Theory of Communicative Action*, first published in Germany in 1981. From this we can note that while Habermas never gives up the impetus for emancipation found in Marx, he is not prepared to accept either a revolutionary or a positivistic means of achieving it. Capitalism ushers in a class society, Habermas agrees, and bureaucratic, or purposive rationality has an ever-increasing hold over individual lives; but it is important, Habermas believes, not to equate the 'self-regulating system whose imperatives override the consciousness of the members integrated into them'[3] with the 'lifeworld': the world of consciousness and communicative action. The greater part of Habermas's later work centres around an exploration of the structures (particularly language and communicative action, and moral consciousness) of the lifeworld. The lifeworld is founded on an interest in emancipation; only a distorted use of reason and language makes this difficult to appreciate. In effect, emancipation is the very basis of social (thus human) life. The task is, therefore, to provide a theory which will make universal lucidity possible on this point.

Specifically, Habermas begins a discussion of the notion of lifeworld in the early 1980s by returning to Durkheim and the phenomenological sociology of Mead and Schutz. For Schutz, the lifeworld was the world of everyday life, the total sphere of an individual's experience, including the stock of previous experiences; it is the biographically determined situation into which the individual is inserted, willy-nilly. This is 'the world as taken for granted' in which individuals seek to realise pragmatic objectives. For Habermas, the lifeworld is a horizon of consciousness which includes both the public and private spheres. It is the sphere of identity formation and communicative action. By the latter, Habermas means action which 'relies on a cooperative process of interpretation in which participants relate simultaneously to something in the objective, the social, and the subjective worlds, even when they *thematically stress only one* of the three components in their utterances'.[4] Communication is, for Habermas, the most important aspect of all the activities in the lifeworld because it is here that, ideally, individuals can gain recognition for the validity of their utterances, as it is here also in which the structures of the lifeworld in general can be modified. These modifications are supposed to react back on to the broader social system, thereby stemming the growth of instrumental rationality.

Concomitant with his investigation of the lifeworld in light of Talcott Parsons's theory of society as a social system, Habermas engages to write a theory of both the evolution of society and of the evolution of the individual within it, particularly as these emerge within specific norms and symbolic forms. Relying on the work of Kolberg and Piaget to develop a theory of moral competence, and on the work of Chomsky for a theory of linguistic competence, Habermas endeavours to show that there must be a normative element dominant in human interaction, as well as a purely instrumental one concerned with the satisfaction of needs. Mistaken, according to Habermas, are those who argue with Weber that a purposive, technical science of action alone is possible, with issues of morals and even true understanding being a matter of personal choice. Norms and values have to be the object of rigorous critical reflection, if only because the very distinction between 'technical' and 'normative' itself depends on a prior distinction of a normative kind. Thus even an ostensibly technical, or strategic interest cannot be seen in isolation from an interest in an ethically-informed set of universal principles.

As a result it becomes crucially important to know what the basic needs of human beings are, just as the nature of undistorted and free communication must be revealed. Always on the look-out for immanent features of the social situation which will give force to his interest in the normative aspects of society, Habermas finds that the very nature of language as communication means that both the speaker and the hearer of speech have an a priori interest in understanding each other. Understanding means participants reach agreement; agreement entails the 'intersubjective recognition' of the validity of the other's utterance. In this process each participant will be drawn into reflecting upon their own position in the communicative process. For Habermas, this means that the structure of language is fundamentally hermeneutic: it calls for participants to engage in interpretation at all levels, thus heightening the degree of each person's self-understanding as this derives from his or her interaction with others. This, Habermas believes, is the very telos of language. Consequently, language must be understood according to a consensus model of rules. One way or another, the proper function of language is to allow communication to take place; where communication fails systematically, there is a pathological form language use.

With regard to 'moral consciousness', Habermas seeks to ground what he accepts (from Kohlberg, Piaget, Mead and others) as moral stages in a 'logic of development'. He aims to show how the moral point of view is grounded in an original element in the structure of human life experience. 'What moral *theory* can do and should be trusted to do is to clarify the universal core of our moral intuitions and thereby refute value skepticism.'[5] Although Habermas denies that this means laying claim to any moral truth, it is difficult to see how 'value skepticism' can escape a substantive claim about what constitutes a moral issue.

Even more problematic than the claim

that a substantive moral position is derived from a 'universal core' of morality is Habermas's concern to pick out the pathologies and disequilibria in modern capitalism. The cultural impoverishment brought about by an excessive emphasis on technical, purposive rationality at the level of the system would thus be an example of a pathological social form. Generally speaking, a pathological situation emerges for Habermas when a disequilibrium – i.e. a fundamental disturbance – occurs in society. Modernity, as a socio-cultural, as well as an economic, form runs the risk of degenerating into a totally pathological state. Correctives found in the modern tradition itself – correctives going back to the use of reason inaugurated by the Enlightenment – must be brought into play if serious consequences are to be avoided. Because correctives are needed, it is imperative that the normative basis of the lifeworld be revealed with all possible clarity. Habermas sees himself as engaged in this process, while others have wondered how Habermas's rather turgid style has contributed to the clarity he seeks to achieve.

From another angle, Habermas analyses what he calls the 'philosophical discourse of modernity' by examining how various thinkers – recalcitrant to the tradition of modernity, as Habermas outlines it – exact 'a high price for taking leave of modernity'. What bothers Habermas about Adorno, Bataille, Foucault and Derrida in particular is their apparent refusal to accept that reason must have its rights, and that, in any case, to mount a radical critique of reason, as Habermas believes is the case, is, without knowing it, still to be beholden to reason. Most of all, Habermas claims, the critics of modernity 'blunt' the distinction between alienation and emancipation; they refuse, in short, to tell us (we, who must be told!) where the road to freedom lies. Here, Habermas is particularly upset by claims – echoing those of Adorno and Horkheimer – that modern reason and enlightenment have participated in political repression of the very worst kind.

Clearly, we are dealing here with an extremely contentious point. And much has been written about the way Habermas's views have been rejected or ignored by key French thinkers. Whatever one thinks about the merits of one side of the debate or the other, a number of basic differences between Habermas and a more structuralist, or a poststructuralist inspired thought need elaboration. Some of these differences are as follows:

First, we note that few can accept in isolation, as Habermas seems to, the totalising effect of Hegel's philosophical system, or the idea that modernity begins with Hegel rather than with other claimants for the mantle, such as Rousseau, Descartes – or Columbus, for that matter. Similarly, Marx's claims about labour and revolution are, in isolation, becoming more redundant by the hour. As the core of Habermas's thought seems to rely on these two thinkers, even though, it is true, he claims to have introduced fundamental modifications to their philosophies, it is to be wondered how a concern for the universal can be reconciled with the maintenance of what is rapidly becoming an idiosyncratic intellectual baggage.

Second, Habermas has an outdated view of modern science which fails to see that – after Einstein, Heisenberg, and Gödel – science is no longer easily reduced to a purely technical interest, one justified in positivist terms. Given his concern with norms and the pathological, Habermas could have profited from a reading of works like Georges Canguilhem's *On the Normal and the Pathological*. There, we see how the history of science can be concerned with the normative dimension of human life.

Third, despite his efforts to constitute a general theory of linguistic competence and undistorted communication at the level of the lifeworld, his approach to language there is based on a number of presuppositions that have been exhaustively questioned in linguistics and semiotics. While a number of commentators have pointed out that poetic language is excluded from Habermas's theory, the more striking thing is that, in his own terms, Habermas insists on giving what amounts to an instrumental interpretation of language by reducing it to a means of communication. And even if he were to reply that this is an unintended result of his theory and can, in principle, be incorporated into it, the difficulty is that Habermas analyses language by way of an ideal model based on a hypothetical sender and receiver of a message. For instance, in *The Theory of Communicative Action*, Habermas speaks of 'what it means for a speaker, in performing one of the *standard* speech acts, to take up a pragmatic relation'[6] to something in the objective, social or subjective 'actor-worlds'. Habermas works with a model of an ideal speaker and hearer of language so that the speaker–hearer couple is effectively prior to language, whereas this couple (if it be only a couple and not a triad) is arguably constituted by language itself. Language thus speaks *in* its users as much as they speak language. Unlike Julia Kristeva's notion of the subject in process, the ideal model based on a standard speech is – even if not fully realised – static, and potentially closed. The point is to work for the openness that 'process' implies.

Hence, even though communication does break down, transparency, for Habermas, is nevertheless language's telos. Clearly, one can note that literary and fictional works of all kinds are also embodiments of language in action; they are rarely entirely transparent in principle – *Finnegans Wake* being a case in point – but are no less language for all that. Opaque works are often instances of language in the process of formation – or deformation in the case of *Finnegans Wake*.

Finally, one of the major difficulties in accepting much of what Habermas writes stems from his insistence on assuming that there can be a relatively fixed universal subject, identical with itself. The existence of this subject is confirmed by the emphasis Habermas – after phenomenology – places on consciousness in the 'lifeworld' to the exclusion of the unconscious, or symptomatic conduct. This is not only a philosophical objection: it arises as a specific problem in some kinds of statements. Thus in speaking of modernity, largely under the influence of Hegel, Habermas writes: 'Modernity sees itself cast back upon itself without any possibility of escape. This explains the sensitiveness of its self-understanding, the dynamism of the attempt, carried forward incessantly down to our time, to "pin itself down".'[7] Here, the whole of modernity is psychologised as though it were a homogeneous, perfectly lucid identity. In this regard, it is not a question of insisting that Habermas accept the notion of the radically de-centred subject he opposes, but rather one of suggesting that to rid modernity – or language, or science, or the subject – of the complexity of its mode of unity is surely inadequate.

Notes

1 Jürgen Habermas, *The Theory of Communicative Action Volume 2. Lifeworld and System: A Critique of Functionalist Reason*, trans. Thomas McCarthy, Boston, Beacon Press, 1987, p. 333. Part VI, Ch. 2., pp. 153–97 is a general discussion of the notion of the separation of system from the life-world.

2 Jürgen Habermas, *The Philosophical Discourse of Modernity*, trans. Frederick Lawrence, Cambridge, Polity Press in association with Basil Blackwell, 1987, p. 4. The lectures were given in Paris, Frankfurt, New York, and Boston in 1983–4.

3 Habermas, *The Theory of Communicative Action Volume 2*, p. 333.

4 ibid., p. 120. Habermas's emphasis.

5 Jürgen Habermas, *Moral Consciousness and Communicative Action*, trans. Christian Lenhardt and Shierry Weber Nicholsen, Cambridge, Polity Press in association with Basil Blackwell, 1990, p. 211.

6 Habermas, *The Theory of Communicative Action Volume 2*, p. 120. Emphasis added.

7 Habermas, *The Philosophical Discourse of Modernity*, p. 7.

See also in this book

Habermas's major writings

The Structural Transformation of the Public Sphere: An Inquiry into a Category of Bourgeois Society (1962), trans. Thomas Burger with the assistance of Frederick Lawrence, Cambridge, Polity Press, 1989

Theory and Practice (1963), trans. John Viertel, Boston, Beacon Press, 1973

Knowledge and Human Interests (1968), trans. Jeremy J. Shapiro, Boston, Beacon Press, 1971

Toward a Rational Society: Student Protest, Science and Politics (1968–9), trans. Jeremy J. Shapiro, Boston, Beacon Press, 1970

On the Logic of the Social Sciences (1970), trans. Shierry W. Nicholsen and Jerry Stark, Cambridge, Mass., MIT Press, 1988

Legitimation Crisis (1973), trans. Thomas McCarthy, Boston, Beacon Press, 1975

Communication and the Evolution of Society (1976), trans. Thomas McCarthy, London, Heinemann, 1979

The Theory of Communicative Action. Volume 1. Reason and Rationalization on Society (1981), trans. Thomas McCarthy, Boston, Beacon Press, 1984

The Theory of Communicative Action Volume 2. Lifeworld and System: A Critique of Functionalist Reason (1981), trans. Thomas McCarthy, Boston, Beacon Press, 1987

The Philosophical Discourse of Modernity (1985), trans. Frederick Lawrence, Cambridge, Polity Press, 1987

Further reading

Bernstein, Richard J. (ed.), *Habermas and Modernity*, Cambridge, Mass., MIT Press, 1985

Braaten, Jane, *Habermas's Critical Theory of Society*, Albany, State University of New York Press, 1991

Ingram, David, *Habermas and the Dialectic of Reason*, New Haven, Yale University Press, 1987

McCarthy, Thomas, *Critical Theory of Jürgen Habermas* (1978), Cambridge, Polity, 1984

Roderick, Rick, *Habermas and the Foundations of Critical Theory*, Basingstoke, Macmillan; New York, St Martins Press, 1986

Thompson, John B. and Held, David (eds), *Habermas: Critical Debates*, London, Macmillan, 1982

White, Stephen R., *The Recent Work of Jürgen Habermas: Reason, Justice and Modernity*, Cambridge, Cambridge University Press, 1988

ERNESTO LACLAU

Together with Alain Touraine, Ernesto Laclau – especially in his book written with Chantal Mouffe, *Hegemony and Socialist Strategy: Towards a Radical Democratic Politics* (1985)[1] – is at the leading edge of political and social theory which aims to revivify political action. Through recourse to the notions of contingency, antagonism, and hegemony, Laclau argues that no social structure is entirely closed; rather, dislocation is its essential feature, the feature that opens the way to socially transformative action. Like Touraine, Laclau offers an optimistic and hopeful approach to politics just when postmodern despair seemed to have left many drowning in a sense of impotence. While Laclau agrees that no one is unaffected by the structure of social relations – to the point indeed where we are partially determined by them – at the same time no identity is entirely determined; a space of autonomy exists, albeit one constituted through dislocation. Identities are formed in social life through the politically potent activity which articulates, and thus links, various social antagonisms. This activity Laclau calls 'hegemony'. At a societal level, we could say that hegemony is the provisional identity of the social structure.

Ernesto Laclau was born in Argentina. He was educated at the Universities of Buenos Aires and Oxford. Since 1973, he has taught in the Department of Government at the University of Essex. In 1971, Laclau came to prominence in Marxist circles when he published a devastating critique of the work of Gunder Frank in an article entitled, 'Feudalism and capitalism in Latin America'.[2] In this piece, Laclau demonstrates the analytical paucity of existing theories (notably Frank's) which reduce capitalism to a (nineteenth-century) notion of the market. Such a notion, Laclau emphasises, is particularly inadequate for grasping the specificity of Latin-American societies, capitalist societies where culture and ideology are just as important as the market.

In his best-known work written with Chantal Mouffe, Laclau first of all proceeds to a critical analysis of the Marxist heritage, and especially to an analysis of the identity and epistemological status of the working class or proletariat in Marxism. Within Marxism the issue regarding social, economic, and eventually cultural change had been to do with understanding how the proletariat, as the oppressed class under capitalism, could become conscious of its oppression and so bring about the transition from capitalism to socialism. A number of thinkers, such as Karl Kautsky, had interpreted Marxism as the theory of the historical inevitability of socialism brought about by the laws of history as these were discovered and formulated by the 'science' of Marxism. For such a dogmatic reading, the economic base – or infrastructure – of society determines the proletariat's role in history, whether or not the latter is conscious of this. Just as pre-capitalist economic formations inevitably gave way to capitalism, so capitalism will inevitably give way to socialism – uneven development and national specificities not withstanding.

Such thinking, characteristic of the Marxism of the Second International, of course had its detractors and critics. Various strands of reformist Marxism (characterised by the British Labour Party), revisionist Marxism (characterised by Bernstein) or Revolutionary Syndicalism (characterised by Sorel) sought to give more weight to ideological or superstructural factors in the realisation of social change. Later, in the 1920s, Gramsci would come to rethink the 'base-superstructure' relation and to attribute a determinate role to intellectuals in bringing about historical change. Despite this, Laclau shows that classical Marxism is determinist and essentialist. It is so, not only because it privileges the economy – 'in the last instance', as Althusser had done – but because it places the working class at the origin of change under capitalism. Whether economistic or culturalist, Marxism is an essentialism because 'socialist intellectuals *read* in the working class its objective destiny'[3] and thereby gave it an ontological status.

Given that classical Marxism is determinist and essentialist, a new theoretical framework is needed, one that can account for the potentially liberatory aspects of the relative fluidity, or 'unfixity', which has 'become the condition of every social identity'. Any productive theory must now start from the position that there is no necessary link between socialism and concrete social agents (such as the working class), that there is no privileged point (such as marginality) from which a progressive politics might be derived, and that everything hinges on the form of conceiving the relation between the different subject relations. Society is no longer to be conceived as an ensemble bound by necessary laws.

Although the determinist aspect of Althusser's view of the economy as being determinate 'in the last instance' is rejected, the concept of 'overdetermination' Althusser borrowed from Freud is not. Overdetermination will give the notion of identity a symbolic form; identity is now conceived as originating in multiple sources, and this gives it its fluidity. Overdetermination and the symbolic entail that the subject is constituted within a plurality of discourses. While, for Laclau and Mouffe, this means that within the context of social relations there is no entity that does not have a symbolic or discursive status, reality cannot be reduced to discourse. Within the domain of social relations, there is no difference between discursive and non-discursive practices. Whether or not agreement can be achieved on this epistemological point, the aim of the writers of *Hegemony and Socialist Strategy* is to go beyond an essentialist and homogenising view of politics and society. It is essentialism, they say, which has led to the fundamentalist and totalitarian regimes of Nazism and Communism.

More precisely, though, it is of importance to know how an identity emerges within the new framework sketched out by Laclau and Mouffe. What indeed is a subject or an identity? The short answer is that while identity is not fixed, in the sense that it is not reducible to the autonomous individual closed in upon him or herself, it is not equivalent to the social structure either. In effect, an identity is neither fixed nor completely fluid. It is rather the product of a contradictory tension between necessity (the social structure) and contingency (individual autonomy). The relationship between identities is the basis of social antagonisms. There is no underlying reason for social antagonisms – this is the key thesis of *Hegemony and Socialist Strategy*. However, antagonisms are unavoidable precisely because identities (including that of the social structure) can never be entirely fixed. Hegemony is the provisional fixity of identities in relation to other identities in the context of social antagonisms.

In his later book, Laclau elaborates on these points by saying that a totally self-determined identity would be equivalent to total autonomy.[4] If such were the case, the issue of individual autonomy would be redundant. Only the fact that identity is partially determined and partially fluid makes it an ongoing political issue. On the other hand, if the subject were nothing but what the social structure determined, it would be the same as the structure – as classical Marxism tended to suppose. Identity is constituted within a system of relations – it is, following Saussure, relational – but it is not reducible to these relations. Identity is relational and autonomous at the same time. Indeed, it is the outcome of the dislocation that comes from this.

This mode of theorising identity has an exemplary status in Laclau's thought. Once it has been understood, it can illuminate his thinking on a range of issues. Thus the social structure is never complete; it is never entirely identical with itself and always subject to dislocation. If it were a homogeneous totality identical with itself, it would be a closed system in which the elements of the structure (e.g., individuals) were identical with the structure itself. Similarly, hegemony is both a necessary and contingent set of relations between identities. Hegemony – like the term democracy – is an example of a floating signifier where meaning is both contextual and also independent of any specific context. The social structure is both 'undecidable' and determined. In fact it is the undecidable nature of the social structure which gives rise to antagonisms – the key element in Laclauian politics. Antagonisms are the basis of politics and politics is what keeps the social structure open. Any political act (an exemplar of contingency) only takes place in relation to a set of 'sedimented' practices. The sedimented practices are the element of necessity without which social life would collapse into pure contingency, that is, into indeterminacy. Politics changes social practices, but in order that there be any politics there must also be relatively unchanging sedimented practices – those bequeathed by history or tradition. Antagonisms become a practice of decentring; but decentring is only possible through centres which form because the structure is never entirely in equilibrium. Centres form through antagonisms and the dislocation of the structural. Finally, representation cannot be entirely transparent because this would lead to the disappearance of the relationship of representation itself. In other words, for representation to succeed in bringing the represented into view, it has to assume a certain opacity.

As has often been noted, such a style of thinking is indebted to the anti-metaphysical and anti-essentialist drive apparent in Derrida's philosophy. In an effort to by-pass a thought which is easily trapped in one or other of the poles of a (sometimes sterile) opposition resulting from a rigid adherence to the law of contradiction, Derrida pushes for 'impurity'. He argues for a logic based, simultaneously, on the one *and* the other. Such an approach has, however, received a reputation for being 'apolitical'. In this regard, the astonishing thing about Laclau's thought is that he turns Derrida's insights into the basis of how the political can finally claim its rights. Indeed, as Laclau reads it, any form of determinism or essentialism is equivalent to the death of politics.

In this light, Laclau's ambition is to show how the key issues and movements in contemporary politics – such as feminism, ecology, multiculturalism, and the anti-war movement – must be understood as autonomously, and contingently constituted. They cannot be seen as the inevitable manifestation of class struggle, or economic issues. Even less can they be seen as the displaced articulation of a working class whose other name is 'necessity', and whose historical destiny would be to assume power in the interests of the whole of society and so usher in the age of socialism. Rather, Laclau intimates, the contemporary period is now the period when politics (whose other names are 'power' and 'contingency'), as autonomous action, has come to assume its rightful place in human affairs now that the era of determinisms at last seems to be coming to an end. In this context, Laclau is able to say that 'the constitution of social identity is an act of power and that identity as such *is* power'.[5]

A key implication of equating identity with power is that the hypothetically autonomous self typical of the American tradition of individualism is rendered problematic. For, as we have seen, to presuppose in effect that the individual is prior to society and is thus a kind of autonomous and isolated monad is just as incredible as presupposing that there is nothing but a social structure which determines individuals in their individuality. The pluralism founded on this notion of autonomous individuality simply becomes the symmetrical obverse of elitism; pluralism and elitism are thus two sides of the same determinist coin: both, in their own way, put an end to politics. If myths with metaphysical connections (such as the myth of the proletariat produced by

economic conditions in Marxism, and the myth of the isolated individual of American individualism) have informed social and political life up to the contemporary era, Laclau wants to put an end to myth. For myth and contingency – myth and politics – would seem to be opposed in such a way that myth would seek to blot out politics.

With specific reference to this last point, however, we must note that any serious reading of Laclau would have to acknowledge the presence of continued references (even in his latest work) to the Marxist tradition – almost to the point where Laclau himself still seems to be organically linked to Marxism. Marx's texts and Trotsky's theory of uneven development still seem to constitute an important springboard for Laclau's own theorising. As a result, the reader might well ask what Laclau's relation actually is to Marxism. Is his position really as 'post-Marxist' as he claims? If Marxism, in all its forms, is deemed to be dogmatic and essentialist, why go on referring to it? More than this, however, Laclau does not appear to have theorised his possible relationship to Marx in light of his own insights. For if we must now recognise that there is no intrinsic link between conditions and forms of political and social practice, and if, in addition, all identities are the result of dislocation, antagonism, and – within limits – contingency, is this not to say that Marxist dogmatism was wrong? For our present has now led us to a fundamental re-evaluation of the past and we cannot claim to know the past independently of this re-evaluation. However much a historicist view might claim to understand the past in its own terms, it is quite out of keeping with the general tenor of Laclau's project that he accept historicism. We cannot then just say that 'for its time' dogmatic Marxism was appropriate, for this would imply that an understanding of Marxism can be independent of the concerns of the present. What Laclau's notions of 'hegemony' and 'dislocation' have enabled us to do is to understand Marxism in a new light; and this light is negative. Hegemony means that we must cut all political links with dogmatic Marxism. Laclau, however, does not seem to be willing to follow up the implications of his own work here.

No doubt connected with this is the question of the precise status of Laclau's theory. To what extent are Laclau's insights related to the very present that he describes and theorises – the present of antagonisms and the drive for hegemony? Quite possibly, Laclau could respond by saying – following the Derridean logic to which he himself subscribes – that his theory 'participates in without belonging to' the milieu it is at pains to articulate. In other words, if we give up the either/or, zero/sum logic so familiar up until now, we can see that the theory of hegemony is itself a stake in the game of 'hegemonizing', and that it need be no less rigorous for all that. This is why hegemony, too, will be characteristic of the 'undecidable' logic first brought to light by Gödel and modern science.

Notes

1 Ernesto Laclau and Chantal Mouffe, *Hegemony and Socialist Strategy: Towards a Radical Democratic Politics*, London and New York, Verso, 1985 (third impression 1989).
2 Ernesto Laclau, 'Feudalism and capitalism in Latin America', *New Left Review*, 67 (1971), collected in *Politics and Ideology in Marxist Theory: Capitalism, Fascism, Populism* (1977), London, Verso, second impression, 1982, pp. 15–50.
3 Laclau and Mouffe, *Hegemony and Socialist Strategy*, p. 85.
4 Ernesto Laclau, *New Reflections on the Revolution of Our Time*, London and New York, Verso, 1990, p. 37.
5 ibid., p. 31. Laclau's emphasis.

See also in this book

Althusser, Derrida, Foucault, Touraine

Laclau's major writings

New Reflections on the Revolution of Our Time, London and New York, Verso, 1990

Hegemony and Socialist Strategy: Towards a Radical Democratic Politics (with Chantal Mouffe), London and New York, Verso, 1985 (third impression 1989)
Politics and Ideology in Marxist Theory: Capitalism, Fascism, Populism, London, Verso, 1977 (second impression 1982)

Further reading

Geras, Norman, 'Post-Marxism?', *New Left Review*, 163 (May/June 1985)
Rustin, Michael, 'Absolute voluntarism: A critique of a post-Marxist concept of hegemony', *New German Critique*, 43 (Winter 1988), pp. 146–73

ALAIN TOURAINE

Alain Touraine is a sociologist who was deeply affected by the events of May 1968 in Paris. As a teacher at the University of Nanterre, Touraine saw that student political action in 1968 had ceased to be reactive: it was no longer contained within existing political forms and power relations. It had become a form of conduct distinguished by its transformative character: fundamental aspects of the social structure were in the process of being changed by what Touraine would come to call a 'social movement'. Despite his numerous studies of workers and students together with a timely study of the American academic system, and along with books and articles on Latin America, Touraine's conceptualisation and study of social movements is no doubt the single most important feature of his sociology of political life. The key element of the social movement, then, is action: action against the social system. Touraine's ambition, especially in his later work, is to show how such an emphasis on action does not inevitably lead to voluntarism or individualism. Neither voluntarism nor individualism provide an insight into the *subject* of action.

Alain Touraine was born in 1929. His father was a doctor who came from a long line of medical practitioners. Although destined for an academic career in entering the Ecole Normale Supérieure, where he passed his *agrégation*, Touraine decided to break with family tradition after the war and went to work in a coal-mine in the north of France. This experience fostered an interest in sociology, and in 1950 Touraine joined the sociologist, Georges Friedmann, at the Centre National de la Recherche Scientifique (the French National Research Organisation). Touraine's first major research piece was a study of work at the Renault car factory in Paris and was published in 1955. His next key work, *Sociologie de l'action*, followed a decade later. In 1952, Touraine left France, and went to study in America with Talcott Parsons and Paul Lazarsfeld. He has also taught at various American universities, including UCLA. This makes him one of the few French sociologists with an inside knowledge of American sociology. In large measure, Touraine's theory of social action is a critique of Parsons's theory of social system. From 1960, Touraine has taught at the Ecole des Hautes Etudes en Sciences Sociales.

Touraine's experience of May 1968 confirmed him in the view that a rigidly conceived theory of society as an organic, functional whole essentially distinguished by its concern to reproduce itself was inadequate. For it did not account for how societies changed, nor did it give due weight to the various forms of social action. Although opposed to the early Foucault as well as to dogmatic versions of structuralism, Touraine, in a recent study of modernity,[1] has recognised the importance of Foucault's later work on the history of the prison and sexuality for the reintroduction of the subject into the study of social life.

Although Touraine emphasises the importance of social action, he is in no sense oblivious of the effects on actors of structure and of 'historicity'. Indeed society is not simply the result of discrete actions or events which would put it into place. Rather, for action to *produce* new elements of social structure (that through which society is reproduced) it must work through and against existing institutions and relatively permanent cultural forms. On the other hand, it would be difficult to underestimate the importance Touraine attributes to action in the constitution of society. To be aware of this, we need only recall the point made shortly after 1968 in *The Self-Production of Society* where Touraine says that society is nothing other than social action, for 'the social order has no metasocial warrant for its existence'.[2] In his work of the early 1970s, Touraine still uses the term 'society', and sociology is still the study of society, as it had been for Durkheim, but with the twist that now society is seen as a system capable of transforming itself. For Durkheim, by contrast, society was an organic system whose normal state was that of equilibrium. Later, in the 1980s in particular, Touraine asks whether sociology can do justice to the notions of action and transformation and still be the study of society. His answer is that it cannot, and that sociology must now become the study of change in light of developments in the natural sciences on such things as the open system. More profoundly for sociology, Touraine argues that class – as the exemplar of a set of given conditions – must give way to the recognition that actions and not given conditions reveal relations of domination and subordination, and that, therefore, 'class' as an explanatory category must give way to 'social movement'.[3] This focus on change should not, however, lead to the view that structural problems no longer exist; for action takes on its real meaning only in relation to structure. In more precise terms, how does Touraine define the nature of 'social movements'?

In the first place, he links his analysis[4] to the designation of three forms of social conflict: (1) defensive collective behaviour, where a specific reform might be demanded; (2) social struggles which aim to modify decisions, or even a system of decisions; and (3) social movements. In the example of the factory floor, given by Touraine to illustrate these three forms, collective action would be manifest in the demand that wage differences between people with equal qualifications be abolished. This is a specific reform relating to an already existing structure. Social struggle would emerge if there was a demand by workers for a greater role in decision-making. Finally, the attempt to bring about a transformation of the social relations of power in the factory, and thence in society at large, would correspond to the emergence of a social movement.

Generally, a social movement is an active rather than a reactive force, unlike collective behaviour which is always reactive. Social movements are in general fighting for control of 'historicity'. Historicity refers to the general cultural forms and structures of social life. If the term 'society' refers to social integration, 'social movement' implies a conflictual action opposing an existing form of social integration. This challenge to existing social integration is not at all the same as a crisis of society as such and the collapse of social organisation. Changes brought by social action are not therefore to be seen as pathological, or as 'dysfunctional', in Parsonian terms. A sociology of social movements thus differs markedly from a study of society as an organic system in the process of gradual evolution from one form to another – for example, the evolution of Western society from tradition to modernity.

A sociology which takes seriously the notion of action as the basis of social life will now see social classes as actors rather than as the simple embodiment of a situation marked by contradiction. Contrary to Marx, Touraine says that there is no class in itself, for there is no class without class consciousness. 'Social class is the category in whose name a movement acts.'[5] As an example of a social movement, Touraine points to the women's movement. Here, the aim is not only to react to existing inequalities by calling upon liberal values, but of working to change the norms and values of cultural and social life. Through the effectiveness of the

women's movement, it becomes possible for men to assume a different position within the household and for women to have new opportunities in public life. The women's movement is also exemplary as a social movement because it cannot be reduced to any pre-existing political form, such as a political party. A social movement always transcends party politics.

For Touraine the emergence of social movements coincides with the disappearance of highly stratified and hierarchical societies. This does not mean that complete equality has been realised, but it does mean that there has been an enormous growth in the middle class in Western industrialised societies, and that social barriers are being constantly lowered precisely because the kind of social formation now in view is one that can intervene to change its own structure. Along with the disappearance of rigidly hierarchical and class-based societies has gone the disappearance of objective conditions which determine action – in the manner, for example, of the Marxist relationship between infrastructure and superstructure. Because action now determines conditions, the sociologist must recognise that it is impossible to study social movements without being involved in them. Cold objectivity, as Touraine has said, fails to make contact with the heat of the social movement. Action, then, must be studied from the inside, but this does not mean that the researcher takes on the ideology of the actors. Just the reverse. The aim is to arrive at a 'reversal' which Touraine calls a 'conversion'. The researcher applies it first to himself, and then tries it out with the actors – the point being to bring researcher and actors together so as to elicit the highest possible meaning of the conflict.

More recently (1992), Touraine has renewed the study of modernity. This has first of all involved a return to prevailing definitions of modernity as being located in the early modern age beginning with Descartes and the Enlightenment. Even in this reading, it is clear to Touraine that modernity is fundamentally secular in orientation and excludes all finality. However, in its commitment to progress, modernity does not exclude a possible end to history, even though such a possibility would seem to be precluded by the dominance of instrumental rationality. Instrumental rationality – Weber's *zweckrationnalität*, or means-ends rationality – leads to the valorisation of means; means (technological, scientific, logical, etc.) become ends in themselves. Instrumental rationality predominates while the Enlightenment values of reason, freedom, method, universalism, and progress are still in force. Similarly, the self, or the individual, embodied in the citizen becomes the central focus of political and social action and gives the modern era its distinctive historical complexion.

With the arrival of the Frankfurt School, the work of the early Foucault, and, latterly, of the 'post-modern', both instrumental and universal reason, the subject, ideologies, and the notion of ultimate values come under intense pressure. Modernity is seen to give rise to the very oppressions it seeks to overcome; instrumental reason is seen to lead to a banalisation of life, and the subject is seen to be the product of ideology, or of a specific epistemological configuration which is now at the point of passing away.

In response, Touraine argues that the critique fails to recognise that modernity is divided against itself: it is 'self-critical' and 'self-destructive'. The writings of Nietzsche and Freud are the clearest evidence of the division, the very same writings which have often been used in the critique of modernity, including that found in post-modern writings. Furthermore, and with particular reference to the Frankfurt School – which he finds insufferably elitist – Touraine remarks that it is all very well to denounce technological rationality in the name of some universal end, but there is always a risk of a totalitarian outcome in such a venture. In any case, he continues,

The weakness of our societies does not result from the disappearance of ends

destroyed by the internal logic of technical means, but, on the contrary, from the decomposition of the rationalist model, broken by modernity itself, and thus by the separate development of logics of action which no longer refer to rationality: the search for pleasure, social status, profit or power.[6]

In a reinterpretation of Freud, Nietzsche, and, to a lesser extent, Foucault, Touraine finds the means to a possible 're-enchantment' of the world. For what all three thinkers do is produce an almost unanswerable critique – not so much of the subject – but of the 'self', the socially consecrated version of the subject. In short, in both their theory and practice, these anti-modernists recognise the singularity which is the subject – the pure actor – the entity which cannot be reduced to a conventionalised set of behaviours or symbolic forms.

In light of this revitalisation of the acting subject, Touraine also presents an impassioned argument against the view that sociology is reductive. In the figures of Nietzsche, Simmel and Weber in particular, an anti-utilitarian sociology is in the making. The leads that they have thrown out are waiting to be taken up. Similarly, in Foucault's writing on the subject towards the end of his life, Touraine detects a shift from the idea that subjectivity is equivalent to a form of subjection to the idea that the subject is capable of self-transformation. There is a need to 'reinvent' modernity on the basis of such scattered insights. There is a need to find a new principle of social integration that does not have the negative aspects of the earlier form of modernity. With Touraine's 'new modernity' the subject and reason become conduits for the broader aspects of social existence ('life', 'consumption', 'nation', and the 'enterprise'). Rather than being the principle of unification, as was the case with the Enlightenment, the subject is the relay who 'reconstructs the fragmented cultural field'.[7] Far from being closed in upon itself – as is the case with purely narcissistic self – the subject becomes the attempt to unify desires and needs within a consciousness belonging to the nation or the enterprise. From a centralised conception of the self one comes to a bi-polar view; this is why the subject cannot be reduced to any of the fragments of the social totality.

Most of all, Touraine wants to reintroduce a subject as actor and as movement thereby replacing, as the key determinants to action, the notions of class and the given situation. Mobilisation of convictions linked to moral and personal issues, replaces the ascendancy of the workplace and of party leadership in the sphere of politics. Overall, the aim is to reinvent hope – not in the populist sense of reinventing origins, but in the sense of action which leads to the production of new social forms as well as to the reproduction necessary for social integration.

Any assessment of Touraine's new modernity would have to acknowledge that it is a powerful antidote to the a priori pessimism often characteristic of so-called postmodern experience. Similarly, through careful attention to the nuances that separate the subject as actor from the self as reactor, Touraine had managed to bring to the fore the issues of action and freedom in a way that scarcely seemed credible less than a decade ago. The question that still remains, in light of Touraine's insights, is that of how we are to understand the passage from the normalised self to the active subject. What precisely is the principle which underlies this movement? Is it Touraine's theory which provides the basis of a new reflexivity? Or is it material conditions – that is, action itself?

Notes

1 Alain Touraine, *Critique de la modernité*, Paris, Fayard, 1992, pp. 198–201.
2 Alain Touraine, *The Self-Production of Society*, trans. Derek Coltman, Chicago, University of Chicago Press, 1977, p. 2. The French edition of this text is called *Production de la société*,

Paris, Seuil, 1973. The translation of *production* as 'self-production' is misleading given that in his later work Touraine endeavours to explain that 'self' is the outcome of a given social form, whereas action relates to a subject, or to an entity distinguished by a singularity that is not given by existing social forms.
3 Alain Touraine, 'Is sociology still the study of society?', trans. Johann Arnason and David Roberts, *Thesis Eleven*, 23 (1989), p. 19.
4 Alain Touraine, 'Social movements: Special area or central problem in sociological analysis?', trans. David Roberts, *Thesis Eleven*, 9 (July 1984), pp. 5–15.
5 ibid., p. 9.
6 Touraine, *Critique de la modernité*, pp. 125–6.
7 ibid., p. 256.

See also in this book

Bourdieu, Foucault, Habermas, Simmel

Touraine's major writings

L'Evolution du travail ouvrier aux usines Renault, Paris, CNRS, 1955
Sociologie de l'action, Paris, Seuil, 1965
The Post-Industrial Society. Tomorrow's Social History: Classes, Conflicts and Culture in the Programmed Society (1969), trans. Leonard F.X. Mayhew, New York, Random House, 1971
The Self-Production of Society (1973), trans. Derek Coltman, Chicago, University of Chicago Press, 1977
The Voice and the Eye: An Analysis of Social Movements (1978), trans. Alan Duff, New York, Cambridge University Press, 1983
(*et al.*) *Solidarity. An Analysis of a Social Movement: Poland 1980–1981* (1982), trans. David Denby, Cambridge, Cambridge University Press, 1983
(*et al.*) *Anti-Nuclear Protest: The Opposition to Nuclear Energy in France*, trans. Peter Fawcett, Cambridge, New York, Cambridge University Press, Paris, Editions de la Maison des Sciences de l'Homme, 1983
'Social movements: Special area or central problem in sociological analysis?', trans. David Roberts, *Thesis Eleven*, 9 (July 1984), pp. 5–15
Return of the Actor: Social Theory in Postindustrial Society, trans. Myrne Godzich, Minneapolis, University of Minnesota Press, 1987
'Is sociology still the study of society?', trans. Johann Arnason and David Roberts, *Thesis Eleven*, 23 (1989), pp. 5–34
Critique de la modernité, Paris, Fayard, 1992

Further reading

Scott, Alan, 'Action, movement, and intervention: Reflections on the Sociology of Alain Touraine', *Canadian Review of Sociology and Anthropology*, 2, 8 (February 1991), pp. 30–45

MODERNITY

Modernity can refer to industrialisation. However, the thinkers in this book who became fascinated by the very real changes that modernity ushered in saw the key to modernity in the changes brought about in consciousness. In fact, modernity could in large part be understood as the valorisation and recognition of consciousness as a force in its own right. Baudelaire's dictum that modernity is the 'transitory, the fleeting and the contingent' could be understood in this sense. Joyce is an author who seriously attempts to work through the consequences of this for the art of writing (the novel).

WALTER BENJAMIN

As scholars of the work of Walter Benjamin have begun to make clear, 'any attempt to establish a unity from a series of texts as clearly diverse as Benjamin's will always be thwarted from the start'.[1] Not only did Benjamin write on an extraordinarily wide range of topics – from German tragic drama, Romanticism, history, language and translation, to film, Paris, Baudelaire, Marxism, and storytelling – but he also moved stylistically between prose, fragment, aphorism and citation, often placing himself between the genres of storytelling, literary criticism, historiography, and philosophy. Influenced variously by Judaism, Marxism, and by what he saw as the progressive aspects of modernity, Benjamin stands at the threshold of a new intellectual era. And yet he lived his own life steeped in the accoutrements of the private scholar – a form of existence which, like the storyteller Benjamin himself described so well, was on the point of disappearing – perhaps for ever.

Walter Benjamin was born in Berlin in 1892, the son of a Jewish art dealer. After his schooling at a humanistic gymnasium he studied philosophy and literature in Freiburg as well as Berlin. While at university, he became leader of the Jewish radical students and, like his friend Gershom Scholem, came under the influences of Jewish messianic and Kabbalistic thinking.[2] Scholem's brand of Zionism mixed with anarchistic political sympathies exerted a strong influence on Benjamin. While studying Hebrew in Munich Benjamin met the Utopian philosopher, Ernst Bloch, and contemplated going with Scholem to Palestine in 1924, but his marriage to the Latvian actress and committed communist, Asja Lacis intervened.

For most of the 1920s Benjamin lived the precarious life of a private scholar, supported mainly by his father, with whom he had difficult relations. In order to ameliorate his financial situation, he set to work to obtain a university post – a fearfully difficult operation at the time – and in 1925 submitted a *Habilitationsschrift*, 'The Origin of German Tragic Drama'. The thesis was rejected by the University of Frankfurt because of its unconventional, and often lyrical, personal style. *The Origin of German Tragic Drama* was Benjamin's only completed book, the rest of his writings being in the form of essays, articles (both academic and journalistic), translations, and fragments, many published posthumously. Through this literary activity, which included translations of Proust and Baudelaire, Benjamin managed to earn some money for himself and his family. With the Nazi rise to power in 1933, Benjamin went to Paris, where he met Hannah Arendt. There, he lived off a modest scholarship awarded to him by the Institute for Social Research. Once in Paris, Benjamin associated with the surrealists, and to a lesser extent, with members of the College of Sociology, run by Georges Bataille, and embarked on an enormous study of Baudelaire and the nineteenth century in The Arcades Project.[3] At the outbreak of war, with the Arcades Project unfinished, Horkheimer and Adorno persuaded Benjamin to come to America via Spain. When he reached the border at Port-Bou, however, he was refused a pass, and, apparently unable to face the thought of being caught by the Gestapo, committed suicide on the night of 25 September 1940. The next morning, the border guards, upon whom Benjamin's death had made an impression, allowed the group he was with to pass through into Spain. 'Suicide', Benjamin had written in his study of Baudelaire, 'is the achievement of modernity in the field of passions.'

Although the whole of Benjamin's *oeuvre* resonates with inspired ideas about modernity in all its aspects, possibly no work has drawn more attention, particularly in the debate over postmodernity, than his essay, 'The work of art in the age of mechanical reproduction'.[4] Although written ostensibly in the tenor of a political analysis of the reproduction of the work of art, particularly in the age of film and photography and mass access to these, Benjamin in fact offers an astute analysis of a fundamental change in the aesthetic quality of the work of art. Once the work of art's aura of authenticity has withered away by its being reproducible, sense perception changes along with humanity's entire mode of existence. The technique of reproduction brings art objects closer to a mass audience. More than this, a certain reversibility develops: the work of art as reproduced leads to the work of art being designed for reproducibility. As always with Benjamin's analyses, there is never a unilateral movement between positions or situations, but a movement to and fro between them.

Thus, despite the title to his piece, Benjamin sees more than the mere reproduction of works of art in the modern age (late nineteenth and twentieth centuries) as being significant. Indeed it is the process of reproduction as such which is revolutionary: the fact, for instance, that the photographic negative enables a veritable multiplication of 'originals'. With the photograph, therefore, the spectre of the simulacrum emerges, although Benjamin never names it as such. The photograph as simulacrum by-passes the simple difference between original and copy. It is this feature of Benjamin's work which is of prime importance for a theorist such as Jean Baudrillard. Not simulacra, but *technik* (German for technique; the term also connotes technology) is the focus of Benjamin's interest. Keeping photography as our example, we note that technique in photography is not an incidental, but an essential part of the art. Hence the photographic work of art might not have the aura of an original classical painting consecrated by tradition, but it is not a simple negation of aura either. This is not to deny that Benjamin also lauds the democratic potential of the reproduction of classical art objects; but it is to suggest that what is of greater interest to him are the new aesthetic possibilities brought to bear in the

wake of *technik*. Reversibility (the effect on the type of art work produced), along with a new conception of 'originality' are just two of the issues opened up by Benjamin's discussion.

Two additional elements stand out. The first is that with the possibility of reproduction a work of art can receive meaning from a diversity of different contexts. In an important essay on this point, Gregory Ulmer speaks of a work, or signifier, being 're-motivated' in a new context, thereby forming the basis for postmodern collage and montage.[5] Ulmer's insight is that a new form of creativity is inaugurated just where people had thought that reproduction tended to lead to the degradation of the art object. The second element of Benjamin's essay worthy of note is his characterisation of film. While some of the early commentators on film had attempted to compare it with Egyptian hieroglyphics or classical painting, Benjamin's approach is once again to see film as a new *technik* of art, one where, unlike the theatre (where the audience identifies with the actor), the film audience occupies the same position as the camera. This implies two things. First, that contrary to expectations, the audience may have quite an active role in the viewing of a film, and, second, that film can change 'our field of perception'. Thus just as Freud and psychoanalysis have sensitised people to the fact of slips of the tongue and to the unconscious generally – even though these clearly existed prior to Freud, but went unnoticed – so the camera sensitises people (with the close-up, for example) to aspects of the environment that were hitherto unnoticed.

Even though Benjamin was clearly enthralled by modernity – as the Arcades Project, as well as his other writings indicate – he has also been seen as a theorist of tradition, which, on the face of it was supposed to be what modernity swept away. Without, at this point, seeking a Jewish motive for this interest, it is possible to suggest that the connecting point between tradition and modernity in Benjamin's work is the notion of reproduction. It emerges in a number of different guises in Benjamin's writing: in the image of the storyteller, in the conception of translation, in the valorisation of Proust's *mémoire involontaire*, in the lyrical aspect of Baudelaire's poetry, and in the notion of cultural transmission in the Arcades Project. Very briefly, let us look at each of these in turn.

In the earliest text, 'The task of the translator' (1923), Benjamin begins by saying that the translator's task is not illuminated if it is looked at from the point of view of the audience. Rather, one has to assume that '[n]o poem is intended for the reader, no picture for the beholder, no symphony for the listener'.[6] Instead it is the text which must be the centre of attention. In this regard, the difference, in principle, between the 'original' and the translation has to be taken into account. And here Benjamin makes a quite singular move. He says that an 'original' should not be understood to be essentially hermetically sealed off from subsequent translations by a quality of purity. Were this the case, no text (and even an interpretation is a translation) would survive the time of its immediate production. The text, or art object, thus has an 'afterlife' which propels it into history via tradition – via translation, we should rather say. To take the concrete case with which Benjamin is dealing, it is a question of how Baudelaire's originally French poetry can be faithfully translated into German. Not by attempting a literal translation, but by 'touch[ing] the original lightly' is the response. A literal translation 'demolishes the theory of the *reproduction* of meaning and is a direct threat to comprehensibility'.[7] The 'reproduction of meaning' is the translation of the poetic element of the work, and it is this which calls for translation. It is part of the work. Reproduction is part of the work. This is Benjamin's most salient argument. To illustrate the point he says that just as the broken fragments of a vessel differ between themselves and yet constitute

the same vessel, so the different, non-literal fragments of a translation can reproduce the whole of the original. The principle of the reproduction of significance (not the literal meaning) is in the word itself. 'In the beginning was the word', Benjamin reiterates after the New Testament. The principle of translation – the principle of reproduction – is original, therefore, not the object reproduced.

In 'The storyteller' (1936), a similar structure is in evidence. What allows the story told by the storyteller to be reproduced is not the content of what is told – not the information, as Benjamin puts it – for it would not survive the moment of its initial telling. Rather, it is the story in the memory which is important. A story is what allows the content to be retained in the memory. Story and memory are thus homologous with news and oblivion. Story is the element of transmission – also called tradition by Benjamin – and transmission is fundamentally the story of a life after death. The story, in effect, is the 'afterlife' of people, just as translation is the afterlife of the poem. The story, which always presupposes a community, is what turns a listener into a storyteller: 'The cardinal point for the unaffected listener is to assure himself of the possibility of reproducing the story.'[8] Here we see that as a principle of reproduction, the story also contains a principle of reversibility, with the listener becoming the storyteller.

Again, with Baudelaire's lyric poetry, as with Proust's *mémoire involontaire*, the difference between 'remembrance' and 'memory' is proposed. Remembrance derives from an experience of memory which was not first of all conscious. Like the Freudian unconscious, remembrance gives rise to experience (Proust's *madeleine*), but is not itself an experience. The same pertains to the lyrical in Baudelaire's poetry: as a traumatic shock, lyricism becomes the principle of poetry's transmission as a kind of aftershock, just as the *mémoire involontaire* carries a life forward, despite the fact that the events at issue may have been forgotten by consciousness.

The subject may have forgotten the basis of the lyricism, or the memory, but these have not forgotten the subject. Once again, in the act of reproducing the experience, reversibility is in evidence.

With regard to the Arcades Project, the situation is much more complex. Scholars are only now beginning to work their way into its labyrinthine structure, a structure which Adorno claimed only Benjamin himself could fully explain. Let us simply note two important aspects of this project: the first is that Benjamin based it on the revolution in architecture that the use of iron and glass had made possible. Here, commentators have noted in particular that Benjamin was fascinated by the new spatial relationships between interior and exterior that the use of glass made possible: the street could be brought inside, and this inside was opened up to the outside. The difference between private and public was thus becoming problematic.

Second, although Benjamin was engaged in working out a philosophy of history, and/or a social and cultural history, as Buck-Morss and McCole have suggested, the question arises concerning the mechanism by which Benjamin saw modernity – as the ephemeral incarnate in Baudelaire's terms – could reproduce itself. How, in short, would the theorist and writer of tradition understand modernity in its ever-changing capitalist variant? Opinion seems to be agreed on the fact that in the most general sense, Benjamin tried to reconcile a version of Marxism with a version of Jewish theology, the Marxist element providing a clinical analysis of the reality of capitalism, and Jewish theology providing an explanation of how a tradition was embodied in this most disembodied of cultural formations. The key, no doubt, is to understand how, for Benjamin, history is embedded in modernity, not separate from it – how the 'original' thing, produced in a moment of time, contains the possibility of its reproduction within it. History, or rather historical understanding might be the 'afterlife' of modernity.[9]

For her part, Buck-Morss illustrates the issue exactly when she refers to Benjamin's fascination with a female wax figure adjusting her garter in Musée Gravin. Buck-Morss comments: 'Her ephemeral act is frozen in time. She is unchanged, defying organic decay.'[10] What remains to be understood is how the wax figure – or its aesthetic equivalent perceptible throughout the labyrinth of society – can become the 'afterlife' – the embodiment – of history. To answer this question is to begin to unlock the sphere of Benjamin's most enigmatic writing.

Notes

1 Andrew Benjamin, *Art, Mimesis and the Avant-garde*, London and New York, Routledge, 1991, p. 143. See also in this regard, an overview of the reception of Benjamin in John McCole, *Walter Benjamin and the Antinomies of Tradition*, New York, Cornell University Press, 1993, pp. 10–21.

2 On the intellectual implications of Benjamin's Jewish experience, see McCole, *Walter Benjamin and the Antinomies of Tradition*, Ch. 1., and Irving Wohlfarth, 'On some Jewish motifs in Benjamin' in Andrew Benjamin (ed.), *The Problems of Modernity: Adorno and Benjamin*, London and New York, 'Warwick Studies in Philosophy and Literature', 1991, pp. 157–215.

3 For an in-depth study of this project, see Susan Buck-Morss, *The Dialectics of Seeing: Walter Benjamin and the Arcades Project*, Cambridge, Mass. and London, MIT Press, fourth printing, 1991.

4 Walter Benjamin, 'The work of art in the age of mechanical reproduction' in *Illuminations*, trans. Harry Zohn, Glasgow, Fontana/Collins, third impression, 1979, pp. 219–53.

5 Gregory Ulmer, 'The object of post-criticism' in Hal Foster (ed.), *The Anti-Aesthetic. Essays on Postmodern Culture*, Seattle, Washington, Bay Press, sixth printing, 1989, p. 85.

6 Benjamin, 'The task of the translator' in *Illuminations*, p. 69.

7 ibid., p. 78. Emphasis added.

8 Benjamin, 'The storyteller' in *Illuminations*, p. 97.

9 John McCole cites a passage from Benjamin which would support this possibility. McCole, *Walter Benjamin and the Antinomies of Tradition*, p. 248n.

10 See Buck-Morss, *The Dialectics of Seeing*, p. 369.

See also in this book

Adorno, Baudrillard

Benjamin's major writings

Illuminations (1955), trans. Harry Zohn, Glasgow, Fontana, 1973, third impression, 1979

Reflections. Essays, Aphorisms, Autobiographical Writings (1955), trans. Edmund Jephcott, New York, Schocken Books, 1986

The Origin of German Tragic Drama (1963), trans. John Osborne, London, NLB, 1977; London, New York, Verso, 1985

'A short history of photography', trans. Stanley Mitchell, *Screen* 13, 1 (Spring 1972), pp. 5–26

Charles Baudelaire: A Lyric Poet in the Era of High Capitalism, trans. Harry Zohn, London, NLB, 1973

'Program for a proletarian children's theatre', trans. Susan Buck-Morss, *Performance* 1, 5 (March–April 1973), pp. 28–32

Understanding Brecht, trans. Anna Bostock, London, NLB, 1973

One-Way Street and Other Writings (1974–6), trans. Edmund Jephcott and Kingsley Shorter, London, NLB, 1979, Verso, 1985

'The destructive character', trans. Irving Wohlfarth, *Diacritics* 8, 2 (June 1978), pp. 47–8

'Theories of German Fascism', trans. Jerolf Wikoff, *New German Critique* 17 (Spring 1979), pp. 120–8

'Goethe: The reluctant bourgeois', trans. Rodney Livingston, *New Left Review* 133 (May–June 1982), pp. 69–93

'Central Park', trans. Lloyd Spencer (with Mark Harrington), *New German Critique* 34 (Winter 1985), pp. 32–58

The Correspondence of Walter Benjamin and Gershom Scholem, 1932–1940, trans. Gary Smith and André Lefevere, New York, Schocken Books, 1989

Further reading

Alter, Robert, *Necessary Angels: Traditions and Modernity in Kafka, Benjamin and Scholem*, Cambridge, Mass., Harvard University Press, 1991

Benjamin, Andrew, *Art, Mimesis and the Avant-garde*, London and New York, Routledge, 1991, Chs. 9 and 10

Benjamin, Andrew, *Translation and the Nature of Philosophy*, London and New York, Routledge, 1989, Ch. 4

Buck-Morss, Susan, *The Dialectics of Seeing: Walter Benjamin and the Arcades Project*, Cambridge, Mass. and London, MIT Press, fourth printing, 1991

Cesar, Jasiel, *Walter Benjamin on Experience and History: Profane Illumination*, Mellen, San Francisco, Edwin Press, 1992

Frisby, David, *Fragments of Modernity: Theories of Modernity in the Work of Simmel, Kracauer and Benjamin*, Cambridge, Polity Press, 1985

Handelman, Susan A., *Fragments of Redemption: Jewish Thought and Literary Theory in Benjamin, Scholem, and Levinas*, Bloomington, Indiana University Press, 1991

McCole, John, *Walter Benjamin and the Antinomies of Tradition*, New York, Cornell University Press, 1993

Nagle, Rainer, *Theatre, Theory, Speculation: Walter Benjamin and the Scenes of Modernity*, Baltimore, Johns Hopkins University Press, 1991

Smith, Gary (ed.), *Benjamin: Philosophy, Aesthetics, History*, Chicago and London, Chicago University Press, 1989

Witte, Bernd, *Walter Benjamin: An Intellectual Biography*, trans. James Rolleston, Detroit, Wayne State University Press, 1991

Wohlfarth, Irving, 'Re-fusing theology: Some first responses to Walter Benjamin's Arcades Project', *New German Critique*, 39 (Fall 1986), 3–24

Wohlfarth, Irving, 'On some Jewish motifs in Benjamin' in Andrew Benjamin (ed.), *The Problems of Modernity: Adorno and Benjamin*, London and New York, Routledge, 1989, pp. 157–215

MAURICE BLANCHOT

In the *Fontana Dictionary of Modern Thinkers* (1983) there are entries for François Mitterand and Michel Foucault (as well as for Marilyn Munroe), but no entry for Maurice Blanchot, one of France's foremost post-war writers and critics, and a thinker who has exerted a powerful influence on Foucault and many others. From his critical writings we can deduce that this fact would not trouble Blanchot at all; in fact, because he sees writing as autonomous, and the outcome of a profound solitude, a biography, or a *curriculum vitae*, is of little relevance for assisting a reader in coming to grips with the enigmas of a truly literary work. In fact, Blanchot's silence on matters biographical constitutes an important part of his literary project. For him the literary object is at one and the same time irreducible (to psychological or sociological explanations) and indeterminate (it is never possible to recover all of the meaning and significance of a literary text). Whether this amounts, as Tzvetan Todorov has argued, to a continuation of Romanticism is perhaps one of the key issues pertaining to an understanding of Blanchot's *oeuvre*.

Despite some stiff competition, Blanchot – who was born in 1907 and devotes his life entirely to literature[1] – has acquired a reputation for writing some of the most enigmatic prose in modern French. In light of the fact that he has himself indirectly clarified some of the motivations for his literary work in his critical writings,[2] the claim is no doubt extreme. On the other hand, as a certain force drives writing towards an unknowable centre of attraction – one that is only dimly perceptible to the one who is writing – a degree of obscurity seems to be built into Blanchot's project. While there are good reasons for refusing the epithet of Romanticism in Blanchot's case (Blanchot's refusal of the notion of the author as origin being one of them), there is a much stronger case for saying that Blanchot is a lucid proponent of artistic modernism. This does not imply an acceptance of a particular version of the principle of original creativity. Blanchot has indeed heeded the warning represented by the Hegelian dialectic, where, in the end, everything will be recuperated within the framework of Absolute Knowledge. Eventually, Hegel argues, history will come to an end; the goal of the system will be united in the process of arriving at it. All of Blanchot's *oeuvre* could be seen as a refusal to accept the basis of Hegel's philosophy of the inevitability of the homogeneity implied in the end of history.

Unlike Joyce, Blanchot does not write 'unreadable' prose; neither does he compose explicitly musical texts, like Mallarmé – although the author of *Un Coup de dés* is an important point of reference for him. On the contrary, the immediate limpidity of Blanchot's fictional writing leads the reader to expect that its meaning will be correspondingly accessible. The opening sentence of *L'Arrêt de mort* (*Death Sentence*), is exemplary: 'These things happened to me in 1938.'[3] Gradually this limpidity of style and meaning gives way to a profound obscurity. Names are erased à la Kafka; the place where events occur seems to be Paris, but full addresses are never given; 'J' is a woman with a terminal illness who seems to die of her own accord, and who, later, seems to be helped to die by the narrator who administers a lethal cocktail of morphine and sedative. The events appear to take place at the time of the Munich crisis, but the narrator also gives the impression that the 'events' concerned are those pertaining to the writing as such of the story – a writing which the narrator continually refuses to assume. In effect, the time of writing is ambiguous. An initial draft of the narrative was destroyed, and this propels the writing into the distant past, while at the point after J's death, the narrator says that the events being narrated have not yet happened. These kinds of features in Blanchot's *oeuvre* have prompted the description of them as swirling in indeterminacy. And in fact Blanchot's own literary theory offers some grounds for this.

From his critical writings of the 1950s, it is clear that Blanchot is opposed to any easy appropriation of the authentically literary text. This frequently happens, however, with few critics actually reading what they claim to have read. Rather, they prefer to write their commentaries on the basis of readings which set new works in pre-existing categories; when the critic does happen to see that a work cannot be thus interpreted, it is too late for reading; for the critic is already an author and thus unable to become a reader. True reading, Blanchot implies, is one that respects the literary work's singularity. True reading, in effect, is a crisis in reading. Such would be the modernist and avant-garde impetus in Blanchot's approach in the 1950s. A number of other features that still figure largely in Blanchot's more recent work accompany it. First of all, against any easy labelling of Blanchot as a Romantic, we note that any truly literary or artistic work is for him anonymous. This does not mean that the author is simply trying to hide in the work; rather, it means that the creative force of the work itself effaces the presence of the author. To be totally aware of the work is to be totally unaware of the author of it. Indeed while an author can be consciously linked to a book or to a painting, his or her true artistic merit is only perceptible at the level of a range of works – the *oeuvre*, in short. Given changes in creative orientation over time, however, the exact nature of an *oeuvre* is never present to any author of it. To understand a work in its singularity it is necessary to grasp the movement that produced it. Thus, to understand writing, one must understand the conditions of possibility of writing. This means, almost inevitably, that the nature of the determination of any singular work is never immediately present.

With regard to the literary work in particular, the nature of determination takes another turn, one that seems to be an important element in Blanchot's own writing practice. It is that, 'the essence of literature is to escape any essential determination, or any affirmation which stabilises or even realises it: it is never already there; it is always to be found or to be reinvented'.[4] In other words, Blanchot's modernist impulse entails that it is far from certain that there is any such thing as an art institution – a mechanism which would be waiting to receive the new work within a framework which would pre-exist it. To give priority to the institution of art over the singularity of the work of art is, effectively, to efface that singularity by turning each work – however different from others it might be – into a repetition of the institution. This is why Blanchot argues that nothing exists prior to the work, every work being a reinvention of the practice of writing.

From the point of view of the institution of literature, therefore, every singular work is characterised by its non-literary quality.

Given the singularity of the literary work, we can see why, earlier in his career, Blanchot had spoken of the significance of the writer's solitude. Solitude refers to the way a literary work and the process giving rise to it is cut off from all others – even if, as is often the case, it alludes to other works. Solitude means that whoever reads the work in question will experience its uniqueness. Solitude is the way in which the work speaks – a speaking which is also the form of the author's silence. Playing on this, Blanchot speaks about the work as being the way that the writer's silence takes shape. In accordance with Blanchot's penchant for the rhetorical figure of the oxymoron, silence becomes the form of the author's speaking. Because the writer is within an *oeuvre*, partially produced in light of his or her unconscious desire, the discovery of the form of the *oeuvre* is of interest to both writer and reader. The *oeuvre* is a source of the writer's fascination precisely because it is not consciously determined. Only the specific work is. Fascination is the look of solitude in the *oeuvre*. The source of fascination *par excellence* is the image; and, interestingly, Blanchot does not automatically accept that the image is an unproblematic reflection of the object. The image, which is essentially visual, is in fact a way of grasping the object through distancing, or objectifying.

Many of Blanchot's fictional works play on the paradoxical status of the image as it is conveyed by the look. The image is a closeness brought about by a distancing. Solitude, fascination, image, and the look thus form a fundamental series of notions which inform Blanchot's writing practice. This practice gives rise to indeterminacy. Whoever is fascinated does not see a real object or figure, 'for what is seen does not belong to the world of reality, but to the *indeterminant* milieu of fascination'.[5] In a characteristically enigmatic move, Blanchot also separates the image from meaning, and relates it instead to ecstasy. Many would argue that such a notion hardly comes through in the somewhat melancholic event of Blanchot's fiction.

While it is impossible to claim to be able to plumb all the depths of Blanchot's modernist project, it is clear that death, forgetting, waiting, and finality constitute another important series of concepts underpinning much of his writing. Death, Blanchot has famously said, cannot be experienced. Rather than attempting to make death the subject of an imaginary projection, or attempting a phenomenological reconstruction of dying, Blanchot writes the experience of the impossibility of the experience of death. No doubt this is the sense behind J's coming back to life in *L'Arrêt de mort*. *L'Attente l'oubli* and *Au moment voulu* both explore the complexities of waiting and forgetting. Waiting is a kind of event that arrives, becomes impossible, while forgetting is caught between the given moment and the wanted moment; forgetting is always a kind of remembering in this sense.

In view of Blanchot's inclination for pointing up ways in which finality does not occur, or at least cannot be experienced, we note that the last man in the book of the same name is, in fact, like all other men; it is as though the last man – one who should be completely singular – is, in fact, everyman. Similarly, the 'last word' is a play on 'there is' which is not itself a word, but that which hints at the being of the word in general. The last word suggests what is given. The last word also calls for explanation, thus for more words.

Around the time of Blanchot's middle to late writings (1960s onwards), chance assumes a more obvious presence. Death only assumes its full significance in relation to chance. In *Le Pas au-delà*, Blanchot refers to the unpredictability of death and of dying.[6] But his most systematic elaboration of chance is found in an essay on André Breton and Surrealism.[7] There, Blanchot talks of chance as a particular kind of experience, one

in which the prevailing system of thought is given a shake. Chance is what existing thought leaves out of account; it is what passes it by, without, on that account, having any less of an effect. Death occurs, then, but exactly when it will occur is a matter of chance. To the extent that chance is not taken into account, therefore, death does not occur; rather, it floats in indeterminacy. In this very specific sense which interested the Surrealists, death escapes a cause and effect logic because causality is the mark of determinacy. Blanchot thus proceeds in his writing according to the principle that chance gives rise to uncertainty and indeterminacy. Implied here is a connection between determinacy, and the reversibility of time, and indeterminacy, which corresponds to irreversible time. Many of Blanchot's fictional texts raise the question as to whether or not something has really taken place – the death of 'J' in *L'Arrêt de mort*, for example. Or again, through chance, a moment comes to pass. At a certain moment in *Au moment voulu*, Claudia seems to stop and look at the narrator, as though invited 'by chance' to do so. A short time later, chance and the moment are once more at issue: 'at such a moment' the narrator sees Claudia's face 'by chance'. 'At such a moment?' the narrator asks, 'and from when dated this moment?' Doubt exists as to whether anything has really happened. The scene is one of indeterminacy. Chance cannot be seen simply as an isolated and discrete occurrence; rather, it spreads its mantle over the whole, like the ink of an octopus.

If the true event is chance, writing the event, clearly, will be equivalent to exploring indeterminacy. Blanchot in fact raises the prospect that writing itself is an event and so is subject to indeterminacy. Already we have seen that this possibility was prepared by the idea of the *oeuvre* as a product of the writer's unconscious desire. There is a sense in which the writer does not go where his writing is going. The writer writes into the void: the white page, in Mallarmé's terms. Thus, largely in terms of an exploration of chance, Blanchot's writing presupposes that nothing exists prior to it; this is the deepest sense of the notion of the solitude and the autonomy of writing.

In his later work, the elementary and fragmentary form of narrative (*récit*) gives way to a series of marked fragments, as though the order could be reconstituted if the reader so desired. Here, Blanchot is effectively writing in order to give as great a reign as possible to indeterminacy. From the reader's point of view this implies giving reign to the greatest range of meaning possible. It would be out of keeping with the logic of Blanchot's enterprise to claim to be able to explain its innermost workings. Instead it is preferable to remain circumspect, and in so doing perhaps move closer to genuine insight.

Briefly, and to conclude, reference should be made to Blanchot's interest in the notion of community. The point that Blanchot wants to make is that a true community has no other end than its own existence. To this extent, it is indeterminate – impossible to represent or to symbolise. The nature of the community is thus incommunicable. For the writer, this community is the audience of unknown readers without whom the writer could not exist, but who have no definable identity. For Blanchot, then – as for Bataille – the indeterminate, unknown reader constitutes the void into which every writer must venture.

Notes

1 Such is the substance of the publisher's note referring to Blanchot.
2 Most notably in *La Part du feu (Sacrifice)*, *L'Espace littéraire (The Space of Literature)*, *Le Livre à venir (The Book to Come)*, and *L'Intretien infini (The Infinite Conversation)*.
3 Maurice Blanchot, *L'Arrêt de mort (Death Sentence)*, trans. Lydia Davis, New York, Station Hill, 1978, p. 1.
4 Maurice Blanchot, *Le Livre à venir*, Paris, Gallimard, 'Idées', 1959, pp. 293–4.
5 Maurice Blanchot, *L'Espace littéraire*, Paris, Gallimard, 'Idées', 1955, p. 26. Emphasis added.
6 Maurice Blanchot, *Le Pas au-delà* , Paris, Gallimard, 1973, p. 133.
7 Maurice Blanchot, 'Le demain joueur (sur l'avenir du surréalisme)' in *La Nouvelle Revue Française*, 172 (April 1967), pp. 283–308.

See also in this book

Bataille

Blanchot's major writings

Thomas l'Obscur, Paris, Gallimard, 1941
Aminadab, Paris, Gallimard, 1942
L'Arrêt de mort (Death Sentence) (1948), trans. Lydia Davis, New York, Station Hill, 1978
Le Part du feu, Paris, Gallimard, 1949
Thomas the Obscure (new version) (1950), trans. Robert Lemerton, New York, Station Hill, 1988
When the Time Comes (translation of *Au moment voulu*) (1951), trans. Lydia Davis, New York, Station Hill, 1985
The One Who was Standing Apart from Me (1953), trans. Lydia Davis, New York, Station Hill, 1989
The Space of Literature (1955), trans. Ann Smock, Lincoln, University of Nebraska, 1982
The Last Man (1957), trans. Lydia Davis, New York, Columbia University Press, 1987
L'Attente l'oubli (Waiting, Forgetting), Paris, Gallimard, 1962
The Infinite Conversation (1969), trans. Susan Hanson, Minneapolis, University of Minnesota Press, 1992
The Madness of the Day (translation of *La folie du Jour*) (1973), trans. Lydia Davis, New York, Station Hill, 1981
The Step Not Beyond (1973), trans. Lycette Nelson, Albany, State University of New York, 1992
The Writing of the Disaster (1980), trans. Ann Smock, Lincoln, University of Nebraska, 1986
The Unavowable Community (1983), trans. Pierre Joris, New York, Station Hill, 1988
Vicious Circles, trans. Paul Auster, New York, Station Hill, 1985
The Sirens' Song: Selected Essays, ed. Gabriel Josipovici, trans. Sacha Rabinovitch, Bloomington, Indiana University Press, 1982, and Brighton, Harvester Press, 1982
The Gaze of Orpheus and Other Literary Essays, ed. P. Adams Sitney, trans. Lydia Davis, New York, Station Hill, 1981

Further reading

Clark, Timothy, *Derrida, Heidegger, Blanchot: sources of Derrida's notion and practice of literature*, Cambridge and New York, Cambridge University Press, 1992

Foucault, Michel/Blanchot, Maurice, *Maurice Blanchot, The Thought from Outside*, by Michel Foucault, trans. Brian Massumi: *Michel Foucault as I Imagine Him* by Maurice Blanchot, trans. Jeffrey Mehlman, New York, Zone Books, 1987

Gallop, Jane, *Intersections: A Reading of Sade with Bataille, Blanchot and Klossowski*, Lincoln, University of Nebraska Press, 1981

Hartman, Geoffrey H., *Beyond Formalism: Literary Essays, 1958–1970*, New Haven, Yale University Press, 1970

Libertson, Joseph, *Proximity, Levinas, Blanchot, Bataille and communication*, The Hague and Boston, M. Nijhoff, 1982

Shaviro, Steven, *Passion and Excess: Blanchot, Bataille and Literary Theory*, Tallahassee, Florida State University, 1990

JAMES JOYCE

In his book on *Ulysses* and *Finnegans Wake*,[1] Jacques Derrida relates how Joyce was present in his very first book, the Introduction to Husserl's *Origin of Geometry* (1962), and present again in a key essay, 'Plato's pharmacy', first published in 1968.[2] Derrida further confirms the importance of Joyce for the understanding of his works, *Glas* (1974) and *The Postcard* (1980). As opposed to Husserl's univocity of meaning, Derrida poses Joyce's 'generalised equivocity'.[3] 'Plato's pharmacy', for its part, refers to Thoth (present in *Finnegans Wake*), the Egyptian god of writing, said by Plato to be the inventor of a false memory: memory as mnemonics (as opposed to lived memory). Thoth would be present as the inspiration of Joyce's mnemonic procedure where links may be forged between the most unlikely elements. For such a procedure, the point is not to produce the thing itself in the memory, but to produce a procedure which would make recall possible. Plato, in the *Phaedrus*, calls mnemonics defective memory without seeming to recognise that it would not be necessary if memory were not already defective. Mnemonics, therefore, is a confirmation of the arbitrary nature of the sign as proposed by Saussure. *Glas*, says Derrida, is also a kind of wake, this time, in the sense of mourning. Finally, Derrida claims that *The Postcard* is 'haunted by Joyce': '[I]t is above all the Babelian motif, which obsesses the *Envois*'[4] – in the sense, among other things, of: meaning as a multiplicity of voices, meaning as always open.

Reference to Derrida reminds us that as well as being a fundamental influence in literature and literary criticism in the English-speaking world and elsewhere, Joyce has also been the inspiration for new ideas – a focus, in the twentieth century, for a new understanding of writing: a force that has brought about a re-evaluation of the relationship between art and reality. Again, reference to Derrida reminds us that there are few philosophers or writers in the latter part of the twentieth century who – either consciously or unconsciously – have not been touched by Joyce. Although Joyce wrote a number of important works – such as *Dubliners* and *A Portrait of the Artist as a Young Man* – in addition to *Ulysses* and *Finnegans Wake*, the focus here will primarily be on the latter two texts, as it is these which have had the greatest impact on thought and writing.

James Joyce was born in Dublin in 1882. He attended Clongowes School and Belvedere College in Dublin, before completing a degree in modern languages at University College, Dublin. Upon graduation in 1902, Joyce was fluent in Italian, French, German, literary Norwegian, as well as Latin. To his chagrin, Joyce never studied Ancient Greek, even though he was fascinated by Greek myths. Determined to make a name for himself, Joyce left Dublin for Paris soon after graduation in order to study medicine at the Sorbonne.

In 1904, Joyce lived in the Martellow Tower made famous by his novel, *Ulysses*, and began to write *Stephen Hero*, the forerunner to *A Portrait of the Artist as a Young Man*, first serialised in the *Egoist* in 1914.

The latter work was published while Joyce was living in Trieste with his wife, Nora Banacle, with whom he had eloped in 1904. Also published in 1914, after much difficulty with the censor, was *Dubliners*, a collection of short stories each introducing a particular aspect of the 'paralysis' (Joyce) of Dublin life. As one critic put it, '*Dubliners* is, in a sense, justification for Joyce's exile.'[5] After spending the remainder of the War in Zürich, Joyce and his family arrived in Paris in 1920. It was there that Sylvia Beach published Joyce's *Ulysses* in 1922 in an edition of 1,000 copies, and it was there, too, that Joyce wrote *Finnegans Wake* from 1923 to 1938. In May 1939, *Finnegans Wake* was finally published by T.S. Eliot's publishing house, Faber & Faber, an advance copy being sent to Joyce in time for his fifty-seventh birthday on 2 February.

One year after the war had begun, Joyce was still undecided about what to do. He had the opportunity to go to America, but elected to apply for Swiss visas for himself and his family, and in December of 1940, the Joyces arrived in Zürich where Joyce had sat out the First World War. Suspected of having a stomach ulcer, Joyce's health progressively deteriorated. In January 1941 he died of a perforated duodenal ulcer and was buried in the Fluntern cemetery in Zürich.

Ulysses is ostensibly a day (16 June 1902) in the life of Molly and Leopold Bloom, presented within the framework of the popular, romanised version of Homer's poem, and containing, in displaced form, biographical elements as well as many details deriving from the history of Dublin and the history of English literature (e.g., Shakespeare). While it is true that Homer's poem and Joyce's biography provide the reader with relatively fixed reference points in relation to which many of the novel's details may be understood, contingency is also a key aspect here. Contingency fascinated Baudelaire, we should recall, and gave him a clue to the nature of a truly modern experience centred on consciousness. 'To be away from home

and yet to feel at home' – this, according to Baudelaire distinguished modern experience from all other.[6] Here, to be away from home means being opened up to the new and the ephemeral, the fleeting and the transient. Prior to modernity, experience could be 'homely' – i.e. predictable and familiar. Modern experience, then, is confronted with, if it does not actively search it out (as did Baudelaire), the unpredictable, the unfamiliar, change and novelty. To be at home, by contrast, is to exist in a closed system, where equilibrium and repetition (of the familiar) always prevails and the new is excluded or repressed.

How can a Baudelairian framework be applied to Joyce's *Ulysses* when, in speaking of the novel, we have just pointed to Homer and biography as two stable – and quite 'homely' – points of reference? An attempt to answer this question should give a deeper grasp of Joyce's project here.

While Homer's *Odyssey* – as well as Catholicism – provides a kind of anchorage for the text, this is only of the most provisional kind. What is notable and relevant in Homer *vis à vis* Joyce, is that the hero of the *Odyssey* leaves home, wanders about, takes undetermined trajectories, even if, in the end, he also struggles to return. So it is with Leopold Bloom. He leaves 7 Eccles Street returning only at the end of the novel, a return which is in no sense predictable. Indeed, apart from the title (what Genette would call the 'paratext') and structure, no other explicit evocation of Homer is visible – Joyce having erased the Homeric chapter titles in the definitive version of the novel. Much of *Ulysses*, then, is 'coincidence of meeting, discussion, dance, row, old salt of the here today and gone tomorrow type, night loafers, the whole galaxy of events',[7] events which serve to make 'up a miniature cameo of the world we live in'.[8] Chance thus plays a role. Joyce's writing is effectively situated at the point where chance – or contingency – and structure coincide. This is his great contribution to literature in the twentieth century – and certainly to the English language version of it.

The problem of writing evident in a text like *Ulysses* is that of how to give a literary – written – form to chance and contingency – in other words, to the events of the here and now. Kristeva has called this aspect of Joyce's writing a 'revelation' – by which she means that the text is a writing of what cannot be predicted by a (symbolic) structure, or framework. This might seem to be an odd thing to say, given that Joyce's writing seems to deal with the very banality of existence, that is, with those things which seem to be as far away as possible from the exotic or the heroic. The kind of passage which brings the issue into sharp focus would be one like the following, from the opening of Chapter 5:

> By lorries along sir John Rogerson's quay Mr Bloom walked soberly, past Windmill lane, Leask's the linseed crusher, the postal telegraph office. Could have given that address too. And past the sailors' home. He turned from the morning noises of the quayside and walked through Lime street. By brady's cottages a boy for the skins lolled, his bucket of offal linked, smoking a chewed fagbutt. A smaller girl with scars of eczema on her forehead eyed him, listlessly holding her battered caskhoop. Tell him if he smokes he won't grow. O let him! His life isn't such a bed of roses.[9]

Bloom's walk is, in almost surrealist fashion, a series of chance encounters. It is a walk of almost pure contingency. 'Almost' – because the text has to be written down. The insignificant, unpredictable detail has to be turned into a sign in order that it might then give up part of its ephemeral status and be communicated, that is, become part of Joyce's novel itself. To avoid denotation, in passages such as the one cited above, from remaining a pure inventory, two strategies emerge: (1) the development of a minimal narrative structure; and (2) the development of a definite style. For Joyce, style makes words – or specific units of writing, like phrases – count for themselves in their relation to other words. Poetry is the ultimate presentation of a style in this sense. If Homer forms a structural, or narrative, backdrop to *Ulysses*, this is to be understood as an open structure which can accommodate an almost infinite series of contents. And few commentators have failed to remark on the poetic quality of Joyce's writing – Molly Bloom's monologue in the last chapter being cited as a prime example. Fewer, however, have been able to link Joyce's style to the problem of writing that he was grappling with. Style is Joyce's answer to the problem of how contingency can appear in the novel. Thus while nineteenth-century realist writers worked to make contingent details appear necessary to the whole of the novel's narrative fabric, Joyce's strategy, by contrast, is to place the very possibility of narrative at risk by making the contingent detail relatively autonomous, subordinate to nothing other than its own (poetic) existence. For a nineteenth-century sensibility, Joyce does the impossible: he founds his novels on contingency and indeterminacy. Indeterminacy arises precisely because a complete narrative structure, founded on a logic of causality, is only ever partially visible. Events that occur by chance, contingently, unpredictably, have no discernible origin. Joyce develops the spoken, active side of language, rather than the side, in Saussure's terminology, of *langue*, or fixed system. As chance, speech–act events are, in principle, unique. They defy the logic of causality. This is what makes them indeterminable. The classical nineteenth-century narrative follows the principle of causality as verisimilitude to the letter. Everything has a reason and there is a reason for everything. If Joyce, too, partially subscribes to verisimilitude in *Ulysses*, the greater part of the novel – its most innovative aspect – defies it. Any doubt as to Joyce's position here is swept away in *Finnegans Wake*.

Ulysses, as Joyce continually proclaimed, is the 'story' of the day. By this he did not simply mean that the events of the novel take place during the day. Nor did he only mean that seeing is the dominant sense used in the work. He also tried to make it known that, in terms of its syntax, grammar, vocabulary, and sentence structure, *Ulysses* is perfectly readable. At an immediate level, in other words, *Ulysses* communicates with the reader. To gain a better grasp of what is at stake in *Finnegans Wake* we first of all return to a key passage in *Ulysses*. In it, Stephen Dedalus ponders a theme that is also important in Homer: namely, the nature of fatherhood. 'Paternity', Stephen says, 'may be a legal fiction. Who is the father of any son that any son should love him or he any son?'[10] Stephen is leading up to the idea that fatherhood is clouded in uncertainty – if only, to begin with, that no one can be absolutely certain as to who their father is. If, second, it is through the father principle that a name is given, the aforementioned uncertainty becomes an uncertainty with regard to one's very identity. As psychoanalysis has emphasised, the father principle – the Name-of-the-Father – is crucial to the communicative function of language. The father principle, then, is the principle of determinacy, meaning, and causality. Joyce challenges this principle in *Finnegans Wake* by rendering meaning entirely fluid. The scene which enables him to do this is the night – the world of dreams. One technique he uses is agglutination: running words and phrases together so as to make them ambiguous. Possible meanings are multiplied – as with 'meanderthalltale',[11] 'automutativeness',[12] 'chaosmos',[13] and 'continuarration'[14] – what could be called, following *Finnegans Wake*, a 'polygluttural' technique.[15] In addition, we find what contributes to the distorting, or 'warping process'[16] (= a work in progress): a writing which uses rhythms, intonations and modulations to render fluid all fixed communicative forms. However, to render meanings fluid is not to render the text meaningless. It is, though, to be made aware of the repressed semiotic (Kristeva) level of language. Once immersed in the text, the reader often finds that it takes over, that criticism of the usual kind – where the critic comments *on* the text – becomes extremely difficult, if it is not made impossible. In short, it becomes difficult to objectify *Finnegans Wake*, the very thing for which the 'father principle' would be the pre-condition.

Questions, then, as to what happens in the novel, who the main protagonists are, who the actual dreamer who dreams is, are impossible to answer with certainty, although many have tried. Joyce himself forecast that, with *Finnegans Wake*, he had set critics a task which would last for three hundred years. Such a claim is misleading – at least in one sense – for it suppresses the possibility that, in the end, *Finnegans Wake* is an indeterminate text, which, as such, has no final meaning, or meanings. Rather, its poetic function renders meaning indeterminate; it definitively challenges the father. It is an analogue of the principle that there is no essential core to language – only a system of differences.

Notes

1 Jacques Derrida, *Ulysses, gramophone. Deux mots pour Joyce*, Paris, Galilée, 1987. The second half of this book is in English as 'Two words for Joyce', trans. Geoff Bennington in Derek Attridge and Daniel Ferrer (eds), *Post-Structuralist Joyce*, Cambridge, Cambridge University Press, 1984, pp. 145–59.

2 See Jacques Derrida, 'Plato's pharmacy' in *Dissemination*, trans. Barbara Johnson, Chicago, Chicago University Press, 1981, pp. 61–171.

3 Derrida, *Ulysses, gramophone. Deux Mots pour Joyce*, p. 28.

4 Derrida, 'Two words for Joyce' in Attridge and Ferrer (eds), *Post-Structuralist Joyce*, p. 151.

5 Armin Arnold, *James Joyce*, New York, Frederick Ungar, 1969, p. 26.

6 C. Baudelaire, *The Painter of Modern Life: Selected Writings on Art and Artists*, trans. P.E. Charvet, Harmondsworth, Penguin, 1972, pp. 399–400.

7 James Joyce, *Ulysses (The Corrected Text)*, London, The Bodley Head, 1986, p. 528.

8 ibid.

9 ibid., p. 58.

10 ibid., p. 170.
11 James Joyce, *Finnegans Wake*, London, Faber & Faber, 1939, third edn (reprinted 1971), p. 19.
12 ibid., p. 112.
13 ibid., p. 118.
14 ibid., p. 205.
15 ibid., p. 117.
16 ibid., p. 497.

See also in this book

Benveniste, Derrida, Kafka, Kristeva, Saussure

Joyce's major works

Chamber Music, London, Elkin Mathews, 1907
Dubliners, London, Grant Richards, 1914
A Portrait of the Artist as a Young Man, New York, B.W. Huebsch, 1916
Exiles, London, Grant Richards, 1918
Ulysses, Paris, Shakespeare & Co., 1922; *Ulysses (The Corrected Text)*, London, The Bodley Head, 1986
Finnegans Wake, London, Faber & Faber; New York, Viking Press, 1939
Stephen Hero, London, Jonathan Cape; Norfolk, Conn., New Directions, 1944. Revised edn 1963

Further reading

Attridge, Derek and Ferrer, Daniel, *Post-Structuralist Joyce*, Cambridge, Cambridge University Press, 1984
Benstock, Barnard, *The Augmented Ninth, Proceedings of the Ninth International James Joyce Symposium, Frankfurt 1984*, Syracuse, Syracuse University Press, 1988. (See pieces by Kristeva and Derrida)
Ellmann, Richard, *Ulysses on the Liffey*, London and Boston, Faber & Faber, 1972. Reissued with corrections 1984
Ellmann, Richard, *James Joyce*, New York, Oxford University Press, 1982
Hart, Clive and Hayman, David, *James Joyce's 'Ulysses': Critical Essays*, Berkeley, Los Angeles, University of California Press, 1977
Lernout, Geert, *The French Joyce*, Ann Arbor, University of Michigan Press, 1990
Litz, A. Walton, *The Art of James Joyce. Method and Design in Ulysses and Finnegans Wake*, London, Oxford University Press, 1964. Reprinted 1968

FRIEDRICH NIETZSCHE

Nietzsche's philosophy has been seminal for contemporary thought, and especially for that thought – exemplified in the work of Michel Foucault – which has taken an anti-humanist stance. That so singular and opaque a thinker could have such an impact becomes all the more surprising when we recall that Nietzsche's biography and supposed influence on Nazism have further complicated the task of interpreting his texts. Despite this, Nietzsche has been the focal point in recent times of a new departure in thought, one which refuses to accept the necessity of a relatively stable subject–object relation.

Friedrich Nietzsche was born in 1844 in Saxony, Prussia. He was the son of a Lutheran minister, Ludwig, who died in 1849 at the young age of 36, after having gone insane a year earlier. The son, who always suffered from poor health, thought that he too was destined to die at 36. As Walter Kaufmann's classic study tells us,[1] from the age of 6 years, following the death of his younger brother in 1850, Nietzsche was brought up by his mother in an entirely female household. From 1858, he attended the old boarding school of Pforta, and excelled in religion, German literature, and the classics, but was poor in maths and drawing.[2] It was at this time that the young scholar first suffered from the migraine headaches that were to be with him for most of his adult life.

After graduating from Pforta in 1864, Nietzsche went to the University of Bonn and studied theology and classical philology. In 1865, he gave up theology and went to Leipzig where he came under the influence of the Schopenhauer of *The World as Will and Idea*. As he was thought to be a brilliant student, the University of Basel called him to the chair of classical philology at the age of 24, even though he had not received his doctorate. Arrangements were hastily made for the doctorate to be awarded after his appointment, and Nietzsche taught at Basel from 1869 to 1879 when he was forced to retire due to ill-health. His productive life continued until January 1889, when he collapsed in Turin with his arms around the neck of a horse that had been cruelly whipped by its coachman. He never regained his sanity, and died in 1900.

Between 1872 and 1888, Nietzsche published nine books, and prepared four others for publication. His magnum opus, *The Will to Power*, based on notes from his notebooks of the 1880s, and first published posthumously in 1901, provides the strongest confirmation of Nietzsche's radically anti-idealist stance. It is this stance in particular which has attracted the attention of postmodern and post-structuralist thinkers alike.[3] Such a thorough-going anti-idealism is what allows us to designate Nietzsche as a radically horizontal thinker. Before proceeding further it is necessary to explain Nietzsche's relation to what we have designated as 'horizontal' thought.

Intuitively, one might think that to invoke the horizontal axis is to place thought on a single level, and that therefore Nietzsche is perhaps proposing a certain equality of thought. Might not horizontal thought be precisely democratic thought? The answer is that horizontal thought has nothing to do with the notion of equality or of democracy. Indeed horizontality does not refer at all to any kind of isomorphism, but to the exact opposite. Horizontal thought, in effect, is incomparable; it cannot be put on a scale; for horizontal thought is the thought of difference, not of identity. On many occasions throughout his work, Nietzsche refers to the conventional idea of equality as the exemplar of the order of the Same. For example, Nietzsche argues that the ideal equality of democracy or Christianity is a fundamentally homogenising equality of a 'herd-animal morality'. Similarly, Nietzsche claims that the idealist[4] principle, often put forward (as he says) by 'physiologists', that all human life is ultimately reducible to the 'drive to self-preservation' is an unwarranted, homogen-ising teleology. Human life, rather, is a venting of life, which is at the same time a 'will to power'.[5] What undermines the credibility of the principle of self-preservation are all the facts (violence, sacrifice, unhealthy living, etc.) which contradict it. Any essentialism or teleology, as versions of idealism, have to deny one or more aspects of life in order to be coherent. This is why Nietzsche says that idealism is life-denying – to the point, in the modern era, of producing pathological consequences. Life is always irreducible; it is a totality of differences, not an identity. An identity can be represented and put on a scale with a common measure. Horizontality, by contrast, refers to the impossibility of ever finding a scale that is adequate to difference. Horizontality opens up the 'ideolectal' (private language) end of the communicative process. And this raises issues regarding Nietzsche's whole project that we shall return to.

What has just been explained regarding idealism and the will to power, is closer to the point of arrival of Nietzsche's thought than to its point of departure. In his first book, *The Birth of Tragedy*, published in 1872 when he was 28, Nietzsche introduces two principles which would be present in his writing to the end: the Dionysian principle – the principle of chaos, dream and intoxication – and the Apollonian principle – the principle of order and form-giving. Both these principles are associated with an aesthetic disposition – of life as a work of art, in effect. Thus, in the first Preface to the work written in 1871, Nietzsche says: 'art represents the highest task and the truly metaphysical activity of this life'.[6] Within this perspective, the Greeks showed how art – as a kind of will to illusion composed of the principles of form-giving and intoxication – could function as the true vantage point of life. Art thus becomes equivalent to a recognition that life is unknowable in terms of any ultimate truth, as implied by an idealist metaphysic. This is life seen as tragedy. Art becomes then a way of not having to deny life. Life as tragic is played out in particular in the spirit of music as the embodiment of the Dionysian principle (the first edition of Nietzsche's book was in fact called, *The Birth of Tragedy Out of the Spirit of Music*). For this reason, Nietzsche focuses on the strategic role of the Chorus in pre-Socratic, Greek drama. Far from being equivalent to the audience (who could hardly mistake the drama for life) as Schlegel had proposed, the Chorus sees the action on the stage as real, and responds to life through rhythmic intoxication. As such, the Chorus gives form to the Dionysian impulse. Apollo, as god of plastic powers and soothsaying, gives rise to the visual, objectifying aspect of the drama. Nietzsche notices, however, that the rise of Platonism destroyed Greek tragic drama from within: Platonism, as high idealism, led to a denial of the tragic tenor of life, and so to a denial of the need for an intoxicating element. Modern philosophy – and certain aspects of modern science – as the heir of Platonism, thus denies life: it blots out the spirit of music – the recognition of the tragic element. So much is knowledge dominant in modern culture, that people have ceased to be able to act. 'Knowledge kills action', Nietzsche says in *The Birth of Tragedy*, 'action requires the veils of illusion.'[7]

While philosophy has become life-denying in the sphere of knowledge, Christianity is so in the sphere of morality. Here Nietzsche relentlessly homes in on the role of Christian guilt. This theme will allow us to touch on another: the relationship between active and reactive dispositions. Christian morality proposes a fundamental principle of equality between human individuals. The difficulty is, Nietzsche points out, that life shows that there are differences – differences between: the strong and the weak, the rich and the poor, the gifted and the mediocre, man and woman; in fact there is in life every variety of difference imaginable. However, to maintain the illusion of (i.e. the ideal of) equality, Christianity invented guilt, or 'bad conscience' which those who judged themselves

to be different in a positive sense would be obliged to turn upon themselves. For with their difference (especially as a sense of superiority) they would be found to be responsible for the suffering of others.

Within the Nietzschean schema, guilt is the mark of reactive thought – the thought of the weak, not necessarily the weak in a strictly physical sense, but in the sense of those who cannot accept life as it is, who are governed by *ressentiment*, and who have to invent ideals in order to cover up their weakness. Guilt, in sum, is the weapon the less endowed use against free and original spirits who often reach new heights. Rather than attempting to raise themselves up to new heights in order to maintain equality, they deny that these heights exist. In his most poetic and famous work, *Thus Spoke Zarathustra*, Nietzsche has Zarathustra – the exemplar of the 'higher man' – come down from the mountain to speak to the people in the market-place. Because the people in the market-place only understand the language of utility (the language of exchange value, and calculability), they fail to understand Zarathustra, and take him for a madman. Dominated by the ethic of equality and the attachment to utility which goes with it, the people of the market-place all want the same thing. 'No herdsman and one herd. Everyone wants the same thing, everyone is the same: whoever thinks otherwise goes voluntarily into the madhouse.'[8] As inexorably reactive, the herd cannot think of any other end than to be happy. This is the happiness deemed to come with equality and utility. The crowd calls on Zarathustra to bring them the Ultimate Man who invented happiness. Zarathustra stands for the higher man, who, as the overcoming of all idealism in favour of life, is the overcoming of man as well; for man, too, is an ideal that does not correspond to anything in reality. Reactive thought, however, wants happiness, not the risks and suffering which often accompany creativeness and originality. The Ultimate Man (equivalent to man in general) is reactive man; the higher man, or

Superman, is the active individual with the determination to be creative and to avoid his life being submerged in the calculating ethic of equality. As an exemplar of the higher man, Zarathustra cannot – almost by definition – be understood; for he embodies horizontal thought; as a result, his language can only rarely be translated into common parlance. The thought of the higher man, is, in short, poetic.

The figure of the higher man reaches its apogee in the posthumously published *The Will to Power*. Interestingly, Nietzsche characterised himself as being a quintessentially posthumous thinker – a thinker out of tune with the times. Despite its posthumous status, *The Will to Power* is the most sustained articulation of a number of key aspects of Nietzsche's thought. These include: the will to power; the eternal recurrence; nihilism; anti-idealism; and a revaluation of all values. We will elaborate here on the first two aspects in particular, as they have recently assumed enormous importance in contemporary thought.

As explained earlier, the will to power is to be understood as the basis of Nietzsche's anti-idealist stance. It is the embodiment of the principle of the affirmation of life. The will to power is, in a sense, equivalent to everything that actually happens in life, making Nietzsche, in the eyes of some, a radically realist thinker. The will to power is the 'world', as our author says; and he continues: '*This world is the will to power – and nothing besides!* And you yourselves are also this will to power – and nothing besides!'[9] There is no willing subject behind power, no reality behind the play of forces, no division into will and its other, or into being and nothingness, or into subject and object – for the division itself is part of the will to power. The will to power is a plurality of forces, from which identities have to be constructed, not an underlying unity behind appearance. The revaluation of values is equivalent to the making of values within the play of forces of the will to power. Values always have to be

affirmed; they do not exist 'in themselves', as Kant thought.

Again, the will to power has no origin or purpose, no beginning or end – for these, too, are idealist and hence metaphysical categories. Or at least, the world has no origin other than the one given to it by a genealogy. Under these circumstances, Nietzsche forges his controversial notion of the 'eternal recurrence', the doctrine of the play of difference and uncertainty. In other words the form taken by the will to power is essentially unpredictable. It is: 'the enjoyment of all kinds of uncertainty, experimentalism, as a counterweight to this extreme fatalism; abolition of the concept of necessity; abolition of the 'will'; abolition of 'knowledge-in-itself'.[10] As the world has no goal, it is in continual, 'aimless' flux of transformation. Everything recurs; the world is not, Nietzsche says, a world of infinite novelty. The system is not in equilibrium, but nor is it infinitely open. It is rather like a game (of dice) played an infinite number of times, so that eventually the outcomes are repeated. The principle of the eternal recurrence is the most enigmatic of this entire philosophy. At times Nietzsche seems to want to link it to the nineteenth-century theory of thermodynamics (hence references to a constant amount of energy, and to the disequilibrium of the system); at other times, the issue seems to be centred on the will to power and a preparedness not to deny any aspect of life – even its most horrific events – such as occurs, Nietzsche says, when life is divided into an acknowledged good side, and a denied evil side; here, the will to power is the will of the eternal return of every event, whatever it might be. *Amor fati* – love of fate – is the phrase used which best evokes this approach.

Clearly, Nietzsche's project is nothing if not exorbitant. But it is not mad, or irrational; it has its own very definite and coherent logic, and this makes it communicable and amenable to being pressed into serving the ends of a *fin-de-siècle* anti-idealism. What then are its difficulties?

To begin with, if the will to power is all there is why is Nietzsche moved to explain it? Perhaps he might have responded by claiming that he is not explaining it, but, through the style of his philosophising, is providing an instance of it. However, no one reading his work can fail to see that there is a message accompanying the style. Nietzsche is unique as a thinker, of this there can be no doubt; but he also says as much himself. He does not write pure poetry. His theories therefore have to be seen as moves in the game of philosophy; to deny this is to deny an important dimension of Nietzsche's thought. To admit it, on the other hand, is to render suspect the possibility of a radically heterogeneous thinker.

Second, Nietzsche's anti-idealism would appear to stand or fall on the possibility that an event can be reduced to a description of it; such a claim is clearly questionable if metaphor is at the very heart of language, as thinkers like Kristeva have argued.

Finally, if Nietzsche is to avoid being a 'denier' of life himself, does he not have to accept that life partly entails the denial of life? – that a will to illusion may not only take the form of art, but might also take the form of a will to happiness?

Notes

1 Walter Kaufmann, *Nietzsche*, New York, Vintage Books, third edn, 1968, p. 22.
2 ibid.
3 Here, one can point to the work of Bataille, Blanchot, Deleuze, Foucault, Derrida, Lyotard, and Irigaray.
4 For Nietzsche, any principle which is proposed as an underlying and coherent truth for the diverse facts of appearance is idealist. In all probability, any form of reductionism (whether in the form of an essence or teleology – purpose) would be idealist according to Nietzsche's scheme of things.
5 See Friedrich Nietzsche, *Beyond Good and Evil*, trans. R.J. Hollingdale, Harmondsworth, Penguin, 1973 (reprinted 1974), p. 26.
6 Friedrich Nietzsche, *The Birth of Tragedy* in *The Birth of Tragedy and The Case of Wagner*, trans. Walter Kaufmann, New York, Vintage Books, 1967, pp. 31–2.

7 ibid, p. 60.
8 Friedrich Nietzsche, *Thus Spoke Zarathustra*, trans. R.J. Hollingdale, Harmondsworth, Penguin, reprinted 1974 , p. 46.
9 Friedrich Nietzsche, *The Will to Power*, trans. Walter Kaufmann and R.J. Hollingdale, New York, Vintage Books, 1968, Sect. 1067, p. 550. Nietzsche's emphasis.
10 ibid., sect. 1060, p. 546.

See also in this book

Bataille, Baudrillard, Deleuze, Foucault

Nietzsche's major writings

Books prepared for publication by Nietzsche

The Birth of Tragedy (1872, 1874, 1886), trans. Walter Kaufmann, New York, Vintage Books, 1967

Untimely Meditations, trans. R.J. Hollingdale, Cambridge, Cambridge University Press, 1983, includes:

First Part: David Strauss, the Writer and the Confessor (1873)
Second Part: On the Use and Disadvantage of History for Life (1874)
Third Part: Schopenhauer as Educator (1874)
Fourth Part: Richard Wagner in Bayreuth (1876)

Human All Too Human. trans. R.J. Hollingdale, Cambridge, Cambridge University Press, 1986 (reprinted 1989):

Volume One (1878)
Volume Two. First Section: Assorted Opinions and Sayings (1879)
Volume Two. Second Section: The Wanderer and His Shadow (1880)

Daybreak: Thoughts on the Prejudices of Morality (1881), trans. R.J. Hollingdale, Cambridge, Cambridge University Press, 1982

The Gay Science: With a Prelude in Rhymes and an Appendix of Songs (1882), trans. Walter Kaufmann, New York, Vintage Books, 1974

Thus Spoke Zarathustra (1883, 1884, 1885), trans. Walter Kaufmann, New York, Viking 1966; edn used: trans. R.J. Hollingdale, Harmondsworth, Penguin, reprinted 1974

Beyond Good and Evil (1886), trans. Walter Kaufmann, New York, Vintage Books, 1966; edn used, trans. R.J. Hollingdale, Harmondsworth, Penguin, 1973. Reprinted 1974

On the Genealogy of Morals (1887), trans. Walter Kaufmann and R.J. Hollingdale, New York, Random House, 1967, Vintage Books, 1989

The Case of Wagner (1888), trans. Walter Kaufmann, New York, Vintage, 1967
The Twilight of the Idols (prepared for publication, 1888; first edn 1889), trans. R.J. Hollingdale, Harmondsworth, Penguin, 1968. Reprinted 1974
Nietzsche contra Wagner (prepared for publication 1888; first edn 1895), trans. Walter Kaufmann (selection) in Walter Kaufmann (ed.), *The Portable Nietzsche*, Harmondsworth, Penguin, 1976 (reprinted 1982), pp. 661–83
The Antichrist (prepared for publication, 1888; first edn 1895), trans. R.J. Hollingdale, Harmondsworth, Penguin, 1968. Reprinted 1974
Ecce Homo (prepared for publication, 1888; first edn 1908), trans. Walter Kaufmann, New York, Random House, 1967, Vintage Books, 1989

Not published by Nietzsche

The Will to Power (selections of excerpts from Nietzsche's notebooks of the 1880s; first edn in 1901; expanded edition 1906), trans. Walter Kaufmann and R.J. Hollingdale, New York, Vintage Books, 1968

Further reading

Kaufmann, Walter, *Nietzsche: Philosopher, Psychologist, Antichrist*, New York, Vintage, 1968
Magnus, Bernd, Miller, Stanley and Mileur, Jean-Pierre, *Nietzsche's Case: Philosophy as/and Literature*, New York, London, Routledge, 1993
Nehamas, Alexander, *Nietzsche: Life as Literature*, Cambridge, Mass., Harvard University Press, 1985

GEORG SIMMEL

As Georg Simmel is a direct contemporary of Ferdinand de Saussure, Sigmund Freud, and Emile Durkheim, many currents in his thought intersect with themes of the most contemporary of thinkers. His writing on sexuality, where objectivity is seen to be male, evokes the feminist concerns of Irigaray; his writing on money and exchange echoes some of the concerns of Mauss and Bataille; and his theory of the event and critique of realism in modernity, that of the early Barthes.

While many of his contemporaries saw Simmel as an idiosyncratic academic and an affront to the university with his undocumented essay style and choice of 'prosaic' subject-matter, in hindsight, Simmel emerges as an innovative and original thinker who saw the need both to analyse contemporary social phenomena, and to be philosophically informed. Even more: for Simmel, to write about sexuality, money, and sociability was also a mode of living these phenomena. Through his analyses – most famously, *The Philosophy of Money* and 'The metropolis and mental life' – Simmel became renowned for a sociological portrait of consciousness in modernity, a consciousness aware of itself as an autonomous individuality.

Born in 1858 in Berlin, Simmel was the youngest of seven children. Throughout his life, he insisted that no one in his parents' house had any idea of a genuine intellectual culture, and indeed, it was a close family friend, the music publisher, Julius Friedländer, who supported Simmel for much of his academic life. At the University of Berlin, which he entered in 1876, Simmel studied psychology, history, philosophy and Italian. In 1881, he obtained his doctorate on the basis of an essay entitled 'Description and assessment of Kant's various views on the nature of matter'. For fifteen years to 1900, Simmel taught as a *Privatdozent* at the University of Berlin, depending on student fees for an income. Although he applied for a number of university chairs (one such being at the University of Heidelberg where he was supported by Max Weber), a combination of anti-Semitism and academic conservatism resulted in Simmel's very late career appointment in 1914 at the age of 56 to the chair of philosophy at Strasbourg University. Four years later, Simmel was dead.

In 'The metropolis and mental life' Simmel offers an analytical sketch of the interaction between individual consciousness and the modern city. Like Ferdinand Tönnies and others before him, Simmel draws attention to the way city life in its modern sense contrasts with tradition. In the city, formal ties between individuals replace the more traditional affective ties; with the rise of bureaucracy and science, life becomes highly differentiated: it no longer has a fixed content, but is rather characterised by abstract forms, of which money is the most important. Before going into more detail, let us note that in the metropolis, money, as a medium of exchange, allows for the transfer of the widest possible variety of goods imaginable because it is a common measure for them all; it is thus a great leveller.

With money as an example, Simmel's essay suggests that the city is in principle woven of forms and mediations of all kinds. Affective ties in and between groups thus give way to formal ties between individuals; and Simmel thinks of this as leading to greater freedom. For just as the seller of produce is able to bring a great variety of goods to market once money has fully replaced barter transactions, so, too, the intellectualist impulse enables the individual to constitute him or herself through a great variety of actions and interactions and so not be limited to the fixed routines and rituals of tradition. Although Simmel does perhaps give the break with tradition a new flavour and atmosphere, it is not this for which he is most original. Rather, his major insight is to propose that city life brings about a fundamentally new psychological disposition: the blasé attitude. The latter is the result of the fact that once freed from the reversible time of tradition – where life is seen as being predominantly repetitive – individual consciousness becomes immersed in the flow of the irreversible time of the city. Experience becomes dominated by Baudelaire's phrase of the 'transitory, the fugitive, the contingent'.

Even though Simmel himself does not put it in exactly these terms, he clearly implies that a modern experience is inseparable from a transformation of consciousness where the self becomes almost hypersensitive to every detail of existence – this very awareness being predicated on the transitory nature of existence. In an odd sort of way, therefore, modern consciousness is a consciousness of death – not death as a once and for all event that is repeated, but death as displaced – mediated – through the multiple facets of ephemeral existence. This hypersensitivity to, and complexity of, modern living, Simmel argues, leads to the need to filter out all but a manageable amount of intellectual and sense stimulation. Beyond a certain point, the psychic apparatus ceases to respond to stimulation and so exemplifies the 'blasé' attitude of the modern city outlook. From being enthralled by distinctions of all kinds, the blasé attitude becomes 'an indifference' to distinctions.[1] A sameness begins to descend on the city when at first (historically? psychologically? – Simmel does not say) there was a sense of fascination and involvement.

Like Marx and Durkheim, Simmel recognises the emergence of the division of labour and the accompanying economic and social differentiation. Unlike Marx, however, he attempts to outline its cultural effects. In particular, Simmel draws attention to what he calls the 'predominance of the objective spirit over the subjective' in modern society. Broadly speaking, the 'objective spirit' is equivalent to the drive to objectify social life. Objectification is the effect of mediations – from money, the law, and writing to the growth of media communications. To objectify an object is to free it from its 'original' context and to translate it into various symbolic forms. For Simmel differentiation is thus inseparable from objectification and to a lesser extent, representation.

In Simmel's book, *The Philosophy of Money*, to which we now turn, objectification is explained with reference to art. In a traditional context, art is almost entirely embodied in a (craft) technique. With modernity, on the other hand, the art object emerges – the object separated from the technique which produced it. Only as an object can the work of art have a monetary, or exchange value. To have an exchange value means, in the most general sense, that art – like so much else in modern life – comes under the law of the Same. For money is the medium of equivalence: exchange value – what Simmel also calls the reduction of quality to quantity – is a general principle which destroys the specific 'form' of the object. For this reason, people often do not like a great work of art (*The Mona Lisa*) being given a monetary value. Or at least if a great work of genius must be given a price, it should be so high as to be almost unimaginable. This is because the uniqueness and originality of the work is the basis of its significance. Its unreproducibility is what distinguishes it from a craft object, where the uniqueness would reside in the technique. What is germane to the realm of art, however, also applies to other domains of modern life, as far as money is concerned.

For instance, in his well-known discussion of prostitution, Simmel says that it evokes human degradation because human beings become a means (whereas Kant argues that the categorical imperative is that people should always be treated as an end in themselves), and because what should in essence be a woman's most personal possession in a human relationship is effectively turned into public property. Simmel himself recognises, however, that there may be a cultural aspect to understanding prostitution because the latter does not everywhere have the negative status it has come to acquire in the West. From a slightly different angle, we could ask about the sense in which the highly developed money economy might lead to prostitution becoming a model of human relationships. Such a notion seems somewhat far fetched: it is based on the idea that every impersonal relationship is potentially a relationship of means, whereas another way of looking at the issue is to say that the notion of professionalisation – living off one's talents – is an equally plausible general development brought about by the money economy.

Within a wealth of historical, ethno-graphic, and psychological references, Simmel outlines what he takes to be the fundamental characteristics of money. Most importantly, money, as has been said, is the principle of equivalence, or mediation which, as such, has no value in itself. Its meaning is to be found in what it can buy. This does not mean that money, used in a perverted way, cannot become an end in itself. The miser, who hordes money, and the ascetic who refuses all monetary dealings are instances of people who exemplify a perverted use of money as an end in itself. A fully developed money economy, however, is one that is always in movement, and money is rarely hoarded.

Another key feature of money in Simmel's analysis is that, as a principle of equivalence, it is entirely abstract, a pure form. As a pure form it can have an infinity of contents. In this sense it is a means of freedom because, unlike a barter situation, many different things can have the same exchange value. Because money is also a form of objectification, it is a knowledge of value through price.

Money is also a means of levelling. It emphasises what things have in common. It can, therefore, lead to the blasé attitude where a feeling for value has been lost: 'Whoever has become possessed by the fact that the same amount of money can procure all the possibilities that life has to offer must also become blasé.'[2] By the same token, cynicism – the sense that no high values exist – is also possible. Typical of the cynical attitude is the belief that anything can be bought.

Because it is itself devoid of qualities, money acts as a stimulus for all kinds of possibilities. In the modern setting, this is the sense in which money opens up greater freedom. As a means of freedom, money leads to depersonalisation as it tends to wrench people away from deep affective ties making them more aware of their 'personal liberty'. Paradoxically, Simmel says that the independence from affective ties that money inaugurates also leads to a certain dependence on others. For money 'has provided us with the sole possibility for uniting people while excluding everything personal'.[3] Thus although there is a sense of loneliness in the modern city, brought about by the severing of affective, informal social ties, when brought to its most complex and highly developed form, individualism increases contact with others and so potentially increases the likelihood of emotional ties being formed with a wider circle of people.

With the development of the money economy the condition of women changes. With the destruction of the narrowness of family life, women can enter the public sphere as paid workers. The rise of the women's movement, says Simmel, is no doubt due to the fact that technological advances accompanied by an intensification of the division of labour have made much of women's work in the home redundant. In effect, the greater the differentiation of tasks in the economy as a whole, the less justification there is for a gender-based division of labour. Although Simmel (following an old tradition) sees women as being closer to 'nature' than men are, the 'fixed forms and habits of married life that are imposed upon individuals run counter to the personal development of the partners'.[4] Because marriage still entails elements of tradition (that is, because there is much about it which has yet to be objectified), it constrains the personal development of women in particular, because women, more than men, have been forced to carry the burden of being the bearers of tradition.

As is perfectly clear from his other writing, Simmel believed that women should, like men, obtain their freedom; freedom, here, should be understood in the modern sense of a freedom from traditional ties. In this regard, Simmel argues that women have to be able to enter objective culture. Although objective culture takes on the appearance of culture itself, and as such is deemed to be gender neutral, Simmel has no hesitation in designating it as male. Indeed the opposition women sometimes exhibit towards the law should not, Simmel urges, be understood as opposition against the law as such, but against the law which has effectively come to embody men's interests. The law still has vestiges of a given purpose behind it, when it should, as an abstract means, be a pure form – like money.

Generally speaking, then, Simmel's support of women – in the family, with regard to the law and justice, in art, love, and the economy – is support that is inseparable from a complete realisation of the project of modernity. Simmel's subtlety, however, is to propose that women enter the public sphere on their own terms, and in terms of their specific abilities as women. Thus, women make better diagnosticians in medical practice than men because they have the ability to empathise with others. On the other hand, Simmel's blindness is perhaps that in order to attribute to women an identity that would be uniquely theirs, he often naturalises their qualities, so that he risks producing a female psychology (for instance, the periphery of a woman's nature is supposedly more closely connected to its centre; female nature is more homogeneous than a man's, etc.). Despite this, we would have to ask whether access to Simmel's limitations can be gained other than by the root of objectification that he marks out. Simmel, after all, is also the theorist of society as conflictual and heterogeneous – themes that bespeak the tenor of postmodern times at the end of the twentieth century.

A more serious limitation for Simmel's approach than that revealed by his analysis of the status of women relates to his insistence on the opposition between tradition and modern life. Consequently, freedom, the city, money, sexuality and love, labour, etc. are all understood to be modern (i.e. are understood to be predominantly forms of mediation) because they have been set free from traditional constraints. Doubts have now arisen, however, as to whether there are empirical instances of societies where mediations in the modern sense do not already exist. In other words, the question to be asked of Simmel is whether modernity itself is not as much mythical (and thus traditional) as real.

Notes

1 Georg Simmel, 'The metropolis and mental life', trans. Edward A. Shils in Donald Levine (ed.), *Georg Simmel, On Individuality and Social Forms*, Chicago and London, University of Chicago Press, 1971, p. 329.
2 Georg Simmel, *The Philosophy of Money*, trans. Tom Bottomore and David Frisby, London, Routledge, second edn 1990, p. 256.
3 ibid., p. 345.
4 ibid., p. 464.

See also in this book

Benjamin

Simmel's major writings

Soziologie: Untersuchungen über die formen der Vergesellschaftung (*Sociology: Investigations of the Forms of Sociation*), Leipzig, Dunker, and Humblot. The work contains many essays – forms of social interaction and social types – that have been translated into English and published separately
Conflict and the Web of Group Affiliations (1908, from *Soziologie*), trans. Kurt H. Wolff and R. Bendix, Hughes, Glencoe, Ill., Free Press, 1955
The Conflict in Modern Culture and Other Essays, (1918), trans. D.E. Jenkinson *et al.*, Sunbury, Middlesex, Nelson; New York, Barnes & Noble, 1968
The Problems of the Philosophy of History (essays), trans. G. Oakes, New York, Free Press, 1977
The Philosophy of Money (1900), trans. Tom Bottomore and David Frisby, London, Routledge, second edn 1990

Further reading

Frisby, David, *Fragments of Modernity: Theories of Modernity in the Work of Simmel, Kracauer and Benjamin*, Cambridge, Polity Press, 1985
Frisby, David, *Georg Simmel*, London, Tavistock, 'Key Sociologists', 1984
Karen, Michael *et al.* (eds), *Georg Simmel and Contemporary Sociology*, Dordrecht, Boston, Kluwer Academic Publications, 1990
Ray, Larry (ed.), *Formal Sociology: The Sociology of Georg Simmel*, Brookfield, Edward Elgar Publishing Co., 1991

PHILIPPE SOLLERS

Just as Georges Bataille used biographical fragments to develop his writing of transposition, so Philippe Sollers (admirer of Bataille) uses his biography to develop a writing of the act of writing: analogical writing, as Philippe Forest says in his scholarly study of Sollers's *oeuvre*.[1] One of the obstacles to grasping the specificity and uniqueness of Sollers's project relates to the emphasis the world of criticism has always placed on the apparently spectacular and perverse changes in Sollers's public persona, rather than on the content of his literary, theoretical and critical writing – a state of affairs for which Sollers is not entirely blameless. From the *Nouveau Roman* (which saw the conventional, nineteenth-century model of the novel as severely limiting) and a critique of literature *engagé*, passing by Maoism and Catholicism, to a return to French eighteenth-century classicism (Voltaire, Crébillon-fils) and to 'meaning', Sollers has always provided media critics with what they needed: a figure who can be both despised and loved (the writer people 'love to hate' is a phrase that would please Sollers) because he also plays their game of mirrors – and plays it well.

Regardless of the position taken regarding his writing or persona, however, there is little doubt that Sollers's founding (with others) of the literary journal *Tel Quel* in 1960, and the publication in it of important works by Foucault, Barthes, Derrida, and Kristeva – among others – transformed the literary environment in France. *Tel Quel*, for many, was the French literary avant-garde. Again, with the foundation of *L'Infini* in 1983 in the wake of *Tel Quel*, the change from the idea of avant-garde writing as concerned with an absence of meaning to the idea of avant-garde writing as the 'return of meaning', would hardly have been marked.

Philippe Sollers was born Philippe Joyaux in 1936 in Bordeaux where the family owned a factory. His parents were Anglophiles – a tendency accentuated by the Occupation. As a result, the young Philippe became a fervent devotee, first of all of jazz, and later of James Joyce. Educated by the Jesuits at the Ecole Sainte-Genviève at Versailles, Sollers was also expelled from the school for indiscipline. He was thus forced to educate himself in the history of literature and philosophy, a notable embarrassment in a culture where formal learning is prized so highly. Opposition to discipline and to all forms of militarism led to Sollers feigning schizophrenia at the time of his military call-up during the Algerian War in 1962. By that time, however, he had already won literary awards, first, for his short work, *Le Défi* (*The Challenge*), published in 1957, and then for *Le Parc* (*The Park*), published in 1961. His first real novel, *Une curieuse solitude* (*A Strange Solitude*) published in 1958 was praised by Louis Aragon, just as the conservative writer, François Mauriac, had praised *Le Défi*.

During his adolescence and youth, Sollers was influenced by Baudelaire, Poe, Proust, Lautréamont, and Surrealism. Later, in 1960, the poet Francis Ponge assumed great importance, with Sollers at the age of 24 giving a lecture on Ponge at the Sorbonne. In 1965, Sollers would point out that Francis Ponge was one of the rare writers to treat language as a milieu providing body and soul for the human being, rather than as a vehicle for an ideology.[2] By 1972 Sollers argued that Surrealism had been responsible for the censoring of Joyce who, together with Artaud, represented 'the greatest revolution in language in the twentieth century'.[3] After supporting some of the aspirations of the *Nouveau Roman*, Sollers, in 1964, distanced himself from it and its originator, Alain Robbe-Grillet. Although critics had detected the imprint of Robbe-Grillet's project in *Le Parc*, for Sollers, the *Nouveau Roman* had become too academic, that is, it had become sterile. From another angle, although Robbe-Grillet's writing confronts a void in reality which cannot be written (it can only be

implied), Sollers aims to speak – write – the void as such. For Sollers, that is, writing is an analogue of the void; just as surrealist writing would be an analogue of *délire* (delirium), rather than being a theory of it.[4]

All analogical writing aspires in some sense to be a practice of writing: it neither seeks to be transparent in a realist sense (a window on the world), nor, on the other hand, does it fall back on being pure poetry in which the opacity of the word would predominate. Although writing is never entirely opaque, this does not mean – far from it – that rhythm is absent. Thus in speaking of his early 1970s novel, *Lois* (Laws), Sollers remarks on the decasyllabic rhythm of the work – a rhythm, however, which issues from the unconscious and evokes the songs of gesture. The rhythm of *Lois* is initially unconscious; gradually, however, its effects can be controlled so that in the unpunctuated novel, *Paradis* (1981), the decasyllabic rhythm is consciously developed as the basis of the force of the writing.

Between 1961 – with the publication of *Le Parc* – and the publication of *Paradis* in 1981, Sollers's writing, at the most general level, moves through the stages of a brief accommodation to certain stylistic strategies of the *Nouveau Roman*, to the highly formalised structure of *Drame*, *Nombres*, *H* and *Lois* – written between 1965 and 1972 – to the unpunctuated and lyrical avant-garde texts reminiscent of Joyce and Mallarmé of the early 1980s.

Sollers has emphasised that he writes to the rhythm of music – inspiration coming in particular from Purcell, Monteverdi, Schönberg, and Webern, and from jazz greats such as Parker, Konitz, and Braxton. The ear, he has said, is the first priority. It is the first priority, but is not the only priority. While Sollers's literary works are far removed from a literature *engagé à la* Sartre, hardly any are not at least indirectly linked to events in the author's biography or to events occurring in the social milieu in which Sollers has always been an active participant. As Forest notes, the biographical element becomes a particularly notable feature of the novels (beginning with *Femmes* (*Women*) of the 1983–93 decade. As a scarcely veiled protagonist in his own later works, Sollers explores, through writing, his relationship to the *fin de siècle* society of the spectacle where sex is obligatory and a rejection of meaning is now the norm. Overall, then, the Sollersian project aspires to produce a writing that is simultaneously poetic (fiction) and descriptive – which is a transcription of the act of writing, and at the same time an intervention as revelatory of the censorship in place to curb the writing of 'exceptions'.

'Exception' is a key term in Sollers's theory of writing, and so it is worthwhile spending a moment to clarify its significance. Like Nietzsche in philosophy, Sollers argues that the writer who is truly imbricated in writing as a vocation is inevitably an exception. For Sollers, exception 'is the rule in art and literature': because to be a writer in the fullest sense, the form and the protocols of writing must be transformed, leaving the writing subject in an often unbearable solitude. As a result, the true writer does not write *within* the already existing conventions of his or her art, but remodels them, or at least is the catalyst of a remodelling. Because writing conventions are always social conventions, the effect of such writing (Joyce is an example) is to shake – and perhaps remake – the social milieu in question. Writing, and perhaps art in general, cannot simply be explained sociologically; rather, it has to be grasped in the sense of set theory where the part is often greater than the power of the whole. Journalistic writing, which often embodies the socially accepted norms of writing (the writing *doxa*, we could say), is in its own sphere a legitimate form of writing; the problem arises for Sollers when writing in the fullest sense ('great' writing) is equated with journalism. Although there is clearly no model with which it can be equated, the true writer's art is always an avant-garde art – always an exception. The

writer, as exception, then, cannot be easily located on an existing scale or table of categories. In relation to society's norms, he or she is always 'other', and is only ever integrated into social life with difficulty, if at all. Here, the risk that writing (art) might degenerate into a self-indulgent narcissism is very real. However, what distinguishes the narcissist from the true writer is that, in the end, the narcissist never really shakes the social milieu because his art never takes in charge the quasi-universal norms of society. The exception, by contrast, takes on the universal as a personal problem; in fact, for the exception, the universal and the exception are inseparable; for the pure narcissist, on the other hand, universality essentially does not exist.

Disagreement with such an argument sometimes centres on its alleged elitism. An elitist theory, however, inevitably proposes a clearly recognisable system of gradations based on inferiority and superiority; it is irrevocably hierarchical. Elites, in short, can only exist within the given system of social relations; they do not challenge the system's competence to judge. A much more horizontal approach characterises Sollers's theory of the exception. Horizontally speaking, the writer is essentially *sui generis*: incomparable – an exception.

A term that is for Sollers almost synonymous with 'exception', is 'singularity'. To get a better grip on this notion in the early 1980s, Sollers, along with some of his colleagues such as Jean-Houdebine, sought an elaboration of 'singularity' in Duns-Scotus's notion of '*haecceitas*'. Literally, *haecceitas* is the 'thisness' of a thing. It is absolute particularity or individuality. In effect, *haecceitas* is what cannot be accounted for by any pre-existing social convention or norm; rather, the norm itself has to be modified to make way for the singularity which is *haecceitas*. The social system inevitably censures singularity; but, like an open system in biology, singularity is also essential for maintaining the vitality of the system.

At the level of the interaction between the writer and the reader of his text, Sollers fundamentally challenges familiar norms of reading; he challenges the reader to transform his or her existing preconceptions and to expand imaginary capacities. For Sollers, a work which does not do this might be good journalism, but it cannot be great writing.

Although 'exception' and 'singularity' could be said to govern the overall economy of Sollers's enterprise, a more specific principle, or practice, governs his writing. This is the principle, first highlighted in *Drame* and *Nombres*, of 'searching for as tight a coincidence as possible between the act of writing and the narrative; the act dictating the narrative, the narrative recounting the act'.[5]

Even after the 'break' with the visibly poetic writing of the 1970s, which culminated with the publication of the entirely unpunctuated novel, *Paradis* in 1981, the concern is still explicitly about producing a writing about writing. Hence in the novel *Femmes*, which marks the transition to a more recognisably conventional style, the narrative is still a narrative of the writing of the novel itself. According to the information provided by the intrigue, 'Will' (an American journalist), *Femmes* will be published in Paris under the name of S, who has previously published an unpunctuated and 'unreadable' novel. To all appearances, S is now in the process of publishing an entirely 'readable' work – something guaranteed to raise a scandal among the critics, given S's 'avant-garde' past. As indeed the Paris critics did respond by criticising Sollers's lack of consistency and lack of loyalty to his avant-garde principles, the response was incorporated by the fictional work, thereby closing the conventional gap between fiction and non-fiction, and between the written narrative and the writing of the narrative.

As Forest points out, the gap between *Paradis* and *Femmes* is, in fact, not as great as one might have thought from the public response to the novel. Rather, *Paradis*, with all its contemporary and historical references, is an unpunctuated *Femmes*; *Femmes*, with all its literary and historical references is a punctuated version of *Paradis*. Or to put it in terms of *Femmes* itself, Will, the American journalist, and S are, as we know, really the same person (this is emphasised by the *roman à clé* aspect of the text). Even in a text as explicitly autobiographical as *Le Portrait du joueur* (*The Portrait of the Player*), with a single narrator, the narrative becomes attracted to the play on the names, Sollers-Diamant. The identity of the narrator becomes fictive (i.e. written) to the extent that, through the name, identity is pluralised.

In 1992, Sollers published a novel called *Le Secret*. Loosely set around the attempted assassination of Pope John Paul II on 13 May 1981, the intrigue partly focuses on a lost note containing information about the attempted crime. The loss of the note leads to the effort to establish what it had to say about the motive and the mechanics of the attempted murder. Like the purloined letter in Edgar Allan Poe's short story, the absence of the letter allows for the projection of imaginary contents onto the note. The contents of the note thus remain a secret. While different aspects of a secret are explored (the secret agent, the secret/private life of the narrator, the secret in military strategy), a key point made by the novel is that the difference between fiction – in terms of strangeness, unreality – and reality is fast disappearing. Especially is this the case with regard to life and death in the context of artificial insemination and proxy parenting, and new media technology.

To write a novel today, says Sollers, is only possible if one starts with the facts. Facts are singularities; they are unpredictable, and beyond the control of a collective consciousness, as this is manifest in the mass media. 'Reality is stranger than fiction' is the principle enunciated. Sollers claims that he 'invents nothing'. The danger is that with the media's capacity for the reproduction of events, and with a medium's role in the reproduction of human life, the exception is in danger:

the exception can be neither reproduced nor collectivised; in short, it cannot be codified. Sollers's great fear, then, is that postmodern society is the society of the pure spectacle, where there is no uniqueness, no surprise, no secret, in fact. Through his later writing, Sollers aims to constitute the exception – not through the violence of an untamed imagination, but through a respect for a reality that he says is fast disappearing. This is the reality of the multiplicity of identities assumed by both writer and secret agent.

Notes

1 Philippe Forest, *Philippe Sollers*, Paris, Editions du Seuil, 1992, pp. 59–61. Although Forest is in fact referring mainly to *Le Parc* (*The Park*), the term is illuminating with regard to Sollers's work as a whole.
2 Philippe Sollers, 'La poésie, oui ou non' (1965) in *Logiques*, Paris, Seuil, Coll. Tel Quel, 1968, pp. 198–205.
3 Philippe Sollers, 'Philippe Sollers: "ébranler le système" ' (interview), *Magazine littéraire*, 65 (1972), p. 12.
4 See Elisabeth Roudinesco, *Jacques Lacan & Co.*, trans. Jeffrey Mehlman, Chicago, Chicago University Press, 1990, p. 26.
5 Philippe Sollers, *Vision à New York. Entretiens avec David Hayman*, Paris, Grasset, 1981, p. 100.

See also in this book

Blanchot, Duras, Joyce, Kafka

Sollers's major writings

Le Défi, Paris, Seuil: 'Ecrire', 1957

A Strange Solitude (1958), trans. Richard Howard, New York, Grove Press, 1959
The Park: A Novel (1961), trans. A.M. Sheridan-Smith, London, Calder and Boyars, 1968
Francis Ponge ou la Raison à plus haut prix, Paris, Seghers, Coll 'Poètes d'aujourd'hui', 1963
Drame, Paris, Seuil: Tel Quel, 1965
Nombres, Paris, Seuil: Tel Quel, 1968
Logiques, Paris, Seuil: Tel Quel, 1968
Writing and the Experience of Limits (1971), ed. David Hayman, trans. Philip Barnard with David Hayman, New York, Columbia University Press, 1983
Lois, Paris, Seuil: Tel Quel, 1972
H, Paris, Seuil: Tel Quel, 1973
Paradis, Paris, Seuil: Tel Quel, 1981
Vision à New York. Entretiens avec David Hayman, Paris, Grasset, 1981
Women (1983), trans. Barbara Bray, New York, Columbia University Press, 1990
Portrait du joueur, Paris, Gallimard, 1984
Paradis II, Paris, Gallimard, 1986
Théorie des exceptions, Paris, Gallimard: Folio/Essais, 1986
Le Coeur absolu, Paris, Gallimard, 1987
Les Folies françaises, Paris, Gallimard, 1988
Le Lys d'or, Paris, Gallimard, 1989
La Fête à Venise, Paris, Gallimard, 1991
Le Rire de Rome, Paris, Gallimard, 1992
Le Secret, Paris, Gallimard, 1993

Further reading

Barthes, Roland, *Sollers Writer*, trans. Philip Thody, London, Althone; Minneapolis, University of Minnesota Press, 1987
Clark, Hilary, *The Fictional Encyclopaedia: Joyce, Pound, Sollers*, New York, Garland Publishing, 1990
Kurk, K.C., *Consummation of the Text: A Study of Philippe Sollers*, Texas, University of Kentucky, 1979

POSTMODERNITY

Although there are various understandings of what postmodernity is, a key notion in this book, deriving from the work of Jean-François Lyotard and Jean Baudrillard, is that postmodernity involves a questioning of a modernist epistemology based on a clear distinction between subject and object. Other things said in describing postmodernity concern the 'incredulity toward metanarratives' (Lyotard) – meaning that no global explanation of conduct is credible in an age of purposive rationality. Moreover, technology is seen to lead to a focus on reproduction, in contrast to the modernist paradigm of production. Or again, postmodern thought takes the implications of modernity absolutely seriously. For instance, if signs and language are the result of differential relations rather than an essential quality, and if, following Foucault, power has no essential quality, postmodernity follows through some of the radical implications of this.

JEAN BAUDRILLARD

In a society dominated by production, Jean Baudrillard argues, the difference between use-value and exchange-value has some pertinence. Certainly, for a time, Marx was able to provide a relatively plausible explanation of the growth of capitalism using just these categories. The use-value of an object would be its utility related in Marx's terms to the satisfaction of certain needs; exchange-value, on the other hand, would refer to the market-value of a product, or object measured by its price. The object of exchange value is what Marx called the commodity form of the object.

Starting with a re-evaluation and critique of Marx's economic theory of the object, especially as concerns the notion of 'use-value', Jean Baudrillard develops the first major phase of his work with a semiotically based theory of production and the object, one that emphasises the 'sign-value' of objects. In the second major phase of his work, Baudrillard argues that even the notion of the sign as vehicle of meaning and signification is too reductive; rather, the Saussure of the anagrams, where words seem to emerge mysteriously, and almost magically, through the letters, is more in keeping with the way language works. Finally, from his writings of the mid-1970s onwards, starting with *Symbolic Exchange and Death*, Baudrillard has taken up the radical consequences, as he sees them, of the pervasiveness of the code in late-modern societies. The code certainly refers to computerisation, and to digitalisation, but it is also fundamental in physics, biology, and other natural sciences where it enables a perfect reproduction of the object or situation; for this reason the code enables a by-passing of the real and opens up what Baudrillard has famously designated as 'hyperreality'.

Although Baudrillard prefers to be without a background,[1] it is possible to ascertain that he was born in 1929 in Reims. While his grandparents were peasants, his own family was in transition to an urban life and jobs in the civil service. The milieu was not an intellectual one, and Baudrillard worked hard at the lycée to compensate for this, becoming the first of his family to do intellectual work in a serious way. Although he attempted the *agrégation* he did not succeed, nor did he ever succeed (he has now retired) in gaining a permanent university post. Personally, Baudrillard prefers to think of his life as one of a 'virtual state of rupture'. In 1966, Baudrillard completed a thesis in sociology at Nanterre with Henri Lefebvre, an anti-structuralist. Later, he became associated with Roland Barthes at the Ecole des Hautes Etudes, and wrote an important article on the object and sign-function in *Communications* in 1969. Baudrillard's book, *Le Système des objets* (*The Object System*) (1968), echoes Barthes's work, *The Fashion System*.

Baudrillard's earliest writings on Calvino, and others published in Sartre's, *Les Temps modernes*, together with his translations of Brecht and Weiss hardly presage the explosive critique of Marx's theory of value that would emerge less than a decade later. Quite unlike Lefebvre, Baudrillard did not reject structuralism; he rather worked through it to the other side. This allowed him to use the notions of the 'sign', 'system', and 'difference' to spell out the limit of the structuralist endeavour, especially as far as the distinction between the real and imagination are concerned.

While Baudrillard's reservations regarding Marx's political economy are largely fuelled by a semiotic conception of the object in capitalism, he has also been crucially influenced by Mauss's theory of the gift and Bataille's theory of expenditure. For the latter two thinkers, no human economy can be reduced to a putative utilitarian base, with equilibrium being its normal state. By contrast, institutions such as the Kula and the potlatch show that waste in the drive for prestige was the original, non-utilitarian basis for consumption. Seen in this light, political economy's distinction between use-value and exchange-value is quite limited. An object also has to be understood to have a symbolic value which is irreducible to either use- or exchange-value. A gift (e.g., a wedding ring) is an object of this nature. The gift still exists – albeit in a reduced form – in capitalist societies; it is the obstacle to any easy theory of the economy as equilibrium.

But even if one were to accept the division between objects of use-value (objects of utility and needs), and objects of exchange-value, the question arises as to where precisely the line is to be drawn between these two forms. In his books which address this issue – *Le Système des objets* (1968), *Consumer Society* (1970), *For a Political Economy of the Sign* (1972) – Baudrillard first broadens the scope of the analysis by adding the symbolic object and the sign object to the category of the object. He then argues that it is necessary to distinguish four different logics: (1) The logic of practical operations, which corresponds to use-value; (2) The logic of equivalence, which corresponds to exchange-value; (3) The logic of ambivalence, which corresponds to symbolic exchange; and (4) the logic of difference, which corresponds to sign-value. These logics may be summarised, respectively, as those of utility, the market, the gift, and status. In the logic of the first category, the object becomes an instrument, in the second, a commodity, in the third, a symbol, and in the fourth, a sign.[2]

With his semiotic writings on the object, Baudrillard, now following Saussure and the structuralists, endeavours to show that no object exists in isolation from others. Instead their differential, or relational, aspect becomes crucial in understanding them. In addition, while there is a utilitarian aspect to many objects, what is essential to them is their capacity to signify a status. In this regard, even denial can be a kind of luxury – as when 'good taste' demands that a room not be overly cluttered with objects. To be emphasised here, is that objects are not simply consumed in a consumer society; they are produced less to satisfy a need than to signify a status, and this is only possible because of the differential relationship between objects. Hence, in a thorough-going consumer society, objects become signs, and the realm of necessity is left far behind – if it ever really existed.

Baudrillard's aim, then, is to render the very idea of needs, or utility, problematic. Needs, he suggests, can only be sustained by an ideologically based anthropology of the subject. Often this takes a psychologistic (needs as a function of human nature), or a culturalist form (needs as a function of society). Once the work of Veblen (on conspicuous consumption), Bataille, and Mauss is considered, and different social and cultural formations are brought into the equation, the notion that irreducible primary needs govern human activities becomes a myth. Subject and object are not joined, Baudrillard points out, on the basis of the eternal qualities of the subject, but – following Lévi-Strauss – are joined through the unconscious structure of social relations. In sum, human beings do not search for happiness; they do not search to realise equality; consumption does not homogenise – it differentiates through the sign system. Life-style and values – not economic need – is the basis of social life.

An important outcome of Baudrillard's analysis of consumption in terms of signs is that it undermines the validity of the distinction – used by Galbraith and the Frankfurt School alike – between true and false, artificial and real, needs. What must be avoided, says Baudrillard, is a critique of consumerism and the notion of *homo economicus* at the cost of a renewed moralism. In elaborating on this, Baudrillard sets out an idea at the end of his analysis of consumer society which will serve as a touch stone for all of his subsequent work. It is that in the discourse of consumption, there is an anti-discourse: the exalted discourse of abundance is everywhere duplicated by a critique of consumer society – even to the point where advertising often intentionally parodies advertising. Everything 'anti-', says Baudrillard, can be recuperated; this is what consigns Marx to another, by-gone era. The society of consumption is also the society of the denunciation of consumption.

On a number of occasions in his early writings, Baudrillard uses the term, 'code' when referring to the system of signs. While this term may have been there as a synonym for system, or language (Saussure's *langue*), in his most important work of the mid-1970s – *Symbolic Exchange and Death* – the notion of 'code' assumes an importance that it would be hard to overestimate. Not that Baudrillard (unlike Eco) spends much time in defining the nature and subtleties of the notion of code. Indeed, we can note in passing that he rarely defines his key terms in anything like an exhaustive fashion, the sense largely being derived from the context, and from the view that Baudrillard accepts the developments in semiotics and other fields as given. Here, though, we can say that the meaning of 'code' is quite straightforward: the code is the binary code of computer technology; it is the DNA code in biology, or the digital code in television and in sound recording, as it is the code in information technology. The era of the code in fact supersedes the era of the sign. None of this is spelled out, but is clearly implied by the context. Central to Baudrillard's concerns is the connection between code and reproduction – reproduction which is itself 'original'. The code entails that the object produced – tissue in biology, for example – is not a copy in the accepted sense of the term, where the copy is the copy of an original, natural object. Rather, the difference between copy and original is now redundant. How redundant? This is a key question. Baudrillard tends to say entirely redundant; but this is also in keeping with his belief that the only way to keep the social system from imploding is to take up an extreme theoretical position. Many would argue, however, that the code has not yet, and

will not, assume the hegemonic proportions Baudrillard sketches out. That the code is of extreme importance, however, cannot be denied. Virtual reality, global communications, the hologram, and art are just some of the areas in addition to those enumerated above where it is exemplified.

In an era when the natural object is no longer credible (structuralism having been the first modern movement to challenge the credibility of the natural object), the code has raised simulation to an unprecedented importance in social life. Simulation and models are the exemplars of pure reproduction. Because the code enables reality – as it was understood in the age of production – to be bypassed, a curious potential emerges; Baudrillard calls it 'reversibility'. Reversibility entails that all finalities disappear; nothing is outside the system, which becomes a tautology. This is seen most starkly with simulation and simulacra.

With regard to simulation, Baudrillard defines three kinds: that of the counterfeit dominant in the classical era of the Renaissance, that of production in the industrial era, and, finally, simulation of the present era governed by the code. With the counterfeited object, the difference between the real, or 'natural' object is made apparent; in industrial production, the difference between the object and the labour process is made evident; in the era of simulation, not the production, but the *re*production of objects becomes crucial. And, as we have seen, the principle of reproduction is contained in the code. With regard to reproduction, it is clear that labour power, or the worker, is also reproduced. Reproduction, therefore, includes what would have been both sides of the equation in the era of industrialism. Now, the origin of things is not an original thing, or being, but formulae, coded signals, and numbers. Given that the origin in reproduction is the principle of generation, and not the object generated, complete reversibility is possible: the last 'original' produced can be perfectly reproduced. The difference between the real and its representation is erased, and the age of simulacra emerges. In its extreme form, therefore, even death can be integrated into the system: or rather, the principle of reversibility implies that death does not really happen.

If, as Foucault's work sought to demonstrate, power no longer has a substantive content – is no longer something possessed and centralised – the continued operation of the institutions of centralised power would become a simulation of a certain form of power relations. In short the claim that power has a content becomes a pretence. Generalised simulation thus accompanies the death of all essentialisms.

Socially speaking, Baudrillard notes that the era of the code begins to penetrate the whole of the social fabric. One of the symptoms of this is that opposites begin to collapse and 'everything becomes undecidable': the beautiful and the ugly in fashion, the left and the right in politics, the true and the false in the media, the useful and the useless at the level of objects, nature and culture – all these become interchangeable in the era of reproduction and simulation.

Baudrillard thus shows how the system is potentially a closed system which risks imploding. Hyperreality effaces the difference between the real and the imaginary. The question to be answered is that of how a political intervention which does not get recuperated by the system is possible. Baudrillard suggests a path with his elaboration of 'seduction' and 'fatal strategies'. In both cases, he argues that it is necessary to give primacy to the object over the subject, fatal theory determined by the object over banal, critical theory determined by the subject. The point is to move to extremes in order to counteract the system's equilibrium. Ecstasy, fascination, risk and vertigo before the object which seduces, takes precedence over the sober reflexivity of banal theory. Banal theory is always tautological: the beginning always equals the end; with fatal (= death and destiny), there is no 'end' in any

representational or teleological sense. Seduction, then, is fatal in the sense that the subject is dominated by the unpredictable object – the object of fascination. The masses who, due to their lack of reflexivity and conformity, were the despair of revolutionary intellectuals now become the model to be followed. For they have always given precedence to ecstasy and fascination, and thus to the object; the masses thus converge towards the potential extremities of the system. In speaking of the masses' relationship to the image, Baudrillard writes: 'There is in this conformity a force of seduction in the literal sense of the word, a force of diversion, distortion, capture and ironic fascination. There is a kind of fatal strategy of conformity.'[3]

A great deal of what Baudrillard has written has raised heated debate – no more so than when he wrote articles in the French daily newspaper, Libération, apparently claiming that the 1991 Gulf War did not take place. The debate is often sterile because people are talking past each other – Baudrillard starting from his position in relation to the implications of the code and developments in modern science and technology, his opponents, often from the humanist position of nineteenth-century science, where the origin was conceived as a real, natural object. What Baudrillard does is demonstrate the very real consequences of changes in symbolic and material forms, and this is important in a world increasingly dominated by media hype and obfuscation. The limit to Baudrillard is very possibly to be found in the limit in modern science itself. And this is that the code is not yet uniformly dominant; the clone version of social reality that Baudrillard effectively presents is not yet true. We still live partly outside the reach of the code; this is what Stephen Spielberg's film, Jurassic Park really shows, even if the principle of its domination is at last fully extant.

Notes

1   See, for example, his response to a letter from Mike Gane, in Mike Gane (ed.), *Baudrillard Live. Selected Interviews*, London and New York, Routledge, 1993, p. 6.
2   See Jean Baudrillard, *For a Critique of the Political Economy of the Sign*, trans. Charles Levin, St Louis, Telos Press, 1981, p. 66.
3   Jean Baudrillard, *The Evil Demon of Images*, trans. Paul Patton and Paul Foss, Sydney, Power Institute, 1981, pp. 14–15.

See also in this book

Bataille, Lyotard, Mauss

Baudrillard's major writings

Le Système des objets, Paris, Denoël, 1968
La Société de la consommation, Paris, Gallimard, 1970
For a Critique of the Political Economy of the Sign (1972), trans. Charles Levin, St Louis, Telos Press, 1981
The Mirror of Production (1973), trans. Mark Poster, St Louis, Telos Press, 1975
Symbolic Exchange and Death (1976), trans. Ian Grant, London, Sage, 1993
Forget Foucault (1977), New York, Semiotext(e), 1987
Seduction (1979), trans. Brian Singer, London, Macmillan; New York, Saint Martins, 1990
The Evil Demon of Images, trans. Paul Patton and Paul Foss, Sydney, The Power Institute, 1981
Simulacres et simulation, Paris, Galilée, 1981
Fatal Strategies. Crystal Revenge (1983), trans. Philip Beitchman and W.G.J. Niesluchowski, New York, Semiotext(e); London, Pluto, 1990
La Gauche divine, chroniques des années 1977–1984, Paris, Grasset, 1985
America (1986), trans. Chris Turner, London and New York, Routledge, 1989
Cool Memories (1987), trans. Chris Turner, London, Verso, 1990
The Transparence of Evil: Essays on Extreme Phenomena (1990), trans. John J. St. John, Baddeley, Routledge, 1992
Selected Writings, ed. Mark Poster, Cambridge, Polity Press, 1988. Reprinted 1989
Baudrillard Live. Selected Interviews, Mike Gane (ed.), London and New York, Routledge, 1993

Further reading

Gane, Mike, *Baudrillard: Critical and Fatal Theory*, London, Routledge, 1991

Gane, Mike, *Baudrillard's Bestiary. Baudrillard and Culture*, London, Routledge, 1991
Kellner, Douglas, *Jean Baudrillard. From Marxism to Post-Modernism and Beyond* (1989), Cambridge, Polity Press, 1989
Pefanis, Julian, *Heterology and the Postmodern, Bataille, Baudrillard and Lyotard*, Sydney, Allen & Unwin, 1991

MARGUERITE DURAS

Marguerite Duras is one of France's most important and interesting intellectual figures. She has excelled at being a writer, film-maker, and dramatist. After the Second World War she also worked for a number of years as a journalist for *France-Observateur*. She has often been at the forefront of political movements, such as the opposition against the Algerian War, May 1968, and feminism. Surprisingly, perhaps, Duras was also in support of the sinking, by the French secret service, of the Greenpeace vessel *The Rainbow Warrior* in 1985, her view being at the time that any impediment - which Greenpeace represented - to French nuclear testing in the Pacific only encouraged Soviet expansionism.

In her extensive *oeuvre*, Duras has particularly explored the emotional disequilibrium brought by love, desire, suffering and death, especially as these affect women and propel them towards the abyss of madness. In addition, however, Duras's writing explores the space between fusion and separation (e.g., in love and sexuality) as it breaks down the boundary between private (family) and public (political and artistic) life - between the symbolic and the imaginary, and between the time of narrative and the event recounted. Often narrative appears as a kind of distancing from the real, so that writing becomes the only reality. Subject and object thus become difficult to separate in many of Duras's key fictional texts. This is illustrated in *The Ravishing of Lol V. Stein*,[1] where the writer/narrator and what is being written about become particularly difficult to determine. For this reason, Duras has come to be seen as a postmodern writer.

Duras's own life has been a crucial source of material and inspiration for her fictional writing. Few have been able to transform everyday life fragments into artistic statements with the combination of intensity and starkness that characterises Duras's prose. Although, as Leslie Hill has pointed out,[2] there is no absolutely true and unchanging set of biographical facts pertaining to Duras's life, certain points can be taken as given.[3]

Marguerite Duras was born Marguerite Donnadieu in 1914 at Gia-Dinh near Saigon in Cochinchina (now South Vietnam). Both her parents had been married previously and had met in Vietnam. Duras's father was a mathematics teacher from south-west France, while her mother came from a poor farming family in the north. Shortly after being posted to Phnom Penh in 1918, the father contracted dysentery and had to return to France, where he later died. Duras's mother was thus forced to bring up Marguerite and her two older brothers alone in various abodes in Cambodia and Vietnam. Until the age of 11, when she completed her first school certificate, Marguerite spoke more Vietnamese than French.

In 1932–3, Duras returned permanently to France and took up the study of mathematics, but soon abandoned this to study political science and law. After her studies, she was employed in the Colonial Office as a researcher and archivist, and shortly before the outbreak of the war, she married the writer Robert Antelme. Between 1940 and 1942, Duras published her first work with Philippe Roques, *L'Empire français*, but her first novel written under the family name Donnadieu, *La Famille Tanéran*, was refused by Gallimard. Also in this period, Duras's first child was stillborn. She would subsequently have a son in 1947 with her partner, Jean Mascolo, her marriage with Robert Antelme being dissolved in 1946. The year 1943 proved to be a major turning point: *Les*

Impudents appeared, Duras's first published novel, and the first piece of writing to appear under the pseudonym 'Duras', and Duras made friends with Georges Bataille, Maurice Merleau-Ponty, Edgar Morin, and others. At the same time, she and her husband joined the French movement for prisoners of war. While active in the Resistance with François Mitterand, Duras, in 1944, joined the communist party, from which she was expelled in 1950. Robert Antelme was arrested and sent to Buchenwald and Dachau. The painful experience of waiting for his return inspired the novel, *La Douleur* published in 1985. In 1984, Duras received the prix Goncourt for her novel, *The Lover*.

Prior to her public acclaim in 1985, however, Duras had become known to a wider public for her script for Alain Resnais's film, *Hiroshima mon amour* (1959), for her own film, *India Song* (1974) based on her novel *Le Vice-consul* (1966), and for two much-discussed novels, *Moderato Cantabile* (1958), and *The Ravishing of Lol V. Stein* (1964).

Generally speaking, Duras's writing does not focus on the elaboration of ideas or on the experimental side of art (although these are of course implicit in everything she does), but rather on emotional experiences which are barely translatable into symbolic form: silences, inarticulateness, deep sadness, sudden and inexplicable violence, loss in love, almost imperceptible – yet fundamental – changes in emotional, or bodily states, odd flights of imagination – it is these which are at the heart of her artistic effort. The focus on emotional states in particular has given Duras's *oeuvre* an allure that feminists have claimed has undermined the supposedly rationalistic and phallocentric narrative of highly regarded male writing.

One can no doubt point to the unique rhythm of the articulation of the fragmentary narrative in the film *India Song* as illustrative of Duras's 'feminine' style – a style contrasting with the tightly ordered realist approach typical of much conventional cinema. Shot in black and white, *India Song* plays on a dissonance between the sound-track and the images; the dialogue is spoken off-screen rather than on, most shots are static, and there is a refusal of the shot/reverse shot technique. Clearly, the film's poetic character sharply contrasts with the diegetic emphasis of a conventional realist film.

Duras's writing style, while clearly singular, often evokes the experimental realism of the *Nouveau Roman*. Short sentences focus on small details, thus slowing the rhythm of the articulation of the intrigue. A look, a sigh, a touch, often seem to be as important in their own right as the significance they are charged with conveying – which is often a mood, or an emotional crisis, rather than an idea. Typically, the novel, *L'amour* (*Love*), does not contain a discussion of what love is; rather, it evokes and denotes love in dialogue and short sentences. As if to reinforce a minimalist, and non-Baroque style, most of Duras's novels are short by conventional standards (around 40,000 words). Such minimalism is more than a stylistic device; it is also part of an effort to focus on the *difficulty* of speaking and writing; it contains a barely suppressed silence.

The features of the Durasian *oeuvre* mentioned above have prompted Julia Kristeva to see Duras's writing as symptomatic of a world where a deficit of language and representation has emerged in light of the terrible events of the twentieth century. While it is true that Kristeva uses a psychoanalytic framework that some might find problematic to interpret features of Duras's *oeuvre*, few commentators seem to disagree about what these features are. Indeed, while Leslie Hill is critical of Kristeva's reading of *The Ravishing of Lol V. Stein*, his insight that indeterminacy is a fundamental feature of the novel in question, would only seem to confirm the problematic status of identity typical of the crisis of representation that characterises the end of the twentieth century.

For Kristeva, then, Duras's work has to be seen against a background of apocalyptic themes: Hiroshima, the Holocaust, Stalinism, Colonialism. She thus participates in the search for a symbolic means adequate to represent the horror of what has happened. Rather than focusing on a public sense of the suffering, the latter is presented in an intensely private context. People become locked in their private grief – or depression – so that their speech, rather than being a means to some kind of catharsis or coming-to-terms with the horror, is in fact a symptom of it. Because it is so intensely evocative and descriptive of sadness, rather than being an analysis of it, Duras's writing, in Kristeva's view, brings us to the verge of madness; her texts fuse with it rather than represent, or transcend it. This madness, though, is now the only way of living one's individuality, so impoverished are the public means of representation.

Leslie Hill's remark in the context of a discussion of *The Lover* confirms the thrust of Kristeva's interpretative insight: Duras's '*L'Amant* does no more than repeat episodes rather than account for them'.[4] Indeed, many scenes and characters in Duras's repertoire are reworked in her novels, and none more, it seems, than those relating to her own autobiography.

Kristeva thus notes the importance of the mother and the theme of separation in Duras. The presence of the mother, from *The Sea Wall* (1950), *The Lover*, and further, to *The North China Lover* (1991) is not only to be seen in the figure represented in a narrative, but also in the writing itself. The mother, on this more psychoanalytic reading, is the emotion of lived experience, it is the madness that cannot be transcended. To begin to understand this one need only refer to how the narrative (such as it is) of *The Lover* stays so close to the well-known facts of Duras's life. As Duras writes in the novel, she wanted to kill her brother because her mother loved him so much. Moreover, she writes that, 'I've written a good deal about the members of my family, but then they were still alive, my mother and my brothers. And I skirted around them, skirted around all these things without really tackling them.'[5] Although setting out to tackle the things concerning her life, 'The story of my life,' she says 'doesn't exist. Does not exist. There's never any centre to it. No path, no line.'[6] Again, what she is doing now 'is both different and the same'.[7]

Duras reworks the same material, but the question is whether she is thereby able to transcend the despair and the hatred depicted in this novel and elsewhere, or whether her writing is indeed an analogue, and thus a confirmation, of it. In other words, does Duras remember her past, and to that extent transcend it, or does she rather have a largely affective and nostalgic relationship to it? In favour of the first explanation, and against Kristeva's view perhaps, is the fact of Duras's undoubted success as a writer – and no more so than with *The Lover* which has become a worldwide bestseller. Therefore, even if she cannot remember for herself, Duras, it seems, remembers for others. To this extent, the work transcends despair. On the other hand, the absence of transcendence may well confirm the despair present in modern society, and it may be this which is at the heart of Duras's success. Just as it is possible to respond to suffering by suffering oneself, so readers may respond to Duras empathetically, in a fascinated rather than an analytical way. Whatever the case may be, it is certain that Duras prompts one to think seriously about the nature of writing today.

One of the most intriguing and renowned of Duras's novels is *The Ravishing of Lol V. Stein*. Its complex narrative – or absence of a clear narrative – has given rise to numerous interpretations, one of the most famous being by Jacques Lacan.[8] Lacan famously sees in Duras's story an exemplification of his own psychoanalytic teaching, even though Duras, in 1964, was not in the least familiar with his theories, nor had she ever attended his seminar. For Lacan, the novel is the repeated attempt at the rememoration of the traumatic primal scene, where Lol Valerie Stein's fiancé goes off with an older woman, Anna-Maria Stretter, at the ball at T. Beach. This event is at least in part doubly filtered: first of all through the narrator, Jacques Hold – also an active protagonist in the events – and through Tatiana Karl (wife of Hold's superior at the hospital where Hold, a doctor, was employed, and also Hold's lover) who, Hold's narrative suggests, had told him what had transpired at T. Beach. What is also clear, however, is that the telling of the story of T. Beach is not separate from the events being recounted. This is particularly so given that part of the narrative describes the attempted re-enactment of the fateful night.

On this night, the shock of her fiancé, Michael Richardson, departing with Anna-Marie Stretter seems to send Lol V. Stein into a state of madness. However, she seems to recover, and leaves her native town, S. Tahla, in order to marry Jean Bedford, with whom she has three children. Eventually, Lol V. Stein returns to S. Tahla after an absence of ten years, and renews her acquaintance with Tatiana, and at the same time meets Tatiana's lover, Jacques Hold. A key element of the novel concerns the ambiguous place of Lol V. Stein. Initially it appears (whether appearance is ever really transcended is a key issue) that Lol is devastated by being thrown over for another woman. A number of things complicate the situation, however, not the least of these being that, later, Lol cannot remember exactly what happened on the fateful night, and claims not to have loved her fiancé from the moment when Anne-Marie Stretter entered the dance hall. Given Lol's forgetting, Tatiana's testimony, filtered through Jacques Hold's narrative, is crucial for the reconstitution of events, that is, effectively, for the story itself. As Lol's story is entirely in the second degree, we suspect that Lol's being unable to tell it herself is part of her condition; the trauma, unable to manifest itself in a symbolic form, is continually acted out. And in fact, the last part of the text concerns Lol's return to the scene of the dramatic events, and their attempted re-enactment.

Very quickly, the reader, increasingly on the alert for new evidence that might throw light on to the meaning of the story, realises that the story is less about an event than it is about how this event can be told. Lol cannot tell it, because she was too close to it; only the witness has the symbolic means to tell the story. Even this is not a simple matter, however; for in Jacques Hold's telling, Lol is placed in the mediating, third position of the symbolic when she becomes the witness to the affair between Hold and Tatiana. It is as though Lol desperately wants to be in the position which allows her to speak of what she sees instead of being the traumatised victim: the object of another's discourse.

Lol V. Stein's relation to her trauma would seem to correspond to Marguerite Duras's relation to her own family (particularly to her mother and brother). Again, the issue is not one of reconstituting the true events of one's past, but of being able to occupy the position of witness to one's own life. How to speak and write at all is at stake, not whether what one says or writes is true or false, fictional or non-fictional. Taking a pseudonym, giving up the family name, should therefore be seen as an essential, and not an accidental part of Duras's art. It is the means whereby she can begin to become a witness to her own life. It entails the separation from (and even denial of) the very real trauma of that life. In this way Duras may well have achieved something that few writers in the twentieth century have achieved: a putting into language – however minimal this might be – of the struggle for language.

Notes

1 Marguerite Duras, *The Ravishing of Lol V. Stein*, trans. Richard Seaver, New York, Grove Press, 1966.
2 Leslie Hill, *Marguerite Duras: Apocalyptic Desires*, London, Routledge, 1993, p. 1.
3 The following biographical details about Duras

come largely from Leslie Hill, *Marguerite Duras*, and Christiane Blot-Labarrère, *Marguerite Duras*, Paris, Seuil 'Les Contemporains', 1992.
4 Hill, *Marguerite Duras*, p. 118.
5 Marguerite Duras, *The Lover*, trans. Barbara Bray, London, Collins, Fontana/Flamingo, third impression, 1986, p. 11.
6 ibid.
7 ibid.
8 Jacques Lacan, 'Hommage to Marguerite Duras', trans. Peter Connor in *Duras on Duras*, San Francisco, City Lights Books, 1987, pp. 122–9.

See also in this book

Irigaray, Kristeva, Lacan

Duras's major works

La Vie tranquille, Paris, Gallimard: folio, 1944
Sea Wall (1950), trans. Herma Briffault, London, Faber &Faber, 1986
Moderato cantabile (1958), trans. Richard Seaver, London, John Calder, 1966
Hiroshima Mon Amour and *Une aussi longue absence* (1960 and 1966), trans. Richard Seaver and Barbara Wright, London, Calder & Boyars, 1966
The Ravishing of Lol V. Stein (1964), trans. Richard Seaver, New York, Grove Press, 1966
L'Amante anglaise (1967), trans. Barbara Bray, London, Hamish Hamilton, 1968
Destroy, She Said (1969), trans. Barbara Bray, New York, Grove Press, 1970
L'Amour, Paris, Gallimard, 1971
India Song, (1973) trans. Barbara Bray, New York, Grove Press, 1976
Outside: Selected Writings (1981 and 1984), trans. Arthur Goldhammer, London, Collins, Fontana/Flamingo, 1987
The Maladie of Death (1982), trans. Barbara Bray, New York, Grove Press, 1986
The Lover (1984), trans. Barbara Bray, London, Collins, Fontana/Flamingo, 1985
La Douleur (1985) (also published as: *The War: A Memoir*), trans. Barbara Bray, London, Collins, Fontana/Flamingo, 1986
Blue Eyes, Black Hair (1986), trans. Barbara Bray, London, Collins, Flamingo, 1988
Emily L. (1987), trans. Barbara Bray, London, Collins, Fontana/Flamingo, 1989
The North China Lover (1991), trans. Leigh Hafrey, New York, The New Press, 1992

Further reading

Hill, Leslie, *Marguerite Duras: Apocalyptic Desires*, London, Routledge, 1993. This book contains an exhaustive English and French bibliography of Duras's works

Woodhull, Winifred, 'Marguerite Duras and the question of community', *Modern Language Studies*, 17, 1 (Winter 1987), pp. 3–16

FRANZ KAFKA

The uniqueness of Kafka stems, in large measure, from the intersection of writing and lived experience. Born into a Jewish family in Prague in 1883, Franz Kafka was the son of a prosperous self-made businessman. Although his parents spoke Czech in their native village, they did everything they could to ensure that their son had a good education, and in particular, that he could speak and write good German – like the privileged German-speaking minority in Prague. The father also wanted the son to know and to appreciate the Jewish side of the family history, a factor which tended to bring Kafka and his father into conflict; for Franz had a very different view of Jewishness, a point brought out in his famous letter to his father, written in November 1919.

From 1893 to 1901, Kafka attended the German gymnasium, after which he studied jurisprudence at the Karl-Ferdinand University. In 1906, he took out his doctorate in Law. In 1902, Kafka first met the critic and novelist Max Brod who introduced him to Prague literary circles. In 1907, he began work in an Italian insurance company before leaving in July 1908 to work, until his retirement in 1922 due to ill-health, for the semi-government Workers Accident Insurance Bureau. The company gave Kafka extended sick-leave, and this allowed him more time to write.

In 1909, Kafka's first story was accepted by a Prague journal and he read to Brod chapters of his novel, *Wedding Preparations*

in the Country. In 1910, he began to keep his diaries and also became involved with the Yiddish theatre company. In 1912, Kafka met Felice Bauer, to whom he was twice engaged and with whom he conducted a voluminous correspondence. He also wrote letters, since published, to the Czech translator of his stories, Milena Jesenská. In 1914, Kafka read the first chapter of *The Trial* to Brod, and in 1918, a year after tuberculosis had been diagnosed, he became engaged to Julie Wohryzek. In the winter of 1920–1, while in a sanatorium for his tuberculosis, Kafka told Brod that he wished all his work to be destroyed after his death, a request subsequently confirmed in writing. After living in Berlin with a Polish Hebrew student, Dora Dymant, Kafka died of tuberculosis in 1924.

Kafka's influence has been profound from at least two points of view. In the first place, his writings – in which an enigmatic, skeletal world has apparently been created – have touched a nerve in the life as lived in modern, industrial society. The nihilism of a society without God, the hyper-rationalism of bureaucratic domination, which strangles the innocent in its web, and the end of all idealism – including perhaps, the end of the notion of causality along with all first principles – is sketched out. Here in Kafka's *oeuvre* is an allegory of a society without any particular end, but which is assuredly destined to come to an end in a material sense. Thus Joseph K cannot find out for what crime he has been arrested in *The Trial*, just as K in *The Castle* cannot enter the castle, but does not know why. At one level, then, Kafka has been taken up as the revealer of the dangers of social and psychological relations that are reduced to nothing but means. And he seems to be all the more successful in creating this world to the extent that he never describes or characterises it, but always only ever suggests or evokes it. Quite possibly, readers looking in Kafka for a message about modernity are able to find it because the suggestion of a message is one of the fundamental traits of Kafka's writing strategy. To suggest and to evoke – to work by way of enigma – rather than to state, gives things a profoundly kaleidoscopic quality. The strangeness of Kafka's writing, that few readers prior to the 1980s could have failed to notice, is to be found in this minimalist style of suggestion. The strangeness has meant that each reader can begin to find there something for him or herself. In other words, the lack of definition and specificity in Kafka's world produces the 'Kafkaesque' – the enigma, the darkness and the mystery within which everyone can find a place, however discomforting and depressing this may be.

The role of enigma and obscurity is by no means the unambiguous outcome of a writing strategy, but often seems to be intrinsic to the object being described. Nowhere is this better demonstrated than in the discussion of the law in *The Trial*. The law, which is supposed to illuminate the case, at the same time obscures it. The law in fact seems to have a blind spot right at its core. For it is unable to answer definitively the question as to who is inside and who is outside the law. In principle, the law is unable to admit its limits; it pretends to be all-powerful. In fact, however, there are always areas outside the law, such as the areas of enjoyment, horror and death – the very areas with which Kafka's text is obsessed.

In the second place, Kafka and his *oeuvre* offer an insight into the mode of being a writer in the twentieth century. Kafka's life in and for writing – a life partially revealed with great force and poignancy in his *Diaries* – raises the question of what it might really mean for someone to be devoted to art in general, and to writing in particular in the twentieth century. Why is this such a difficult question to answer? Why is it not simply that some people are called to the vocation of 'writer', just as some are lawyers or doctors? A response to this question hinges on what it is that the writer qua writer in modern society feels called upon to do. If he or she is content to conform to the existing conventions of writing, there is really no problem; the doors of journalism and writing within well-established genres (e.g., the detective novel) are open to them. Rightly or wrongly, however, the category of literature has, since the middle of the eighteenth century, emerged in modern society. Literature, from one point of view at least, is the 'canonisation' of a truly singular writing. In Kafka's case, this entails the consecration of his most intimate inner-experience. This consecration, or the becoming-literary of writing, sets up a profound tension. For after the writer has made his play, burned his bridges, put his own being on the line, and set the scene of his challenge to the deepest conventions of the art of his day, he may not be recognised; it may all be for nothing. The possibility of the most profound failure has to be entertained. The stakes have thus been raised very high, the temptation to compromise is extremely strong.

From this angle, a writer not only lives for his writing, but more profoundly lives *in* his writing, and is even formed by it in a physical sense. This is writing as the expenditure of a certain energy without return. Certain traits of Kafka's biography confirm and illustrate what is at stake. For instance, rather than becoming a fully professional writer who lived from his work, Kafka remained working in the government insurance office during the day, and only wrote at night, or in the late afternoon. Second, as is known, Kafka told his literary executor, Max Brod, that he wanted all his extant works (with a few exceptions) burned. Just as the origin of the events in Kafka's fiction is shrouded in the mists of enigma, so, too, is this request. Why would Kafka, who was still correcting the proofs of one of his works on his death bed, have made such a request? As Max Brod refused to go along with his protégé on this crucial point, and instead set to work producing a five-volume set of Kafka's complete works, Kafka has become immortalised; his writing has become literature. He did, finally, gain recognition on his own terms, but, tragically, did not live to see it.

Although there are undoubtedly elements in Kafka's fiction which lend themselves to an allegorical reading, and thus to a political use, the main way in which Kafka's writing can be seen to have political effects is a more indirect one, achieved through the valorisation of a practice of writing. Kafka's writing is not engaged, in the manner of Sartre; for the ideal truth necessary for such a political stance is missing from Kafka's fiction. Indeed, the impossibility of such an engagement is more in keeping with Kafka's approach. The practice of writing is writing produced despite the despair and obscurity of the world, despite the absence of rational protocols that could be followed with a degree of certainty. In this sense, Kafka's is a writing of sacrifice. Its enigmas become essential to it; the effort it cost is also essential to it: Kafka exhausts himself in writing. On one now well-known occasion he wrote his story *The Judgement* in one sitting on the night of 22–3 September 1912. As he comments in his diary:

> I was hardly able to pull my legs out from under the desk, they had got so stiff from sitting. The fearful strain and joy, how the story developed before me, as if I were advancing over water. Several times during this night I heaved my own weight on my back ... At two I looked at the clock for the last time. As the maid walked through the ante-room for the first time, I wrote the last sentence.... The slight pains around my heart. The weariness that disappeared in the middle of the night.[1]

Although they, too, do not see the political effect of Kafka's writing as being committed in the Sartrian sense, Deleuze and Guattari argue that Kafka's fiction is political in the sense that it constitutes a 'minor' writing within a major linguistic formation.[2] Thus as a Czech Jew – that is, a member of a minority group – writing in German, Kafka manages to make his own way in the dominant language by constructing a minor idiom in it. Kafka plays with the tonality of German; refuses metaphors; writes so as to defamiliarise (deterritorialise) the language; refuses genealogical connections and focuses on the very small things around him; produces a flood of letters rather than an overall vision. In short, Kafka changes the nature of German significantly, if imperceptibly, and makes a unique place for himself in it, one that was in no sense anticipated by the current usage of the language at the time when he was writing.

Without analysing this turn of events any further, let it suffice to say that Kafka's life brought to the fore a new way of understanding the link between writing and life. This may be summarised in the following way: Kafka showed in his writing practice that writing is a way of life, that it demands a concentration of forces;[3] he also made visible the real stakes at play in the constitution of the literary object; finally, through the use of enigma, he set writing free from a sociological, or psychological determinism that would seek to explain writing in terms of material conditions or a writer's biography. After Kafka, writing (literature) is no longer a product of conditions, but is also constitutive of those conditions.

According to the French critic, Marthe Robert, Kafka makes use of the anonymity of his key characters like K in order to bring out their transcendent quality.[4] In other words, they are freed from the environment in which they may have originated and can take root in many different environments. This character is thus an exile – like the Jews (although none of Kafka's fiction ever says this) – capable of transgressing boundaries of all kinds – moral, legal, cultural, psychological. The character is the anonymous, rootless person always in search of a community, much as many displaced persons are today in Europe at the end of the twentieth century. Kafka's own life, being half Jewish, half German, also embodies this theme of exile and 'extraterritoriality'.

Absence of fixed boundaries can be seen as a feature of Kafka's novels from another angle. This time, the collapse of boundaries evokes an absence of transcendence. The source, or origin, is erased: the origin of the law, the origin of change, of sexuality, the cause in cause and effect all evaporate into an enigma. 'Why', in short, finds no answer. In this sense, Kafka becomes Nietzschean and radically anti-idealist. As Georges Bataille put it,[5] there is no promised land in Kafka; Moses's goal is unattainable because it is human life – the physical material world – we are dealing with, and not with any transcendent realm. No doubt Kafka tends to fit into some of the features designated as 'postmodern' in his effort to render all boundaries, and thus all identities more fluid.

The spectre of death, together with anguish and despair haunts Kafka's fiction. Faith may be excluded, but not the search for faith. As Maurice Blanchot has said, there is an uncertainty about meaning because despair and anxiety are literary equivalents of death within life.[6] Despair arises here because existence is an exile; there is no true home where one could avoid the anxiety of modern life. To be modern is to be Jewish in a way. Few have better summarised the uniqueness of Kafka than Blanchot when he argues that Kafka's work shines forth despite itself, that is, despite its preoccupation with death: 'This is why we only understand [Kafka's *oeuvre*] in betraying it; our reading turns anxiously around a misunderstanding.'[7]

Notes

1 Franz Kafka, *The Diaries of Franz Kafka 1910–23*, ed. Max Brod, trans. Joseph Kresh and Martin Greenberg, Harmondsworth, Peregrine/Penguin, 1964, p. 212.
2 Gilles Deleuze and Félix Guattari, *Kafka: Toward a Minor Literature*, trans. Dana Polan, Minneapolis, University of Minnesota Press, 1986, 16–18.
3 On this point, see Franz Kafka, *The Diaries of Franz Kafka 1910–23*, p. 163.
4 Marthe Robert, *Franz Kafka's Loneliness*, trans. Ralph Manheim, London, Faber & Faber, 1982, p. 5.
5 Georges Bataille, 'Kafka' in *La Littérature et le mal* in *Oeuvres complètes, IX*, Paris, Gallimard, 1979, p. 272.
6 Maurice Blanchot, *De Kafka à Kafka*, Paris, Gallimard/Idées, 1981, p. 66.
7 ibid., p. 74.

See also in this book

Bataille, Blanchot, Duras

Kafka's major writings

The Trial (1925), trans. Willa and Edwin Muir, New York, Schocken Books, 1968
America (1927), trans. Willa and Edwin Muir, New York, Schocken Books, 1962
The Castle (1926), trans. Willa and Edwin Muir, New York, Schocken Books, 1974
Metamorphosis and *In the Penal Settlement* (1919 and 1933), trans. Eithne Wilkins and Ernst Kaiser, London, Secker & Warburg/Octopus Books, 1976
The Great Wall of China and *Investigations of a Dog* (1931), trans. Willa and Edwin Muir, London, Secker & Warburg/Octopus Books, 1976
Diaries (one volume), ed. Max Brod 1910–13 (1948), trans. Joseph Kresh, 1914–23 (1949), trans. Martin Greenberg and Hannah Arendt, New York, Schocken Books, 1988
Dearest Father (Letter to His Father) (1953), trans. Ernst and Eithne Wilkins, New York, Schocken Books, 1954
Letters to Milena, ed. Willy Haas, trans. Tania and James Stern, New York, Schocken Books, 1962
Letters to Felice, ed. Erich Heller and Jürgen Born, trans. James Stern and Elisabeth Duckworth, New York, Schocken Books, 1973
Wedding Preparations in the Country and Other Stories (also includes: *Letter to His Father*; *Meditation*; *The Judgement*; and *A Country Doctor*), Harmondsworth, Penguin, 1978

Further reading

Anderson, Mark (ed.), *Reading Kafka: Prague, Politics and the Fin de siècle*, New York, Schocken Books, 1989
Bataille, Georges, 'Kafka' in *Literature and Evil*, trans. Alastair Hamilton, London, Calder & Boyars, 1973
Benjamin, Walter, 'Franz Kafka on the tenth anniversary of his death' in *Illuminations*, trans. Harry Zohn, Glasgow, Fontana/Collins, third impression 1979, pp. 111–140
Blanchot, Maurice, *De Kafka à Kafka*, Paris, Gallimard/Idées, 1981

Deleuze, Gilles and Guattari, Félix, *Kafka: Toward a Minor Literature*, Minneapolis, University of Minnesota Press, 1986

Robert, Marthe, *Franz Kafka's Loneliness*, trans. Ralph Manheim, London, Faber & Faber, 1982

JEAN-FRANÇOIS LYOTARD

Jean-François Lyotard was born in 1924 at Versailles. For ten years to 1959, he taught philosophy in secondary schools, and later became a professor of philosophy at the University of Paris VIII (Saint-Denis) – a post which he held until his retirement in 1989. From 1956 to 1966, Lyotard was on the editorial committee of the socialist journal, *Socialisme ou barbarie* and the socialist newspaper, *Pouvoir ouvrier*. As well as being an active opponent of the French government over the war in Algeria, Lyotard participated in the events of May 1968.

Although a political activist of Marxist persuasion in the 1950s and 1960s, Lyotard became the non-Marxist philosopher of postmodernity in the 1980s. Postmodernity thus marks a fundamental disengagement from the kind of totalitarian thought Marxism (but not only Marxism) represents. Before the appearance of, arguably, his most important book of philosophy – *The Differend: Phrases in Dispute* – Lyotard had already signalled this change of philosophical direction in both his doctoral thesis, *Discours, figure*, and in *Economie libidinale*. The latter work looks to escape from the theoretical 'coldness' of Marxism by way of Freud's economy of libidinal energy and the notion of the primary process. Now, a libidinal economy becomes the basis of the political instead of a political economy. This extreme break with Marxism in *Economie libidinale* becomes much more nuanced in the philosophy of postmodernism.

Despite his prolific output in recent years, especially in the area of aesthetics, almost all of Lyotard's truly innovative (or experimental) thinking – and certainly the thinking for which he has become renowned – comes together in just two books: *The Postmodern Condition*, and *The Differend*.

The *Postmodern Condition*, written as a report on knowledge for the Quebec government, examines knowledge, science, and technology in advanced capitalist societies. Here, the very notion of society as a form of 'unicity' (as in national identity) is judged to be loosing credibility. Society as unicity – whether conceived as an organic whole (Durkheim), or as a functional system (Parsons), or again, as a fundamentally divided whole composed of two opposing classes (Marx) – is no longer credible in light of a growing 'incredulity towards' legitimating 'metanarratives'. Such metanarratives (for example: every society exists for the good of its members; the whole unites the parts; the relation between the parts is just, or unjust, depending on the situation) provide a teleology legitimating both the social bond and the role of science and knowledge in relation to it. A metanarrative, then, provides a 'credible' purpose for action, science, or society at large. At a more technical level, a science is modern if it tries to legitimate its own rules through reference to a metanarrative – that is, a narrative outside its own sphere of competence.

Two influential metanarratives are the idea that knowledge is produced for its own sake (this was typical of German idealism), and the idea that knowledge was produced for a people-subject in quest of emancipation. Postmodernity, on the other hand, implies that these goals of knowledge are now contested, and, furthermore, that no ultimate proof is available for settling disputes over these goals. In the computer age where complexity is perceived to be ever increasing, the possibility of there being a single, or even dual, rationale for knowledge or science, becomes remote. Before, faith in a narrative (e.g., religious doctrines) would have resolved the potential difficulty. Since the Second World War techniques and technologies have, as Weber anticipated, 'shifted emphasis from the ends of action to its means'.[1] Regardless of whether the form of narrative unification is of the speculative or of the emancipatory type, the legitimation of knowledge can no longer rely on a 'grand narrative', so that science is now best understood in terms of Wittgenstein's theory of 'language game'.

A language game signifies that no concept or theory could adequately capture language in its totality, if only because the attempt to do so itself constitutes its own particular language game. Thus, again, grand narratives no longer have credulity, for they are part of a language game which is itself part of a multiplicity of language games. Lyotard has written of speculative discourse as a language game – a game with specific rules which can be analysed in terms of the way statements should be linked to each other.

Science, therefore, is a language game with the following rules:

1 Only denotative (descriptive) statements are scientific.

2 Scientific statements are quite different from those (concerned with origins) constituting the social bond.

3 Competence is only required on the part of the sender of the scientific message, not on the part of the receiver.

4 A scientific statement only exists within a series of statements which are validated by argument and by proof.

5 In light of (4), the scientific language game requires a knowledge of the existing state of scientific knowledge. Science no longer requires a narrative for its legitimation, for the rules of science are immanent in its game.

For science to 'progress' (i.e. for a new axiom, or denotative statement to be accepted), the individual scientist, or group of scientists, must win the approval of all other scientists in the same field. And as scientific work becomes more complex, so do the forms of proof: the more complex the proof, the more complex the technology necessary in order to achieve generally accepted levels of validation. Technology, crucial for understanding the form of scientific knowledge in the society of the last quarter of the twentieth century, follows the principle of optimal performance: maximum output for minimum input. Lyotard calls this the principle of 'performativity', and it now dominates the scientific language game precisely because a scientific discovery requires a proof which costs money. Technology thus becomes the most efficient way of achieving scientific proof: 'an equation between wealth, efficiency, and truth is thus established'.[2] Although 'wildcat' discoveries (where technology is very minimal) can still take place, technology tends to link science to the economy. Although inexpensive, pure research in search of truth is still possible, expensive research is becoming the norm; and this means obtaining funding assistance. To get funding, the long-term relevance of the research has to be justified; and this brings pure research under the auspices of the language game of performativity.

Once performativity dominates, truth and justice tend to be the outcome of the best-funded research (best-funded, therefore most convincing); 'by reinforcing technology, one "reinforces" reality, and one's chances of being just and right increase accordingly'.[3] And if those who have wealth to fund research also have power (and they have power, according to Lyotard, because they profit from research), the postmodern era would be one in which power and knowledge come into contact with each other as never before.

On the other hand, performativity can remain in a hegemonic position in the scientific language game only if the issue of its legitimacy is kept out of play. This is easily done if the question of legitimation is the same as the question: What is science? Once the performativity of the question is made an issue, however, the limit of performative rationality emerges, in as far as performativity cannot justify itself except through a metanarrative.

Systems theorists such as Luhmann propose that performativity is the basis on which the (social) system maintains itself, in the wake of the disenchantment of the world brought about by science and technology. As the perfect system is deemed to be the most efficient, the goal is to eliminate all dysfunctions. For the systems theorist, human beings are part of a homogeneous, stable, theoretically knowable, and therefore, predictable system. Knowledge is the means of controlling the system. Even if perfect knowledge does not yet exist, the equation: the greater the knowledge the greater the power over the system, is, for the systems theorist, irrefutable.

By contrast, Lyotard shows that systems theory is located within a modernist epistemology. For within the very terms of the system as performativity, control through knowledge lowers its performance, since uncertainty increases rather then decreases with knowledge (cf. Heisenberg). Now, a new, postmodern paradigm is coming into being, one that emphasises unpredictability, uncertainty, catastrophe (as in René Thom's work), chaos, and, most of all, paralogy, or dissensus. Dissensus challenges the existing rules of the game. Paralogy becomes impossible when recognition is withheld and legitimacy denied for new moves in the game. Silencing – or eliminating – a player from the game is equivalent to a terrorist act. The notion of being unable to present a position that is at variance with the dominant rules of argumentation and validation, provides an appropriate point of transition to Lyotard's later work, *The Differend*.

As though having sensed the political issues at stake – especially with regard to justice – Lyotard proceeds to develop his philosophy of the differend – the real philosophical basis of the more sociological work, *The Postmodern Condition*. The differend is the name Lyotard gives to the silencing of a player in a language game. It exists when there are no agreed procedures for what is different (be it an idea, an aesthetic principle, or a grievance) to be presented in the current domain of discourse. This is graphically illustrated when revisionist historians refuse to recognise the existence of the Nazi gas chambers unless a victim of the gas chambers can be brought as a witness. To be a victim, one must have died in the chambers. Many historians have been justifiably outraged by this perverse use of the rules of evidence, and refer to the bad faith of the perpetrators. Lyotard, on the other hand, emphasises that the problem arises because too much has been invested in what amounts to an empiricist historiography. The latter assumes that the mere existence of the referent (e.g., the gas chambers) is sufficient for a cognitive phrase (e.g., 'the gas chambers existed') to be accepted as true. It also accepts that this principle of proof deriving from the simple existence of the referent is universally valid. The proof is deemed to be universally valid because reality is deemed to be a universe (a totality) which can be represented, or expressed in symbolic form. However, even in physics no such universe exists which can be put fully into symbolic form. Rather, any statement which lays claim to universality can be quickly shown to be only *part* of the universe it claims to describe.

For Lyotard it is necessary to adopt a regional, rather than a universal approach to issues in history, politics, language, art, society. Instead of speaking of language games, Lyotard speaks, in *The Differend*, of 'regimes of phrases', and 'genres of discourse'. Like language games, regimes of phrases have their rules of formation, and each phrase presents a universe. There is thus no single universe, but a plurality of universes. A phrase regime presents a sentence universe, or type of phrase: prescriptive, ostensive, performative, exclamatory, interrogative, imperative, evaluative, nominative, etc. A genre of discourse, on the other hand, attempts to give a unity to a collection of sentences. A genre of discourse must be invoked to identify a phrase regime, since phrases can be cited and imitated. A cognitive (factual) phrase in a fictional work is not the same as a historian's cognitive phrase. Because the genre of historiography has tried to conflate history and the cognitive genre, it has enabled Faurisson – a revisionist historian – to mount a case against the existence of the gas chambers. He is able to undermine the procedures of the historical genre because within this genre it has been claimed that history is only about what is knowable via a cognitive phrase. In short, cognitive phrases deal uniquely with the determinable; the unknowable and the indeterminate are beyond their ken. Just as science is inseparable from conditions of proof (it is not a simple reporting of reality), so the rules for establishing the reality of the referent determine the 'universe of cognitive phrases', 'where truth and falsity are at stake'.[4] True statements do not automatically result from the simple existence of the referent. This is why there will be not only disagreements as to the true nature of the referent, but also claims by those (of bad faith) who refuse to accept that the rules of proof have been adhered to, or who interpret the rules in such a way as to subvert them – by claiming, for example, that only a dead person can be a witness.

The possibility of this subversion of the cognitive gives rise to the differend. Its existence cannot be established cognitively; for it is the sign of an injustice which, qua injustice, cannot be given expression in cognitive terms. Whether someone is or is not a victim of an injustice cannot be validated by cognitive phrases because, qua victim, he or she is the subject of a differend. The differend marks the silence of an impossibility of phrasing an injustice.

In a discussion 'The Sign of History',[5] Lyotard takes up the issue of interpreting historical events in light of Kant's notion of the sublime in *The Critique of Judgement*. For Kant, the sublime feeling does not come from the object (e.g., nature), but is an index of a unique state of mind which recognises its incapacity to find an object adequate to the sublime feeling. The sublime, like all sentiment, is a sign of this incapacity. As such the sublime becomes a sign of the differend understood *as* a pure sign. The philosopher's task now is to search out such signs of the differend. Again, because no universal – be it humanity, freedom, progress, justice, the law, beauty, society, or language – can correspond to a real object, the attempted link between the universal and a real object can only result in totalitarianism and the consequent exclusion of otherness. Kant, however, was a keen observer of the French Revolution. He looked to it as an event signalling that humanity was progressing. He had the *enthusiasm* of its many interested, external spectators. Was Kant therefore going against the logic of the sublime and confusing a strong sentiment (enthusiasm) with a concrete historical event: the Revolution? He was not because enthusiasm is a sign that the Revolution has a sublime – that is, an unpresentable – aspect; and this, precisely because it *is* a historical event. A true historical event cannot be given expression by any existing genre of discourse; it thus challenges existing genres to make way for it. In other words, the historical event is an instance of the differend.

Unlike Hegel, Kant does not try to make a speculative phrase equivalent to a cognitive phrase. Speculative phrases always relate to signs (i.e. sentiments and emotions), and Hegel was wrong to think that a speculative phrase could have a concrete realisation. Hegel in this way was tied to a philosophy of the result – of how things would turn out in a determinant way. The indeterminant – the sign, emotion, event, differend – is entirely absent from the Hegelian system.

Like Kant's critique of history, the problematic of obligation is taken up in Lyotard's book *Just Gaming*. The search for the basis of an ethical phrase, and thus for the basis of being obligated, guides Lyotard's discussion. He concludes, perhaps paradoxically, by saying that the basis of obligation cannot be specified – first, because an obligation cannot be explained descriptively; if it could be, the obligation qua obligation would evaporate. One can only be obligated if – as Kant says – one is free not to accomplish the obligation. A description can only show why an obligation *cannot* be avoided. In short, 'ought' cannot be derived from 'is'.

Second, though, obligation is not the outcome of 'my' law, but of the 'other's' law: I can only be obliged if the obligation comes from outside my own world: from the world of the other. The other's law which obliges is evidence of the impossibility of ever constructing an adequate representation of it. The ethical phrase can only be a sign indicating an obligation that never has concrete form. At stake is whether Kant's categorical imperative could ever be the basis of an ethical community. Here, we see the pertinence of Levinas's philosophy which invokes Jewish theological sources in order to show the necessary primacy of the other (the 'you') at the origin of the moral law. Not only does Kant refuse to compromise by not reducing the genre of discourse of obligation to the cognitive genre, but he also offers a way of thinking about the way genres of discourse are 'connected' to each other. Each genre of discourse is analogous to an 'archipelago', while judgement is a means of passing from one archipelago to another. Unlike the homogenising drive of speculative discourse, judgement allows the necessary heterogeneity of genres to remain. Judgement, then, is the way of recognising the differend – Hegelian speculation, a way of obscuring it.

The force of Lyotard's argument is in its capacity to highlight the impossibility of making a general idea identical to a specific real instance (i.e. to the referent of a cognitive phrase). Philosophers, mathematicians, and scientists now recognise the paradoxes arising when a general statement about the world is forced to take its own place of enunciation into account. Lyotard's thought in *The Differend* is a valuable antidote to the totalitarian delirium for reducing everything to a single genre, thus stifling the differend. To stifle the differend is to stifle new ways of thinking and acting.

On a more problematical note, however, Lyotard's promotion of the phrase to a privileged position in relation to the differend itself seems to risk obscuring a differend. For here there is no non-phrase. A silence, an interjection, a shrug of the shoulders are all phrases. Moreover, there is no first or last phrase because there is always a linking of phrases. To say that there is no other of the phrase surely implies that the phrase emanates from itself – that it is its own law. But this claim is in danger of becoming a restrictive totalisation which flies in the face of the principle of allowing the differend to emerge from silence. Lyotard might reply that this is to deny the (radically) heterogeneous status he has attributed to phrase regimes – a status ensuring the differend. What kind of heterogeneity can it be, however, which denies otherness? To say that there is always a phrase – that there is always something rather than nothing – does not eliminate the problem of 'nothing', even if nothing is an impossibility. This problem indicates that a more intricate elaboration of the 'phrase' is necessary before Lyotard's claim that a philosophy of phrases is the way to gain an insight into the differend could be accepted.

Notes

1 Jean-François Lyotard, *The Postmodern Condition: A Report on Knowledge*, trans. Geoffrey Bennington and Brian Massumi, Minneapolis, University of Minnesota Press, 1984, sixth printing, p. 37.
2 ibid., p. 45.
3 ibid., p. 47.
4 Jean-François Lyotard, *Le Différend*, Paris, Minuit, 1983, p. 35.
5 Lyotard, 'Le signe de l'histoire' in *Le Différend*, pp. 218–60.

See also in this book

Baudrillard, Habermas, Levinas

Lyotard's major writings

Phenomenology, (1954) trans. Brian Beakley, New York, State University of New York Press, 1991

Discours, figure, Paris, Klincksieck, 1971

Dérive à partir de Marx et Freud, Paris, Union générale d'éditions, 1973

Des dispositifs pulsionnels, Paris, Union générale d'éditions, 1973

Libidinal Economy (1974), trans. Iain Hamilton Grant, Bloomington, Indiana University Press, 1993

Instructions païennes, Paris, Galilée, 1977

Just Gaming (with Jean-Loup Thébaud) (1979), trans. Wlad Godzich, Minneapolis, Minnesota University Press; Manchester, Manchester University Press, 1984

The Postmodern Condition (1979), trans. Geoffrey Bennington and Brian Massumi, Minneapolis, Minnesota University Press; Manchester, Manchester University Press, 1984

The Differend: Phrases in Dispute (1983), trans. George ven den Abeele, Minneapolis, Minnesota University Press; Manchester, Manchester University Press, 1986

L'Enthusiasme: la critique kantienne de l'histoire, Paris, Galilée, 1986

Peregrinations: Law, Form, Event, New York, Columbia University Press, 'The Welleck Library Lectures', 1988. Contains a 'checklist' of writings by and about Lyotard

Heidegger and 'The Jews' (1988), trans. by Andreas Michel and Mark Roberts, Minneapolis, University of Minnesota Press, 1990

The Inhuman: Reflections on Time (1988), trans. Geoffrey Bennington and Rachel Bowlby, Cambridge, Polity Press, 1991

The Postmodern Explained to Children: Correspondence 1982–1985 (1988), trans. Julian Pefanis and Morgan Thomas, Sydney, Power Publications, 1992

The Lyotard Reader, ed. Andrew Benjamin, Oxford, Basil Blackwell, 1989. Contains a wide-ranging selection of articles and chapters by Lyotard, with a special emphasis on aesthetics and representation. Also has a select bibliography (to 1988) of Lyotard's articles and chapters translated into English

Further reading

Bennington, Geoffrey, *Lyotard: Writing the Event*, Manchester, Manchester University Press, 1988

Descombes, Vincent, *Modern French Philosophy*, trans. L. Scott-Fox and J.M. Harding, Cambridge, Cambridge University Press, 1980, pp. 180–6 and *passim*

Pefanis, Julian, *Heterology and the Postmodern: Bataille, Baudrillard, and Lyotard*, Sydney, Allen & Unwin, 1991